GRAND CANYON TO HEARST RANCH

*One Woman's Fight to Save Land
in the American West*

ELIZABETH AUSTIN

Foreword by Stephen T. Hearst

TWODOT®

GUILFORD, CONNECTICUT
HELENA, MONTANA

For our children and grandchildren

A · TWODOT® · BOOK

An imprint of The Rowman & Littlefield Publishing Group, Inc.
4501 Forbes Blvd., Ste. 200
Lanham, MD 20706
www.rowman.com
A registered trademark of The Rowman & Littlefield Publishing Group, Inc.

Distributed by NATIONAL BOOK NETWORK

British Library Cataloguing in Publication Information available

Library of Congress Cataloging-in-Publication Data
Names: Austin, Elizabeth, 1954– author.
Title: Grand Canyon to Hearst Ranch : one woman's fight to save land in the American West / Elizabeth Austin ; foreword by Stephen T. Hearst.
Description: Guilford, Connecticut : TwoDot, [2020] | Includes bibliographical references and index. | Summary: "In the 1950s, Harriet Hunt Burgess persevered in the face of daunting obstacles and took extraordinary risks to conserve hundreds of thousands of acres of land in the American West. Without Burgess, places like the Lake Tahoe region and the California coast would be much different today. Grand Canyon to Hearst Ranch is the story of her struggle, but it is also the story of author Elizabeth Austin's search to find Burgess and tell her more personal story. Austin searches beyond documents and interviews, traveling in Burgess's wake and, in the case of the Grand Canyon, taking a life-changing rafting trip through its depths. Austin has interwoven her journey through the Grand Canyon and Harriet's experiences there with explorations of her early life and five of her most significant and representative conservation achievements as the founder of the American Land Conservancy"— Provided by publisher.
Identifiers: LCCN 2019041004 (print) | LCCN 2019041005 (ebook) | ISBN 9781493048342 (cloth) | ISBN 9781493048359 (epub)
Subjects: LCSH: Burgess, Harriet Hunt. | Conservationists—United States—Biography. | Nature conservation—West (U.S.)
Classification: LCC QH76.5.W34 A97 2020 (print) | LCC QH76.5.W34 (ebook) | DDC 333.72092 [B] —dc23
LC record available at https://lccn.loc.gov/2019041004
LC ebook record available at https://lccn.loc.gov/2019041005

Tell me, what is it you plan to do
With your one wild and precious life?

—MARY OLIVER, *THE SUMMER DAY*

Contents

Contents

Foreword

OUR COMPANY WAS FORTUNATE THAT WE CHOSE HARRIET BURGESS AND her team at the American Land Conservancy (ALC) as the lead conservation partner for our work to preserve the Hearst Ranch at San Simeon as a working cattle ranch. When I met with Harriet in late 2002 to discuss the possibility of a partnership, I shared our vision and laid out our conservation goals and objectives for the Hearst Ranch. Without hesitation, Harriet immediately and fully committed the ALC team to our project, which we successfully completed after two-plus years of intense and continuous effort.

The story of Harriet's life is timely and compelling, and it traces the arc of profound and enduring changes in American culture and society over the past sixty years. How did Harriet transform herself from a full-time mother of five living in suburban Virginia in the early 1960s to a nationally recognized conservationist by the late 1980s? How did she assemble a team of supporters and advisers that included many of the most celebrated conservationists of this era? How did she become the "go-to" conservationist, ready and willing to take on the projects that other conservation organizations considered too difficult or risky?

Harriet's story shows us how one person can make a difference and an enduring contribution to a better world through passion, commitment, and perseverance. Her story also shows how a young woman from a modest background was able to navigate the changing standards and expectations for women in the workplace over the past sixty years to achieve national recognition and success. Finally, Harriet's story showcases just a few of her many successful conservation projects, including the preservation of Hearst Ranch.

Harriet's story reminds us that conservation of our vital land and water resources is not easily accomplished, and that it requires the passion, commitment, and perseverance that Harriet personified in her life and her work. With the ever-increasing threats to those vital resources, Harriet's story may help inspire another generation of leaders to carry on this critically important and essential work.

Stephen T. Hearst

Introduction

"I AM HERE TO SPEAK FOR THE EARTH," HARRIET HUNT BURGESS declared to a congressional committee in the 1970s. And speak she did, repeatedly and for the rest of her life, both in words and actions. Hiking trails, public beaches, open rangelands, dense forests, and coastal wetlands across the American West bear witness to her unwavering commitment to conservation. Without Harriet's passion for preserving these outdoor sanctuaries, many of them would have been lost forever.[1]

At first glance, Harriet was an unlikely conservation crusader. Going down the same path many of her contemporaries followed in the 1950s, she married young without finishing college. Her family expanded rapidly to include five children. She was active in her local church, she joined the League of Women Voters, and she volunteered in her community. Still, Harriet longed to do more.

Transported by the breathtaking beauty of the Grand Canyon on her first dory trip down the Colorado River with uncompromising environmentalist Martin Litton in 1973, and captivated by Martin's zealous and eloquent orations on nature and the imperative of conservation, Harriet returned home to Virginia convinced that she had discovered her purpose in life. She had found a solution to the "problem with no name" that Betty Friedan had identified in *The Feminine Mystique* as the source of the dissatisfaction and yearning that women often felt in their limited roles as wives and mothers. She dedicated her life to conservation because, as she told a crowded room of admirers in 1999, "The land we save is our legacy. It's what we give to our children. It's what future generations can cherish thanks to our perseverance."[2]

Harriet mixed limitless energy, fierce determination, and dedication to her conservation mission with charm, compassion, and convincing arguments in favor of her projects. It was a powerful combination. "Leaning in" long before Sheryl Sandberg coined the phrase to describe women who pursued ambitious goals, Harriet persevered in the face of daunting obstacles and took extraordinary risks to conserve land.[3]

At the peak of her conservation career, after many successful years at Trust for Public Land (TPL), Harriet Burgess founded the American Land Conservancy (ALC) to take on projects that other conservation organizations were not willing to tackle. For the most difficult, high-risk, complex projects, Harriet was the one to call. If she felt a project was important, Harriet did it. She did not take no for an answer.

Intrigued by her transformation from a busy housewife with many family and community responsibilities into a relentless risk-taking advocate for saving the only Earth we will ever have, I came up with the idea of telling Harriet's story in 2008. After years of hearing about her projects from my attorney husband as he worked closely with Harriet on hundreds of ALC deals, I assumed Harriet's story would be a straightforward biography and history of a successful woman and the organization she founded. As an historian and librarian, in-depth research including scrutinizing documents and conducting interviews was my métier. I had used that approach for my first book, *To Be the Change You Wish to See*.[4]

I soon realized that the research for this book would be different. There was no finding Harriet in diaries or journals, and little trace of her in personal letters. Unlike conservationists from Aldo Leopold to Wallace Stegner, from Rachel Carson to Terry Tempest Williams, Harriet was not a writer. Her business letters and newsletters often were written or edited by others. But as the outspoken environmentalist and author Edward Abbey once wrote, "One brave deed is worth a thousand books."[5]

Harriet's legacy is the land she saved. To find her, I had to go beyond the thousands of pages in the files that document her deals. Not only did I have to talk to her friends and colleagues, but I also had to go where she went. See what she saw. Imagine her life. And, in the case of the Grand Canyon, do what she did. The Grand Canyon is at the heart of this story, both for Harriet and for me. The Grand Canyon was the catalyst for Harriet's conservation mission and the spark for my account of her life and work.

I have interwoven my journey through the Grand Canyon and Harriet's experiences there with my explorations of her early life and five of her most significant and representative conservation achievements as the founder and president of ALC. Harriet left TPL and started ALC to save Lower Topanga Canyon for the enjoyment of the millions who live in the Los Angeles area. She engineered the Nevada Land Exchange to prevent the construction of a ski resort on the slopes of Mount Rose. She struggled for years to add the few acres of the John Muir gravesite in Martinez, California, to the John Muir National Historic Site. Harriet often "bet the farm," as she liked to say about her approach to risky undertakings; and, on a few projects, she came close to losing her bet. Thunderbird Lodge on the shores of Lake Tahoe is a case in point. She concluded her career in a blaze of glory with the conservation of the Hearst Ranch on California's central coast. She completed many more projects, some of which are mentioned in my discussion of the five listed here with the others detailed in appendix 1.

Harriet's strategy for saving land was simple and straightforward: "You have to know what should be done. You have to have the determination to do it. You have to start." A woman in a man's world, she took on the tough projects and dared the impossible. And perhaps I, too, dared the impossible by attempting to depict the life of a multifaceted woman who embraced her family and her conservation mission with unwavering zeal.

George Bernard Shaw captured Harriet's passionate approach to life perfectly:

> This is the true joy in life, the being used for a purpose recognized by yourself as a mighty one; the being thoroughly worn out before you are thrown on the scrap heap; the being a force of nature instead of a feverish selfish little clod of ailments and grievances complaining that the world will not devote itself to making you happy.[6]

Harriet's purpose was mighty. She was both a force of and a force for nature.[7]

Grand Canyon to Hearst Ranch is the story of the power of one woman to make a difference and the power of place to inspire.

Overture

Grand Canyon

In the Grand Canyon, Arizona has a natural wonder which, so far as I know, is in kind absolutely unparalleled throughout the rest of the world. I want to ask you to do one thing in connection with it. In your own interest and in the interest of the country keep this great wonder of nature as it now is. I hope you will not have a building of any kind, not a summer cottage, a hotel, or anything else, to mar the wonderful grandeur, the sublimity, the great loneliness and beauty of the canyon.

Leave it as it is. You cannot improve on it. The ages have been at work on it, and man can only mar it. What you can do is to keep it for your children, your children's children, and for all who come after you, as one of the great sights which every American should see. —THEODORE ROOSEVELT, 1903[8]

"I AM NOT HARRIET. THIS IS SO NOT ME."

I am in the Grand Canyon with my husband, Russell, and our son, Michael. Russell and I lie sweltering in our tent on unopened sleeping bags spread on thin yellow foam pads hoping for sleep. Nearby in his tent, Michael already is sound asleep.

I have survived the almost ten-mile hike down Bright Angel Trail from the South Rim to the Colorado River carrying my backpack. I have been indoctrinated in the ways of life on the Colorado River. I have met the river guides, the baggage raft crews, and the thirteen other people making the journey with us. I have run my first rapid in a small wooden boat called a dory.

The whole idea of going down the Colorado River through the Grand Canyon in a dory started with Harriet Hunt Burgess, founder and president of the American Land Conservancy (ALC) and a client of my attorney husband. Running the Colorado River through the Grand Canyon was Harriet's refuge and inspiration. She did the trip at least nineteen or twenty times. Nobody knows for sure exactly how many times she escaped to the freedom and solace of the Grand Canyon. It was the primary source of her passionate commitment to conservation and the reason she turned her life upside down. She is the reason I am here.

At fifty-seven years old, I am going to camp for the first time in my life. I am going to risk my life in monstrous rapids. I am going to scramble on rocks up narrow canyons. And I'm wondering why I ever thought I should go on this trip. I'm wondering why I didn't back out before it was too late. How is it that the trip that sounded like a fabulous adventure seven months ago now seems like a big mistake?

Early in the morning, before the sun was up, we had filled our water bottles, strapped on our loaded backpacks, and left our comfortable room at the Maswik Lodge on the South Rim of the Grand Canyon. The night before, we had dropped off our duffels, packed almost to the thirty-pound limit with our clothing and other necessities, at the Bright Angel Lodge for transport to the Colorado River on mules.

We had also met with the folks from O.A.R.S., the company taking us on this trip. They told us to gather at the top of Bright Angel Trail at 5:30 a.m., and we are there promptly at the appointed time. The three of us start down the trail with Peter and Barbara, another couple in our group. Liz, in her mid-seventies, and her granddaughter, Marguerite, preceded us. They left at 4:30 a.m. to give themselves the benefit of extra time to make the hike. The remaining nine members of our group will follow soon.

I see the dark outline of the canyon stark against the pale grays and eye-popping whites of the sky. Peachy pinks, brick reds, pale yellows, glowing oranges shade from one color to another as the sun hits the rock walls of the canyon, then shifts farther overhead or disappears behind cloud hazes.

Blues, grays, and browns, too, accented by the surprise of green agave, green mesquite, green pine and juniper.

The canyon is a visual feast of shapes and colors. Stair-stepping or ramping down the wide but often uneven red dirt trail, I absorb image after image juggling my trekking poles to record as many as I can with my camera without falling too far behind my family. I often walk alone down the path that I share with the ghosts of prehistoric and historic Native Americans and nineteenth-century miners. Few of the more than one hundred thousand of my contemporaries who hike this way every year are present at this early hour, but the occasional unperturbed squirrel belies the frequency of their passage.

Rock of ages from the Vishnu Schist to the Kaibab Formation. Limestone, sandstone, shale, granite. Jagged and smooth. Stacked like pancakes, and rounded like mushroom caps. The rock strata speak of two billion years of the Earth's history, but I cannot comprehend such immensity. However, I am intensely aware of my body as I make my way through these layers of time. I nearly fall over backward as I descend a steep step, unbalanced by my heavy backpack. I feel the pain that develops on the outside of my left knee ameliorated somewhat by stepping down with my left foot first. My back complains, and my right big toe protests. But I keep putting one foot in front of the other and try to think only of where I am and not how far it is to where I am going.

Starting at 5:30, we have had the advantage of the early morning cool. Our first respite on the trail, Mile-and-a-Half Resthouse, offers water and a toilet. Later in the day, it will be staffed by a park ranger whose primary duty is to caution hikers about the dangers of the trail. Running out of water and succumbing to the heat are two of the primary pitfalls. Hikers who have not heeded the rangers' warnings—warnings repeated on signs posted along the way—have died on Bright Angel Trail.[9]

Three-Mile Resthouse, built like Mile-and-a-Half by the Civilian Conservation Corps in the 1930s, is our next chance for water. Then Indian Garden with its natural springs. When we reach Indian Garden, we are about halfway to the jumping-off point for our adventure on the Colorado River—a beach near Phantom Ranch.

The trail levels for a short distance after Indian Garden but soon returns to steep descents with steps and switchbacks. It's hot and getting hotter. Any advantage gained from our early start has evaporated. But I am prepared with water and my wide-brimmed Tilley hat, sunscreen and sunglasses, sun-shielding shirt and pants, and the determination to make it. I soldier on.

I may not be an experienced camper, but I am a veteran walker. Russell and I have walked three marathons and hiked twelve to seventeen miles a day on a weeklong trip through northern England. I walk several miles every day at home. I figured the hike would be the easy part of the trip.

Still, I have never gone down this much for this long. O.A.R.S. warned us, "Remember, your hike into the canyon is *downhill for 9.7 miles*," and offered two single-spaced pages of training advice observing that hiking downhill is harder than hiking up and recommending warm-up hikes on dirt trails with ups and downs. All well and good. I followed many of their recommendations. But, like so many things in life, you can't know what it's like until you do it.

Eight miles and six hours into the hike, I see the Colorado River. It is dirt brown, carrying about eighty thousand tons of sediment daily, and flowing rapidly along at some fifteen thousand cubic feet per second with occasional flashes of whitewater. Two more miles to go. I start on the trail along the river that the Civilian Conservation Corps built in 1936, the year after Harriet was born. If that confluence of events had any significance, it escapes me now as I single-mindedly focus on the goal of getting to the boat beach on the other side of the river. The Silver Bridge span beckons. I am on it and across. A few minutes more, and I am parked on a concrete coping, elbows on my thighs, a smile on my face. Four dories and two baggage rafts round a bend in the river and tie up on the beach in front of me.

An expert river guide rows each dory. Our group leader, Kerstin Dale, is rowing *Dark Canyon*, a gift from Martin Litton to her father-in-law, Regan Dale, who later gave it to his wife and Kerstin's mother-in-law, Ote Dale. Kerstin is married to Duffy Dale, who is rowing *Escalante*. Duffy's uncle, Roger Dale, rows *Paria*—a dory that Duffy built. Roger has nine siblings, which partly explains why being a boatman with O.A.R.S. is a family affair. Morgan Holpuch rows *Lost Creek*. Morgan is the odd man out—it is his first time on the Colorado River, and he is no relation to the Dales. The much larger baggage rafts are rowed by Amber Shannon and Brian Rudd with Jim Varney and Megan Maibach along for the ride and for helping out when needed.

Dories like *Dark Canyon* have been slicing through the Colorado River in the Grand Canyon since Martin Litton introduced them in the early 1960s. Martin's fascination with running the Colorado River began with his 1955 trip in cataract boats with Pat Reilly and seven others. He was the 185th person to make the run. John Wesley Powell, a one-armed Civil War veteran, was the first in 1869. Martin was a passenger on that 1955 trip because he had dislocated his shoulder in a horseback riding accident. He rowed his next trip in 1956 in a cataract boat and many more in dories. He made his last trip with Harriet in 1997 at the age of eighty, but he was still rowing rapids in 2004 at the age of eighty-seven. He made his final run through the Grand Canyon in 2009 at the age of ninety-two.[10]

Martin Litton's first boats were modified Grand Banks cod-fishing dories called McKenzie driftboats that he bought from two Oregon boat-wrights. Just for fun, Litton began inviting friends to join him in these boats for excursions on the Colorado River through the Grand Canyon. Every year, Litton ordered more boats. With each order he made changes in the design until he created the dories like the ones on our trip.

The dories are sixteen or seventeen feet long, about six feet wide, and two feet deep. Usually they are painted with brilliant reds, blues, and whites, like *Dark Canyon*, *Escalante*, and *Lost Creek*. Occasionally, they are painted Colorado River brown like *Paria*. They weigh anywhere from 350 pounds (*Paria*) to 700 pounds (*Lost Creek*). Their bows and sterns sweep to graceful points, though the stern may be squared off and decorated with an intricately drawn design like *Dark Canyon*'s yellow butterfly and blooming cacti. Their sides are flared, and their bottoms are flat. Following a tradition started by Martin Litton, they are named after places that people have spoiled or destroyed.

When we were making plans for this trip, I asked Carrie, one of the office staff at O.A.R.S., about the differences between going down the Colorado in a raft and going down the Colorado in a dory. Carrie compared the two by saying that rafts were like Hondas and dories were like Lamborghinis. That alone made our decision to choose dories easy. Besides, rafts really were not an option. They were Martin Litton's dories, and Harriet's first trip (and many subsequent trips) had been in a dory.

According to Martin, "The dory is an ancient design. We didn't originate it. It goes back into antiquity. There's a kind of magic about the shape of the boat in terms of its stability and its ability to recover from extreme situations—self-righting, practically. The boat is something beautiful to look at: it has lines that belong on the water. The dories really were adapted by us because they handle so well, they're enjoyable to row, you get response from them, they respond to the oars. They're safe, relatively, and secure. They have places to put things. There's a mystic thing about a dory, to those of us who know them. I feel that anyone who looks at a dory and then has to ask why you use that, will never understand, no matter what kind of answer you give." Dories were the only way to go.[11]

Once the passengers who are leaving the trip at Phantom Ranch have disembarked and emptied the dry bags that have protected their belongings during the journey down the river from Lees Ferry, they enjoy the lunch that was put together efficiently by the O.A.R.S. crew from provisions stored on the baggage rafts and in the dories. Making lunch appear just a few minutes after tying up is one of the many talents of our hosts.

But we don't get to eat yet. While the departing and continuing passengers lunch sumptuously, we transfer the contents of our backpacks and duffel bags into dry bags. I shove my stuff into the small bag quickly but, to my later chagrin, in no particular order. The bag is only twenty inches tall and fourteen inches across, so it was a tight fit because I have not followed Harriet's advice that "all you need to pack for a trip down the Grand Canyon is a toothbrush and a bathing suit." I also have another even smaller dry bag (seventeen inches by nine inches) that I can use for daily necessities because the bigger bag will be on the baggage raft and inaccessible during the day.

Closing the dry bag correctly is crucial. First, I push as much air as possible out of the bag. Then I press the lips of the bag together forming a band that I fold over itself three times before pulling the two ends of the clip located on opposite sides of the band toward me and snapping the clip ends together. Even working together with Russell and Michael, it takes several tries to do it right.

After our turn at lunch, we gather on the beach to hear Morgan's talk on river safety. First comes the obvious advice, such as always wearing a life jacket, and the less obvious, wearing a helmet when going through some of the rapids. Falling out of the dory happens. If you fall out, your head may hit a rock. Then there's what to do if the dory flips. What you're supposed to do is use the flipline tied around the outside of the dory to pull it right side up again.

Dories haven't always had flip lines. Martin Litton never liked them, claiming that they slowed down the boat, but without flip lines, the boats have to be pushed to shore to be turned upright, and they often hit rocks on the way. Repairing the damage caused by the rocks is difficult and time consuming, so some of the boatmen started using flip lines in the 1970s to right the boats in the deep water away from the rocks. All of the dories have flip lines now.[12]

If dealing with the dry bags hadn't already made me feel incompetent, contemplating the prospect of turning a sixteen-foot wooden boat right side up while being whisked along in a cold, rushing river, probably in the middle of serious whitewater, did. I also was more than a little apprehensive, especially because even Martin Litton once said, when asked about adventures in dories and near misses, "A couple of times I thought, was I drowning or not?"[13]

It's just about time to get in the dories. Figuring that it would be my last chance to use a toilet, I ask Kerstin, "Is there a toilet?" Answer, "No, you pee in the river." She elaborates. "Ladies pee upstream and men downstream. But that's not a hard and fast rule. I always want the ladies to go to the easiest location."

One of the reasons I have always been reluctant to camp involves the lack of bathroom facilities. I knew ahead of time that some provision would be made to take care of that deficiency, but beyond assurances that the accommodations would provide a modicum of privacy, I had no idea what to expect. So here we are on the beach with the dories lined up ready to go, and I'm supposed to pee in the river?

I ask, "Where exactly?" Kerstin points to the last dory and suggests going on the other side.

I am joined by several other ladies and get it done, hovering over the cold water and envying the guys. No room for modesty here.

Russell, Michael, and I are assigned to Kerstin's dory. Each dory holds four passengers in addition to the river guide. Our fourth is Gail, a woman of about my age from Ventura who began the trip at Lees Ferry. A former dressage trainer/instructor who's into photography and history, we have a lot in common. One thing Gail and I do not share: she has been down the Colorado River through the Grand Canyon four or five times whereas this is my first. Gail is the most experienced of the passengers and frequently offers much appreciated advice and assistance to us newbies.

Before climbing into *Dark Canyon*, I pull on my orange life jacket and attach the three clips that hold it snugly around my upper body. The life jacket is a foam-filled vest with a pillow hanging behind my head like a hood. If I make an unplanned exit from the dory, I should float and even be turned faceup by the life jacket if I'm unconscious. Nice to know, but I don't want to put it to the test.

It's time to go. I grab my yellow helmet and the small dry bag that holds my camera, waterproof journal, and other items such as chapstick and sunscreen that I might need to use during the day, and follow Gail into the dory. Obeying one of the rules of dory etiquette, I swish my river sandal–clad feet in the Colorado River to wash off as much sand as possible before grabbing the dory's side and hauling myself in. Gail and I climb over the raised platform where Kerstin will sit to our assigned seats in the stern. Kerstin explained earlier that it's best to have heavier passengers in the bow to help balance the dory so Russell and Michael will sit up front. I don't mind sitting in the back of the dory. It seems somehow safer.

Kerstin takes her seat in the middle of the dory. At about five feet five, she looks more like the community college instructor of art studies that she is during the off-season than the strong and skillful boatman that she is when rowing the Colorado River. Tanned, with her blonde hair pulled back in a ponytail and hung over the band of her white visor, she projects a reassuring air of confident competence.[14]

Kerstin made her first trip through the Grand Canyon on the river when she was twenty-three. It was a life-changing experience that she has repeated more than seventy-five times. It's where she met and married Duffy, whose parents also met on the river. It's where she returns every year to reconnect and recharge. She started with O.A.R.S. in 2000 as an assistant cook after meeting O.A.R.S. owner George Wendt while waiting tables and then convincing Regan Dale, manager of O.A.R.S. Grand Canyon operations at the time, to take her on. The next year she began rowing baggage boats and later dories.

As she rows away from the beach with easy strokes into the quietly running river, Kerstin explains our responsibilities as passengers. It turns out we are not just along for the ride. First she instructs us to throw our body weight toward oncoming waves. It's called high siding, and the idea is to prevent the waves from unbalancing and flipping the dory. Then she tells us to use the plastic gallon milk jugs with cutaway tops that are roped to the dory in front of each of us to bail water out of the dory after we go through a rapid.

Starting from Phantom Ranch at mile 89—the miles are counted from Lees Ferry, the beginning of the Grand Canyon and the first put-in point for whitewater trips—we have an immediate opportunity to practice our newly learned skills. Within minutes, at mile 91, we go straight into Horn Creek Rapid. It's rated from seven to nine on a scale where ten is the most difficult. Whether it's a seven, eight, or nine depends on how fast and how full the river is running—and on how the boatman goes through it.

I hear the rapid before I see it. The water roars and gives fair warning as it churns over rocks and boulders washed into the river over the years by floods from side canyons and in pre-dam years by river floods. I feel the prickly sensation that always accompanies the appearance of real or imagined dangers. It spreads through my chest like a swarm of bees. Then the rapid's tongue sucks *Dark Canyon* into the maelstrom.

Anxiety and fear abruptly vanish into the immediate demands of the moment. Walls of water surge toward me. I push my body at the waves. And if the dory dips near the waterline on one side, I lean all my weight to the opposite side. Kerstin stands to use her full weight against the power of the rushing water. Is that a bad sign? Are we in trouble? Waves douse and cool us as Kerstin wrestles the dory through the swirling, seething river.

We shoot out the other side of the rapid, wet and bailing water out of the seat well as fast as we can. I have survived the first test.

Kerstin rows easily through the placid river that succeeds the rumble and tumble of Horn Creek. Her eleven-foot wooden oars dip and rise, dip and rise, hypnotically propelling the dory forward. Tension and fatigue drop away with every stroke. The cold river, fifty degrees but colored warm like cappuccino, cradles our dory after tossing it around like a ping-pong ball. The steep walls of the Grand Canyon rise thousands of feet overhead, channeling the rushing waters of the river. I am enclosed. There is no horizon line. There is no escape.

Harriet was here for the first time thirty-eight years before. Her enthusiasm for running rapids and conserving land was fanned into a burning passion by her first trip down the Grand Canyon in 1973. Roger began rowing the river in 1976. It's his 178th trip. He says there is very little difference between now and then—just more people and fewer beaches. What I see is what Harriet saw. Different times, different people, but the Grand Canyon is steadfastly there.

Harriet had been on other rivers, been through other rapids. She had run the New River in West Virginia with her family. She had gone down the Youghiogheny River in Pennsylvania with the Sierra Club. But this river is different. For 297 of its 1,450 miles, it runs through the Grand Canyon. It is heavily silted, muddier than the muddy Mississippi. It drops an average of eight feet per mile as it cuts through the canyon. Its depth may change suddenly from a few inches to many feet. Its rapids are more treacherous than any in the United States.

Harriet made her first trip to the Grand Canyon with her thirteen-year-old daughter, Julie. No one else in her family wanted to come along. She asked her oldest daughter, Leslie, who said, "Are you insane? No." Then she asked Linda, the next oldest. Same answer. Julie, the third oldest, enthusiastically said, "I'll go. I'll go."

Harriet saved housekeeping money for months to be able to afford the trip. She baked her own bread to save three cents per loaf. She purchased dry milk to save a few more pennies. She canceled the trash pickup, leaving it to her husband to haul their garbage to the dump. She painted the house herself so she wouldn't have to hire a professional painter. Eventually she had enough for the two of them to travel to the Grand Canyon and join one of Martin Litton's dory adventures.[15]

CHAPTER ONE

Two Husbands and Five Children

Beginnings

If I am right, the problem that has no name stirring in the minds of so many American women today is not a matter of loss of femininity or too much education, or the demands of domesticity. It is far more important than anyone recognizes. . . . We can no longer ignore that voice within women that says: "I want something more than my husband and my children and my home." —BETTY FRIEDAN, *THE FEMININE MYSTIQUE*[1]

Memories may escape the action of the will, may sleep a long time, but when stirred by the right influence, though that influence be light as a shadow, they flash into full stature and life with everything in place. —JOHN MUIR, *A THOUSAND-MILE WALK TO THE GULF*[2]

HARRIET HAD TWO HUSBANDS. RUSSELL AND I VISITED HER FIRST HUS-band, Robert G. Hunt, at his home in Springfield, Virginia, in June 2010. In his late seventies, Bob Hunt still lives in the same two-story brick and clapboard house on Cromwell Drive that he built with Harriet in 1962. The house where they spent most of their married life together. The house where they raised their five children: Leslie, Linda, Julie, John, and Gregg. The house that Harriet left behind in 1978 to move as far away from Bob Hunt as she could get.[3]

When I talked with Bob by telephone several months before our visit, he was willing—indeed, eager—to talk about Harriet. Although he was scheduled for replacement pacemaker surgery two days after our call—it would be his third pacemaker—his voice was strong, and his memory was sharp. He had asked for my questions in advance, and he was ready with his answers.

When we arrived for our late-afternoon visit, Bob and Harriet's daughter Julie greeted us at the front door. Bob followed slowly behind her. While recovering from his pacemaker surgery, he had suffered a small stroke. A nurse was still in attendance twelve hours daily assisted by a home helper for shopping and other errands, but Harriet's first husband and the father of her children was just as prepared and eager to share his memories as he had been on the phone. Sitting together around the dining-room table, Bob and Julie regaled us with stories about Harriet as we looked at photos that Bob had selected and arranged in chronological order.

After our visit, Bob shared more about his life with Harriet from the 1950s to the 1970s in a series of e-mails. As he remarked, "When you sit down and dig into your memory, you come up with all sorts of things." Although I did not rely exclusively on Bob's memories for the details of Harriet's early life, they opened windows into her world that otherwise would have been closed forever.

Harriet and Bob first met in 1953 when she was called "Hattie"—a nickname she hated—and was living with her parents in Loveland, Colorado. Harriet's father, Clair Vaughn McNeel, was the minister at the Presbyterian Church in Loveland, where Bob was a member. Bob said her father was "bullheaded and opinionated and had difficulty getting along with people," but her mother was "an exceptional woman much like Harriet." He described Harriet in the 1950s as beautiful, charming, thrill seeking, complex, ambitious, tireless, and driven—adjectives that many others would use to describe her throughout her life.[4]

Clair Vaughn McNeel was a dedicated Presbyterian from a solidly Presbyterian family. As a young boy, he was active in the Presbyterian Church in Bellwood, Pennsylvania, where his father was the Sunday school superintendent and choir director. By the time he turned eleven and became a member of the church, he knew that he had a calling for the ministry.

He went straight from Cedarville College in Cedarville, Ohio, to Western Theological Seminary in Pittsburgh, Pennsylvania.[5]

Clair McNeel found the perfect helpmeet in Harriet's mother, Frances Adella McKibben. She was the daughter of a Presbyterian minister and as dedicated to the church as he was. They married in 1932 when he graduated from seminary and dreamed of becoming missionaries together in Africa. They applied. They passed the physical and written tests. They were sure the Board of Foreign Missions was notifying them of their appointment to Africa when they received a rejection letter instead. The board informed them that no missionaries would be sent that year because of the Depression.[6]

The Depression may have disrupted Clair McNeel's plans to become a missionary in Africa, but it did not stop him from creating his own mission enterprise. He decided to dedicate his ministry to small, rural churches that had difficulty attracting pastors. Coming to the rescue of struggling churches began "a life of real romance" for Harriet's father. Many years later, Harriet, too, would forge her own path and dedicate herself to taking on tough challenges.[7]

Once a church was doing well with a strong membership, Harriet's father would leave for the next small congregation that needed his help. The McNeel family moved every four to seven years. Harriet was born in 1935 about halfway through Clair McNeel's first pastorate at Clifton Presbyterian Church in Clifton, Ohio—the hometown of Harriet's maternal grandfather. Clifton was so small that Harriet was born at the nearest hospital in Xenia, twelve miles away. Clair and Frances McNeil named her Harriet Gertrude after her grandmothers.[8]

Shortly after the birth of Harriet's sister Jean in late 1936, the McNeels left tiny Clifton for a Presbyterian church about seventy miles to the west in Liberty, Indiana. With a population of about fifteen hundred, Liberty was a little bit bigger than Clifton. One of its upstanding citizens at the time, attorney and Republican Party official Walter F. Bossert, had been a Grand Dragon of the Ku Klux Klan in the 1920s. It's possible that the Klan still was active in Liberty when Harriet was growing up. Harriet once told Tim Richardson, ALC's director of government affairs in Washington, D.C., that her father warned her to crawl when she passed the windows in their house at night so she wouldn't be an easy target for the Ku Klux

Klan. Apparently Pastor McNeel had gotten on the wrong side of the racist, anti-Semitic, anti-Catholic, anti-immigrant right-wing organization.[9]

When McNeel started his ministry at the church in Liberty, the congregation was filled with people who were out of work during the Depression, just like the congregation in Clifton. He offered to serve without a salary, but every month they managed to pay him. By the time he left seven years later, the growing church was able to pay the new pastor an adequate salary.

Another church, another challenge. The United States was in the middle of World War II when McNeel was installed as pastor of Sharon Presbyterian Church in Carnot, Pennsylvania, in September 1943. Gas rationing limited the number of church services and meetings. One church elder resigned from Session (the governing body of the church), explaining that he was not able to attend meetings because he had no gas for his car. And the members of Sharon Presbyterian were suffering through a thirty-year division over its building program. It took three years, but McNeel reconciled the opposing factions and supervised the remodeling of the sanctuary.[10]

World War II ended, and an era of postwar prosperity began. The McNeel family moved on to Minnesota. Pastor McNeel had two churches under his wing there and had to go from the one in Rushford to the other in Houston like a circuit rider. Harriet told Bob that she loved the snowy winters and ice-skating on a pond near their house that froze every year. In the summer, she'd go up in the hills above Rushford with her friends to look for rattlesnakes. Whenever they found one, they'd pin down its head with a forked stick and pull off its rattles because a bounty was given for killing rattlesnakes. Proof of a dead rattlesnake was required to collect the bounty. But Harriet and her friends never killed the rattlesnakes because that would have meant killing off a good source of income.[11]

The two-year stint in Minnesota was followed by a five-year stay in Savannah, Ohio. Savannah was another tiny town. Its high school didn't teach Latin, which Harriet's father thought was a big hole in the curriculum, so he sent Harriet and her sister off to the Wasatch Academy, a private Presbyterian boarding school near the Wasatch Mountains in Mount Pleasant, Utah. That at least was the ostensible reason for sending them away from home, but Bob told me that teenaged Harriet, with her own ideas of what she should think and do, believed that she was an embarrassment to her father who wanted her out of sight and out of mind.[12]

Harriet loved Wasatch Academy. It was her first taste of freedom and the best thing that had happened in her young life. No longer watched like hawks by the members of her father's congregation and out from under her father's constant oversight, she blossomed. She became involved in drama and debate. She was a twirler for the school band. She won a state high-school oratory contest. She found a mentor in one of the academy's teachers.[13]

And she drank in the beauty of the Wasatch Mountains that glowed red and gold after the leaves of the oak and aspen trees changed in the fall, that disappeared beneath heavy snow often until late spring, that emerged again after snowmelt covered in green and adorned with wildflowers and free-flowing streams. Extending 160 miles south from the Utah-Idaho border through central Utah, the rugged Wasatch Mountains dominated Harriet's view from the Wasatch Academy, and she remembered those magnificent mountains for the rest of her life.

The Wasatch Mountains weren't Harriet's first exposure to striking landscapes and the outdoors. Growing up in small rural towns, she had spent her childhood in close proximity to nature. Harriet's mother, whose accomplishments included teaching high-school biology, often had taken her children into nearby woods to explore the natural world. Every summer, the whole family vacationed at Chautauqua Lake in southwestern New York as part of the educational Chautauqua Institution where outdoor discoveries went hand in hand with exposure to opera and theater.[14]

Harriet had just graduated from Wasatch Academy when she joined her parents at their new home in Loveland, Colorado, at the base of the Rocky Mountains. Pastor McNeel had taken on another church that was near failure and that eventually would thrive under his care. Sometime during her first summer there, she met Bob Hunt. Bob, a student at Colorado State College, was a couple of years older than Harriet. Shortly after they began dating, Harriet gave him a wallet-sized photo of herself at seventeen. Showing it to me, Bob called it "the most precious photo of the bunch" that he had gathered.

When Harriet went off to college at Colorado A&M fifteen miles from Loveland in Fort Collins, Bob was conveniently nearby in Greeley. Harriet had chosen Colorado A&M in spite of her father's plan for her to attend Maryville College, a Presbyterian institution in Tennessee. Her father figured she could meet a nice young man there who would become a Presbyterian minister just like him. She had already met a nice young man—who didn't want to become a Presbyterian minister—and she went to Colorado A&M.[15]

Harriet majored in engineering math. She had a heavy class load in a field dominated by men and completed three years' work in two years. She swam on the college water ballet team. She belonged to the math honorary society. She worked two jobs: grading papers for the math department and selling tickets at the local movie theater. And in the midst of going to class and working, she took care of her mother as she lay dying in the family home from colon cancer at a time when nobody talked about the dread disease. Cancer was the feared C-word, as unacceptable in polite company as the F-word.[16]

$$\mathscr{I\!\!\!G}$$

Harriet's mother died on February 5, 1955. Harriet married Bob Hunt on June 10, 1955, ten days after Bob graduated from college. As Bob put it, "she wanted to be married, so we did." Harriet was not quite twenty years old. It was the 1950s, and marriage was the end-all and be-all for most young women. Everybody was either getting married or trying to get married. It almost didn't matter who you married as long as you married, though it was best to find a solid, reliable man with a good future.

Television shows and articles in women's magazines often glorified the role of housewife. *Father Knows Best, Leave it to Beaver,* and *The Adventures of Ozzie and Harriet* were three popular shows from the 1950s that featured happy housewives in suburbia. Ads for detergent, vacuum cleaners, ketchup, refrigerators, beauty products, and even beer played to the image of the happy housewife. A sampling of articles in *Ladies' Home Journal, McCall's, Redbook,* and other popular magazines promote the same theme: "Have Babies While You're Young," "Are You Training Your Daughter to be a Wife?," "Cooking to Me is Poetry," and "The Business of Running a Home."[17]

Betty Friedan hadn't yet coined the phrase "feminine mystique," but the notion that the ultimate fulfillment for a woman was to be married, have children, and stay at home permeated life in the 1950s. Besides, as one author writing about women in the 1950s asserts, "The importance of sex as a motive for marriage can hardly be overestimated." Harriet loved Bob and wanted to get married, but she may also have realized that marriage had the advantage of being considered highly desirable at the same time that it offered a way to move out of her father's house now that her mother was gone. They both also realized that as soon as Bob graduated from college, he would lose his student deferment and would be subject to the military draft in the aftermath of the Korean War.[18]

Bob showed me a photo of the two of them on their wedding day. He and Harriet are beaming as they walk hand in hand down the aisle of the First Presbyterian Church in Loveland after the ceremony. Harriet's hair is pulled back and held by a gauzy veil except for rolled bangs that spill down the left side of her forehead. A double strand of pearls encircles her neck above the lacy V-necked bodice of her long-sleeved white gown. She grips a bouquet of white flowers in one hand and holds tightly to Bob's hand with the other. Bob strides beside her in a formal white jacket with a perfectly knotted black bowtie and black pants. With his rimmed glasses and broad smile, he looks enough like 1950s rock star Buddy Holly to be his brother. A picture of a very happy couple.

Harriet never finished college. Only about one-third of women attending college in the 1950s did graduate. Still, she later added to her formal education with two quarters in education at Colorado State College, a semester of courses in landscape architecture at the University of Maryland, and a semester in the University of Southern California's Washington, D.C., master's program in public administration. But, like conservationists John Muir and David Brower, she had no formal degree.[19]

Right after their marriage, Bob spent the summer editing and managing the summer newspaper at his alma mater, then spent the next year teaching junior high school in Twin Falls, Idaho, before he decided to do graduate work at Syracuse University's Maxwell School of Public Affairs in Syracuse, New York. Harriet did her two quarters at Colorado State, then worked as a bookkeeper for a department store in Twin Falls. The summer before Syracuse, she worked as a food concession waitress at a dog-racing track. She got a job as a statistician in the actuarial department of an insurance company in Syracuse until Bob was awarded his master's degree in public administration and the federal government recruited him for an internship program in an agency that later became part of the Department of Housing and Urban Development (HUD). Bob was a dedicated public servant. He devoted his entire forty-one year career to working for HUD and its predecessors.[20]

Shortly before Harriet and Bob moved to Washington, D.C., for his new job, their first child was born. Leslie Lynn was two months old when they loaded up the car with her in a basket in the back seat for the drive to D.C. Linda Jean joined her sister in December 1958. Julia Gail followed in April 1960. By then, the apartment that they had rented in Arlington when they first arrived in D.C. was becoming a little crowded. They found a lot about ten miles away in suburban Virginia and began building their Springfield house in November 1962.

Harriet did door-to-door sales for Avon to help raise money to purchase the house when she wasn't participating in a neighborhood mom's babysitting club, being involved with a co-op preschool, playing bridge, singing with a Washington, D.C., choral group, or attending services at the New York Avenue Presbyterian Church. Their new home was completed in May 1963, at about the same time as the birth of their fourth child and first son, Gregg Brian. Their fifth child, Robert John, arrived eighteen months later in 1964, the last year of the baby boom.[21]

Having a family followed close behind marriage as the thing to do in the 1950s. According to Brett Harvey, author of *The Fifties: A Woman's Oral History*:

> Nothing you could do elicited such universal and unstinting approval. Motherhood has always been a socially sanctioned condition, but not since the late 1800s had motherhood been so glorified and enshrined. The "baby boom," which began as a national response to the end of hard times, a gesture of confidence in the future, turned into a decade-

long celebration of maternity. . . . In fact, motherhood couldn't really be described as a "choice" in the fifties. For one thing, the ideology that equated womanhood and motherhood was powerful and ubiquitous. . . . The project of rearing children was touted as the ultimate challenge to women's skill, resourcefulness, organizational, and even scientific talent. It was also her exclusive domain, the one area in which she could exercise complete control.[22]

The baby boom tsunami of the 1950s began to ebb by 1960. The introduction of the birth control pill gave women the ability to decide how many children they would have and when they would have them. After years of childrearing, many women were beginning to look beyond the confines of domesticity. One indication that not all women were satisfied with just being happy homemakers: twenty-four thousand women responded to *Redbook* magazine's 1960 survey of its readers that revealed, "Why Young Mothers Feel Trapped."

Betty Friedan's *The Feminine Mystique*, published in 1963, labeled the sense of dissatisfaction "the problem that has no name." Friedan argued that women were denied the opportunity to "grow and fulfill their potentialities as human beings" outside of their roles as wives and mothers. But she did not suggest that women discard their roles as wives and mothers. She suggested that women take classes or volunteer until they could begin or resume careers when their children were older.[23]

I don't know if Harriet read *The Feminine Mystique*, though she may very well have because she was an avid reader of newspapers and books. She'd take whatever chance she could to read, even sitting on the floor to peruse a book while doing the laundry. Whether or not she read Betty Friedan's book, she did exactly what Friedan recommended. She volunteered in her new community by joining the Fairfax County League of Women Voters. Soon she was a member of the league's board of directors, serving as chair of the planning and zoning committee and tackling the problem of soil siltation in Fairfax County. To raise public awareness of the problem, she and her committee spoke before fifty county organizations, and their efforts prompted the county to adopt a revised siltation ordinance. Two years later she served on the board as treasurer and chaired a committee looking at ways to redistrict county magisterial districts. The committee proposed the "community of interest" districting plan used by the new Fairfax County Urban Government.[24]

A recommendation from the League of Women Voters put Harriet in charge of the 1968 campaign to win approval of a $67.5 million bond referendum for local schools. After spending five or six nights a week during the month of March at school board meetings that deliberated the form and amount of the bond issue, Harriet had six weeks before the election to convince the citizens of Fairfax County to support the renovation of old schools and the construction of new schools. She organized volunteers to raise campaign funds, to prepare brochures and press releases, and to write and deliver more than one hundred speeches. Harriet joined the volunteers going door-to-door to encourage people to vote. Ten thousand bumper stickers in support of the bond referendum featured photos of two of her children, Julie and Gregg. Her big concern was voter apathy. She told the local newspaper, "There seems to be a mood of indifference to this referendum"; then asked, "How can anyone be indifferent to good education for their children?"[25]

Responding to Harriet's zealous campaign, voter turnout was the largest ever for a school bond referendum in Fairfax County. The referendum passed by a huge margin, but Harriet's celebration of the victory was cut short by the assassination of Robert F. Kennedy on June 6, 1968. After hearing the news, she canceled the victory party for key volunteers. Active in local Democratic politics, Harriet had been a regular delegate to state conventions and had hoped to become a delegate to the national convention to nominate Kennedy as the Democratic candidate for president.[26]

Harriet's all-out efforts on behalf of Fairfax County schools were recognized by the leaders of the Federation of Citizens' Associations, Chamber of Commerce, Council of PTAs, and League of Women Voters when they selected her as the recipient of the *Washington Evening Star* Fairfax County's 1968 Citizen of the Year award. A photograph of Harriet is in the program for the 1969 awards dinner. She is sitting in a chair with a pile of knitting in her lap, needles poised for the next stitch, a big smile on her face and her short hair puffed around her face like an abbreviated nun's wimple. Harriet hadn't had time to knit in years, but looking directly into the camera, long legs demurely crossed, she looked exactly like a housewife who just wanted her kids to have a good education.[27]

Harriet also volunteered in her community by joining the Chelsea Garden Club. Garden clubs had served as a means for women to be involved in environmental issues since the early twentieth century and were especially popular in the 1950s. Harriet again moved into a position of leadership. She served as cochair of a committee that designed the landscape plan for the new local elementary school. The design received community beautification awards from Sears and honorable mention in the national Reader's Digest Civic Beautification Contest. Perhaps her committee work motivated her to do that semester of coursework in landscape architecture at the University of Maryland.[28]

Accolades for Harriet's achievements also came from friends and colleagues. She kept some of the letters written to praise and thank her for her work in a manila envelope labeled "H2 Mementos." One of those letters, penned by a woman named Sarah in April 1968 during the tough battle for passage of the school bond, captures the essence of Harriet Hunt. Sarah wrote:

Dear Harriet,

Two things, as a result of my own private post mortem of last night's briefing:

1. In re-reading the Questions and Answers deal I was simply stunned at the sheer <u>volume</u> of the thing. Migawd did I really write, rewrite, and rewrite again all that stuff? No wonder my head shrieked and my stomach snarled at me! But having worked with the material so intensely, I thought I detected several editorial changes, all of which made the information more clear and meaningful. Thank you very much!

2. During this last ghastly weekend I began to see a "new" Harriet Hunt reveal herself, one who must have always been there

behind the sweet, ready smile, the quick humor, the enormous energy, the highly organized way of getting absolutely impossible projects done competently. This new Harriet has the toughness, the steely determination to persist in the face of unbelievable odds, to firmly, pleasantly, and oh so thoroughly plow through road blocks, and boobie traps, side-stepping diversionary tactics, winding up where she always intended to get at the time she always meant to arrive there.

In short, Harriet, you're a born "battle-axe," and this quality is very hard to find. It is a must for real leadership. I'm happy as a clam to have "found you out"!

Warm regards,

Sarah[29]

Harriet's energy knew no bounds. In the same year that she engineered the school bond referendum victory, she chaired the planning and zoning committee for Kings Park Civic Association, a neighborhood organization, and was the citizen representative to the Fairfax County Planning Commission's advisory committee on the comprehensive plan for the Pohick watershed. One year later she was the coordinator of women's activities for Northern Virginia in the William Battle for governor campaign and she cochaired Omer Hirst's 1971 campaign for Virginia state senator.

Building on her zoning experience with the League of Women Voters and the Kings Park Civic Association, Harriet was tapped to chair the Fairfax County Zoning Ordinance Study Committee (ZOSC) in 1970. Fairfax County had contracted with a Chicago consultant to develop a zoning ordinance for the rapidly growing area. Dissatisfied with the ordinance created by the consultant, the Fairfax County Board of Supervisors appointed a committee to study the zoning issue. Harriet's committee included developers, zoning attorneys, and citizen activists.

After studying the old zoning ordinance, the members of ZOSC concluded that an entirely new ordinance was needed to respond to the intense pressure of development that was devouring open space. Over the four years that Harriet chaired ZOSC, she hired and supervised staff, secured funding, and explained the proposed ZOSC ordinance to public agencies, elected officials, and community organizations. As one of the committee members said, "She ran the thing." The draft ordinance proposed by ZOSC was approved in principle by the County Board of Supervisors in 1974 and officially adopted in 1978. Harriet initiated one of its key provisions that permitted cluster housing for the less-developed western part of the county to preserve as much open space as possible. Her reputation in land-use matters led the *Fairfax County Newsletter* to claim that Harriet probably qualified "as another countywide organization" before quoting her extensively in connection with a zoning issue.[30]

To keep up with all of her commitments, Harriet needed to have her own car. She purchased a small, used Fiat convertible. It was forest green with a black top, two seats, and a luggage rack on the trunk with a ski rack. The car reflected Harriet's move away from the happy housewife portrayed in her photograph in the Citizen of the Year program to a liberated woman of the 1970s. Although she did not join any women's liberation groups or attend protest rallies, she let her hair grow longer and began wearing popular fashions. One-piece swimsuits were out. Bikinis were in, along with miniskirts during the day and long skirts with thigh-high slits for evening events.[31]

At the same time, Harriet had a busy family life. She loved to take her children exploring outdoors. Her daughter Leslie told me, "Nature was the big thing. Her little bible was Rachel Carson's *The Sense of Wonder.*" Harriet had read Carson's *Silent Spring* that exposed the dangers of the widespread use of pesticides such as DDT when it was published in 1962. Bob said that *Silent Spring* was "a real eye-opener for Harriet" and remembered that she stopped using DDT in their yard and tried to find fresh fruit and vegetables that had not been contaminated with the deadly pesticide.[32]

When Carson's *The Sense of Wonder* was published posthumously in 1965, Harriet took her message to heart. Carson hoped that her book would inspire both adults and children to "drink in the beauty and wonder at the meaning of what you see." She believed that "if a child is to keep alive his inborn sense of wonder without any such gift from the fairies, he needs the companionship of at least one adult who can share it, rediscovering with him the joy, excitement and mystery of the world we live in." It was essential to give children the gift of discovering nature for themselves by using all of their senses to see, hear, smell, and touch the world around them. Harriet walked in the woods with her children, letting them sense the wonders of nature, just as Rachel Carson had experienced the natural world with her nephew Roger.[33]

Family camping trips took Harriet, Bob, and their children beyond the limits of their immediate surroundings. They hiked and backpacked from West Virginia to the Colorado Rockies. One holiday weekend, they headed for Spruce Knob, the highest point in West Virginia. In the Monongahela National Forest, Spruce Knob is part of the first National Recreation Area designated by the Forest Service in 1965. Years after hiking there with her family, Harriet was responsible for having forty thousand acres added to the Monongahela National Forest when she worked for Trust for Public Land. On their weekend visit, Harriet and the kids were gathering wild blueberries in a cow pasture when their foraging was interrupted by an irate bull. Instead of dropping the berries and running to safety, Harriet pulled out her T-shirt to make a basket for them before dashing out of the field ahead of the charging bull.[34]

On one hike in Rocky Mountain National Park, they searched for Rocky Mountain bighorn sheep. Scarce in those days, though now some three to four hundred live in the park, they located sheep on Specimen Mountain near the timberline. A backpacking trip took them to Thunder Lake and Wild Basin in Rocky Mountain National Park. They crossed the Continental Divide on another Colorado backpacking adventure, making their way through Indian Peaks Wilderness within Roosevelt National Forest. When the family reached the timberline, hail bombarded everyone and bounced off the boulders, prompting John, Harriet's youngest child, to say, "You didn't tell me it was going to rain ice cubes."[35]

Harriet needed to be outdoors and enjoyed being there with her children. Its importance to her is clear from the draft of a letter she wrote—and perhaps never sent—asking about a job that would allow her to spend the summer in the Idaho wilderness with her two sons. It is undated but must have been written in 1975 based on her references to the ages of her sons and to a newspaper article.

Dear Mr. Campbell,

Today I talked to Ms. Saules about ways I might arrange to spend the summer months in Idaho wilderness. She said you might have job openings so I am sending a resume.

I am trying to find a way to give my two boys a summer away from suburban living. We live in a Virginia suburb of Washington, D.C. where there are a lot of children with not much to do. That provides fertile soil for mischief or at least boredom. The boys are 10 and 11, love fishing and backpacking, and would love a summer spent out of doors.

I am not looking for a job to make me rich but rather a way of earning enough to cover our expenses or at least a part of them.

I love outdoor activities including backpacking, whitewater rafting, spelunking, skiing, etc. so a summer spent in high country would be as much fun for me as for the boys.

Our backpacking experience has been primarily in the Colorado Rockys [sic] and the mountains of Virginia and West Virginia but also includes trips along wild areas of the Virginia seacoast and the New Jersey Pine Barrens. I sometimes backpack alone and am often out alone with children.

I would be glad to send personal references if you would like them. I have included a newspaper article done last fall. I belong to all the PTAs though PTA really isn't my thing. Neither is my hair always in place [a reference I expect to her photograph with coiffed hair captioned "Environmentalist" that appeared in the 19 October 1974 *Alexandria Gazette*].

Thank you,

Harriet Hunt[36]

Harriet was a stay-at-home mom who didn't stay at home. She channeled her drive and energy into community activities before her last child was born and only increased her involvement as her children grew older. She seemed to be the epitome of what psychologist Abraham Maslow once called a "high dominance woman." Based on a late 1930s study of 130 women "of college education or comparable intelligence, between 20 and 28, most of whom were married, of Protestant middle-class city background"—women like Harriet—Maslow drew distinctions between high-dominance women who were self-confident and self-assured with "feelings of general capability or superiority, and lack of shyness, timidity, self-consciousness or embarrassment" and low-dominance women who lacked self-confidence, self-assurance, and self-esteem who were timid, shy, fearful, and self-conscious. High-dominance women "prefer to be independent, stand on their own two feet . . . Many of the qualities that are considered in our culture to be 'manly' are seen in them in high degree, e.g., leadership, strength of character, strong social purpose, emancipation from trivialities, lack of fear, shyness, etc. . . . These individuals customarily have some mission in life, some task to fulfill, some problem outside themselves which enlists much of their energies." Sure sounds like Harriet, who jumped into the socially acceptable arena of community service with both feet.[37]

Busyness devoted to children's activities and community improvement fit right in with the parameters of the feminine mystique, as did marrying young, having five children in rapid succession, and living in a comfortable home in a new subdivision in suburbia. Harriet was living the feminine dream. But it wasn't enough. It wasn't enough to satisfy the basic human need to grow, to take life seriously, and to find one's identity in meaningful work. As one woman with four children who left college at nineteen to get married told Betty Friedan, "I've tried everything women are supposed to do—hobbies, gardening, pickling, canning, being very social with my neighbors, joining committees, running PTA teas. I can do it all, and I like it, but it doesn't leave you anything to think about—any feeling of who you are. . . . I love the kids and Bob and my home. There's no problem you can even put a name to. But I'm desperate. I begin to feel I have no personality."

Most women suffered in silence or ignored the gnawing feelings of dissatisfaction. Some, such as Harriet, did not.[38]

Betty Friedan controversially compared living in a suburban house to living in a German concentration camp. She asked, "Have not women who live in the image of the feminine mystique trapped themselves within the narrow walls of their homes?" Friedan answered her own question with a definitive "yes": "They have learned to 'adjust' to their biological role. They have become dependent, passive, childlike; they have given up their adult frame of reference to live at the lower human level of food and things. The work they do does not require adult capabilities; it is endless, monotonous, unrewarding." She acknowledged that "American women are not, of course, being readied for mass extermination, but they are suffering a slow death of mind and spirit." But, she continued, "there are women who have resisted that death, who have managed to retain a core of self, who have not lost touch with the outside world, who use their abilities to some creative purpose. They are women of spirit and intelligence who have refused to 'adjust' as housewives." Harriet did not lose touch with the outside world. She, like her husband, took an active role in her community.[39]

Harriet waited until her youngest child was in school before taking on responsibilities that involved going away from her home base. She often told the story of how she became a volunteer at the Sierra Club's Washington, D.C., office. "I started volunteering on conservation work when my youngest son went to first grade. I walked into the Sierra Club office in Washington and said, 'I'm a housewife. I'm available from 9 to 3, three days a week. What would you like me to do?' They didn't know what to do with me but I did everything. I stuffed envelopes. I wrote articles. I even went in and talked to congressmen from time to time which was a really scary thing for me at the time."[40]

It was 1973, and the Sierra Club office was on Pennsylvania Avenue right above Roland's grocery store. The smells from the grocery store wafted up into the offices that were cluttered with files. It was an old, dirty place with rats and cockroaches. Brock Evans had just been given the job of managing the Sierra Club's D.C. office when Harriet showed up. Brock told me "this attractive younger woman walks into my office. Harriet wanting to do something. . . . There she was, eager to work and the Sierra Club works off volunteers. . . . There was plenty to do. She didn't come in every day I don't think but came in a lot of days. Whatever there was to do. Sometimes she'd file for me, things like that."[41]

It didn't take long for Brock to realize that Harriet's abilities went beyond filing. He recognized that "she could handle things." He'd tell her, "Go over to such-and-such's office and talk to them. Here's what we want. Here's the file on the case. Let's talk about it and you go on over there and see them." He started sending her as a citizen representative of the Sierra Club. Brock was used to fighting battles over national parks and forests, but he did not know much about appropriations, so he asked Harriet to "go talk to the appropriations committee and see what's going on. How can we weigh in here and things like that." Harriet was a quick study. She figured out what was going on, and her knowledge of the ins and outs of appropriations and her connections with appropriations staff served her well throughout her career. Brock said if he'd had the money, he would have hired her because "she was so competent and so good. Not afraid to ask questions."[42]

Harriet's successes in the community led to the prospect of new opportunities that excited her but alarmed Bob. She was thrilled when friends encouraged her to run for public office—perhaps the County Board of Supervisors or even Congress. Harriet had run campaigns for other candidates and was ready to take on more responsibility, to further broaden her horizons beyond her local community, but Bob was afraid that her political ambitions would lead to the end of their marriage.[43]

Bob's concern was not unwarranted. He may have remembered the national news stories about Coya Knutson, the first congresswoman from Minnesota. Knutson won two terms in the House of Representatives before she was the only Democratic incumbent to lose the 1958 congressional election after the publication of her alcoholic husband's letter that begged her to leave politics "and make a home for your husband and son." Knutson and her husband divorced soon after the election loss. And Bob told me, "We had a couple of friends who had been involved in a political campaign the previous year. And he lost, and it tore up the marriage. I felt she would get hurt, frankly, and it would tear up the marriage." Harriet believed that Bob had sabotaged her plans to run for office.[44]

Even though Harriet did not run for office, her marriage to Bob was in trouble. Bob admitted, "At that point, the girls were teenagers. Things were pretty tense. The family was sort of unraveling anyway." The tensions that had developed in their marriage were evident to Brock Evans, who felt that Harriet "had all the aura and all the angst that I've learned to recognize as a broken home or a divorce."[45]

Between Harriet's demanding volunteer commitments and the business trips that were part of Bob's job at HUD along with his community activities, the two of them were going their separate ways as their lives traveled divergent paths. They increasingly spent more time apart than together. As a member of the Virginia Governor's Electricity Costs Commission, Harriet was in Richmond, Virginia, for weekend meetings for several months. She was a regular delegate from the Fairfax County Democratic Committee to Democratic state conventions. She often was gone on weekend camping trips with the Girl Scout troop that she led. As a member of the Board of the Girl Scout Council in Washington, D.C., she traveled to cities throughout the United States to meet and interview candidates for the council's executive director position. In the last year that Harriet and Bob lived together, she was gone overnight 191 days. Bob was typically out of town on HUD business seventy days every year.[46]

Harriet's work at the Sierra Club's D.C. office was not her first involvement with the club. She had taken her kids on lots of Sierra Club outings as they were growing up. She had helped arrange for rooms and rides from the airports for attendees at the Sierra Club's twelfth Wilderness Conference held in D.C. in September 1971. Bob Hunt speculated that she first encountered Martin Litton at this conference. It was probably because of her connection with the Sierra Club that she received Litton's brochure in the early 1970s that advertised trips down the Colorado River through the Grand Canyon with his company, Grand Canyon Dories.

Harriet's fascination with the Grand Canyon may have been sparked by all of the publicity associated with the Sierra Club's campaign against dams on the Colorado River in the 1960s.

Marble and Bridge Canyon Dams had been proposed as part of the Pacific Southwest Water Plan developed by the Department of the Interior in 1963. They were both in the Grand Canyon itself—the first at mile 40 and the second farther downstream at mile 237. Interior Secretary Stewart Udall praised the dams for their ability to generate enough electricity to pump Colorado River water to Phoenix and Tucson with power left over that could be sold to private utilities. Floyd Dominy, commissioner of the Bureau of Reclamation that would oversee the dams, and others, called the dams "cash registers."[47]

David Brower, executive director of the Sierra Club, was determined to stop the dams and enlisted Martin Litton's help in persuading the Sierra Club to oppose them. At the meeting of the Sierra Club's board of directors in Oakland on May 4, 1963, the question of the Grand Canyon dams was sandwiched on the agenda between consideration of a boundary realignment for Sequoia National Park and the report of the club's Washington representative.[48]

First, board member Bestor Robinson spoke in favor of supporting the dams. After all, he said, the dams would only submerge the first few hundred feet of the canyon and the reservoirs would be hidden from viewpoints most frequently visited by tourists. Robinson recommended that the club approve the dams but stipulate that elevators must be built to transport anglers to the great trout fishing that would be created by the dams.

Enraged by Robinson's pro-dam position, Martin Litton began his argument against the dams by quoting from Theodore Roosevelt's 1903 speech delivered while standing on the South Rim:

In the Grand Canyon, Arizona has a natural wonder which . . . is in kind absolutely unparalleled throughout the rest of the world. I want to ask you . . . to keep this great wonder of nature as it now is. I hope you will not have a building of any kind, not a summer cottage, a hotel or anything else, to mar the wonderful grandeur, the sublimity, the great loneliness and beauty of the canyon. Leave it as it is. You cannot improve on it. The ages have been at work on it, and man can only mar it.

Litton continued by saying that it didn't matter if you couldn't see the reservoirs. What mattered was that dams would violate the sanctity of the river itself. The dams would take the river's soul. Greater access to the river and the canyon would further destroy the very isolation and solitude that drew people to the Grand Canyon in the first place. The government had no right to impose its plan for dams on the Grand Canyon because it belonged to the people. "It's *our* canyon. It's *our* national park," he said. The board listened to Litton and then voted unanimously to give Brower the go-ahead to attack the dams.[49]

The battle against the dams made headlines in the national press. The onslaught included books, pamphlets, letter-writing campaigns, magazine articles, movies, and testimony at congressional hearings. Politicians and other celebrities signed up to experience the Grand Canyon for themselves. A regular reader of the *Washington Post* and Robert Kennedy supporter, Harriet probably saw Art Buchwald's July 1967 column about Kennedy's Colorado River rafting trip through the Grand Canyon. Guests on that trip included Buchwald, Andy Williams, and George Plimpton.[50]

Harriet also may have seen the powerful Sierra Club ads in the *New York Times* that were reproduced in newspapers and magazines across the country. The most well known of these ads asked, "Should We Also Flood the Sistine Chapel so Tourists Can Get Nearer the Ceiling?" Another urged, "Now Only You Can Save the Grand Canyon From Being Flooded . . . For Profit." The ads included coupons addressed to President Johnson, Interior Secretary Stewart Udall, Representative Wayne Aspinall of the House committee that was considering the bill that included the dams, and others to encourage readers to register their protest against the dams in writing. Letters by the thousands poured into Udall's office. At the Bureau of Reclamation, Dan Dreyfus "never saw anything like it. Letters were arriving in dump trucks. Ninety-five percent of them said we'd better keep our mitts off the Grand Canyon and a lot of them quoted the Sierra Club ads."[51]

Even the Internal Revenue Service took notice. Only one day after the first ad appeared, the IRS sent a letter to the Sierra Club suggesting that the club's tax-exempt status was now in jeopardy. It was an unprecedented action that cost the Sierra Club hundreds of thousands of dollars in contributions, but the financial loss was offset by the public support generated by what was perceived as an attempt to intimidate conservationists who were just trying to save the Grand Canyon. The Sierra Club continued its ads. Membership in the club soared. More letters arrived in Washington.[52]

Prompted and inspired by Martin Litton, David Brower and the Sierra Club refused to compromise. At one of the many congressional hearings on the dams, Brower testified, "We have no choice. There have to be groups who will hold for these things that are not replaceable. If we stop doing that we might as well stop being an organization, and conservation organizations might as well throw in the towel." Brower and the Sierra Club triumphed. The final version of the bill that authorized the Central Arizona Project in 1968 prohibited dams in the Grand Canyon.[53]

By the time the battle against the dams was over, the publicity generated by the fight had triggered widespread enthusiasm for experiencing the Grand Canyon. As Kevin Fedarko, author of *The Emerald Mile: The Epic Story of the Fastest Ride in History Through the Heart of the Grand Canyon*, observed, "a Grand Canyon white-water trip had emerged as the classic American wilderness experience, a pilgrimage at the top of the bucket list for anyone who loved the country's natural wonders." Harriet decided that she wanted to make the pilgrimage; that she wanted to go down the Colorado River through the Grand Canyon. She had been on several rafting trips already but never down the Colorado River. Never in the Grand Canyon. Never in a dory. She made plans to embark on this great adventure. With her daughter Julie, Harriet joined one of Martin Litton's dory expeditions in 1973.[54]

Martin Litton started his company, Grand Canyon Dories, after he resigned his position as travel editor with *Sunset Magazine* in late 1968 over a disagreement about a story on threats to the California redwoods. As he tells it, "I was having somewhat of a feud with the management at *Sunset* and one day I said, 'That does it. I quit.' And walked out. Threw away my security blanket and what was left was the dories." Litton had been taking folks on dory trips in the 1960s mostly because he loved the Grand Canyon and wanted "to help them see enough so they could care more. Have them on that river. Let them feel its life. The way it stirs and rumbles and moves you along at its own pace. It has tremendous force and appeal. Getting people on that river means *they* can understand it." His 1964 expedition that included David Brower, Philip Hyde, and François Leydet was re-created in the Sierra Club book *Time and the River Flowing* to describe the wonders of the Grand Canyon and to protest the proposal to put dams there. Friends wanted to have the same experience, then friends of friends, and then there were so many that Litton began charging for the trips. He incorporated Grand Canyon Dories in 1971.[55]

Journeying through the Grand Canyon with Martin Litton, Harriet no doubt heard him extol the virtues of the canyon and its river while excoriating the greed that threatened it and other wilderness areas. Rowing down the river or hiking the side canyons, Martin was known for taking advantage of every opportunity to share his passionate beliefs about saving the earth from destruction. I imagine that what he said then was much like what he said to Lew Steiger in 1994:

> There are several reasons why the Colorado River should be natural, one is the joy of running on a natural river, and knowing that you're as close to nature as you can be. And the other is, whether we run it or not, nature has its right. It has a right to be here untrammeled, unfettered. Man doesn't have to screw everything up, and yet we go out of our way to do so. Greed is the motive and it's important to frustrate greed. . . . Do we have a right even to interrupt nature, even for a short time? To exterminate species? To kill the last fly? That's not really our right.

He also liked to pepper his orations with quotes from his favorite works of literature, like Kenneth Grahame's, "There is *nothing*, absolutely nothing, half so much worth doing as simply messing about in boats," from *The Wind in the Willows*. Or a few quotes from Grand Canyon pioneer John Wesley Powell. Martin was an eloquent, charming, and convincing advocate for conservation.[56]

Martin Litton advocated a no-compromise approach and is famous for declaring over and over again, "People often tell me not to be extreme. Be reasonable! they say. But I've never felt it did any good to be reasonable about anything in conservation, because what you give away will never come back—ever. When it comes to saving wilderness, we cannot be extreme *enough*." Litton also said, "Well, of course, to compromise is to lose. When you're willing to compromise your principles, you've given up, you abandon them. As Dan Luten said, 'When you compromise, nature gets compromised.' It's gone, it's hurt, it's injured. You gain nothing back, ever."[57]

Harriet absorbed Litton's message. He's been called a "world-class charmer," and Harriet fell under his spell. Back from her first trip through the Grand Canyon in Martin Litton's dories, Harriet plunged into her volunteer work at the Sierra Club's Washington, D.C., office. She began her work at the Sierra Club with his words ringing in her ears. Conservation, saving land from development, always had been important to Harriet, but now it became her mission. In her testimony before a congressional committee soon after she began volunteering at the D.C. office, Harriet proclaimed, "I am here to speak for the Earth because it can't speak for itself." Harriet had found her purpose in life.[58]

When I asked Martin about Harriet, one story he told me was about the time the two of them worked together to prevent the transfer of parts of Grand Canyon National Park to the Havasupai Indians. I think it was his favorite Harriet story, because I heard him tell it on several occasions. For hundreds of years, the Havasupai gardened in the side canyons of the Colorado River during the summer and ranged over the nearby Coconino Plateau to hunt in the winter. Their traditional lands covered more than two million acres. By the late nineteenth century, ranches, mines, and railroads had pushed the Havasupai onto a reservation of slightly more than five hundred acres divided between two parcels above Havasu Falls. Use permits from the National Park Service allowed the Havasupai access to the plateau land. The reservation was enlarged by twenty-five hundred acres in the 1940s, but that addition fell far short of Havasupai hopes.[59]

Although the tribe voted to accept $1.24 million in 1968 as compensation for the loss of more than two million acres of its traditional lands, the drive to expand the Havasupai reservation did not end. In 1972, the Havasupai persuaded Senator Barry Goldwater to add a provision to his Grand Canyon National Park enlargement bill that transferred approximately 185,000 acres of land to the tribe.[60] Spearheaded by the Sierra Club and Friends of the Earth, environmental groups and the National Park Service opposed the land transfer. The struggle between the Havasupai supporters and the environmentalists lasted for almost two years.[61]

Not surprisingly, Martin Litton jumped into the fray. Harriet joined him. They worked closely together to oppose the land transfer. In 1974, as lobbyists on both sides were exerting themselves to gain support among House committee members, Harriet wrote Martin on July 2:

> Dear Martin,
>
> This is the list of Interior committee members. If you have time to get a wire off to Taylor before July 10 it would be great. Ask him to defer if he can and remind him of his responsibility to the parks. I sent him a letter, the one I read you, over your signature. Leydet called and signed the letter also. The club is doing a mailer to the districts of Interior committee members. Can you bring pressure to bear on Owens from folks in Utah? John thinks he will vote pro-Indian. Maybe the other outfitters would write to him, call or wire.
>
> Love, Harriet
>
> We may be able to get further delays in the vote in the Interior Committee. I'll let you know.

Then Harriet adds on July 3:

> The Wilderness Society has agreed to send the Sierra Club action letter to their membership, the Friends of the Earth is doing a mailing. I've spent the last week visiting other conservation organizations urging them to join the fight. It's a slow business but personal visits carry more weight than a phone call.
>
> Ann Sutton is taking up the battle. I called her yesterday and she's going to wire and rally others she knows. (You probably know she & her husband wrote a book on the canyon several years ago.)
>
> Sorry this letter is such a mess but I wanted to let you know where things were.
>
> HH

At this point, Harriet only had been working with Brock Evans at the Sierra Club's D.C. office for about a year, but she knew how to bring pressure on the members of Congress whose votes were crucial for blocking the Havasupai land transfer.[62]

Sometime during the debate over the bill known as the Grand Canyon National Park Enlargement Act, Harriet and Martin called on congressmen during a long day on Capitol Hill. When Martin told me the story many years later, he said that the Havasupai hoped to become rich by claiming land on the rim of the canyon and developing aerial tramways. He said the politicians in Arizona were for it—anything to make money. Mo Udall was one of the congressmen from Arizona who supported the bill. Martin felt "he was going to be our stumbling block," so he planned to see Udall when he and Harriet went to Washington, D.C. Udall was their last appointment after calling on congressmen all day trying to stop the desecration of the Grand Canyon. They were an hour late for the appointment. By that time, no one was in the anteroom of Udall's office, but the congressman had waited for them.

Martin and Harriet showed Udall a map that revealed the damage to the Grand Canyon if the legislation to expand the Havasupai reservation and develop the rim of the Grand Canyon passed. Mo Udall did not seem to be interested in listening to their argument. Martin thought maybe Udall was looking at Harriet more than at the map and that Harriet made the difference. Udall offered to push the line for the development one-quarter mile back from the river. Harriet suggested one-half mile back. Martin said, "He couldn't say no to Harriet. Harriet was telling Congress what they had to do to save the Grand Canyon. They were charmed by Harriet." By the time Martin and Harriet left Udall's office, they believed they had convinced him to revise the map as Harriet wanted. Martin concluded that Harriet had "changed the course of history by the way she could charm a member of Congress into doing what she wanted to be done. And what she wanted done was always the right thing."[63]

Harriet may have charmed Mo Udall, and he may have at least temporarily agreed to her suggestion that the boundary line for the Havasupai reservation be pushed back one-half mile instead of his recommendation of one-quarter mile. In September or October 1974, Jeff Ingram, a Sierra Club lobbyist, heard Udall talk about moving the boundary farther back from the rim, but when the Grand Canyon National Park Enlargement Act finally passed Congress in December, it delineated "a boundary line generally one-fourth of a mile from the rim of the outer gorge of the Grand Canyon of the Colorado River" for the 185,000 acres of land that were transferred to the Havasupai. It's possible that Harriet's achievement was getting one-quarter mile instead of nothing. The Havasupai were also granted the use of approximately 95,300 acres of land for grazing and other traditional purposes within Grand Canyon National Park.

The Sierra Club and its allies had failed to persuade Congress to stop the Havasupai land transfer, but the 1974 act did enhance Grand Canyon National Park by declaring that the entire Grand Canyon is "a natural feature of national and international significance" that should be protected and interpreted "in accordance with its true significance." Grand Canyon National Monument and Marble Canyon National Monument were abolished and incorporated into the park. The park's approximately 1.2 million acres now included the entire Colorado River from the Paria junction to the Grand Wash Cliffs—progress if not total victory.[64]

The Grand Canyon changes people. Not usually those who simply peer over the rim at its immensity for an hour or two, but those who go down into the heart of the canyon and feel its pulse. Those who are cut off from the amenities and distractions of civilization for days as they make their way through the mile-deep canyon on the Colorado River. Especially those who go slowly and silently in oar-powered rafts or dories.

Martin Litton believed that "the most important thing is the majesty of the Canyon. And what it does to people's lives to be away from their normal routines for a while. Even a short while." Expanding on the impact of the Canyon, he said:

> Many people . . . make quite a thing of how the Grand Canyon experience, going down the river, has changed their lives . . . how the experience has somehow opened their eyes to something bigger and greater in life. It's made their lives better. They understand . . . the whole universe better because of having been in the Grand Canyon and isolated from other things and having time to think. A river trip has been called "The Voyage of Life" [like] the famous series of paintings from the National Gallery [by Thomas Cole]. It's about a voyage down this river of life. It begins with a little baby in a little

floating cockleshell, shaped like a swan, floating into this canyon and then the paintings go on and the party ages. You see the roughness of life by the rapids in the river. The obstacles and all that.

And that's where you have a young man able to grip all these things and master them, the problems of life. It's all related to a voyage down a river. And then you see suddenly the calm and the sun shining through the clouds and this old, old man comes out of this canyon onto the calm water. And it's amazing how like a Grand Canyon trip that is. . . . There's something very fine and ennobling and serious about the whole experience. It is a microcosm of life when you go down that river. You start, a kind of lighthearted effect and the challenge isn't so great at the beginning and then it develops and develops and you find yourself able to cope with it and finally you've done it. You've done the whole thing.

As one passenger who joined Martin in 2004 for her fourth trip down the river said, "I've seen a few people go down this canyon and not get changed, but not many. There's just something about how minuscule you feel compared to how long it took to put this place together. It seems to put things in balance. It wakes you up. It opens your eyes. And afterwards, things are not the same."[65]

Things were not the same for Harriet. She was drawn irresistibly back to the Grand Canyon. Leaving her husband and kids in Virginia, she made at least two more trips with Martin Litton and his Grand Canyon Dories in the early 1970s. Photos taken on one of those trips—probably by Martin—capture Harriet reveling in the freedom and glory of the Grand Canyon. Harriet smiling up from between two boulders with a waterfall directly behind her. Harriet walking a canyon path clad in her bikini. Harriet in another world far removed from PTA meetings, Girl Scout Council meetings, and zoning committee meetings.

Harriet's trips to the Grand Canyon created friction in her marriage. Once Harriet just left a note for her husband on the kitchen table: "I'm going to the Grand Canyon. I'll see you again in eight weeks. I was going to tell you but we would only have fought about it."[66] I think this was the trip to the Grand Canyon that Harriet took shortly after she was appointed Park and Recreation Authority commissioner for her district in Fairfax

County in 1976. This time she went early and came back late. She was not available for answering calls about Park and Recreation Authority business. She did not tell her husband her plans. She ran the rapids and climbed the canyons. On one hike, she lost her balance when a ledge broke and she fell. She was saved from crashing to the canyon floor when her ankle caught on the broken ledge. Her ankle was smashed. She had to be carried everywhere she went for the rest of the trip.

Harriet eventually resurfaced in Virginia and officially separated from Bob Hunt on August 20, 1976.[67]

After filing for divorce, Harriet loaded her two sons and their dog into the wood-paneled family station wagon and started driving west—away from her conventional life in the suburbs, away from Providence Presbyterian Church where she was a charter member, away from her friends, away from her husband, away from her daughters. Just before leaving, Harriet and the boys leaned against the side of their car and posed for a photograph. Harriet is dressed in a sleeveless white turtleneck. Long bangs obscure most of her high forehead. A whisper of a smile plays on her grimly determined face.

Harriet called Bob from somewhere on Interstate 70. She told him that she was on her way with Gregg and John to join Natalie Roush, a woman she had met on one of her Grand Canyon trips, at her Lopez Island sheep ranch. One of the San Juan Islands, Lopez Island is located off the coast of northwestern Washington State.

A converted granary on the ranch became their new home. The basic living quarters were not quite the hayloft that Bob Hunt remembered when we talked, but the bathroom facilities were limited: a sink, an outhouse, and a shower one-quarter of a mile away in the ranch bunkhouse. The boys attended a small school with a total of about fifteen kids in the combined fifth and sixth grades.

Some nine months after their arrival, Harriet—perhaps in response to her husband's demands or perhaps because she realized that Gregg and John needed to be home in Virginia—put her sons on a United flight out of Seattle. Eventually Harriet drove back to Virginia, but not before leaving Lopez Island and trying unsuccessfully to find a job in San Francisco.[68]

Harriet did not return to the family home on Cromwell Drive. Living on her own, sleeping on the couch at a friend's house, she needed a job. Her experience as a volunteer for the Sierra Club on Capitol Hill paid off, though not at first. When she went looking for a job as a congressional staff member, she started with her congressman, Herb Harris. Harriet and Bob both knew him well. Harriet had worked on both of his first two campaigns for office. But Harris refused to hire her. He told her, "If I hire you, you'll be running against me in two years. Go home and help Bob raise your five kids."[69]

Harriet had better luck at Congressman Pete Stark's office. Stark represented the ninth congressional district in California. Harriet first had made contact with Stark's office on one of her congressional forays for the Sierra Club. When she told Brock Evans that she was going to work for Stark, he congratulated her. He "could tell she was in pain," and the job "was exactly what she needed."[70]

Harriet continued to develop her skills as Stark's legislative assistant. She researched, analyzed, and drafted legislation. She advised Stark on pending legislation that involved environmental, urban, and agricultural issues. She drafted statements and briefing reports. She served as Stark's liaison to the District of Columbia Committee and the National Capital Regional Planning Commission. She supervised staff interns. In remarks published in the *Congressional Record*, Stark called Harriet "an exemplary member of my legislative staff in Washington, D.C."[71]

Harriet's tenure at Stark's D.C. office lasted as long as it took for her divorce to be finalized. The divorce proceedings dragged on for almost two years. Actions were filed, counter-filed, and venues changed before the final decree was issued on July 10, 1978. Harriet's attorney told Bob, "I would bet that within six months she will be back with you. Right now she needs time to get her head straight." Harriet's attorney lost her bet. Harriet left for Stark's district office in Oakland, California, shortly after her divorce was granted.[72]

Harriet later said she wanted to get as far away from Bob Hunt as possible. But two months after the divorce, Bob flew out to California to see her. Harriet was bored with her work at the district office and her spirits were low. They spent Columbus Day weekend traveling the California coast from Big Sur to San Francisco together. At the end of the weekend, Bob asked Harriet, "What would you think about getting married again?" Possibly feeling guilty and homesick, Harriet said, "I think I would like that. Can we do it on a bicoastal basis? I'd like to see what I can do with the job here in California and you're in San Francisco on business quite a bit. I'm in Washington on business. There are vacations. There are holidays. We could be together those times."

A bicoastal marriage was not what Bob had in mind. It probably wasn't really what Harriet wanted either. Bob flew back to Virginia, and Harriet stayed in California, but she kept Hunt as her middle name and informally signed herself as H2 or HH throughout her career.[73]

Because Harriet had decided to stay in California, she needed to find a place to live. She had a temporary home with her friend Kate, who ran Stark's district office, but she wanted a place of her own, so she started checking out rentals listed in the classified section of the newspaper. And that's how she met Joe Burgess, the man who would become her second husband.

Joe had placed an ad in the local paper to find a tenant for his house in the Montclair district of Oakland after his recent divorce. Harriet had been looking at all of the houses she could afford and didn't like any of them, so she decided to look at houses she couldn't afford. She figured she'd get a roommate one way or another to share the cost of the house. Located high in the Oakland hills, with a 270-degree view of the bay, Joe's house was definitely outside her price range. But as fate would have it, she looked at the house anyway.[74]

Walking down Joe's street in high heels and a very stylish outfit, Harriet spotted a good-looking man in front of the house and said, "Joe?" He answered, "Harriet?" They went into the house, looked around a little bit, then sat in front of the fireplace talking and drinking wine together. Joe was supposed to check out Harriet as a tenant, but he didn't ask for references or a deposit. Harriet was supposed to check out the house. When Harriet went back to Kate's place, Kate asked, "How was the house?" Harriet answered, "Great!" When Kate asked about the kitchen, Harriet said, "I never got to the kitchen. I don't even know if it has a kitchen."[75]

Eventually Harriet moved into Joe's house and became well acquainted with the kitchen. But first, she negotiated the lease. She told Joe she would have to find a roommate to be able to afford the house. And that her son, John, would be joining her as soon as she was settled. And her dog, too. Joe didn't hesitate. He said, "Sure, no problem. Son, dog. You need a roommate, fine, I'll help you. No problem at all." He could not resist the sexy, long-legged, beautiful, smart woman who had shown up on his doorstep.

Joe, an attorney, wrote the lease that they both signed. Harriet found a roommate. John and her dog joined her. Joe's six-year-old son, Evan, often was at the house, too. And Joe's dog was there. Joe planned to live in the apartment that he was constructing below the house, but it wasn't finished yet, so he subleased space from Harriet. Soon they were sharing the same bedroom. The roommate left, and they made no effort to replace her.

After a few years of living together, Harriet and Joe decided to get married. About fifty friends gathered in Cazadero at Green Glen, ten acres of redwoods that belonged to Joe, for the ceremony on May 24, 1981. Bob Stephens was best man. Harriet's cousin, Lou, was maid of honor. It was an informal wedding in a grove of trees. No church. No minister. Several dogs in attendance.[76]

Joe showed me a photo of the two of them on their wedding day. Harriet and Joe are grinning as they stand amid the redwoods. Harriet's auburn hair falls loosely to her shoulders. A small brooch is pinned to the lace that borders her scoop-necked dress of lavender sprigged cotton. She clasps a casual bouquet of daisies, iris, baby's breath, and ferns. Joe stands beside her in a dark suit and red-striped tie with his arm around her waist. A very happy couple.

Russell and I made several trips to visit Joe Burgess at the home he shared with Harriet on Inverness Ridge. We navigated a steep, twisty, narrow road to get there. Every time we drove that road, I was amazed that so many people were so strongly attached to that place that they were willing to drive it regularly. They must possess a fortitude that I do not have—but I am willing to negotiate the climb up to the ridge to visit with Joe, and my amazement fades every time I look out the windows of the house or stand on its deck to see nothing but the forested slopes Harriet saw every day of the twelve years she lived there with her husband.

During each visit, Joe told me more about the woman he described as "fiercely determined; a loving wife, mother, grandmother and friend; fearless and adventuresome; exceptionally capable at most things she tried; intelligent; an unselfish person who genuinely cared about other people and causes; someone who always wanted to do the right thing; a practical idealist."

He added, "She had the kind of superhuman energy that allowed her to cook a family dinner, make her 'red-eye' flight to Washington with ten minutes to spare, change and take a quick shower, spend all day walking the halls of Congress, meeting with and cajoling congressional staff, jump on a westbound plane that very same day and return home."

And Harriet was "a voracious reader, a political junkie, sexy, an opera lover from childhood, a scuba diver, an enthusiastic hiker and trekker who never seemed to tire out, an avid white-water/Grand Canyon enthusiast, the perfect crew member . . . possessed of boundless energy, courage, and will in the cause of saving land and nurturing her family, a 'force of nature.'" For Joe, that was Harriet.

We talked about Harriet while Joe prepared lunch. Joe remarked that he cooks, but Harriet would "sling hash." Harriet always needed something to eat before taking on the day, otherwise she was "cranky." She had to have her coffee.

We talked about Harriet while sitting around the kitchen table or on a sofa in front of the fireplace. Harriet loved music, especially the opera and symphony. Except in the Grand Canyon, Harriet did not do well in hot weather. She was an ebullient extrovert, connecting with people wherever she went.

We talked about Harriet while walking on nearby Kehoe Beach. Harriet had a bucket list of all the places she wanted to experience, all of the adventures she wanted to have. Early in their relationship, Joe took Harriet sailing off Vancouver Island in the wilds of British Columbia. She had no sailing experience, but she was "totally game" and responded intuitively to Joe's nautical commands. It was the first of their many travels all over the world.[77]

Harriet did not make the same copious notes on her personal life that she recorded for many of her conservation projects. She left no diary or journal for historians to scrutinize. Instead, it is clear from talking to Bob and Joe—seeing the earnest eagerness on Bob's face as he recalls one of her many adventures or the delighted look in Joe's eyes as he relives one of their bucket-list trips—that she is deeply inscribed in the memories of those she loved and who loved her.

Harriet with her sister, Jean, and parents, Frances and Clair McNeel

A young Harriet in the mountains

Harriet and Robert Hunt on their wedding day, June 10, 1955
FAMILY OF HARRIET BURGESS/LESLIE KING COWAN

Harriet and her family in Colorado, August 1969; from left to right, the children are Leslie, Gregg, Linda, John, and Julie.

Harriet in the 1960s

Harriet (on the far right) in the 1960s with the Kings Park Elementary School
Landscape Committee reviewing landscape plans

Harriet in the living room of her home in Springfield, Virginia, after receiving the *Washington Evening Star* Fairfax County 1968 Citizen of the Year award

Harriet and the group that went with her on her first trip through the Grand Canyon in May 1973. Harriet is in the first row, second from the left. John Blaustein sits next to her on the right. Harriet's daughter Julie is in the second row, second from the right with her arms crossed over her knees. Martin Litton stands in the back row in a white T-shirt and no hat.

JOHN BLAUSTEIN

Harriet, John, and Gregg just before leaving for Lopez Island with their dog, Sam, 1976

Harriet and Joe Burgess on their wedding day, May 24, 1981

Harriet trekking in Nepal, 1984

Harriet on vacation

Harriet Burgess, circa 1995
FAMILY OF HARRIET BURGESS/JOSEPH BURGESS

Harriet on one of her first Grand Canyon trips in the mid-1970s
JOHN BLAUSTEIN

John rowing Bob Stephens past a hole in Crystal Rapid at mile 98.2
FAMILY OF HARRIET BURGESS/JOHN HUNT

Joe and Harriet in the Grand Canyon, mid-1980s
FAMILY OF HARRIET BURGESS/JOSEPH BURGESS

Harriet and a boatman running Crystal while everyone else walks around the dangerous rapid
RICHARD ANDERSON

Harriet in the Grand Canyon
FAMILY OF HARRIET BURGESS/LESLIE KING COWAN

John rows Harriet in the Grand Canyon
FAMILY OF HARRIET BURGESS/JOHN HUNT

Harriet and friends scouting a Grand Canyon rapid; Harriet is wearing her favorite Grand Canyon shirt
FAMILY OF HARRIET BURGESS/LESLIE KING COWAN

Interlude

Grand Canyon

AT MILE 92, *DARK CANYON* GLIDES ONTO THE BEACH AT TRINITY CREEK. Kerstin hops out and secures the dory, then we follow her. It is our first campsite. Harriet may also have camped here on one of her numerous Grand Canyon trips, though the exact dimensions of the beach, the arrangement of its rocks, and the display of its vegetation undoubtedly have altered with the passage of time.

According to a 2009 National Park Service inventory, there are 235 campsites between Lees Ferry and Diamond Creek on sandy beaches formed by deposits of sand and sediment carried by the river. Before the Colorado River was blocked by Glen Canyon Dam sixteen miles above Lees Ferry in 1963, annual sediment flows of one million tons created and maintained long stretches of wide sandy beaches along the shores of the Colorado River. According to Kerstin's mother-in-law, at one time you could go for miles through the Grand Canyon without leaving the sandy banks of the river.

Recently instituted annual flooding caused by large releases of sediment-filled water from Glen Canyon Dam is intended to help retain and rebuild beaches, but the controlled floods don't begin to duplicate the impact of a wild river flowing. The beaches are narrow. Sand deposited by the annual floods erodes quickly. Vegetation is taking over many of the beaches, including the invasive and ubiquitous tamarisk. Spacious and comfortable campsites are few and far between.

Our first task on reaching the campsite is to find a good place for our tent. What constitutes a good place depends on the camper, but most of us are looking for a flat area at least somewhat screened by brush from neighboring tents. Sand, rocks, and vegetation dictate our options. Tent sites are first come, first served so we quickly learn to exit the dory expeditiously to scout the best locations. We don't know this the first day, and we don't know exactly which features are especially important to us. After looking at some possibilities and weighing the advantages of each, we select a spot that is fairly flat and open. We share the area with several others.

Leaving our dry bags to mark our tent site, we head over to where Roger and Kerstin are gathering the group together to cover the basics of Grand Canyon camping. Roger explains and demonstrates what we need to do to put up our two-person dome tent. He makes it look easy. It's not. Not for a first-time camper like me.

The tent components are in a dry bag that we have taken from the stack unloaded onto the beach from one of the baggage rafts. After spreading our ground cloth over the sand, we remove the pieces of the tent from the bag and look at them.

I am tired, hot, and hungry. I suck it up and try to remember what to do.

"So where do we start?"

"Put all the poles together."

We do that by sliding the end of one piece of a pole into the end of another. The pieces are all strung together with stretchy cord. They are very flexible and difficult to control.

"Now what?"

"Beats the shit out of me."

We have to attach the tent to the poles but have no idea how to do it. Russell tries something that doesn't work, then I try something that doesn't work.

"God damn fucking tent."

Harriet, a very experienced camper, often simply constructed a tent by stringing a rope between two trees and hanging a sheet of plastic over it when she went on backpacking trips with her young family in the wilds of Virginia. In the Grand Canyon, I suspect she rarely used a tent at all, choosing to sleep out in the open. And if the boatmen hadn't advised against it because of forecast rain, I would have been tempted to choose that option myself.

The tent still is lying in a pile on the ground cloth when Russell finally yells, "Get over here!" at Michael, who has quietly and efficiently assembled his own tent nearby. Within ten minutes, our tent is up and ready for us. It is not very big. It has just enough space for two sleeping pads butted up against each other, leaving narrow strips around the edges for our stuff. I crawl in through one of the two door flaps and lay the sleeping bags on the pads. I am reminded of the fun I had building tents out of furniture and blankets in the living room when I was a kid. But now I'm really camping, and there is no retreating to a comfortable bed under a solid roof in a house with a bathroom.

I may regret the absence of the "comforts" of home, but I am sure that Harriet never did. For her, the Grand Canyon was home. And there she lacked for nothing.

After Roger explains tent construction, Kerstin explains Grand Canyon toilet etiquette—or how to use "The Unit"—while in camp. The Unit is the name for the white toilet-seat topped gray metal ammo box next to the black toilet-seat topped yellow plastic bucket that together constitute the closest to a bathroom that we will see for ten days. The ammo box is for shitting and the bucket is for peeing. It is important to keep the two separate because the contents of the ammo box have to be carried out of the Canyon whereas the contents of the bucket can be dumped in the river. The ammo box gets too full and heavy if the two are combined. Kerstin especially cautioned the ladies against using the ammo box for anything but shit. Toilet paper goes in the ammo box. Very bad if you forget and drop it in the pee bucket. The contents of the ammo box are dusted with bleach powder after every use, unfortunately reminding me of dusting brownies with confectioner's sugar. The ammo box—14.5 inches high, 18 inches long, and 8 inches wide and originally intended to hold antitank grenade rockets for M1A1 bazookas—is also known as the Groover. In the early days of Grand Canyon expeditions, the nicety of a toilet seat was accidentally omitted once and sitting on the can left grooves wherever the can touched skin.[78]

Finding The Unit is easy. Located at every campsite in a spot chosen with both privacy and views in mind, its entrance is marked by a reflector stake. Next to the stake are two buckets. One is filled with water, the other sports a spigot and soap dispenser hanging from its rim. A hose runs from the water bucket to a foot pump on the ground between the two buckets to the spigot. Pump soap on your hands. Pump water to rinse them. The first step—and the last step—for using The Unit is hand washing. The boatmen are always reminding us to wash our hands to minimize the chances of getting any kind of digestive upset or other illness while on the river, which would be extremely inconvenient and unpleasant for everyone.

The next step is to determine whether The Unit is available. All twenty-four of us share it. If the plastic container holding a roll of toilet paper is near the hand washing buckets, then the coast is clear. More reflector stakes mark the path to the O.A.R.S. version of a Grand Canyon toilet. The round red reflectors at the top of the stakes are essential for nighttime trips to The Unit, though everybody is provided with a small lapis blue bucket to keep just outside the tent for peeing in the middle of the night. Emphasis on keeping the bucket outside—we were told a story about the unfortunate consequences of trying to use the bucket inside your tent.

It's your responsibility to dump the contents of the blue bucket in the river the next morning, a task that Russell gallantly assigned himself with no objections from me. For safety reasons, peeing directly into the river at night is strongly discouraged.

I check out The Unit and conclude that, indeed, toilet seats on two containers sitting on sand visible from the river are going to put me way out of my comfort zone—probably not as far, though, as I would have been had I gone with Martin Litton in his early days of running the river. Then it was just take a roll of toilet paper and go up in the rocks, far away from the camp. Find a crack in the rocks. Then burn your toilet paper. Sometimes big fires resulted from people burning toilet paper. Everybody would get buckets and carry up water to put out the fire. One time Martin inadvertently started a really big fire at Lower Lava. So I guess it could have been worse.[79]

I wake early the first morning to beat the crowd to The Unit. I wriggle into my clothes, scoot over to the tent flap, unzip it, stick my legs out the opening, and try to stand up. Overnight, my whole body has stiffened in reaction to the long downhill hike, the cold bath I'd taken in the river, and the thin pad on firm sand that had served as my bed. I stagger for a few painful and wobbly steps before my muscles warm enough to allow me to navigate my way to The Unit entrance about one hundred feet from our tent.

Back in the tent, I try for some semblance of my normal routine. I wash my face with Cetaphil, which has the big benefit of requiring no water, just a towel to rub it off. I do as many of my exercises as I can manage—constrained both by the limitations of the tent and the soreness of my muscles. I scribble a few notes in my journal. I help Russell repack the tent and sleep kits in dry bags that we deliver to a staging area near the boats on our way to join the group for breakfast.

The drill for every meal is first, and always, wash hands! I soon realize the multipurpose value of the bandana I'd brought to shield my neck from the sun. Handy for drying hands after washing them, and for serving as a napkin during meals. I serve myself from the bountiful array of remarkably good food. On offer for our first night were chicken, broccoli, and potatoes, with birthday cake for dessert in honor of Russell and several others celebrating birthdays in September. Breakfast is pancakes.

The boatmen rotate cooking responsibilities. When Martin first started Grand Canyon Dories in the 1970s, he staffed the trips with cooks. Usually women were the cooks, the only position available to them on the river because Martin initially didn't allow women to row the dories. On one of Harriet's early trips, an inexperienced cook quit in a huff after six days. Harriet said, "Don't worry, I'll cook." And she did, even though the previous cook had planned poorly so they hardly had enough food to go around.[80]

All of the plates and utensils are reusable, and four large metal buckets are lined up on a table to clean them after eating. The first two are filled with soapy water, the third with water for a plain rinse, and the fourth with water and bleach for a chlorine rinse. Forks, knives, and spoons are then dropped in a container hanging at one end of the table. Plates and bowls go in a net hanging from one of the kitchen prep tables nearby. Yet another remarkably efficient camp system.

Blue canvas chairs arranged in a circle form the camp dining and living rooms. I balance my plate of pancakes on my lap to eat, having wedged my cup of orange juice in the sand below my chair, and chat with a few other early risers as the rest of the group joins us one or two at a time. Our group is mostly older, professional men and women. We'd had a chance to get to know one another a little before dinner the night before.

All of the six married couples on this trip (with one possible exception) have been married to each other for a long time. Two of the couples are traveling together to celebrate their fortieth anniversary. Russell and I have been married thirty-six years. I am a bit surprised at the number and length of one-time marriages because divorce and second marriages are so common. Included are two doctors, so we're in good shape if we have a medical crisis, and two lawyers, an engineer, an art curator, and a businessman. Everyone is friendly and pleasant.

CHAPTER TWO

Another Canyon

Topanga Canyon

*My wife and I have lived here for over thirty years, and have traveled to many places, from China to Africa and from England to Greece. We have crisscrossed the United States more times than we can remember, in the air and on the ground, from the Pacific to the Atlantic, and from the Arctic Ocean to the Gulf of Mexico. But nowhere have we seen the combined beauty that Topanga offers, with its peaks and gorges, its wildlife and its wildflowers. Nowhere is there a place like this, a community that exists in all dimensions. —*AL MARTINEZ[1]

My feeling has always been, you can't always win, but you can always try. And that we're not as poor for the battles we've lost as for the ones we never fought. Win or lose, there's a measure of victory in the endeavor. —MARTIN LITTON[2]

ABOUT 420 MILES SOUTHWEST OF THE GRAND CANYON, A MUCH shorter and younger canyon cuts a path from the San Fernando Valley to the Pacific Ocean. Located in the Santa Monica Mountains almost entirely within the Los Angeles city limits, this canyon is surrounded by densely populated urban areas on three sides—the San Fernando Valley to the north, Malibu to the west, Santa Monica and Pacific Palisades to the east—and the Pacific Ocean on the fourth side. Its rugged terrain is covered with chaparral and coastal sage scrub. Stands of oak woodland dot its rolling hills. A year-round creek winds it way through the canyon toward Santa Monica Bay and the Pacific Ocean. It is called Topanga Canyon from the Shoshonean word that means "above place," possibly in reference to heaven or to the sky. For many of those who call Topanga Canyon home, it is like living in paradise.

Early one weekday morning in January 2016, Russell and I ventured into paradise in the rental car we had picked up at the airport the day before. We were going against the traffic as we left the Pacific Coast Highway and headed north on Topanga Canyon Boulevard. I stared in amazement at the long line of waiting cars that extended more than a mile back into the canyon. Some twelve thousand people live in Topanga Canyon, and it looked like they were all on their way to work, though many of the drivers likely were not residents but commuters making the trip from the San Fernando Valley to Santa Monica and Interstate 10.

As we drove the two-lane road to Topanga State Park headquarters at Trippet Ranch, I tried to spot Topanga Creek. The curves of Topanga Canyon Boulevard follow the twists and turns of the creek as it slips along the canyon floor, but the flow of water was low and hidden from us as we whizzed by in our car. We had to pull off the road to be rewarded with a view of water cascading over and between boulders worn smooth by its passing. Topanga Creek is a peaceful waterway, home to endangered steelhead trout and the more commonly found Arroyo chub. But at times the steelhead trout almost disappeared, times when the water has blasted through the canyon, flooding roads and homes, reminding those who live there that nature will have its way with them.

Mule deer munching grass were the only witnesses to our departure from the parking lot at Trippet Ranch on the fire road that leads to Parker Mesa Overlook. The wide, packed dirt road—dust free because of recent rains—makes for easy hiking, but its primary purpose is to slow or stop the wildfires that sweep through the canyon from time to time, most notably the Santa Ynez fire in 1961 and the Old Topanga Canyon fire in 1993. The road follows the up-and-down curving contours of the ridge that marks the edge of one side of Topanga Canyon.

A few early blooming wildflowers emerged from the surrounding vegetation. Low growing evergreen chaparral covered the downslopes on either side of the road. The small, tough leaves of ceanothus, laurel sumac, and other shrubs shielded the steep inclines. On that sunny, cloudless, calm day, I was glad for the towering slabs of sandstone that offered occasional shade on the otherwise open and exposed road.

No boundary line marked our passage from Topanga State Park before and Topanga State Park after Harriet engineered the addition of 1,659 acres, but I guesstimated its location from maps. My guesstimate coincidentally put it at the point on our hike where I stopped seeing houses. I imagined similar houses spilling down the sides of the canyon all the way to the beach but for Harriet's intervention.

It was a weekday, so we mostly had the road to ourselves. Russell disappeared ahead of me as I lingered to take photos. Then he suddenly reappeared as the road doubled back and just as suddenly disappeared again, almost as if he were an apparition and I was alone.

But not completely alone. This is, after all, a state park serving a metropolitan area populated by more than ten million people. It is entirely within the city limits of Los Angeles. I could see development peeking over nearby hills. As I drew closer to the end of the road, particularly after I passed the intersection with a trail from Paseo Miramar and Los Liones, my solitude was broken by other hikers. A couple chatting nonstop about business matters. A few runners. A fast-walking elderly man who sped by with a curt, "On your left." He must have been in his eighties, lean though his flesh sagged around his middle, unable to defy the laws of gravity. His walk was steady but looked awkward, one foot turned out almost forty-five degrees and one shoulder hiked up. He wore no hat to protect his balding head fringed with thin black and gray strands of hair. I wanted to ask him if he walked the ridge regularly, but he clearly did not want to be disturbed. It is a place for people and nature, this Lower Topanga Canyon that Harriet snatched from the jaws of potential development.

The road ended at Parker Mesa Overlook, 1,525 feet above the Pacific Ocean. We sat on a bench and absorbed the view. All of Los Angeles and beyond spread out in front of us. The towering office buildings of Century City and downtown L.A. A helicopter rumbling overhead. An airplane taking off from LAX. The curving beaches. The snow-capped mountains. The canyon ravines. The houses. The ocean sliding into the far horizon. The urban and the wild, side by side.

Topanga Canyon grabbed Harriet's attention in the 1980s when she was working for The Trust for Public Land (TPL). State Parks had acquired 7,200 acres of northern Topanga Canyon in the early 1970s. Topanga Beach was added to the park system through eminent domain proceedings in 1973. There had been a few other Parks' acquisitions in the canyon since the 1970s, but the 1,659 acres of Lower Topanga Canyon between the park and the beach were still privately owned and largely undeveloped except for a few businesses and a motel along the Pacific Coast Highway along with about fifty houses near the coast that were leased on a month-to-month basis. After a failed effort to condemn Lower Topanga Canyon in 1979, State Parks still was looking for an opportunity to complete Topanga State Park by adding the land that would connect the mountains to the ocean. Harriet was looking for a way to make that happen.

Topanga Canyon is next door to Malibu Canyon, a place near and dear to the heart of Harriet's mentor and close friend, Martin Litton. Martin had explored and enjoyed Malibu Canyon while growing up in nearby Inglewood. When he left to serve as a glider pilot during World War II, Malibu Canyon was a place where "the quiet of the steep-walled gorge was broken only by bird songs and the splashing of perennial Malibu Creek. There were trout, and deer, and wild orchids, and massed phlox and monkey flowers spilling out of the mossy crevices like a bride's bouquet." When he returned, he flew "over the cherished spot . . . and [experienced] the shock of discovering the ugly white scar pushing into the gorge from both ends." Hardly believing what he saw, he "went there on the ground and found the County Detention Camp, the dirty, debris-choked trickle that had been the crystal stream, the piled-up skeletons of sycamores and the rubble of the blasted sandstone cliffs. The road gangs had sneaked into the wonderful place under the cover of war and wiped out its beauty." Martin always regretted the loss of the beautiful canyon of his youth. He lamented, "There was never a place quite like little Malibu Canyon and there never will be again." And he named one of his Grand Canyon dories *Malibu Canyon* in keeping with his tradition of naming dories after lost places. Harriet was determined to prevent a similar fate for 1,659 acres of neighboring Topanga Canyon—another canyon where Martin had roamed in his youth.[3]

Harriet was on good terms with the owners of Lower Topanga Canyon, the Los Angeles Athletic Club, and its parent company, LAACO, Ltd. The Los Angeles Athletic Club (LAAC) had first purchased a four-ninths interest in the Lower Topanga Canyon acreage in 1924. Frank Garbutt, an oil magnate and sportsman who had revived and incorporated the moribund Athletic Club in 1905, envisioned a new beach and yacht club there with easy access from the Club's recently constructed Riviera Country Club in Pacific Palisades. Garbutt's dream had yet to be realized by the late 1920s, when William Randolph Hearst acquired ownership of the remaining five-ninths interest in the property.[4]

Hearst did not support Garbutt's pet scheme for the development of Lower Topanga Canyon. Instead, he favored building a beach hotel similar to the New Breakers at Palm Beach. Ultimately, neither project moved beyond the planning stages. Meanwhile, to squeeze some income from the property, ground leases cancelable on ninety-days' notice were negotiated on fifty-foot-wide beachfront homesites. The leases led to the construction of 125 homes built over fifteen years. Initial rents of $15 per month increased to $50 per month after World War II.[5]

When LAAC became the sole owner of Lower Topanga Canyon in 1946, development of Lower Topanga Canyon still was under consideration. Although LAAC did not develop any of the land itself, it did sell eighty hillside acres called Parker Mesa in 1957 for $500,000 that later were subdivided and renamed Sunset Mesa when homes were built there in the early 1960s.[6]

Further development always was a possibility. The Malibu Local Coastal Program land use plan certified by the Coastal Commission in December 1986 permitted mixed-use development at the intersection of the Pacific Coast Highway and Topanga Canyon Boulevard. It also allowed residential, low-intensity commercial development for recreation. Outside the commercial area, zoning varied between one house per five or ten acres and one house per twenty acres.[7]

The possibility of development became a probability in 1989. A September 9 article in the *Los Angeles Times* reported that LAACO intended to sell or do a joint-venture development of the Lower Topanga Canyon land. The article said that LAACO was talking "to various potential buyers or partners." It also pointed out that selling the mostly undeveloped Topanga property might be as controversial as LAACO's recent sale of the Riviera Country Club. An article in the *Topanga Messenger* headlined "Mini-Malls & Motels at Mouth of Canyon?" said that even the challenges of the rugged terrain might not be enough to prevent some development given "L.A.'s hyperinflated real estate market."[8]

Still, LAACO's spokesman, Alex Auerbach, claimed that LAACO was conservation oriented. He said, "We're not an exploitation-oriented company at all. The Hathaways are an old California family and are aware of the role that the environment plays. . . . they have a record of safeguarding the environment of any property that they are involved with." The *Topanga Messenger* article concluded with a quote by Joan Shaffran, an aide to U.S. Congressman Tony Beilenson, who authored the bill that created the Santa Monica Mountains Recreation Area in 1978. "It's near existing parkland, it's a priority acquisition for many agencies, it's covered by the Coastal Commission and the county's zoning regulations, and it contains a flood plan that's a threat. . . . it's amazing that anyone's considering developing it." But someone was.[9]

When Harriet read the *Los Angeles Times* article and learned that a developer had made an offer, she called Frank Hathaway, LAACO's president and Frank Garbutt's grandson, and asked, "How can you sell the property without giving TPL a chance?" Harriet had been talking to Frank off and on for ten years, trying to find a way to get the beautiful canyon into public ownership. They had become good friends. Frank had always told Harriet, "You can't afford this property." When she called him, he said he still didn't think she could afford it, but he agreed to a meeting in late November.[10]

Two weeks after their face-to-face meeting at the LAACO office in Los Angeles, Frank Hathaway called Harriet and gave TPL until December 31, 1990, to put together a transaction with a public takeout, even though a developer had offered $35 million for the property, and he had two other serious offers from developers. Over the telephone, they worked out the basics of the transaction: LAACO options the property to TPL with a signed option agreement in place by April 1, 1990; TPL makes a $50,000 option payment; the option expires on December 31, 1990; the purchase price is $25 million, an all-cash transaction that closes by December 31,

1990, and reduces the purchase price by 2 percent; and the purchase price is discounted by an additional one-half percent for every month that the transaction closes before December 31.[11]

It took until the end of January and many more telephone conversations before Hathaway made a written proposal in a letter to Harriet and TPL. Hathaway confirmed that TPL intended to place Lower Topanga Canyon in public ownership for park purposes. He reiterated Harriet's belief that TPL would be able to pay $25 million in cash for the Topanga property before the end of 1990. He agreed not to make a commitment to any developer to sell Topanga prior to April 1, 1990, to give TPL and LAACO the opportunity to draft a letter of intent or an option to buy the property acceptable to both organizations. Frank Hathaway and LAACO were willing to work for a conservation outcome, but Hathaway also advised Harriet that LAACO may continue to negotiate with developers and may enter into a binding agreement with a developer if LAACO and TPL have not signed a purchase and sale agreement by April 1.[12]

Harriet had her foot in the door, but she was a long way from closing the deal.

She had to negotiate the terms of the sale, then find $25 million to purchase the property, and she had less than one year to do it. Harriet acknowledged that all potential funding sources were just "a gleam in my eye," but she had decided that Lower Topanga Canyon had to be saved. In her mind, she had no doubt she could make it happen.[13]

Harriet's confidence in her abilities had been confirmed by her successes at TPL. She began at TPL's San Francisco office in late 1978, at about the same time as attorney Ralph Benson, who would become one of her close friends and supporters. TPL was in transition at the time because of the departure of Huey Johnson, its founder and president, who had been tapped in 1976 by recently elected Governor Jerry Brown to be secretary of California's Resources Agency. When Johnson's replacement as president left to become the director of a regional office in the state of Washington two years later, TPL founding member and board member Marty Rosen took a sabbatical from his law firm to serve as interim president. Rosen was persuaded by the TPL board to take the position of president permanently at the end of his law firm sabbatical. He felt it was the right thing to do. Besides, it was more fun than being a lawyer.[14]

Rosen was just taking the reins at TPL when Harriet appeared. She had been working for Congressman Stark in his district office in Oakland capitalizing on the skills she had developed as one of Stark's legislative staff in Washington, D.C., and, earlier, as a volunteer in the Sierra Club's Washington office. She also had started managing some of Stark's personal real estate investments, a valuable background for doing land conservation deals.[15]

Working in Stark's district office was a job that allowed Harriet to support herself now that she was on her own in California, but it did not offer her the opportunity to wholeheartedly pursue her mission of saving land. She wasn't at the district office very long before she called Steve Costa, The Trust for Public Land's national urban land project director, to ask him about job possibilities at TPL. Harriet knew Costa from his time as Stark's district office manager from 1973 until 1976, when TPL's Huey Johnson had asked him to help set up a program in Oakland to bring land conservation to an urban setting. Costa introduced Harriet to Marty Rosen.[16]

Harriet said that she got the job at TPL because of her answer to one interview question. The TPL interviewer—probably Marty Rosen—asked why she wanted to work in conservation. She told him about taking her kids to a place in Colorado that she had loved. She had hiked there and wanted to share its beauty with her children. Only when they arrived at the place, it had been strip-mined. Harriet was devastated. While she was telling this story, she started crying. She was hired on the spot.[17]

Harriet joined other project managers at TPL who competed among themselves to find land to save in a highly entrepreneurial sink-or-swim environment that suited her perfectly. She gravitated to the spectacular Columbia River Gorge as early as 1979 for its own sake and because her contacts at the Forest Service told her it was a top priority. Because the gorge was on the border between Oregon and Washington, Harriet hoped that the good relationship that she had developed with Oregon's Senator Mark Hatfield during her days in D.C. would be helpful, especially given his position as chair of the Senate committee on appropriations.[18]

The Columbia River Gorge is an eighty-five mile long river canyon that cuts through the Cascade Mountain Range on its way to the Pacific

Ocean. The gorge features diverse ecosystems from wetlands and forests to cliffs and grasslands. Waterfalls spill down its sides, and rolling farmland frames its edges. It was an unprotected environmental treasure endangered by encroaching development.

The proposed development of a subdivision in Washington's unzoned Skamania County directly across the Columbia River from Oregon's 611-foot Multnomah Falls drew Harriet's attention in the early 1980s. The first attempt to develop a twenty-four-lot subdivision called Columbia Gorge Riverfront Estates in 1980 had failed after Yvonne Montchalin, owner of land adjoining the property, sued to defeat it.[19] The Friends of the Columbia Gorge organized in response to the development proposal and participated in Montchalin's lawsuit against it. Then, in 1983, the owner of the land tried again with a proposal for a twenty-one-lot subdivision. This time he ran up against Harriet and TPL.[20]

The owner of the land proposed for development was a retired military man named Colonel George Rizor, who was all in favor of the lands around his property remaining undeveloped so that the houses on his lots retained unobstructed views. Harriet made the case at TPL that the organization should go after the Rizor lands on the Washington side to begin the process of establishing federal protection for the whole gorge. She believed that stopping the Rizor subdivision was a crucial first step. If the subdivision were not stopped, it would open the door for development all along the Columbia River Gorge.[21]

Ralph Benson joined Harriet in the effort to convince Rizor that he should give up his development plans and sell the property to TPL. An eccentric man and a devout Christian, Rizor often called Benson late in the night to tell him, "Harriet Burgess was sent to me by God." Harriet had gotten to him. Still, Rizor was a tough negotiator, and TPL had to pay a high price for the land because it already was entitled for subdivision lots.[22] The Rizor purchase in November 1983 was a big risk for TPL because there was no guarantee that it eventually would become part of a greater protected area.

At about the same time Harriet was working on the Rizor deal, she took Nancy Russell to see another tract of land on the Washington side of the Columbia River that was slated for development. Nancy Russell was the organizing founder of Friends of the Columbia Gorge, which had been involved in the lawsuit that stopped Rizor's first effort at developing his land. Like Harriet, she began as a homemaker with a love for the outdoors. Like Harriet, she had five children. Like Harriet, she had a vision for the preservation of the Columbia River Gorge.

Driving Washington Highway 14 to Cape Horn, Harriet and Nancy pulled up to the large sign advertising Rim View Estates. "For Sale" in big red letters announced the availability of beautiful view property. Four of the sixteen narrow lots in the subdivision already had been sold. Taking in the dramatic and expansive views of the Columbia River Gorge from Cape Horn, Nancy Russell was awestruck. And as she did many times in her work to save the gorge, Nancy, along with her husband, Bruce, provided the financial backing to protect land from development. They borrowed $300,000 from a bank and then made a no-interest loan to TPL for the purchase of twelve of the sixteen lots.[23]

These early acquisitions paved the way for future purchases by both Nancy Russell and The Trust for Public Land. Nancy and Bruce Russell funded the purchase of a total of thirty-three parcels and more than six hundred acres of protected land before Nancy's death in 2008. Building on Harriet's strategic approach to acquiring land in the gorge that she initiated in 1979, TPL eventually protected more than 17,200 acres through more than sixty-five projects.[24]

The risk that Harriet and TPL took with the purchase of the Rizor property paid off. Harriet's vision of federal protection for the gorge was realized when Congress passed and President Ronald Reagan signed the Columbia River Gorge National Scenic Area Act in 1986. Although many worked for the creation of the National Scenic Area, Harriet's contributions were crucial. She made the Columbia River Gorge a priority. She redefined the boundaries of the gorge through land acquisitions that stretched the boundaries both farther east and farther west than they had ever been. She used her political connections and lobbied tirelessly.[25] She had had no guarantees of success, but by convincing TPL to acquire the Rizor property, Harriet took a chance and jump-started the fight to gain federal protection for the entire Columbia River Gorge.

When Lower Topanga Canyon came up for sale in 1989, land that had long been on her list of must-haves, Harriet was more than ready to take another chance. She faced both the problem of finding $25 million in less than a year to purchase the property and the challenge of convincing Marty Rosen that she had the time and the staff to do it. Between her responsibilities as TPL's senior vice president and manager of the Western Region and her role as TPL's lobbyist in Washington, D.C., she was swamped with work.

When Harriet called Marty in late March to tell him that the members of the Sierra Club's Quercus Fund advisory committee chaired by Elden Hughes had voted to allow TPL to use $100,000 of the Santa Monica Mountains acquisition revolving fund to pay for costs associated with the Lower Topanga Canyon acquisition, he insisted that Harriet give him a memo that clearly described the transaction; her strategy for the project including option costs, fund-raising, and risks; staffing requirements; and the impact on existing TPL commitments. He reiterated what he and Ralph Benson had told Harriet before: spending $100,000 on a nine-month option for a project with a $25 million takeout, together with the relatively heavy staff requirements, would have a major unsettling effect both on the Western Region and on TPL as a whole.[26]

Harriet addressed Marty's concerns in her April 5 response.[27] She described the transaction: option the property for $50,000 with an incremental approach to refunding the option payment still under negotiation. She listed possible funding sources: drawing on the Santa Monica Mountains Conservancy for some of the $30 million that it should have available; $2 million in state money from Proposition 70; Los Angeles and Long Beach Port Authority mitigation funding; and State Parks funding. She designated two members of the TPL staff to manage the project with outside assistance from consultants for fund-raising and publicity. She noted the strong support of the Quercus board of directors and the Santa Monica Mountains Conservancy, though State Parks' support was qualified by concerns about cost and relocation of tenants living on the property. She sidestepped the question of the impact on other TPL commitments but remarked on TPL's earlier successful Santa Monica

Mountains efforts in Solstice and Cheeseboro Canyons along with her behind-the-scenes efforts to help protect Rustic, Sullivan, and Mission Canyons in the Santa Monica area.

And then Harriet made her pitch:

> Topanga offers the opportunity of doing *the* most spectacular coastal canyon acquisition in the Mountains. . . . This is an opportunity that we should not let slide through our fingers. It would be a tragedy to lose this wonderful place. I think that you and I need to go to the Santa Monicas and take the "Harriet Burgess" tour, or at least do the "map" tour with me. I think we can do this project with present staff if Neil Gaston is aboard. I cannot do it if I have to do it alone, obviously you are as aware of that as I am. I need your help and support on this.[28]

Marty Rosen was not persuaded. He agreed that Topanga was a wonderful place, but after considerable thought and with regret, he directed Harriet to drop the project. He felt that Harriet was overloaded with her responsibilities both as TPL's federal liaison and Western Region manager, which only would be exacerbated by taking on the Topanga project, where essentially she would be the project manager. He reminded Harriet of her responsibility for the newly implemented and extremely demanding Western Region action plan that listed Topanga as a low-probability project. He considered Topanga to be a formidable project—almost $200,000 in up-front expenditures with no firm prospect of funding from any public agency by the time the deal was supposed to close. It was, he said, "no more than a crapshoot on which you plan to 'bet' the region, if not the whole organization."[29]

But Harriet would not give it up. She kept working on it. As she had done from time to time with staff at government agencies on other projects—and as she would continue to do when she thought it was necessary—she went over Marty's head. She went to TPL's board of directors to plead her case for taking on the Topanga project. Ralph Benson couldn't believe that she expected the board to back her over TPL's president. "People just don't do that. Any board will back its president. They may fire a president or CEO but they will not have somebody directly go around them." It was no surprise to Ralph when Harriet's ploy did not work.[30]

Harriet confronted Marty after the board refused her request to overrule his decision to drop Topanga. Angry over not being allowed to do the project, she may have threatened to quit. It probably was not Harriet's intention to leave TPL. She later said, "Separating from The Trust for Public Land after twelve years was a difficult emotional experience."[31] Harriet may have believed that her many successes, both with projects such as the Columbia River Gorge and especially at securing funding—according to Ralph Benson, "anything we asked for we got funded"—would be sufficient to protect her. That Marty would cave and say, "Don't leave Harriet. Okay, do Topanga." Instead, he accepted her resignation as soon as she suggested quitting. As far as Rosen was concerned, his decision to accept Harriet's resignation was final. There was no going back. Harriet may have been bluffing, but Marty was dead serious. As far as Harriet was concerned, she was fired.[32]

Ralph Benson tried to negotiate a rapprochement. Although he was in Connecticut on personal business, he phoned Marty and Harriet. In the era before cell phones, he used two public telephones to talk to both of them simultaneously. He beseeched them, "Can't we just get along?" The answer, at least from Rosen, was a definitive "No." In his view, Harriet's charismatic presence at TPL had become divisive. People in the organization either supported Harriet or supported Marty—and that made it difficult for TPL to fulfill its mission. Perhaps, to paraphrase a popular song, TPL just wasn't big enough for both of them.[33]

When Harriet told Martin Litton about the break with TPL, he encouraged her to create her own organization. That way, she would be able to tackle all of the tough deals. She would have the chance to save land that otherwise would be lost forever. Harriet wasn't sure. She wondered whether she really should try starting her own organization. Martin said, "Go for it," and Harriet took Martin's advice. After talking it over with her husband, attorney Joe Burgess, and longtime friends and neighbors Bob and Marian Stephens, while working their way through several glasses of wine and dinner, the American Land Conservancy was born on Earth Day, April 22, 1990.[34]

Then, urged on by her husband, Harriet threatened to sue TPL on the grounds of wrongful termination. Arguing that he had just accepted her proffered resignation, Rosen disputed the allegation. Joe admits that Harriet probably would not have considered suing except for him. "Harriet's not a litigious person so it was pretty shocking. Harriet's one of those people who would move on with life rather than dwell on that kind of thing," but he was "very pissed off." He probably would have filed a lawsuit and "tried to make life miserable for a few people." But, acting as Harriet's attorney, Joe worked out the terms of her departure over the next few months without going to court. The terms included a substantial financial settlement that was the seed money for starting the American Land Conservancy.[35]

Leaving TPL did not stop Harriet. Leaving TPL did not even slow her down. Barely breaking stride, she went to work as a consultant to complete the acquisition of Lower Topanga Canyon. Marty's memo to Harriet directing her to drop the Topanga project is dated April 18, 1990. By April 23, 1990, Harriet had left TPL and was working on an agreement with the Mountains Conservancy Foundation (MCF) to serve as an independent contractor on the Topanga deal.

In a memo describing the project to Ruth Kilday, MCF's executive director, Harriet wrote that she expected to have a signed agreement with LAACO by the end of the week. She concluded, "Obviously this is not a simple project but one that I believe is doable with a lean team of committed professionals." The MCF board unanimously approved the effort to acquire Lower Topanga Canyon and contracted with Harriet on May 3, 1990.[36]

MCF had been created in 1983 in part to support the work of the Santa Monica Mountains Conservancy (SMMC), the state agency led by Joseph Edmiston, by buying property and holding it until it was transferred to a public agency. Harriet already had involved Edmiston in the effort to acquire Lower Topanga Canyon. She had taken him on an aerial tour of the property in mid-December and kept in touch with him. Edmiston was enthusiastic about the prospect of the acquisition because Lower Topanga had been a priority for SMMC and State Parks for many years.[37]

Harriet did not wait for the signed contract with MCF to begin work. She immediately flew to Los Angeles on April 24 for a meeting with Frank Hathaway. She also discussed the proposed agreement for the acquisition of Lower Topanga Canyon with Karen Hathaway, Frank's daughter and LAACO's vice president and general counsel, on April 24 and 27. Based on her discussions with Karen, Harriet revised the TPL option agreement for Lower Topanga Canyon. The Trust for Public Land was crossed out as buyer and replaced with Mountains Conservancy Foundation, c/o Harriet Burgess. Harriet flew back to Los Angeles to finalize the agreement. She used a TPL form to keep track of her expenses.[38]

An agreement between LAACO, seller, and Mountains Conservancy Foundation, buyer, for the purchase and sale of Lower Topanga Canyon was executed on May 4, and LAACO issued a press release announcing that it "had reached an agreement to sell its Topanga Canyon Property, totaling some 1,600 acres to the Mountains Conservancy Foundation for $25 million in cash. The sale of the property is subject to funding of the transaction and certain other contingencies. The sale is scheduled to close on January 31, 1991. The Mountains Conservancy Foundation, headquartered in Solstice Canyon Park, Malibu, intends to use the property as a public park."[39]

According to Joe Edmiston, MCF was just acting as an agent for SMMC because LAACO wanted to sell the land to a tax-exempt, nonprofit organization. SMMC granted MCF $100,000 to fund the acquisition process. The $25 million purchase price for Lower Topanga Canyon ultimately would be given to MCF by SMMC. While SMMC was working to raise the necessary funds—and MCF was contracting with Harriet to achieve that goal—the $50,000 option payment that the Quercus Fund had made available through TPL was transferred to MCF to be used as a nonrefundable deposit to hold the property until the sale closed.[40]

Now—to find the money. Although Ruth Kilday had told the *Los Angeles Times* that she was confident money would be available to buy Lower Topanga Canyon, funding was far from certain. Over the next few months, Harriet waged a nonstop campaign to secure the necessary funds and to satisfy the other prerequisites for acquisition. Working out of her Oakland home and her husband's San Francisco law office, Harriet made phone calls and wrote letters. Flying to Los Angeles, she met with LAACO's

Fred Zepeda and LAACO's Lower Topanga Canyon tenants. Flying to Washington, D.C., she lobbied her contacts in Congress in search of appropriations for the Topanga purchase. She hired Marc Litchman to do private fund-raising, community organizing, and public relations. She arranged for conservation photographer Robert Glenn Ketchum to photograph Lower Topanga Canyon to persuade prospective supporters visually that it was land worth saving. She took a Topanga slide show to *Sunset Magazine*. She contracted with Robert Flavell to do the appraisal. She scheduled the environmental assessment. She attended meetings with State Parks and the Coastal Commission. She set up tours of Lower Topanga Canyon for elected officials and others. She contacted the Port of Los Angeles to look into the possibility of mitigation funding. She even met with a few developers to explore the possibility of developing part of the property as a way of raising funds to keep the rest of it undeveloped. Then she negotiated an amendment to the purchase and sale agreement because she needed more time. The deadline for showing LAACO convincing evidence of available funds was shifted from July 4 to August 1. She kept working.[41]

But Harriet's determination, hard work, and perseverance were not enough. She drafted a termination letter for Ruth Kilday's signature at the end of July to notify LAACO that MCF had not met the terms of their agreement:

The terms provided that by July 4, there be a minimum appropriation of $20 million for the Santa Monica Mountains National Recreation Area in the Department of Interior Fiscal Year 1991 appropriation legislation as passed by The House of Representatives Interior Appropriations Sub-Committee. We appreciate your willingness to extend the time for compliance to August 1, 1990 to accommodate delays in the appropriation legislation. Unfortunately, only $12 million was earmarked for the Santa Monicas in the House of Representatives Sub-Committee mark-up on July 24, 1990. Therefore, we have not met the terms of our agreement and are relinquishing our right to purchase Lower Topanga Canyon. We wish to thank you for your cooperation in making this very special property available for public acquisition. We are disappointed that we are unable to proceed with this transaction.

Harriet conceded defeat—at least for the time being. Her contract with MCF for the Topanga acquisition was also terminated, effective August 24.[42]

LAACO announced the termination of the agreement with MCF for the sale of Lower Topanga Canyon on August 8. In the LAACO press release, Frank Hathaway "praised the Mountains Conservancy Foundation Staff and consultants who worked on the project, commending them for their untiring and diligent efforts to put the Topanga property into public ownership. There are no other immediate plans for the property." In the Santa Monica Mountains Conservancy press release, Ruth Kilday said, "We are very disappointed that the transaction cannot be completed at this time." Joe Edmiston said, "The Topanga property will remain a high priority acquisition for the State of California." Harriet was not mentioned.[43]

It looked like Marty Rosen had been right. Now was not the time for the Lower Topanga Canyon acquisition. But that didn't mean Harriet was giving up. In ALC's first newsletter, Harriet pledged to continue to seek funding for the purchase because "we do not consider Topanga a dead issue." The wildflowers, the sweeping vistas, the scrub-covered slopes, the meandering creek that I had seen that January morning in 2016 were at stake.[44]

Interlude

Grand Canyon

WE PUSH OFF INTO THE COLORADO RIVER UNDER A CLOUDLESS BLUE SKY. The four of us are with Kerstin again in *Dark Canyon*, though the usual routine is to ride in a different dory every day. We have broken with routine because of the photo op that Kerstin offered that morning. She's going to pull over before Hermit to let us get out to take photos of the dories as they go through the rapid.

Granite is the first significant rapid of the day. Then Hermit. We hop out and run to a good vantage point. I have my small camera encased in hard plastic. It's awkward to use, but at least it stays dry and sand free. Gail carries a full-sized SLR that she keeps safe in a dry box when she's on the river.

The eye-opening view from the shore is stupendous. Roger guides *Paria* into the crisscrossing waves. *Paria* surges up and dives down. It disappears behind a wall of water, then emerges on the other side. The stern of Duffy's *Escalante* is swamped. It's bow soars and shatters a wave into bits of sparkling crystal. Flying into another wave, only the bright yellow and white helmets worn by two of the passengers are visible. The dory is exuberantly alive. Oblivious to its cargo of passengers and seemingly acting of its own volition, it is one with the river. As Martin Litton once said, "It rides the waves beautifully. It has grace to it."[45]

After the second baggage raft shoves its way through Hermit, we hightail it back to *Dark Canyon* for our turn.

Three miles farther down the river, we exit the dories again. This time everyone gets out—not to take photos but to walk around treacherous Crystal Rapid. Crystal is so notorious for flipping boats that the boatmen don't want to risk dumping the lot of us in the churning water.

As we hike downstream to the other side of the rapid, I catch glimpses of the river, where the boatmen are making solo runs through Crystal's craziness.

Until a flash flood added debris to Crystal in 1966, it was not especially formidable. But when Martin tried to run Crystal with four dories not long after the 1966 flood, he flipped three of them. Martin Litton tells the story:

> it was a very difficult day in the early history of Crystal Rapid that we got there with four boats and one old basket-boat raft and it looked bad. . . . I thought I could see the way to go, but I didn't want to damage the boats if I could help it. I also felt I didn't want people to damage the boats and then feel bad about it. So I thought if anybody were to feel bad about it, it ought to be me. So I told them I would take all the boats through. . . . I took the first boat and went into the big hole. . . . Went into the big hole, went up on the crest and turned over and the boat went upside down through what we call "the rock garden," which was just a real scattering of big boulders all down through there, all kind of pushing me along as it went, and ripping its decks off and its bow and its stern and everything, and tearing itself up generally. And the gear kind of oozing out through all the open places that were torn out. Anyway, it ended up down there, and I ended up with it, way down at the bottom of the rapid and so I couldn't right it and I just tied it up there and went back up to get another one—flipped the same way! . . . Got the third boat, and then a boatman named Plenty Andrews wanted to go with me. . . . So he got in the boat and we went down and it went over the same way, and there we are, two of us swimming now instead of just one. . . . And I was ready to take the fourth boat, but before I got up there, Curtis Chang decided he could do better, I guess. But he didn't wait for me, he got in the boat and

took it through and flipped the same way I had. And so we had four upside-down boats, all wrecked down there.[46]

Another time, almost twenty years later, Bruce Babbitt was on a river trip with Martin and a number of his political advisers. Babbitt, then governor of Arizona, was planning to run for president and all the talk was about campaign strategy. Like us, Babbitt and his advisers walked around Crystal. Regan Dale, the trip's leader, said Crystal "was still very ominous. It had changed and become a really big, big ride, and big rapid. Tough to row, a lot of laterals that you had to bust through, and another classic example of where we were walkin' our people around. But we [the boatmen] were goin' with each other." Dale had gone through once without mishap, but on his second go, he hit a big wave four feet over his head that just buried him and the boatman with him. The dory, *Lava Cliff*, flipped. Dale describes what happened next:

I made a couple of efforts to grab it and couldn't. The next thing I knew we were in the old hole. I remember goin' down, and the boat was in front of me, and it was goin' up, and all of a sudden it was comin' back at me, and I reached for it and got ahold of it, went under it, and was able to hang onto it, finally crawled out from underneath it, just as we went down. I got up on the bottom of it and looked around for Dale [Delomas, the other boatman in his dory], and he was about thirty feet downstream of it. . . . And we proceeded to go down and get stuck on that big pink rock, upside down. We hit it and stopped, instantly. And then the boat started sinkin'. Within seconds it started goin' under. . . . I got washed through the rest of the boulders there, and kinda got beat up a little bit. . . . By that time I was pretty wasted. I was totally spent. I walked back up to where Martin and Babbitt and all these guys were, and they're sittin' there still talkin'. They didn't even see it happen. They had no idea.[47]

Crystal is still too dangerous. Martin told a *New York Times* reporter, "The river ordinarily would have pushed that stuff out and reestablished its channel. But the river can't move rocks around like it used to. Not since the dam." And so we walk around to reunite with the dories and the boatmen after they have conquered Crystal.[48]

Roger sets off on a hike shortly after we make camp just past mile 108 near the foot of South Bass Trail. He's leading us up a trail to William Wallace Bass's early-twentieth-century River Camp. We clamber over boulders as we make our way along the side of the canyon. I want to hug the angled rock slope to keep my footing, but Roger advises walking fully upright. Roger's logic is that the soles of our river shoes are most effective at preventing slips and falls when we have centered our weight on them. I'm sure Roger knows what he's talking about, but I still slant my body to mirror the angle of the rock. I need the reassurance of its solidity. Harriet must have hiked this way, probably more than once, her long legs striding confidently and energetically over the smooth, rounded rock.

We reach our destination without mishap. William Bass set up his small River Camp here for visitors to spend the night before crossing the river or returning back up South Bass Trail to Bass Camp on the South Rim. Bass was one of the first to recognize the tourist potential of the Grand Canyon. He began advertising its attractions in 1885 while still carrying on mining operations in the canyon. Over thirty-six years, he hosted several thousand visitors at Bass Camp. Zane Grey, Thomas Moran, John Muir, and Henry Ford were among his guests.

River Camp was simply a tent with a stone fireplace. The fireplace is still there. Smoothly hewn rectangular rocks stacked neatly together form its sides and support the much larger slab top. Bass did his job well—the fireplace looks much as it must have looked when he used it. Rusted bits of metal implements laid on and around the fireplace did not fare so well but suggest the presence of those who were there more than one hundred years before.

Bass accommodated early tourists and others who wanted to cross the Colorado at River Camp by building Bass Ferry, a wooden boat that he constructed from lumber transported to the site by burro. He replaced the ferry with a cable tramway anchored in the schist cliffs in 1906. Tourists, animals, hunting parties, and asbestos from the Bass mines then were able to make the trip across the river more conveniently in a wobbly wooden cage hung from four steel cables. Remnants of the cables still hang from the cliffs, and we will see them and a ruined cable car from the river the next day. In addition to mining asbestos on the other side of the river at Shinumo Creek, Bass planted a garden and an orchard of fig, peach, and apricot trees. From there Bass completed one of the most challenging trails in the Grand Canyon, the Shinumo Trail (later renamed the North Bass Trail) to the North Rim.[49]

Bass was an explorer, an entrepreneur, a miner, a trail builder, a poet, a photographer, and a politician. And he was far more successful during his long sojourn in the Grand Canyon than the snakebitten Charles Russell, whose abandoned boat, the *Ross Wheeler*, lies nearby. The boat is wedged among the rocks not far off the trail that we hiked to River Camp.

Russell hoped to film his whitewater trip down the Colorado River. He began his expedition in 1914 in partnership with Bert Loper—known as the "Grand Old Man of the Colorado," Loper was a river-running pioneer in the West—but sank his first boat in Utah's Cataract Canyon just above the Grand Canyon. The partners left Loper's boat and hiked out. Loper designed and built another boat—this one out of galvanized steel—that they christened the *Ross Wheeler* after a local steamboat pilot.

Loper left after the two partners argued, but Russell went on with the *Ross Wheeler* and a new crew. They found Loper's boat but soon sank it. The replacement for Loper's boat—its fate secured when they named it the *Titanic II*—also sank. Russell acquired yet another boat. It foundered on the rocks at Crystal Creek Rapid and sank there after an effort to save it. Finally taking the hint after going another ten miles in the *Ross Wheeler*, Russell gave up his movie plans and left the boat behind on the beach at South Bass Trail in 1915.

A miner named John Waltenberg—who has a rapid and a canyon named after him around mile 113—later found the *Ross Wheeler* and hoisted it up on the rocks, where it lies like a beached whale to this day, a testament to man's folly. Perhaps Harriet saw it before its oars, pulleys, and other accoutrements that had remained untouched for more than fifty years vanished.[50]

CHAPTER THREE

It's Still There

Topanga Canyon

Please rest assured that I have not forgotten Lower Topanga Canyon.
That is one of my "life projects" that I am determined to finish.
—HARRIET BURGESS TO ELDEN HUGHES, 1997

ELDEN HUGHES DROVE PAST LOWER TOPANGA CANYON IN LATE 1996 AND wrote Harriet that the canyon had not changed. Hughes, a strong advocate of saving wild places, was chair of the Sierra Club's Quercus Fund when Harriet tried to negotiate the canyon's purchase and transfer to public ownership in 1990. With his leadership, the Quercus Fund had provided the financing for the $50,000 option payment. Harriet had not been able to protect the canyon in 1990. But it was still there, and LAACO was still interested in selling the property to a conservation organization for transfer to public ownership. Harriet was still interested in finding a way to make the transfer possible.[1]

It wasn't the first time since the 1990 deal fell through that Hughes had contacted Harriet about Topanga. After a Los Angeles meeting with Harriet in the fall of 1991, he had mailed photos of the canyon to her that showed its beauty and how that beauty was compromised by the "trashy houses" near Topanga Beach. Thanking Hughes for the photos, Harriet told him she had not given up on the project. Twenty months later, Hughes forwarded a copy of a letter to the editor in the *Los Angeles Times* from

LAACO's Karen Hathaway regarding the company's sale of a nearby country club to a Japanese firm.[2]

Harriet also had stayed in contact with Joe Edmiston of the Santa Monica Mountains Conservancy. Edmiston and SMMC had closed escrow in April 1994 on 662 acres of land in upper Topanga Canyon's Summit Valley that a Disney family trust had sought for almost sixteen years to develop as Canyon Oaks Estates, a subdivision with ninety-seven luxury homes and a private golf course. Topangans had protested the proposed development with road signs that played on the Disney connection: "Disney's Eighth Dwarf: Greedy" and "Topanga is Nature's Niche; Please Don't Make It Disney's Ditch." The first installment of $14.1 million for the land had been paid; the remaining $5.8 million was due in August. Edmiston expected to fund the final installment through a park bond initiative on the June 1994 ballot.[3]

The park bond initiative, Proposition 180, included $30 million for "acquisition, restoration and enhancement of coastal canyons," not less than $20 million to be designated for acquisitions in the Topanga Canyon watershed. Jerry Meral, head of the Planning and Conservation League sponsoring the initiative, told Harriet that after $6 million was used to complete the Canyon Oaks acquisition, the purchase of Lower Topanga Canyon would be the perfect use for the remaining $24 million. Edmiston told Harriet the same thing. Meral believed that Proposition 180 funds were "the last real hope that a reasonable offer can be made on the property." He also said, "I suppose that some day in another lifetime, there might be such funds specified for the Topanga purchase, but it will probably be very far in the future." Voters however, coping with the economic recession of the early 1990s, were not interested in spending lots of money on conservation. Proposition 180 failed, and its failure pushed the prospects for the acquisition of Lower Topanga Canyon into the distant future.[4]

The possibility of funding from Proposition 180 for the purchase of Lower Topanga Canyon had reopened the lines of communication between Harriet and Karen Hathaway. Harriet met Hathaway and Edmiston for lunch in Los Angeles in the spring of 1994 to discuss the use of Proposition 180 funds for the Lower Topanga purchase. Shortly after their meeting, Hathaway advised the LAACO partners that the firm's Topanga lands were included in Proposition 180's list of possible properties for public acquisition, that the Santa Monica Mountains Conservancy still was interested in acquiring the property, and that a public announcement would herald any agreement made to sell Lower Topanga Canyon. LAACO was willing to consider a sale to SMMC but other buyers—perhaps developers—also might be considered. At about the same time, LAACO made a $5,000 contribution to the American Land Conservancy.[5]

Harriet also had maintained her connection with Frank Hathaway, Karen's father. Frank had been instrumental in Harriet's first effort to acquire Lower Topanga Canyon in 1990. Harriet and her husband, Joe, visited Frank and his wife on several occasions after that deal collapsed, including a lunch that the Hathaways hosted at their home. The Hathaways were friends as well as potential partners in achieving one of Harriet's top conservation goals.[6]

In August 1998, Harriet heard from Chris Harrer, who had been reviewing the status of the Lower Topanga Canyon property, to tell her that market conditions were good. Harrer, an assistant director at the real estate consulting firm of Julien Studley and Karen Hathaway's husband, was a vice president at LAACO in the mid-1990s. After Harrer called Harriet again in October, she decided to get the Topanga files out of storage. Time for another run at putting Lower Topanga Canyon into public ownership.

But Lower Topanga Canyon suddenly ceased to be one of Harriet's top priorities. Shortly after Harriet met with Karen Hathaway at the Biltmore Hotel to discuss the project in late October or early November, Joe Burgess was rushed to the hospital for emergency open-heart surgery. Harriet's work at ALC was put on hold for several weeks while she took care of her husband. Ame Hellman, ALC's vice president, worked on Topanga in Harriet's absence.

Ame began working at ALC in August 1996 as a project manager. She remembers the date clearly because just after she started at ALC she was a delegate to the Democratic National Convention in Chicago, where "you are for seven days in a row, right there with the governors, the senators, the congress people. You've got their ears." She took advantage of the "very casual environment" to bend "[Nevada] Senator Bryan's and Senator Reid's ears" about ALC's Thunderbird Lodge project for half of the time she was there.[7]

Ame first connected with Harriet at a meeting of the Douglas County (Nevada) Planning Commission. She was there to represent a small group of citizens who were trying to persuade the developer of Jobs Peak Ranch in Gardnerville, Nevada, to provide an easement through the development for public access to Faye-Luther Canyon in the Humboldt Toiyabe National Forest. No other access points were available to public lands from the Carson Valley into the Carson Range of the Sierra Nevada between Carson City and the California state line. Harriet was there with ALC Nevada consultant Grant Barbour for the same reason. She had been invited to assist in the public access issue by Mary Wagner, district ranger for the Carson Ranger District, and Bill Van Bruggen, the Carson Ranger District's land specialist.[8]

Harriet and Ame didn't talk long at their first meeting, but when Harriet came back a second time, they spent a lot more time together and established a great rapport. Before Harriet left for home, she said, "I don't know if you're interested in a job, but if you're free next week, I'll buy you a plane ticket to San Francisco, and we'll sit down and talk about it. I need to hire an attorney because Grant Barbour is leaving."[9]

Ame wasn't sure she had the right background for a conservation organization. She said, "Well, Harriet, I'm not a conservation attorney. I'm actually a divorce lawyer. I worked for a big firm in Denver doing pots-and-pans divorce work."

Harriet came back with, "Do you have children?"

Ame replied, "Yes, I've got two."

Then Harriet asked, "Do you pack their lunches in the morning and make sure they do their homework and send them to school every day?"

Again Ame said, "Yes."

And Harriet said, "Well, you'll be perfect for working with BLM because that's basically all you need to do—make sure they get up in the morning and think about the things they need to do for the land exchange, make sure their title clearances are working through the process, and the appraisals are getting done." Ame called those "the truest words that I've ever heard about the tedious process of land deals."[10]

Explaining later how Harriet selected and hired people to work for her at ALC, Ame said:

> I really credit Harriet. Harriet was the kind of person who saw qualities in people that no one else necessarily did. She was a visionary. She was a people visionary. She could see someone's personality or their strengths that came through in their personality. If she saw that in a person, she really went all out like a mother would. I think she hired a lot of people like me.

Once hired, Harriet turned her employees loose. She let them jump into the deep end to sink or swim according to their own abilities. She put Ame right to work on the Faye-Luther deal. Trail access for the public had been secured, but more land was needed for a trailhead with enough room for parking and for horse trailers to turn around. Harriet told her, "Look, find a parcel to buy. Raise the money." Ame rose to the challenge, found a willing seller of a 2.35 acre parcel, and raised $57,000 in three months to purchase it from Charles Paya. The construction of the Faye-Luther trailhead was completed in 2000.[11]

Ame no longer lives in Nevada, but whenever she returns for a visit, she hikes Faye-Luther Canyon. She loves seeing all of the hikers, bikers, and horseback riders enjoying the popular trail. She told me, "It would mean a lot to Harriet because I think more than anything that's what it was about for her. People and nature."[12]

Harriet was back in the saddle by mid-December, writing to Karen Hathaway to apologize for the delay and explain her belief that "the time is right to rekindle our effort to see beautiful Topanga Canyon a centerpiece for both the California State Park system and the Santa Monica [Mountains] National Recreational Area." Harriet thought that a new governor and administration in Sacramento would "be more supportive and sympathetic to preservation of public open space than the previous administration." She reported that a new legislative initiative for a state park bond to fund open-space acquisition was already in the works. But, if funding were going to be included in that initiative, ALC needed to have a signed option agreement for the purchase of LAACO's 1,659 Lower Topanga Canyon acres.[13]

Ame already had started negotiating the terms of the option agreement with LAACO while waiting for Harriet's return. A central issue that needed to be settled involved the relocation of the tenants who occupied forty-nine homes near the intersection of the Pacific Coast Highway and Topanga Canyon Boulevard. LAACO had rented the properties on a month-to-month basis for decades with the intention of developing the land eventually. But many tenants viewed the short-term rental agreement as a permanent arrangement. Many of them had lived there for years, had built and improved their homes at their own expense. If the land were sold to ALC for transfer into public ownership, the tenants would have to leave. Paying below-market rents in homes that they maintained located no more than one mile from the beach, almost all of the tenants were very reluctant to move. Neither LAACO, ALC, nor the state of California wanted the responsibility of relocating them.[14]

When Harriet wrote Karen Hathaway in mid-December, she proposed optioning the Lower Topanga Canyon property for one year and making an option payment of $500,000 with a commitment from LAACO to remove the tenants. ALC's responsibilities included the appraisal, the phase-one toxic survey, and necessary title work. She assured Hathaway, "American Land Conservancy's financial resources are quite different from our resources at the time when we last held an option from you. I'm confident in our ability to succeed in this undertaking now."[15]

Harriet often used options and bargain sales to secure land for her conservation deals. Options permitted ALC to tie up a property without being obligated to purchase the land if the deal didn't work. In an option agreement, the seller gives the buyer the exclusive right to purchase land within a specified period of time. The buyer gives the seller something of value, generally a monetary fee, in return. The fee can be as low as one dollar or may range into the millions. The option agreement states all the terms for buying the land, including the cost of the option and the price of the land. It may include conditions that must be satisfied before the sale can be completed. In most cases, the option fee is credited to the purchase price. If the option to buy is not exercised, the option fee generally is nonrefundable.[16]

Bargain sales are used by conservation organizations to acquire land for less than fair market value. The difference between fair market value as determined by an independent appraiser and the sales price is a charitable deduction for the seller and income for the nonprofit buyer when the organization sells the land for the appraised value to a public agency or other buyer. The seller also is saved the trouble of marketing the land and is able to make a contribution to conservation. In many cases, the conservation organization is able to act quickly to save land that otherwise might be lost. Dealing with a private nonprofit organization also offers the benefits of confidentiality and flexibility. The land may be sold to the public agency for less than the appraised value, saving public acquisition funds. Bargain sales facilitate the transfer of desirable lands to the public while also financing future conservation transactions.

Bargain sales were as crucial to the financial success of ALC as they had been for TPL when Harriet worked there. TPL used bargain sales and outright gifts extensively in its early years to finance operation costs. Harriet learned the ropes of bargain sales at TPL and used that knowledge for ALC transactions. Bargain sales allowed ALC to save land and fund its operations through project transactions rather than through fund-raising. ALC's purchase of Lower Topanga Canyon would be a bargain sale preceded by an option agreement.[17]

The back-and-forth between ALC and LAACO over the terms of their bargain sale option agreement lasted for months. Tenant relocation and the appraised value of the 1,659 acres of Lower Topanga Canyon were the focus of most of the discussions. Who will handle the relocation effort? Who will pay for the relocation? What are the legally mandated relocation benefits? Are any historic preservation issues involved? Are there building code compliance issues? Is a public agency ready to take ownership? What is the appraised value of the property?[18]

Harriet, Ame, and ALC's attorneys, Russell Austin and Julie Turrini of Murphy Austin, worked with LAACO's Karen Hathaway, Charles

Michaels, and Fred Zepeda and their outside attorneys to find answers to these crucial questions. In early September, Harriet was getting impatient. She wrote in her notes, "Let's make a move. We're ready to go." But the appraisal that LAACO commissioned from Kauttu Valuation was not completed until the end of October, and the bargain sale option agreement was not signed until the first week of 2000.[19]

ALC's initial bargain sale option agreement proposal specified a one-year option with a $100 option payment for LAACO's thirteen hundred acres. The purchase price was set at 90 percent of fair market value as determined by a full narrative appraisal. The appraisal had to be approved by both ALC and LAACO or the agreement was terminated.[20]

The terms of the bargain sale option agreement finally signed by Harriet Burgess for ALC as buyer and by Karen Hathaway and Charles Michaels for LAACO as seller on January 6, 2000, differed substantially from the first proposal. The payment for an exclusive option to purchase the Lower Topanga Canyon property—either all 1,655 acres owned by LAACO or all but the approximately 52 acres of the commercial and residential areas—increased from $100 to $50,000. The option expired in just over three months on March 15. The purchase price of $65,070,720 for all of the property was based on the Kauttu appraisal. The Kauttu appraisal had concluded that the highest and best use of the undeveloped acres of Lower Topanga Canyon was mitigation or preservation.[21]

The likelihood that ALC would be ready to exercise the option—commit to buying the LAACO property within three months—was remote. The agreement allowed for the probability that ALC would need more time by including a provision to extend the option for a year to March 15, 2001, if two conditions were satisfied. First, Proposition 12, the "Safe Neighborhood Parks, Clean Water, Clean Air and Coastal Protection Bond Act of 2000" had to be approved by California voters on March 7, 2000. A $2.1 billion bond measure for local and state parks and other public land uses, Proposition 12 was the most promising source of funds for the purchase of the Lower Topanga Canyon property by a state agency. The agreement automatically was terminated if the bond measure failed.

To satisfy the second condition, ALC had to make another nonrefundable option payment of $250,000 that would be credited toward the purchase price. The high cost of the second option payment necessitated several amendments to the agreement. The first amendment shortened the extension to April 28, 2000, and reduced the option payment to $20,000. That still was not enough time, and the option again was extended to March 15, 2001, for $250,000 payable in two payments, $150,000 on or before April 28, 2000, and $100,000 on or before January 5, 2001. Yet another amendment was needed to break the $100,000 payment into two payments of $10,000 due on or before January 5, 2001, and $90,000 due on or before January 19, 2001.[22]

The twenty-page legal document and its five exhibits spelled out all of the details of the agreement between ALC and LAACO. Not all of the questions about the acquisition were resolved, but ALC's second attempt to preserve Lower Topanga Canyon for public, open space, and recreational purposes was officially underway.

ALC cleared the first hurdle when the voters passed Proposition 12 in March. With the passage of Proposition 12, money was available for the Topanga purchase if the governor included funding in the May revision of his 2000–2001 fiscal year budget. Sheila Kuehl, California Assemblymember for the district that includes Topanga Canyon, wrote a persuasive letter to the governor on April 4 in support of funding for the acquisition of Lower Topanga Canyon. She emphasized that Lower Topanga Canyon had been an acquisition priority for California State Parks for the past thirty years. It was

> the celebrated canyon in the Santa Monica Mountains that links Topanga State Park with Topanga State Beach. Public acquisition of this property, which includes the entire lower canyon, would complete an amazing and unique mountains-to-the-sea park, easily accessible to the densely populated Los Angeles Basin.

She went on to say that ALC had the property under contract and was working to put together a funding package that probably would include local, state, and federal partners. Beyond recreation, she listed the environmental and public health benefits offered by the acquisition that ranged from saving the threatened steelhead trout in Topanga Creek to wetland restoration and pollution prevention. She concluded:

> Because of its extraordinary public recreation, environmental and health benefits, the Lower Topanga Canyon should be State Park's number one acquisition priority in Southern California. We have tried and tried to acquire this parcel in the past and failed. With the passage of Proposition 12, now is the perfect time to seize an opportunity that may never come again.

Harriet herself, who had written in notes dated April 3, "Shila Quel [sic] close to gov," could not have said it better.[23]

The state budgeted $40 million of Proposition 12 money to acquire Lower Topanga Canyon. As the *Malibu Times* reported on September 7, "that money is currently sitting in the bank waiting to be used." But the money could not be used until LAACO, ALC, and State Parks agreed on Lower Topanga Canyon's appraised value. How much was the state going to pay for LAACO's 1,659 Lower Topanga Canyon acres? Although the Kauttu appraisal of about $65 million commissioned by LAACO was used to set the price in the option agreement, an independent, state-approved appraisal was needed to determine the purchase price paid by State Parks to LAACO through ALC. Even if the state-approved appraisal came in above $40 million, Harriet still was optimistic that additional funding could be located. She was "very excited about our prospects this time around." She said, "The owner is still committed to selling the property, and the state has made the acquisition one of its priorities this year. It's looking very good."[24]

Months before Proposition 12 passed, Harriet had been looking at the key question of the Lower Topanga Canyon appraisal. An appraisal is only one professional's opinion of the value of a property, so it is not set in concrete and may be reviewed and challenged. Harriet asked Karen Hathaway for the appraisal that Kauttu did for LAACO, which set the value of Lower Topanga Canyon at $65,070,720. She, in turn, sent it to Steve Morgan at Wildlands, Inc., in February for his input on the issue of mitigation credits.

Kauttu had calculated a value for the undeveloped Lower Topanga Canyon acreage based on using it as a mitigation bank for the sale of mitigation credits. Mitigation credits are purchased by developers and others to compensate for the impact of development or pollution on the environment. Morgan's associate reviewed the appraisal and suggested that the value given to potential mitigation credits in Lower Topanga Canyon was higher than warranted.[25]

Harriet also sent the Kauttu appraisal to Andrea Gaston, an appraiser with the firm of Nichols and Gaston, for a full review. Gaston responded with a number of questions and concluded that she did not have enough information to determine whether the "analyses, opinions and conclusions are appropriate and reasonable." Kauttu maintained, "I am confident that the questions and issues raised by both Ms. Gaston and Mr. DeYoung of Wildlands, Inc. can be answered in a formal revision of the appraisal documents," but a subsequent review of the Kauttu valuation by the appraisal firm of Mason and Mason for ALC criticized it because "the 'leap of faith' between data and conclusions is too great," and it was impossible to "conclude that the analyses, opinions, and conclusions expressed in the appraisal report appear appropriate and reasonable."[26]

Given the concerns expressed about the Kauttu appraisal report, Harriet arranged to have another full appraisal completed by Fran Mason and her firm, Mason and Mason. Fran Mason and her staff began work on the appraisal in October. The bills received by ALC for the appraisal process itemized their painstaking approach. Hours and hours of data collection and analysis went into the final report that was ready on February 19, 2001. The 1,659± acres of Lower Topanga Canyon owned by LAACO were valued at $43 million.[27]

The California Department of General Services (DGS) had to review and approve the Mason and Mason appraisal of Lower Topanga Canyon for the Department of Parks and Recreation (DPR) before funds could be used to purchase the property. ALC's attorney, Russell Austin, accompanied Fran Mason to a meeting with DGS on February 22 to discuss the appraisal. Russell told Harriet,

This morning's meeting with the DGS review appraisers went well. On Topanga, Fran provided the DGS review appraisers with an overview of the valuation problem raised by the Topanga Canyon property and how her report approached the valuation problem. In response to their inquiry about priority, I asked them to make their review of Fran's appraisal a very high priority.... All in all, I think it was well worth the effort for Fran to meet with them face to face.

On May 1, DGS notified DPR that "the content, analysis, and conclusions stated in the report under review are in compliance with applicable standards and requirements. The value opinion of $43,000,000 stated in the appraisal report is adequately supported."[28]

The deadline for Harriet and ALC to exercise the option to purchase LAACO's Topanga property was March 15, so Harriet had to decide whether to move forward with the purchase before receiving DGS approval of the appraisal. She asked Russell to join her in two conference calls to discuss the appraisal with LAACO's Karen Hathaway and Fred Zepeda. The calls must have persuaded Karen and Fred to accept the $43 million appraisal, because Harriet notified them by March 12 that ALC would exercise its option to purchase Lower Topanga Canyon.[29]

In Harriet's letter to Karen Hathaway announcing ALC's intention to purchase Lower Topanga Canyon, she reiterated LAACO's agreement to "reduce the purchase price to support ALC's charitable purposes and programs." It was, after all, a bargain sale. The reduction would be a donation to ALC equal to a 4 percent interest in the property. Because the purchase price was $43 million, ALC's share of the sale proceeds was $1,720,000. The donation was a charitable contribution tax deduction for LAACO. All of the $320,000 that ALC had paid to option the property was nonrefundable and would be credited to ALC when the sale closed. The sale had to close no later than July 13, 2001.[30]

Harriet was moving closer to fulfilling her elusive dream of protecting Lower Topanga Canyon. She had negotiated an agreement with LAACO to purchase the property and secured most of the funding. But one potentially deal-breaking obstacle stood in the way of achieving her goal: the tenants who resided in forty-nine houses and ten businesses on approximately fifty-two acres at the mouth of the canyon where Topanga Canyon Boulevard meets the Pacific Coast Highway. Since the Lower Topanga Canyon purchase would be funded by Proposition 12 funds, which prohibited the purchase of improved land, the tenants would have to vacate the houses and businesses that some had occupied for decades for the deal to work.

The tenants were a closely-knit group of artists, writers, filmmakers, surfers, local business owners, photographers, students, and retirees who enjoyed the proximity to the ocean and the canyon. They lived in one- and two-story wood framed houses owned by LAACO but maintained by the tenants in varying states of repair that were described by appraisers as being in fair to poor condition.

The tenants had been free to improve their residences however they wished, and many did so even though the improvements also were LAACO's property. Small sheds, garages, and covered storage areas were constructed near many of the houses. Art studios, offices, sunrooms, and bedrooms were added to some of the houses. Lawns and gardens existed side by side with abundant uncontrolled vegetation. Abandoned vehicles, scrap equipment, garbage, and building materials were scattered about the compound. Unpaved roads connected the houses that were arranged in several small villages. The road to the Rodeo Grounds—named after the rodeos held there in the 1800s on a Mexican Ranch—led from Topanga Canyon Boulevard across Topanga Creek. An area called the Snake Pit was accessed from the Pacific Coast Highway. The village of Brookside lay north of the Rodeo Grounds, and other houses fronted on Topanga Canyon Boulevard.

The commercial tenants operated ten businesses on the Pacific Coast Highway: three restaurants (Cholada Thai Beach Cuisine, Something's Fishy, and Reel Inn), a hair salon (Ginger Snips), a realty business (The Money House), the Topanga Ranch Motel, the Topanga Ranch Market, a bait shop (Wylie's Bait), an animal feed and supply store (Malibu Feed Bin established in the 1960s), and a home furnishings retail business (Oasis).[31]

LAACO's tenants had been threatened before with the loss of their homes and businesses. After LAACO sold its Topanga beach property to the state in 1971, the state evicted the tenants from more than 115 building sites on the beach. Some of those tenants moved across the highway and resumed leasing homes from LAACO. An effort by the state to condemn the remaining Lower Topanga Canyon acreage in the late 1970s foundered in part because of the cost of relocating tenants. When Harriet made her first attempt to purchase Lower Topanga Canyon for a public agency in 1990, she began early in the process working on the question of removing the tenants. She considered the possibility of eviction and wanted to review tenant files. A spokesman for LAACO said then that he was unsure about what would happen to the tenants if the property were sold as park land, but "the transactions don't mean anyone will be kicked out." The tenants were saved again when Harriet was unable to secure funding. But this time it looked like their luck had run out.[32]

The issue of tenant relocation resurfaced early in Harriet's second effort to purchase Lower Topanga Canyon. Her first proposal to Karen Hathaway in December 1998 asked for a commitment from LAACO to remove the tenants. When ALC's negotiations with LAACO began, the possibility of LAACO's giving thirty-day notice to the tenants was considered but rejected, apparently because LAACO did not want to be solely responsible for tenant removal. The bargain sale option agreement ALC and LAACO signed in January 2000 made no direct reference to tenant relocation, but Harriet considered relocation to be a critical step on the path to public ownership. By March 2000, ALC had agreed to be responsible for the relocation plan mandated by California Relocation Assistance Law.[33]

ALC was responsible, but LAACO still was involved in the relocation process. At LAACO's direction, Pacific Relocation Consultants (PRC) prepared an assessment of Topanga Canyon relocation issues if the LAACO property were acquired by a public agency. Karen Hathaway forwarded the analysis to Harriet in July. It described the existing conditions, including a survey of residential housing and business establishments. It gave an overview of available replacement housing and commercial properties. PRC concluded,

> In order to determine a more accurate estimation of relocation issues, needs of those residential and business occupants that may

be potentially displaced, schedule and budget, it will be necessary to prepare a detailed relocation plan which will entail an individual interview with each residential and business occupant.

Eventually, ALC would sign an agreement with PRC to prepare the relocation plan, but not yet.[34]

In August, LAACO's Fred Zepeda sent a letter to the tenants to notify them that ALC had an option to buy Lower Topanga Canyon. He assured them that there was a long way to go before the sale to ALC for transfer to a state agency occurred. He also told the tenants that laws existed that provided for compensation if they had to leave their homes.[35]

Most of the tenants probably already knew that ALC had optioned Lower Topanga Canyon. A June article in the *Topanga Messenger* headlined "A New Park in Our Future?" reported that ALC had acquired the option in January and that Governor Gray Davis recently had designated $40 million for state parks from Proposition 12 in his May state budget revision. Jeff Stump, ALC's Lower Topanga Canyon project manager, said then that the relocation of the tenants is "a key concern." He continued, "We are trying to come up with a solution that works for everybody. ALC will work closely with LAACO to come up with a plan on this." He said, "We think we can help them in a very fair way."[36]

The tenants were not so sure. Many feared the loss of their homes if the property were sold to ALC and transferred to State Parks. They didn't want to be evicted and have their homes bulldozed. They knew that their below-market rents could not be duplicated elsewhere. They hoped for a plan that left their homes untouched, but Roy Sterns, deputy director of DPR for communication, made it clear that there was no chance the homes would remain if the land became a park. He said, "The bond act [Proposition 12] restricts our ability to buy land with improvements. We are trying real hard to make parks and open space for people, but somebody is always unhappy. We expect LAACO will proceed in a kindly fashion to relocate people. Until successful, we are not interested in buying the property. We are going to continue to sit on the side lines, waiting for the property owner, the American Land Conservancy and the renters, possibly, to come to some sort of agreement that would open the door for us to purchase."[37]

Either the tenants had to leave, or there would be no park. For Harriet, the choice was clear. The tenants had to go. But the chance was still there that ALC would fail again in its attempt to purchase Lower Topanga Canyon or would purchase only the undeveloped acreage of the property, and the tenants would survive another threat to their community.[38]

The LAACO tenants received the news that ALC had exercised its option to purchase the entire Lower Topanga Canyon property in advance of the public announcement of the sale. In a letter dated March 12, Fred Zepeda informed them that ALC planned to purchase the property and transfer it to the state to be added to Topanga State Park. Zepeda made it clear that the LAACO leases were in effect until the close of escrow, which would occur later in the year. He indicated that ALC was in charge of the relocation timetable. Nothing suggested that relocation was a choice. Zepeda offered to answer any of the tenants' questions and concerns. He concluded, "We take our responsibilities to our tenants and the community seriously, even as we look forward to the day when this unique and wonderful property will pass into the public domain to be enjoyed for generations to come."[39]

With the deal to acquire Lower Topanga Canyon dependent on the need to relocate the tenants, Harriet moved to make it happen as quickly and painlessly as possible in accordance with state law. Since PRC already had completed a preliminary relocation analysis at LAACO's request and had facilitated a number of relocation projects in the Los Angeles area, Harriet decided to retain the firm to prepare the required relocation plan. Explaining her choice of PRC to the tenants, Harriet said, "We really spent some time investigating relocation companies. This was not the least expensive. These guys were at the top of the list." She also explained that the purpose of the relocation plan was to determine "who's out there and what kind of help they need . . . under any number of scenarios. This is a process that needs to be started and I don't have an agenda beyond that. The people have a right to know what their rights are."[40]

PRC needed to develop a relocation plan before the scheduled close of escrow in mid-July, and they needed to comply with the requirement of the

California Relocation Assistance Law that informational material be prepared and distributed to each occupant of the property as early as practicable. They went right to work and scheduled a series of three general meetings at the Topanga Community House to explain the relocation process to the tenants. The first and third meetings on April 25 and 27 were intended for residents, the second meeting on April 26 for business owners. Notice of the meetings was included in letters mailed on April 17 and 18 to tenants with current rental or lease agreements with LAACO. The letters also informed the tenants that they would be relocated because ALC intended to purchase the property where they lived for use as public parkland and that PRC would be preparing the relocation plan. If any tenants were unable to attend one of the scheduled meetings, PRC underlined their request to call and schedule an appointment. PRC further advised the tenants that they planned to meet individually with each of them after the community meetings to determine their specific needs and to explain available benefits. Contrary to newspaper reports, no specific relocation date was given in the letter, but a LAACO spokeswoman told a *Topanga Messenger* reporter that "our goal is to have relocation completed by the end of the year."[41]

Refreshments at the meetings were arranged for one hundred people, but only a few tenants attended. Some objected to the short notice. Others refused to attend without an attorney. If more of the tenants had gone to the meeting, they would have heard Harriet introduce herself and explain the work of the American Land Conservancy. They would have heard her share her vision for Lower Topanga Canyon. Priceless coastal woodlands and canyons protected from future urban development. More than sixteen hundred acres of open space between Malibu and Pacific Palisades provided for the enjoyment and enrichment of all Los Angeles County residents. Topanga State Park completed. Topanga State Park connected to the Pacific Ocean. The Topanga wetlands restored. They would have heard her say, "We work on a pretty slim margin. Payment for ALC services comes from the seller discounting the price as a charitable contribution. In this instance, ALC has made a substantial investment in optioning and appraising the property and now in hiring a relocation company to facilitate acquisition of Lower Topanga for parkland." They also would have heard Barry McDaniel of PRC discuss the relocation process, including timing, benefits, and relocation alternatives. They would have heard him say, "We are going to be there hand-holding you through this process. Moving on your own can be a horrendous thing. . . . We pride ourselves on being very caring people."[42]

But most of the tenants did not go to the meetings. Tenants reacted to the relocation notice with fear, confusion, regret, and anger. Longtime resident and president of the recently formed Lower Topanga Community Association Scott Dittrich said relocation "will kill these people, especially the older people. Old people can't pick up and move again." He called the immediate relocation of tenants "mean-spirited and unprecedented with State Parks acquisitions."

Thirty-two-year resident Carol Winters said she understood why LAACO wants "to get rid of this land, it's a pain in their side, but we are human beings and I want all the legal rights for the people, especially the elderly."

Katie Wood, who lived in a house with her husband that was moved from the beach in 1932, said, "This imminent purchase by the Conservancy will be an especially difficult loss because we are elderly now. Our roots here go deep and we have loved living and raising our children here."

Richard Jo, owner of Topanga Ranch Market, said, "There's nowhere to relocate me. An ABC [liquor] license is next to impossible to get in another neighborhood. I put my life savings into this place. It's all the money I had. I was going to fix it up, but I kept on hearing rumors. It seems like now the rumors are becoming truths. It looks very grim for me."

Another commercial tenant, Andy Leonard, owned the Reel Inn Fresh Fish Market and Restaurant. He said, "I'd hate to see them knock down the Reel Inn and then in three years decide they'd like to have a restaurant here. I think it's a noble goal to save property for future generations, but I'll be damned if I can find anybody who has thought through what is really going to happen."

Martin Morehart and his wife, Patricia, had operated the Malibu Feed Bin for thirty-five years. Martin said, "There is no such thing as relocation. We're an old feed store. It doesn't work unless we have the old rent."

Bernt Capra, a LAACO tenant for twenty-one years, lamented the loss of a vibrant community. He said, "A wise city planner should preserve this area. There is nothing like it. This is a beautiful beach community. People are getting kicked out. . . . There is more profit culturally and socially that can't be expressed in dollar signs." He and others hoped that relocation would be delayed until a land-use plan for the residential and commercial area was developed.[43]

Frank Angel, the attorney representing the Lower Topanga Community Association, questioned ALC's authority for handling the relocation. He believed that it was illegal for the state to transfer the relocation responsibility to ALC. He complained about the short notice for the April 25–27 meetings and recommended that tenants refuse to schedule individual interviews with PRC. He protested that LAACO had asked some tenants to sign leases that waived their rights to relocation assistance even though Fred Zepeda explained that the new leases were simply being offered to current tenants in place of leases signed by tenants who no longer lived on the property, and the new leases did not affect rights to relocation assistance. Angel supported long-term leases with definite termination dates for the tenants as the "only humanly, politically and fiscally responsible solution here." He also may have hoped to limit the Lower Topanga acquisition to the undeveloped portion of the property or to delay the deal in an effort to defeat the whole transaction.[44]

What the tenants and the attorney for the Lower Topanga Community Association seemed to have overlooked was the possibility that LAACO would sell the land to a developer if ALC did not acquire Lower Topanga Canyon and transfer it to DPR. The tenants' leases would then be terminated immediately, and they would receive no relocation assistance to help them move elsewhere.

Harriet reminded them that the fact that most of the land is undeveloped "doesn't mean the land will continue to be undeveloped in the future. The property is zoned by the county for multiple uses, including business and residential uses. If we don't buy this magnificent parcel now, it will be developed. Designating the site as public parkland is the only way to protect its natural beauty so that it can be enjoyed by future generations." She sympathized with the tenants but said, "This is not my position. This is State Park's position. They don't want to be a landlord. They want open space and natural landscapes for people to enjoy. State Parks will not buy the property without a relocation plan."[45]

By May, with little progress made toward relocating the tenants, DPR's acquisitions chief Warren Westrup raised tenants' hopes when he said State

Parks may only purchase the undeveloped portions of Lower Topanga Canyon and that Parks has not made a final decision on the acquisition of either all or part of the property. But just one day later, Westrup said, "One alternative considered was to buy just the undeveloped land because the dollars don't add up. But negotiations are ongoing [to find additional funding], and we are hopeful that we will move ahead with the whole 1,659 acres."[46]

Westrup also dashed tenant hopes that their homes would be preserved as an artists' colony. He said, "We do living history programs in State Parks all over. But we don't do them in areas where we pollute the ocean." Westrup was referring to the problem of leaking septic tanks that were suspected of polluting Topanga State Beach.[47]

After several weeks of escalating conflict over the relocation issue, with the goal of a canyon and its creek preserved almost lost in the acrimony, Harriet and ALC along with LAACO and PRC directed their energies toward reducing tensions with the tenants and increasing understanding of the Lower Topanga Canyon acquisition. Their efforts were aided by Senator Sheila Kuehl's May 18 agreement with the tenants that relocation by the end of the year was too soon. Kuehl said, "I have a very simple goal. I don't want them to have to be out until they *have* to be out because work needs to go on. I want the amount of time that is 'just right.' I'd like to try to be the person who finds the middle ground. From my point of view, there is not a need to relocate these tenants by the end of the year."[48]

Harriet and ALC project manager Jeff Stump met with Frank Angel at the PRC offices in Long Beach on May 15. Representatives and attorneys from PRC and LAACO also attended. Harriet explained that ALC's objective was simply to develop a plan for relocation that would be submitted to the state and that ALC had no ability to grant the long-term leases that Angel proposed. Angel was not satisfied with ALC's response and continued to advise his client, the Lower Topanga Community Association, to file a lawsuit to prohibit ALC from acting as an agent of the state. Angel and his client also threatened to file a lawsuit to force the state to grant them leases for as long as three years while the state determined how the land would be used.[49]

Fred Zepeda wrote to individual tenants on May 15 explaining the basis for and the terms of relocation. He was firm but sympathetic. He acknowledged the desirability of living in Topanga Canyon. He reminded the tenants that LAACO always had offered only month-to-month leases. He emphasized that LAACO always had intended to sell or develop the land. He reiterated that relocation assistance was available because of the sale to the state rather than to a private developer. In another letter dated May 24, Zepeda reassured LAACO tenants that Frank Angel's claim that the new leases some were asked to sign included a waiver of rights to relocation assistance and benefits was incorrect. He told them that it had never been and was not then LAACO's intent or objective to request a waiver.[50]

PRC's David Richman sent letters to tenants who were unable to attend one of the April meetings. He explained, "One of the discussions at the meeting was PRC's involvement in the preparation of a Relocation Plan. A Relocation Plan is an information gathering process, establishing the needs of the residents and businesses, along with identifying the available housing and commercial resources in the surrounding communities. The Relocation Plan is simply an information resource to be used at such time that relocation becomes necessary." Richman asked again for an opportunity to interview each tenant to determine individual needs.[51]

Harriet responded to one of several newspaper articles that were less than complimentary when describing ALC's role in the Lower Topanga Canyon acquisition by writing a letter to the editor of the *Malibu Times*. She explained ALC's mission and approach to preserving land and water throughout the United States. She wrote, "ALC does not seek to own land. Rather, its strategy is to option environmentally sensitive lands that public agencies wish to acquire, arrange appraisals, surveys, toxic assessments, and the other pre-sale requirements and then transfer the land to local, state or federal agencies for conservation." She denied a belief held by some tenants that "the sale to ALC really masks a future real estate development on a portion of the property near PCH [Pacific Coast Highway]. ALC has no such plans. When we purchase the Topanga Canyon property, we will immediately transfer the property to state ownership. ALC . . . work[s] on the slimmest of margins and seek[s] only to recover our costs of doing business." She sympathized with the disruption that relocation causes but noted, "With the cooperation of the current owner, LAACO, Ltd., we are developing the relocation plan in order to protect the rights of the tenants to receive relocation benefits."[52]

Harriet and Jeff Stump also joined Barry McDaniel and others at a meeting on June 4 to update representatives of Assemblywoman Pavley, State Senator Sheila Kuehl, and Supervisor Fran Zev Yaroslavsky on the relocation process and to ask for their help in completing the Lower Topanga Canyon acquisition. Harriet highlighted the benefits of an expanded Topanga State Park. She painted a future of restored wetlands, the return of steelhead trout to Topanga Creek, a visitor center on the Pacific Coast Highway, and trails along the creek to connect the beach to the mountains—all within easy reach of hundreds of thousands of Angelenos.[53]

The conflict over relocation was at least partially defused by the inclusion of $8 million in Governor Gray Davis's May budget revision to cover the $3 million shortfall in funding for the purchase of Lower Topanga Canyon and to provide $5 million for relocating tenants and other expenses. Assemblywoman Pavley and Senator Kuehl worked together with Governor Davis to secure the additional funding. Kuehl explained, "The wild beauty of Southern California is an irreplaceable treasure that each generation is responsible to preserve for the next. I'm proud that we are doing our part."[54]

With the expectation of the additional funding, Warren Westrup said, "We are stepping up to the plate. We're looking very closely at the relocation issue." State involvement would take one of the tenants' main objections to relocation off the table—the participation of a private, nonprofit organization in even just the planning stages of the state's relocation obligation. Ever since PRC had written the first letter to the tenants to notify them about relocation, tenant opposition had been focused on ALC. Senator Kuehl called it "a disconnect between the ALC, the relocation agency folks, Parks, and the tenants." Whatever it was, ALC had become part of a problem that stood in the way of the Lower Topanga Canyon acquisition. Taking immediate and direct action to solve that problem, Harriet facilitated the state takeover of the relocation process by donating the cost of relocation services contracted with PRC to State Parks. She signed the donation agreement on

June 1. PRC was now a state contractor reporting to and working under the direction of State Parks.[55]

By the third week in June, State Parks had notified LAACO's Lower Topanga Canyon tenants that it had assumed responsibility for the relocation process. State Parks then scheduled a meeting on June 28 at Topanga Elementary School to discuss the relocation process. The tenants showed up in force for the Parks meeting. They seemed to agree with Anne Soble's message printed in the *Malibu Surfside News* before the meeting that it was the first civil step taken to address relocation. Soble suggested, "State Parks can be a much better dispenser of both fairness and empathy than the private consultants and special agents who seemed to want to pit neighbors against each other in the interests of an arbitrary and possible fee-related timetable." State Parks, for the moment, was cast in the role of the white knight riding to the rescue. The distorted view of ALC's relocation efforts persisted but was no longer a bone of contention.[56]

The seventy-five Lower Topanga Canyon tenants at the two-and-one-half-hour meeting on June 28 had plenty of questions and comments for State Parks. Emotions ran high as they asked:

"How can you compare living somewhere else to this paradise we're living in now?"

"Why are you trying to move us so fast?"

"What are you going to do with some of our eighty-year-old citizens? A move will kill them."

"Some of our homes go back fifty to seventy years. Would it not be possible to keep them and let them be part of the historical culture of the land?"

"Will you replace us with park rangers?"

"We're meant to be here. We're the keepers of this land. My children have spent their whole lives here. Where am I going to take them?"

But State Parks' answers were no more reassuring than the answers PRC and ALC had provided:

"It's premature to talk about what we might do with these structures."

"We're in the business of clean water, parks, preservation. We aren't in the business of providing housing."

"We've used [PRC] before and they are very good. They will look out for you."

"Some visitor-serving businesses may be allowed to stay."

"Tenants will be gone by June 2002."

"Our commitment is that you will get everything you are entitled to under state law."

State Parks also laid out some of the basic benefits of relocation assistance:

Rental assistance for forty-two months or replacement housing payment for residential tenants wherever they choose. Moving expenses will be paid.

Reimbursement for moving expenses or a payment in lieu of moving expenses for commercial tenants and possible compensation for loss of goodwill.

Meet the new boss. Same as the old boss. Except for saying that relocation would be delayed by six months, State Parks' message during the almost three-hour meeting was no different from what the tenants had heard from ALC. But now they had no "outside agency" to blame.[57]

In the midst of the relocation brouhaha, Harriet had to negotiate a new closing date. ALC and LAACO originally had agreed to close escrow on the sale of Lower Topanga Canyon on July 13. That date had been a big factor behind the urgency of getting a relocation plan in place quickly.

With the addition of $8 million in the governor's May budget revision, Harriet knew she had the money to complete the purchase, but she also knew that she didn't have enough time before the July 13 cutoff date to conduct the two meetings that state law required before the funds could be used: a public meeting to review the state's acquisition proposal and a meeting of the Public Works Board to approve the expenditure of Proposition 12 funds.

Once Harriet had advised Karen Hathaway that the state would not be able to fund by July 13, she worked out an agreement in a phone call with Karen, Russell Austin, and Charles Michaels that extended the closing date to August 29. The extension came at a price: a one-time fee of $25,000 plus $4,000 per day from July 14 to July 26 and $8,000 per day from July 27 to the closing date.[58]

One day after the meeting with the tenants, State Parks issued a press release announcing the July 9 date for the public hearing on the acquisition of Lower Topanga Canyon. The purpose of the mandated hearing was "to hear and record comments from the general public and local public officials on the reasons why this property should or should not be acquired by the State Department of Parks and Recreation." After describing ALC's role and the source of funding, the release referred to the problem of pollution in Topanga Creek and at Topanga State Beach caused by septic tanks in the residential area and said State Parks "intends to stop the pollution and restore the creek." The property would be added to Topanga State Park and would become part of "what is already considered the world's largest wildland within the boundaries of a major city, Los Angeles." Growing to 12,659 acres, Topanga State Park would offer "extensive recreational opportunities for the Los Angeles region."[59]

Leading up to the public hearing, Harriet and Jeff Stump joined State Parks Director Rusty Areias for a tour of Lower Topanga Canyon with a *Los Angeles Times* reporter and photographer. Areias told the reporter, "The governor wants parks close to where people live. This is it. It's a fabulous wildlife corridor. And you will be able to walk from the San Fernando Valley to the beach and never cross a road." Areias was photographed leaping across rocks in Topanga Creek. Harriet sent the very favorable article with its account of the environmental benefits of the acquisition to the ALC board.[60]

In a letter to Friends of the Santa Monica Mountains, Harriet encouraged members to attend the public hearing. She wrote, "We need you to be there to show your support." She described the impact of the acquisition and concluded, "To date, the media coverage of this acquisition has focused solely on the relocation of the residential and business tenants and not on the fact that the transfer of Lower Topanga Canyon to public stewardship and its restoration as part of California's natural heritage is a unique opportunity to provide truly priceless benefits to current and future generations." She may have sent similar letters to other organizations such as Trout Unlimited and the Sierra Club.[61]

Campaigning to generate support for the Lower Topanga Canyon acquisition, Harriet wrote, "Topanga Parkland a True Dream Come True," for the *Daily News of Los Angeles*. Published the day of the public hearing, Harriet sang the praises of adding 1,659 acres of prime coastal property to Topanga State Park. She wrote, "It's difficult to imagine a better, more appropriate or enduring investment than this." She called it a "magnificent piece of property" that would "create a gateway to the Santa Monica Mountains National Recreation Area." She urged, "This purchase makes good sense—for the environment, for the public and for our future." Not being much of a writer, it's entirely possible that Harriet didn't write this article herself, but it certainly captured the intensity of her support for the Lower Topanga Canyon acquisition.[62]

Some 250 people crowded into the Topanga Elementary School auditorium on July 9 to share their views on the acquisition of Lower Topanga Canyon by State Parks. Sitting in rows of folding chairs, they heard Mark Schrader, State Parks deputy director of acquisitions, open the meeting and caution that the only subject for discussion that night was the acquisition—how the parkland would be used would be considered at future meetings. Schrader presented the reasons that State Parks had pursued the acquisition of Lower Topanga Canyon since the 1970s. He remarked on its easy accessibility to more than eleven million people; on its importance for both habitat and public recreation linkage; on its value as a home for endangered species;

and on the necessity of ensuring the water quality of Topanga Creek. He concluded that the $43 million price tag "seems like a pretty good deal."[63]

Schrader sat down and the first of sixty-eight speakers took the floor. Joe Edmiston, director of the Santa Monica Mountains Conservancy, praised the purchase and pledged $2 million for park improvements. Arthur Eck, superintendent of the Santa Monica Mountains National Recreation Area, gave the acquisition his unqualified support. Marianne Webster, chair of the Sierra Club's Santa Monica Mountains Task Force, conveyed the club's strong support of the acquisition. She added, "We do feel the pain of the forty-nine families . . . but we also feel the pain of the park-poor people of L.A."[64]

Almost all of the speakers supported the park acquisition, including some of the large contingent of tenants who attended the meeting, but nearly half commented on the value of the tenants' unique Lower Topanga community. Tenants who spoke in favor of the purchase also argued either for more time before relocation or for leaving their homes and businesses in place. Derrick Von Driesen emphasized his support of the acquisition but denied that he and his fellow tenants were polluters. He pushed for extending the leases to ease the hardship caused by relocation. David Haid, owner of Oasis, pleaded for more time. He said, "The time I'm asking for is not a year. Let's get off the fast track and breathe, slow down." Scott Dittrich continued to oppose the acquisition because of the relocation. He claimed the tenants had been stewards of the land and should be allowed to remain at least until State Parks has a plan for the land. Bernt Capra again expressed his opposition to forced relocation asking, "Why get rid of us in such a hurry?" And tenant attorney Frank Angel, proclaiming himself a friend of State Parks and an environmentalist, said, "The big question here is at what price, at what human, at what economic, at what social toll to the tenants and at what cost to the taxpayer?"[65]

Near the end of the meeting, Fred Zepeda shared LAACO's perspective. He said, "We see this, not just a win win, but we see it as a win win win, three wins." The first win would be the creation of a park as the voters requested when they approved Proposition 12. The second win would be some money for LAACO. The third win would be the availability of relocation money for the tenants.[66]

State Parks Director Rusty Areias wrapped up the public hearing on the acquisition of Lower Topanga Canyon after almost four hours of testimony. He said, "I'm always impressed by your community. One thing you have no shortage of is passion." He responded to the speakers who had argued for creating a land-use plan before relocating the Lower Topanga tenants by expanding on the State Parks experience at Crystal Cove. Located on the coast south of Los Angeles in Orange County, Crystal Cove was purchased as parkland from the Irvine Company in 1979. State Parks had been trying to evict tenants from Crystal Cove ever since. The Crystal Cove controversy had been exacerbated when a proposed plan for the park that included a luxury resort was strongly opposed by the local community.

Once burned, twice shy. State Parks now approached planning by consulting the public throughout the process. After an interim plan was developed, a long-term plan for Lower Topanga Canyon would only be finalized after public meetings. Areias said, "Hopefully consensus will come that we can all embrace." He ended by saying, "We must seize the opportunity and purchase the land before we are once again faced with an uncaring governor and an unforgiving economy. Parks are not a luxury for good times, they're a necessity for all times."[67]

After the public hearing, Areias reported on the meeting in letters to John Burton, president pro tem of the California Senate, and five other elected officials. He concluded the letter with his recommendation "that the California Department of Parks and Recreation purchase the LAACO property, add it to Topanga State Park, and provide relocation assistance in a fair and equitable manner as required by existing state law."[68]

The public hearing was one requirement that had to be met before the Lower Topanga acquisition would be considered by the Public Works Board (PWB). Without PWB approval, the deal was dead in the water. Harriet's attention was focused on the all-important PWB meeting before the end of June. Faxing "talking points" for the PWB meeting to Russell on June 22, she wrote, "We need to jam—on final title, legal deed, etc. for closing!!"

And jam they did. They convinced PWB to consider both site selection and acquisition at one meeting on August 10 rather than the usual two meetings by arguing that the option on the property expired soon, so an August closing was necessary; the transaction is straightforward; all acquisition requirements would be satisfied by August; and having State Parks take over the property would facilitate relocation and park management plans. They completed all of the requirements for site selection and acquisition before August 10.

On August 10, at an open public meeting, PWB approved State Department of Parks and Recreation consent item no. 3790 and State Department of General Services consent item no. 1760 authorizing the site selection and acquisition of Lower Topanga Canyon and funding for ALC's purchase of the property.[69]

ALC had nineteen days after PWB approval to close the deal to purchase Lower Topanga Canyon by the agreed upon date of August 29. With every day costing ALC $8,000, ALC was ready to close in seven days but LAACO was not. LAACO was trying to work out a way to grant the property directly to the state without going through ALC. Russell Austin e-mailed LAACO's attorney on August 22:

> ALC is ready, willing and able to proceed with closing this transaction immediately. While ALC has endeavored to work cooperatively with LAACO over the last week to accommodate LAACO's planning objectives, it is not willing to continue to do so at ALC's expense. ALC was prepared to submit to State Parks a deed conveying title solely from ALC to State Parks last Wednesday, August 15, which would have permitted the parties to close the transaction on Friday, August 17.[70]

By August 24, ALC and LAACO had worked out an agreement to accommodate LAACO and compensate ALC for the delay. The closing date was extended to August 31, and ALC would not be charged the $8,000 per day extension fee for five days from August 18 to August 22. On August 27, ALC agreed to convey title to LAACO's Lower Topanga

Canyon property to the state at the same time that LAACO conveyed title to ALC. All LAACO's tenant leases also would be simultaneously transferred to the state.[71]

Karen Hathaway wrote Harriet a personal letter on August 24 to clear the air after LAACO's last-minute jockeying to alter the terms of the deal. She referred to their recent telephone conversations focused on negotiating the timing of the closing and compensation for the delays caused by LAACO's effort to sell directly to the state. She assured Harriet that they were diligently working toward closing early the next week. She concluded, "Not everything has gone our way in this sale, but the bottom line is, it's finally going to happen and I am very pleased about that. I hope you feel the same way—I'm sure you must." Harriet faxed this letter to Russell. She marked the fax "Urgent" and added a handwritten note: "We need to get this done! I give up! H2." It had been more than ten years. It was time to get this deal done.[72]

E-mails and phone calls and faxes were flying back and forth among ALC; LAACO; State Parks; the lawyers for ALC, LAACO and State Parks; and the escrow officer at Commerce Escrow to close the Lower Topanga Canyon sale as quickly as possible. Lease assignments, closing checklists, letter agreements, rent statements, escrow instructions, option payment amounts, grant deeds, transfer taxes, recording fees, tax credits, tax prorations, and closing statements were scrutinized. Documents were reviewed, discussed, signed, and shuttled from one office to another.

Harriet replied to Karen's letter on August 27:

Dear Karen:

Thank you for your note of August 24. All of us at ALC appreciate the hard work and cooperative effort demonstrated by all of you at LAACO and your professional advisors as we come to the final stages of closing. Indeed, we appear to have resolved all of the documentation issues to complete the conveyance of the property to State Parks in the next day or so. I've signed and have enclosed with this letter the "side letter" requested by LAACO's counsel, as revised to incorporate the revisions requested by Russell.

As we've also discussed over the last several weeks, LAACO and ALC will still need to work together after closing to resolve some questions and issues. . . . We will continue to work with LAACO on this aspect of the project in the same cooperative spirit.

Thanks again for your continued support in bringing this project to a successful conclusion.

Sincerely,

Harriet Burgess
President

The enclosed "side letter" reviewed the basics of the original agreement between ALC and LAACO, then made it clear that the "possession, management, and control of the Subject Property will directly pass to the State from LAACO through American Land Conservancy."[73]

Finally at 12:13 p.m. on August 30, Russell e-mailed Jeff Stump, copying Harriet, "You can now pop your cork—we are on record." The next day, Russell sent Jeff copies of the two state warrants paying a total of $43 million for Lower Topanga Canyon. Russell e-mailed Charles Michaels, "Congratulations to LAACO on being the proud former owner of the Topanga Canyon property and thanks again to you and everyone at LAACO for all of your help and support in completing this important project."[74]

Harriet told the *Los Angeles Times*, "It's such a wonderful purchase. It completes the most magnificent urban coastal park in the state system." She later told her Board of Councillors, "One of our greatest achievements was the successful acquisition of the 1,655-acre Lower Topanga Canyon in the Santa Monica Mountains." LAACO announced the sale in a press release that said, "LAACO intends to reinvest the proceeds in other real estate through a tax deferred exchange which is scheduled to close later this week." And Roy Stearns, State Parks spokesman, said, "We are delighted to have acquired the property."[75]

As soon as the sale closed, State Parks prepared letters to the tenants "assuring them of just treatment." Frank Angel said, "It's good to hear they will be treated fairly. Now we have to see deeds following their words. We were encouraged that all options, including long-term leases are on the table."

State Parks continued to work with Pacific Relocation Consultants to relocate the Lower Topanga Canyon residents.[76]

Still more protests and lawsuits over tenant evictions followed, but they were unsuccessful. Demolition of the Lower Topanga Canyon houses and businesses began in 2003 and was mostly completed by 2006. Only Wylie's Bait & Tackle Shop, Malibu Feed Bin, and the Reel Inn and Cholada Thai Beach Restaurants remained in operation, with the Topanga Ranch Motel still standing but unoccupied.[77]

The State Park and Recreation Commission approved the Topanga State Park General Plan on September 28, 2012. A map of the plan for the park near the intersection of Topanga Canyon Boulevard and the Pacific Coast Highway delineated areas for day use parking, a trail system, outdoor classrooms, and creek restoration. The plan finally in was place, but the planned park facilities had yet to be constructed when I visited in 2016.[78]

One of Harriet's primary reasons for purchasing Lower Topanga Canyon was the restoration of the wetlands at the mouth of Topanga Creek. During the acquisition effort, ALC's project manager Jeff Stump had said, "Our vision for that property is to restore the wetlands which used to be larger than Malibu Lagoon. Eventually, it could be an amazing restored wetland area. This is especially important because California has lost almost all of its wetland habitat areas—less than 3 percent remain." Saving threatened steelhead trout and preventing pollution were part of that vision.[79]

The first step toward restoring the lagoon wetlands was to fix the impacts to the creek just upstream. Rosi Dagit, senior conservation biologist of the Resource Conservation District of the Santa Monica Mountains, has called the lower Topanga Creek restoration a "massive undertaking." When staff from the state and federal fish and wildlife agencies toured the site in 2008, they told her, "You're going to be dead and gone before this is restored." But then Rosi and a dedicated group of volunteers went to work. When the fish and wildlife staff returned five years after their first visit, they said, "This is awesome. We didn't think we'd ever see this again."

On a foggy day in March 2016, Russell and I joined Rosi for a tour of the restoration project. As we started our tour, Rosi warned us about the presence of ticks and rattlesnakes. She was dressed in running shoes, patterned socks, and loose light blue pants that ended just above her ankle. She didn't seem to be too worried herself. I had worn my hiking boots and long pants. I figured I could deal with ticks but didn't know what I'd do with a rattlesnake. As it happened, neither appeared.

We walked single file down the road the tenants had used, now a rather narrow dirt path. Only chunks of asphalt here and there suggested that cars once had passed that way. After a short distance we reached the creek whose smooth surface belied its steady flow toward the ocean. We used rocks as stepping stones to cross the creek that was no more than eight or ten feet wide because there had been little rain recently. The creek expands in rainier years, sometimes far beyond its current confines, as it did in the flood years of 1960, 1980, 1995, and 2011. Near where we crossed, a wide slab of paving was easily visible under the clear, shallow water.

Motivated by the destructive 1960 flood, LAACO's tenants had constructed a berm to protect their rental houses from future floods. The unpermitted berm they built without plans gradually grew into a levee 1,000 feet long, 20–25 feet high, and 20–40 feet wide. It was filled with just about whatever the tenants could find or wanted to discard, including asphalt from the repaving of Santa Monica's Lincoln Boulevard in the late 1960s. Testing revealed that some areas of the berm contained lead-contaminated soil.[80]

Restoration of lower Topanga Creek required removal of the berm, and removal of the berm required several years of fund-raising. Grants and in-kind contributions yielded the estimated $3.3 million removal cost. Rosi and the Resource Conservation District of the Santa Monica Mountains spearheaded the grant-writing process.

For two months in 2008, sixty twenty-ton trailer trucks formed a long line on the Pacific Coast Highway just before Topanga Canyon Boulevard at 5:30 in the morning. Different trucks carried different materials—some for concrete, some for green waste, some for contaminated soil. Beginning at 6 a.m., the trucks entered the floodplain. By 9 a.m., all of the trucks were loaded with excavated material. In a choreographed dance, the trucks were released one at a time into the traffic cycle. More than twenty-six thousand tons of fill were hauled out in 1,934 truckloads. Except for the ninety-six loads of lead-contaminated soil, all of the material removed was recycled as landfill soil cover, composted green waste, or rocks for road base.[81]

Near the end of the removal job, one truck knocked into a fallen pine close to the edge of the project. The jolt to the tree exposed black, oozing soil where tenants had dumped at least two fifty-five-gallon drums of diesel fuel. The diesel-soaked soil was just outside the project boundaries. Although the contractor was under no obligation to remove the contaminated soil, he took the initiative to negotiate a trade with the State Parks contract manager. He'd take out the oozing soil instead of doing work that he otherwise would have done elsewhere on the site.

With the demolition of the berm, Topanga Creek gradually is returning to its natural path as it responds to storms and sediment accumulation. The restoration of natural creek flow and the creation of newly formed scour pools in the creek are encouraging the return of the endangered steelhead trout. No steelhead were found in the creek between 1980 and 1998, but their numbers exceeded 325 in 2008. Until the long drought that began in 2012, they seemed to be well on their way from near extinction to reestablishment in the waters where they once flourished. Even with the expanded spawning opportunities in the restored areas, the drought took a heavy toll on the population. The return of the rains in late 2018 began to reverse the decline. The fish numbered only eleven in February 2019 but had increased to fifty by the end of March 2019. Rosi and her team monitor the trout using the fish lab located near the entrance to the property.[82]

The restoration of lower Topanga Creek is a work in progress. Eradicating invasive nonnative species is a high priority. Arundo, a perennial grass planted by the tenants that grows up to thirty feet tall, is a serious threat to the riparian habitat. A macerator borrowed from State Parks chewed up a lot of the bamboo-like arundo, but stands of the invasive plant persist because of the moisture provided by the revitalization of Topanga Creek. The drought has fostered the spread of another invasive plant, *Euphorbia terracina*. Its removal has yet to be attempted, but it is a threat because it tends to spread rapidly and can interfere with the germination of native plants.[83]

Funding for floodplain restoration is limited, but the goodwill and efforts of community volunteers are not. Every year three hundred UCLA freshman arrive to do a day's work as part of a mandatory community-service project. All dressed in blue, they tackle the arundo and remove it by hand. The California Conservation Corps has used jackhammers to break up concrete. Groups of Scouts have undertaken restoration projects. Volunteers from Mountains Restoration Trust and TreePeople have planted coastal sage scrub and coast live oaks. The Topanga Creek Stream Team volunteers have taken out hazardous waste such as paint cans and batteries. The Stream Team volunteers also walk four sections of the creek every year in the spring to count all of the wildlife they can find. In 2002, the Stream Team discovered a small population of southwestern pond turtles making a comeback in Topanga Canyon's upper watershed. Part of the planning for the floodplain restoration includes creating areas of safety for the turtles when flash floods sweep down the canyon.

Much work remains, but much has been accomplished since Harriet gave potential supporters the "Harriet Tour" of the site. The rental houses and tenants are gone. The buried septic tanks that polluted Topanga Creek and Beach are gone. The roads are gone. The berm is gone. Instead, taking the "Rosi Tour" on a foggy morning in 2016, we saw newly planted oak saplings marked by orange flags and surrounded by protective tubes and chicken wire. We saw a narrow dirt path instead of a road wide enough for cars. We saw a fallen sycamore tree that has created a scour pool for breeding fish. We saw a meandering creek working its way to the ocean unimpeded.[84]

Interlude

Grand Canyon

DAY BY DAY, MOMENT BY MOMENT, THE LAYERS OF CIVILIZATION SLIP away. The separation from the rest of the world is total. No cell phones. No television. No automobiles. No obligations beyond the rules of the river and the daily routines of departure and arrival as we move from camp to camp.

We travel a short distance in Duffy's *Escalante* to the mouth of Shinumo Creek for our first hike of the day. River sandals are just the thing for splashing through the creek in clear, shallow water that hits me at mid-calf to mid-thigh. Dike intrusions of pink and white granite cascade through the darker rock of the creek's narrow side canyon like waterfalls. Like the waterfall that spills in a spray of white water as Shinumo Creek drops down over a rock ledge to form a small pool no deeper than my hips—perfect for a cool dip on what promises to be another hot day. Fully dressed, we frolic in the pool and under the waterfall like kids. Wearing goggles, Roger disappears into the pool's depths. Not wearing goggles, one of us slips under the surface after taking a wrong step. I join several others—including all of the boatmen—to lounge on the surprisingly comfortable slope of smooth rock that edges the pool and creek.

It is a day for waterfalls. After lunch near Buckhorn Canyon under umbrellas striped in all of the colors of the rainbow, we hike about a half-mile over and among boulders to the waterfall at Elves Chasm on Royal Arch Creek. I negotiate the sometimes very narrow trail with aplomb, if not always in the fully upright position that Roger advocates. In contrast with the big spray at Shinumo, the waterfall at Elves Chasm is elegant and restrained as it streams in thin ribbons over and through the massive rocks adorned with pockets of greenery.

Climbing up through the rock, Roger demonstrates the thrill of leaping from a ledge partway up the waterfall. Michael, Marguerite, and Gail all follow suit. I admire their fearlessness but take photos instead of jumping fifteen or twenty feet into the water, even knowing that Harriet surely must have taken the plunge. But if I ever go again, I'm jumping.

The rapids—another kind of waterfall that forms periodically as the river drops about two thousand feet in stages from one end of the canyon to the other—punctuate the otherwise smoothly flowing Colorado River. In the silence the oar-driven dories afford as we slice through the unruffled stretches of the river, I study the steep walls of the Grand Canyon rising thousands of feet overhead. The different layers of rock stacked on each other or interlaced when molten rock filled gaps in rock that had already hardened. Streaks of solidified black travertine dripping down canyon walls like a Jackson Pollock painting. Rocks called Tapeats Sandstone that look like mushroom gills. Rocks atop the canyon rim like strategically built medieval fortresses. Fallen rocks, balanced on an edge, soon to fall again. Giant faces formed in rock. Watching, watching as I drift by.

All of the Grand Canyon is a lesson in geology. Geologists have been discovering the earth's secrets there since the mid-nineteenth century when Dr. John Strong Newberry visited the canyon as a member of an 1857–1858 surveying expedition sponsored by the U.S. Army. He described it as "the most splendid exposure of stratified rocks that there is in the world." In 1870, John Wesley Powell wrote, "the thought grew into my mind that the canyons of this region would be a book of revelations in the rock-leaved Bible of geology."[85]

But one area remains a mystery: the Great Unconformity, a one- to two-billion-year—geologists do not know the exact figure—gap in the history of the earth. Five hundred to 550 million-year-old Tapeats Sandstone (sedimentary rocks) rests directly on top of one- to two-billion-year-old Vishnu Schist (metamorphosed sedimentary rocks). Erosion has removed most of the intervening geologic record, so no one knows exactly what happened in those billion or more years.[86]

Leaving our third camp at Big Dune—and it is, indeed, a large expanse of open sand, located between miles 119 and 120—in Roger's *Paria*, we soon arrive at Blacktail Canyon, one of the best places to see the Great Unconformity. Roger leads us over rock-strewn ground into a narrow, high-walled chasm. He stops when he reaches a spot where the narrow passageway widens a bit and unrolls a map that he has carried from the dory in a white tube over his shoulder. He spreads it on the ground anchoring its corners with small rocks. We position ourselves around the map on comfortable rocks and smooth ledges to hear the story of Grand Canyon geology and the Great Unconformity.

I wander deeper into Blacktail Canyon, further into this eerie corridor that bends and twists its way through the mysteries of time. Hundreds of thin pancaked layers of golden sandstone top a base of dark, rounded schist. Occasional dike intrusions interrupt the schist with jagged streaks of white and pink where cracks have allowed molten rock to invade the ancient stone. I touch the walls of time before time.

The Grand Canyon is a monumental reminder of our human puniness. In the grand scheme of things, we humans are mere blips. We have been on Earth for such a short time compared to the surrounding rock canyon. Our individual passage here is brief. Harriet made the most of her moment. I wonder if it will be possible to say the same of me.

Bright Angel Trail on the way to the Colorado River, September 6, 2011

Elizabeth and Russell in the Grand Canyon at the Phantom Ranch boat beach awaiting the arrival of the O.A.R.S. dories on September 6, 2011

Duffy's dory, *Escalante*, tied up during lunch on a Colorado River beach, September 7, 2011
AUTHOR'S COLLECTION

Kerstin Dale rowing *Dark Canyon* after running Hermit. Russell and Michael are seated in the bow, September 6, 2011
AUTHOR'S COLLECTION

Morgan's dory, *Lost Creek*, on the Colorado River, September 8, 2011
AUTHOR'S COLLECTION

Duffy rows *Escalante* after our hike up Blacktail Canyon to see the Great Unconformity, September 9, 2011.
AUTHOR'S COLLECTION

As we hiked up Stone Creek Canyon between miles 132 and 133, we paused to look at the mescal oven and granaries in the canyon walls, September 10, 2011

The start of the day on September 11, 2011, as we head for Tapeats Rapid then pass through the Colorado River's narrowest point in the Grand Canyon, a mere 76 feet wide

Kerstin, Duffy, and Amber scouting Lava Falls on September 13, 2011
AUTHOR'S COLLECTION

Lava Falls survivors celebrate! September 13, 2011
AUTHOR'S COLLECTION

The dories lined up for the takeout at Diamond Peak, mile 226; from foreground to background: *Dark Canyon, Lost Creek, Paria, Escalante*; September 15, 2011
AUTHOR'S COLLECTION

CHAPTER FOUR

No Good Deed Goes Unpunished

Galena and the Nevada Land Exchange

The land ethic simply enlarges the boundaries of the community to include soils, waters, plants, and animals, or collectively: the lands . . . In short, a land ethic changes the role of Homo sapiens *from conqueror of the land-community to plain member and citizen of it. It implies respect for his fellow-members, and also respect for the community as such.* —ALDO LEOPOLD, *A SAND COUNTY ALMANAC*

Something will have gone out of us as a people if we ever let the remaining wilderness be destroyed. . . . We simply need that wild country available to us, even if we never do more than drive to its edge and look in. For it can be a means of reassuring ourselves of our sanity as creatures, a part of the geography of hope. —WALLACE STEGNER, *WILDERNESS LETTER*

We need wilderness whether or not we ever set foot in it. . . . No, wilderness is not a luxury but a necessity of the human spirit, and as vital to our lives as water and good bread. . . . What we need now are heroes and heroines, about a million of them, one brave deed is worth a thousand books. Sentiment without action is the ruin of the soul. —EDWARD ABBEY, *DESERT SOLITAIRE* AND *BEYOND THE WALL*[1]

ABOUT A MONTH BEFORE OUR TRIP TO THE GRAND CANYON, I HIKED THE Mount Rose Trail with Russell and Michael. Michael had accepted a spur-of-the-moment invitation to climb Tanzania's 19,341-foot Mount Kilimanjaro in early August, and we decided it would be a good idea to help him get ready to tackle the highest mountain in Africa by climbing to the summit of Nevada's 10,776-foot Mount Rose together just before his big adventure. The hike also would take us through lands that Harriet Burgess had saved from development many years before.

The Mount Rose Trail begins at Mount Rose Summit—which is not the actual summit but the mountain pass on the Mount Rose Highway (SR 431) that winds its way some twenty miles from Reno to Incline Village— at an elevation of 8,900 feet. Sacramento, our home base in California, is just a bit lower at thirty feet.

Blue skies, a gentle breeze, and a cool morning blessed our undertaking. It was the middle of summer, but snow still lingered along the trail. Patches of wildflowers—lupine, mule's ears, buckwheat—punctuated broad, rolling meadow. Fragrant evergreens soared overhead. The crisp, clean air was an open invitation to walk briskly up the narrow, mostly flat trail.

After an easy two and one-half miles, we reached a waterfall formed by Galena Creek tumbling over rocks on its way down the mountain to join the Truckee River. Many casual hikers stop here, perhaps resting awhile to enjoy the wonders of the great outdoors, then returning to the parking lot and heading home. We were not among them. We kept going, entering the Mount Rose Wilderness and continuing our trek to the summit. The gentle trail that led us to the waterfall became steeper and rockier.

I was exhilarated by the climb and maintained my pace as we ascended Mount Rose. I dismissed my aching head and my heart that was now beating with noticeable rapidity. After all, I was in shape. I walk all the time. But, when we stopped for a break one mile below the summit, I realized that I was in trouble. I began the last ascent, and forced myself forward over the first one hundred yards before nausea convinced me that I could go no farther.

I flashed on a story that Joe Burgess told me about climbing to the Mount Everest base camp in Nepal with Harriet. Joe said Harriet wanted to be the first woman to climb Mount Everest—it was on her bucket list— but settled for a trek to the base camp. They flew into Lukla, an airport carved into the side of the mountain and considered the most dangerous in the world, in a twin engine De Havilland Otter. It has only a short runway, on an upward slope to help slow the landing plane. It's at 9,100 feet. The base camp is at 17,598 feet. Trekking up the mountain, Joe came within 1,000 feet of the base camp but couldn't go any higher. He remembered:

> Every ten steps I was out of breath. Harriet being Harriet, either she wasn't as affected or was so determined she was going to get to the top of Kala Patthar, she did it. The funny thing is I trained for a month beforehand to get in good shape and I had a touch of altitude sickness almost every night whereas Harriet was too busy to train or do anything special and she never had any problem whatsoever. She had no problem at all.

Harriet had no problem at all.[2]

As I stumbled wretchedly back down the mountain defeated by altitude sickness, Michael hiked the final mile to the top of Mount Rose. For the last two hundred feet, he covered rocky volcanic ground above the tree line. When he reached the summit, sixty-three hundred feet above downtown Reno, he saw spectacular views of Lake Tahoe to the southwest, Mount Lassen to the north, and Reno to the northeast. He did not see the Galena Resort that developers almost built into the southeastern side of Mount Rose because it's not there. And it's not there because Harriet put together a land exchange that traded scattered lots in the city of Las Vegas for pristine forest and meadows in the Carson Range of the Sierra Nevada.

Land exchanges are a mechanism for trading surplus federal lands that have been determined to have little or no public benefit for desirable privately owned properties. The publicly owned lands may be scattered small parcels or lands that are otherwise difficult to manage. The private properties may offer significant conservation, recreational, or other benefits that fit within the mission of a federal land agency. The fair market value of both the "selected" lands of the federal government and the "offered" lands of the private owners must be equal as determined by federally approved appraisals, although small differences can be addressed through cash payments. Land exchanges are an effective method for acquiring and preserving lands for the public without the need for appropriating funds for land purchases.[3]

When Bruce Babbitt became Bill Clinton's secretary of the interior in 1993, land exchanges offered him a way to protect open space and conserve natural resources without having to spend scarce funds on land acquisition. In his initial testimony as secretary of the interior before the House Natural Resources Committee, Babbitt acknowledged that "this is a time of austerity and the Interior Department is doing its share to reflect the President's determination to keep spending down." Clinton's 1994 budget request for purchasing land was more than $150 million less than Bush had requested the previous year, but Babbitt still wanted to expand the national park system. He told the Natural Resources Committee, "I will be focusing on ways to expand and infill the national park system through the use of land exchanges. . . . I continue to believe out of my own experience that in addition to the Land and Water Trust [sic] Fund for outright acquisition that the use of the public land base for infill and expansion of the park system is a powerful way in times of budget austerity to continue this process."[4]

Babbitt was no stranger to land exchanges, having been among the first to use them when he was governor of Arizona in the 1980s. He exchanged parcels of state land isolated within federal landholdings for scattered tracts of Bureau of Land Management (BLM) land near Phoenix and Tucson that had high development value. As Interior secretary, he included $3.5 million in his budget to identify and facilitate potential land trades.[5]

A land exchange was exactly what Babbitt had in mind when he called Harriet in July 1993. The BLM was about to sell a single block of seventy-five hundred acres of public land to the city of North Las Vegas for development. The land was adjacent to the city and fit in with its plans for expansion. Developers were lining up for a chance to acquire the land. But Babbitt didn't want the BLM to sell the land to the city because sale proceeds would go into a general fund at the Treasury and would not necessarily be used to purchase environmentally sensitive land. Plus he was interested in acquiring 3,864 acres on the slopes of Mount Rose near Reno that were in imminent danger of being developed by the Galena Resort Company.

The BLM land was worth $50 to $60 million. The Galena land near Reno was worth about $20 million. For a land exchange to work, Harriet needed to secure more land in Nevada worthy of conservation with a value of approximately $30 million. She also needed the city of North

Las Vegas and BLM to switch from a purchase and sale to an exchange. And Babbitt wanted her to close the deal quickly. They talked about the exchange as a "sixty-day wonder"—even though exchanges often took several years to complete.[6]

When Babbitt asked Harriet if she could find land in Nevada to make an exchange work, she said, "Yes, and I'd love to do it."[7]

Harriet first connected with Bruce Babbitt and his wife, also named Harriet, on one of her many trips down the Colorado River through the Grand Canyon. Growing up in Flagstaff on his family's ranch, the Grand Canyon had been a constant presence during Babbitt's childhood. He hiked the Grand Canyon looking for fossils and dinosaur tracks. He built on his interest in the layers of time revealed in the rock walls of the Grand Canyon by earning a geology degree at the University of Notre Dame.[8]

The affinity for the Grand Canyon that Babbitt and Harriet shared formed the basis for their long friendship and led to their working together with others to create the Grand Canyon Trust in 1985. I can easily imagine Harriet and Bruce Babbitt gathered with Martin Litton and others on a sandy beach in the depths of the Grand Canyon. Harriet, with campfire flames reflected in her hazel eyes, perhaps using her experiences at TPL to urge the creation of a similar trust focused exclusively on the canyon. The stars—so visible in the darkness afforded by the absence of artificial light—were overseeing an animated conversation as the dedicated conservationists explored ways to preserve the glory of the Grand Canyon.

When Harriet asked Babbitt and his wife to serve on her Board of Councillors when she organized ALC in 1990, they agreed. They joined other big names in conservation, giving Harriet's organization immediate credibility. Babbitt already had served as Arizona's attorney general and governor. After an unsuccessful bid for the presidency, he was leading the League of Conservation Voters when he accepted Harriet's invitation. Harriet Burgess also bonded with Harriet Babbitt because they shared the nickname "Hattie"—although Harriet Burgess hated the sobriquet.[9]

Harriet "loved Babbitt because he was pushy. He wanted to get things done." Babbitt had absorbed the messages of writers such as Aldo Leopold,

Wallace Stegner, and Edward Abbey. Inspired by Leopold's land ethic, Stegner's geography of hope, and Abbey's fierce defense of wilderness, Babbitt recognized the unique qualities of the Western landscape and was a strong advocate for protecting it. Harriet credited Babbitt, along with Martin Litton, with igniting her passion to save land.[10]

Babbitt resigned from ALC's Board of Councillors when he was appointed secretary of the interior, but knowing Harriet's abilities and willingness to take risks, she was the one he called when he needed somebody to facilitate the complicated Nevada land exchange and get it done in a hurry.

The fight to save Galena had been going on for more than a decade by the time Babbitt asked for Harriet's assistance. It started soon after Nell Redfield died in 1981. Redfield had been the sole owner of the Galena property since her husband's death in 1974. When she died, the family trust invited AMOT, Inc., the owner of Alpine Meadows, California, and Park City, Utah, ski areas, to assess the feasibility of developing Galena as a destination ski resort.[11]

After three years of preliminary studies examining the terrain, climate, snow conditions, and marketability, AMOT, the Nell J. Redfield Trust, Quadriga Development Company of Nevada, and local developer Robert Weise joined together as partners in the Galena Resort Company to begin the development process. In February 1983, the Galena partners announced plans for a year-round destination ski resort to be constructed on 2,615 acres of land contributed by the Redfield Trust and 1,920 adjoining acres acquired by AMOT.[12]

The development envisioned by the Galena Resort Company on the slopes of Mount Rose boasted eleven ski lifts; 1,900 acres of skiable terrain, with 836 acres of ski runs and 176 acres of machine snowmaking; 34,500 square feet of day-use facilities and the equipment required to operate the ski facilities; a regulation eighteen-hole golf course on 150 acres; 195,000 square feet of commercial space; a parking garage for 1,900 automobiles; condominium sites for 1,460 units; one hundred single family homesites; four hotel sites with a total of 720 rooms; a 125-unit employee apartment complex; and a water and sewer plant to serve the development. Located along the Mount Rose Highway, the scenic mountain road connecting Reno and Incline Village, the resort site is just thirty minutes from the Reno airport and ten minutes from Lake Tahoe's North Shore. In the eyes of Nick Badami, the president of Alpine Meadows and the driving force behind the Galena Resort Company, it would be "an absolutely outstanding family resort."[13]

Almost immediately after the announcement of the Galena Resort Company's plans, a group of environmentalists and area residents joined forces to protest the development. They formed the Friends of Mount Rose to oppose the Galena Resort because "of the scale of the proposed project, the potential environmental, social, and fiscal impacts of the massive development, and the loss of their traditional access to both Forest Service and private lands with high recreational values." The development would burden the already busy Mount Rose Highway with more traffic and would take away the scenic views of the Mount Rose slopes.[14]

One of the founders and leaders of the Friends of Mount Rose, Rose Strickland, became a strong ally of Harriet's. Active in the Toiyabe Chapter of the Sierra Club, Strickland may have been responsible for sending Harriet the September/October 1983 issue of the chapter's newsletter that featured several articles on the Galena development. The threat to Galena was on Harriet's radar screen long before Babbitt contacted her ten years later.[15]

The Galena Resort Company's plans were initially welcomed by local and other government agencies. The Regional Planning Commission unanimously supported the project in August 1983 after reviewing it for more than four months. The Washoe County Board of Commissioners also approved the project and issued a special use permit in June 1984. The Nevada Department of Environmental Protection certified that the project would not violate state water quality standards in May 1986. The final subdivision plat for Galena Village was recorded in April 1990. The U.S. Army Corps of Engineers issued a permit to place fill in wetlands in October 1990. The development plans had been adjusted along the way, but Galena Resort was on track.[16]

Then strong opposition to the resort resurfaced in the summer of 1990. Rosemary Osborne jump-started the effort to defeat the Galena development when she helped organize the Save Galena Group and placed signs for miles along the busy Mount Rose Highway. One sign said, "Take a Look/Imagine the View if They Built a Resort." Another proclaimed, "A Terrible, Irreversible, Tragic Mistake." Some of the signs marked the locations of resort buildings.[17]

Osborne had just moved to Incline Village when she learned of the planned development of the Galena Resort. Talking to local residents about it, she realized that many didn't know the extent of the project. She said, "I know it sounds bizarre, but I felt I had to let the people know. It was almost a voice coming from the land." The signs were a wake-up call to the community. In two months, six thousand motorists stopped to sign petitions protesting the resort. Osborne capped her campaign by calling Nevada's Senator Richard Bryan to let him know and ask for his help.[18]

Perhaps in response to Osborne's campaign, Senator Bryan introduced legislation in February 1991 authorizing the secretaries of the Interior and Agriculture to acquire the Galena Resort through land exchanges. Bryan's bill directed the Agriculture secretary to form a negotiating committee to advise on possible land exchanges that would best serve the public interest and directed the the Interior secretary to provide technical assistance to identify parcels of federal land available for disposal and suitable to exchange. Bryan's bill also required the Agriculture secretary to develop a plan to acquire Galena through eminent domain if negotiations for a land exchange were not successful after one year. Reacting to the news of the bill, Galena Resort spokesman Werner Schuster said, "Obviously, we have not gone through the whole ten-year planning process just to sell the land. But if there is any value or realism to Bryan's bill, we'll consider the desires of the majority of the people of northern Nevada." The bill didn't move beyond introduction and referral to committee, but it added to the pressure to prevent the development of the resort.[19]

Even before the introduction of Bryan's bill, efforts were underway to facilitate a land exchange that would save Galena from development. The pressure of community protests may have led Nick Badami to contact Harriet in early January 1991. Harriet's notes of their conversation are sketchy, but they probably discussed doing a land exchange for Galena. In a letter written the next day, Harriet thanked Badami for calling and said, "Your comments on the Galena ski resort development were most helpful. It was nice to talk to you again after all these years." Badami had not forgotten Harriet—I suspect she often made such deep impressions on the people that she met. When he wanted to explore conservation options for Galena, he reestablished contact. Harriet enclosed a newsletter with her note that described the American Land Conservancy and its activities.[20]

Whatever Badami and Harriet discussed, it was not the American Land Conservancy but the organization that Harriet had left less than a year before that went to work on a land exchange to save Galena. In the same month that Harriet talked to Badami, The Trust for Public Land secured an option to purchase the Galena Resort property after Rosemary Osborne helped to bring TPL and the Galena developers together. TPL's Margaret Eadington immediately set out to find federal land for an exchange.[21]

Eadington zeroed in on the seventy-five hundred acres that BLM was planning to sell to the city of North Las Vegas but was faced with the problem of converting the sale to an exchange. BLM denied TPL's July 1991 exchange request in November and advised TPL to resubmit the request. Eadington and TPL continued to work the deal, but in the middle of ongoing negotiations with BLM, the city of North Las Vegas, environmentalists, and potential developers, their effort cratered because of a disagreement with the owners of the Galena Resort Company over who should be doing what in the negotiations. Galena's spokesman, Werner Schuster, said, "We were frustrated at not being in the communications loop every step of the way. We made it very clear we wanted to remain directly and actively involved in the decision-making process because time is of the essence." TPL withdrew in February 1992, and the question of whether Galena would be saved from development loomed large.[22]

Saving Galena was exactly the kind of project that Harriet founded ALC to undertake. It was large, complex, and risky. It was an inholding in the

Toiyabe National Forest. It was a high priority for the local community. For Harriet, "the Galena property represents the heart of the Carson Range. Starting just below the summit of Mount Rose, this property encompasses important wild lands from which most of the Truckee waters flow. The gentle slopes and meadows offer easily accessible recreation opportunities for year-round sports activities." It had to be done.[23]

Harriet already was working on a land exchange in Nevada when Babbitt contacted her about Galena. In early June 1993, she proposed an exchange of privately owned lands in Nevada for Nevada lands owned by the federal government. She detailed her proposition in a letter to BLM's state director for Nevada, Billy Templeton:

> The lands we offer in exchange [for the 7,500 acres of BLM lands adjacent to the City of North Las Vegas] will include several inholdings in the Pyramid Lake Indian Reservation in Northern Nevada, several inholdings in the Spring Mountains area of Toiyabe National Forest in Southern Nevada, and inholdings in the Red Rock Canyon Conservation Area in Southern Nevada. Many of the lands we offer in exchange are currently under purchase option contracts, and we are in negotiations with the owners of additional properties in all three target areas. We have a purchase contract with a buyer for the Government lands.

Harriet concluded by noting that the exchange would be a complex transaction, involving several federal agencies, and perhaps being realized in multiple transactions. Galena wasn't mentioned in her letter to Templeton, but it did come up in at least two telephone conversations in late June. She also had been tracking the TPL effort to acquire Galena. There was still a lot of work to do after Babbitt called, and Harriet was eager to get started.[24]

With the challenge of producing a "sixty-day wonder," Harriet tackled the land exchange in Nevada with her usual focused ferocity. Her sense of urgency was matched by the Galena owners' push to get the deal done as soon as possible. The Galena Resort Company had an agreement with Washoe County to build sewer and water facilities for the development.

Bonds had been issued, and the company had to make payments on the indebtedness either by developing the resort or by selling the land to the public. The city of North Las Vegas was also on the hook with developers who had been waiting to purchase the selected BLM lands for more than four years while appraisal issues were being resolved.[25]

Harriet prepared a long list of the offered lands that she already had chosen as possibilities for a land exchange in Nevada and that could be added to the Galena property to make the exchange with the seventy-five hundred acres near the city of North Las Vegas work. Harriet had selected most of these environmentally sensitive lands because public agencies—usually the Forest Service—wanted to acquire them. They were often within or adjacent to existing national forests. Harriet's connections at the Forest Service were essential resources for determining desirable private lands for transfer to public ownership.

Harriet's list included property in the California desert, seven properties at Pyramid Lake, Massacre Ranch, two properties in the Red Rock Conservation Area, a property on Peavine Mountain, and three properties in the Las Vegas area. Eight of the properties were still in negotiations. Appraisals either were completed or underway.[26]

Harriet met with Secretary Babbitt, Nevada's Senator Reid, and BLM's Director Jim Baca in late July to discuss strategies for the Galena transaction. One proposal involved adding privately owned land in California to the aggregation of offered lands needed to balance the value of BLM's selected lands in the city of North Las Vegas—a proposal that would require legislative approval because land exchanges legally were restricted to one state.

Harriet captured the need for immediate action in a letter she wrote to BLM's California state director, Ed Hastey, after the meeting:

> Because the Galena transaction is ready with appraisals and clearances in place, there is considerable urgency in assembling these additional lands to be included in this transaction. Some of these lands are ready to go, particularly certain parcels in Nevada. The expectation is that the transaction can be completed in sixty days. This is a challenge of magnificent proportion. But with concentrated attention, I think it is possible.
>
> The time urgency on this transaction is critical because the owners of the Galena property are paying, I've been told, some

$50,000 a month in sewer fees. I have not verified that number and I would not want to be held to it because I have no personal knowledge that it is correct. I do know that the Galena owners are very anxious to complete this transaction.

In addition, the City of North Las Vegas is very concerned that the developers who are buying these surplus BLM lands, may not wait patiently much longer for this transaction to be completed.... Other's [sic] speculate that the developers may be losing interest in pursuing this transaction. The City of North Las Vegas is most anxious to close this while they still have their buyers lined up. That of course, is central to the success of this whole transaction. The urgency of a timely completion cannot be too strongly emphasized.

This was discussed at some length at the meeting in Secretary Babbitt's office. All parties agreed that they would press full speed ahead to see this through to completion.

Harriet's longtime friend Ed Hastey and his BLM staff in California would be essential to making the Galena deal happen as quickly as possible. Hastey probably received the letter just before his telephone discussion with Harriet and the Nevada state director, Billy Templeton, on the status, scope, tasks, process, and schedule for the land exchange that would protect Galena.[27]

Getting the Galena deal over the goal line within the allotted time was a daunting task, even for Harriet. In all likelihood responding to Babbitt's strong support for the exchange, BLM's Jack Peterson was assigned in mid-August to assist and coordinate the complicated transaction for the Department of the Interior. He managed a special departmental task force of senior specialists in complex project management, negotiation, realty actions, mining law, and public land law.[28]

At about the same time that Harriet was writing to Ed Hastey, Peterson faxed a fifteen-item list of "updated tasks and a schedule for the Nevada and California land acquisition/exchange." Key tasks included the completion and review of the appraisals for all of the proposed acquisitions in Nevada and California, HazMat review and clearance for all lands proposed for acquisition, and completion of the preliminary title report review. The target date for completion of the land acquisition/exchange: September 30, 1993.[29]

Harriet also enlisted the aid of the attorneys at the San Francisco and Sacramento law firm of Marron Reid and Sheehy. She had worked with the firm's Lew Reid and Russell Austin on TPL projects in the 1980s and reconnected with them after two members of her staff, project manager Aaron Peskin and his domestic partner and future wife, attorney Nancy Shanahan, abruptly quit in early March 1993, leaving Harriet in the lurch with sixteen active projects.[30]

Peskin and Shanahan were barely out the door when Harriet contacted Lew Reid in San Francisco about doing work for ALC. Reid called his partner, Russell Austin, in Sacramento.

"Remember Harriet Burgess?"

"Of course I remember Harriet."

At one of Russell's first meetings with Harriet, he had accompanied Lew Reid as a junior attorney to the TPL office with documents for Harriet to sign. She had aggressively cross-examined Lew about whether he actually had read the documents or whether he had simply had Russell do them. Remembering that early meeting, Russell said:

> At one point, she noticed a typographical error in the transmittal letter to her, the cover letter explaining and listing the documents. The letter was addressed to Dear Harry, H-A-R-R-Y, not Dear Harriet. She pointed that out to Lew as evidence that Lew had not thoroughly read the package. To which Lew responded by grabbing her pen, scratching out Harry, H-A-R-R-Y, and writing in Hairy, H-A-I-R-Y, and telling her to sign the documents. She broke out into a laugh and started signing the documents.

Lew continued, "Well, Harriet needs some help. Can you be down here tomorrow?"

Russell said, "Sure," and joined Lew the next day at the offices that Harriet was subleasing from her husband's law firm. Joe had arranged for Harriet to use the offices at 44 Montgomery Street in San Francisco, but the space was empty when she started work there. It wasn't built out. It didn't have walls. It didn't have carpet. It didn't have phones. It didn't have furniture. It didn't have file cabinets.

After Harriet's daughter Leslie helped her move some desks from home to the new office, and offered to correct a contract Harriet was drafting by using a computer instead of using white-out and a typewriter, Harriet asked, "Can you come in and help me for a few days? Just get me organized?"

After one week Harriet asked Leslie, "When are you coming to work?"

Together they installed phones, bought used furniture and file cabinets, and set up a filing system that replaced sticky notes on the walls and organized the piles of paper all around the office. Leslie remembered, "It was easy for me to work with her because I knew how she liked things. And she could yell at me and it wasn't going to hurt my feelings." Leslie worked with Harriet at ALC for many years and became its "institutional memory."[31]

When Lew and Russell showed up, the office was fully functional. Harriet seemed pleased and relieved to see both of them. After she gave them an overview of the projects that needed immediate attention, Lew and Russell walked out of the meeting with their arms full of files. Lew took some of the projects. Russell took some of the projects. By the time Bruce Babbitt called Harriet to put together the Nevada land exchange a few months later, Russell had established a strong working relationship with Harriet. They were getting things done. They were closing projects. They were an effective team.

Harriet first negotiated the purchase contract for Galena with support from Russell and then, as the scope of the land exchange grew, the contracts for the other offered lands. Sometimes Russell had a significant role in the negotiations. Other times he had a collaborative role. Occasionally he simply was given the deal sheet after Harriet did all of the negotiating. If Russell took the lead in negotiating, as he did with the developer who owned offered land on Peavine Mountain, he would report to Harriet on the negotiations to make sure she knew and understood what the negotiations were, what worked for her, what didn't work for her.[32]

Just as Harriet was ramping up to make the land exchange in Nevada a success, she left on a long planned trip with Joe to Africa. Harriet and Joe loved to travel together, and they usually calendared their trips a year in advance because of their busy work schedules. She was out of the country from July 29 to August 15. While she was gone, she kept her commitment to her husband and did not dwell on the challenging deal that she had left behind in the capable hands of her staff and advisers.

Harriet had a laser-like ability to train her attention on the matter at hand to the exclusion of whatever else was happening in her life. The same ability she used in pursuing deals she applied in her personal life. She gave her all to her trip with Joe.

Joe once shared another example of Harriet's single-minded focus under extremely difficult circumstances:

> Harriet and I were just getting certified for diving and so we were down in Monterey doing our certification dive. The night before we got the word that [Harriet's daughter] Linda was in this terrible [automobile] accident. We had to decide whether to pull the plug on the whole thing. She couldn't get her flight out to Denver until a certain time so Harriet decided to do the certification dive. I remember it well. We dove. We got out of the water and she ripped her wetsuit off, her flippers, because she was going to go from the dive into a cab, to the airport, to Denver. And that's what she did. It was a hard day. But she did it. Very few people would have had the grit to finish the dive.[33]

Harriet was serious, focused, and unrelenting in the pursuit of her mission to save Galena and other lands in Nevada. It was a frame of mind that some referred to as Harriet's "blowtorch mode." She had a job to do, and she would take on any and all obstacles placed in the way of achieving her goal. But she had made a personal commitment to her husband to go to Africa, leaving her job behind, and she kept it.[34]

Harriet was back to work on August 19. Galena was ready to go. BLM had accepted the appraised exchange value of $19.4 million for the property. Commenting on the extreme complexity of the appraisal described in a report that filled two volumes and more than 450 pages, the BLM's Gerald

Stoebig said, "In my twenty-year career as a real estate appraiser . . . I have never seen an appraisal that remotely compares to this one in terms of complexity and difficulty." Appraisals often were stumbling blocks in doing land exchanges, but whatever issues there had been in establishing the fair market value of Galena, there were none now. Environmental clearances also had been completed and accepted.[35]

Galena was ready to go, and its owners were very anxious to close the deal, but not all of the other pieces of the land exchange were in place. While Harriet was in Africa, an all-hands-on-deck meeting convened at the Las Vegas Airport to discuss the situation with the city of North Las Vegas (CNLV) land. BLM was well represented by Jack Peterson, Billy Templeton, Ed Hastey, Butch Hayes, and six others. Bonnie Cohen, the Department of the Interior's assistant secretary for policy, management and budget was there along with Interior's regional solicitor. Jim Nelson, supervisor of the Humboldt-Toiyabe National Forest, was there for the Forest Service. Lauren Ward and Al Jahns, another attorney at Marron Reid, represented ALC. Marlene Lockard, state director for Nevada's Senator Bryan, attended. Nick Badami attended for the Galena Resort Company. The CNLV sent an attorney and the city's director of economic development. The developers interested in purchasing the CNLV land sent their attorney. But, as Lauren Ward reported to Harriet, the upshot of the meeting was to schedule another meeting on September 2.[36]

The CNLV had started the process of acquiring thousands of acres of BLM land within the city limits in 1988. The city planned to sell the land to selected developers to transform an underutilized public land asset into innovative, aesthetically pleasing, environmentally sensitive, quality master-planned residential communities that provide their residents with high amenity values, civic pride, housing at affordable price levels, and related benefits for project site residents, users and the City in general, and mixed-use commercial projects.

A lofty goal with tremendous economic benefits for the city.[37]

Significant progress had been made toward the sale of the land to the CNLV when the Interior Board of Land Appeals directed the BLM to reconsider the deal in September 1992 after the Sierra Club Legal Defense Fund on behalf of the Sierra Club's Toiyabe Chapter and the Nevada Outdoor Recreation Association filed an appeal in protest against it. The Sierra Club Legal Defense Fund insisted that any settlement of the appeal "must include an exchange for federal lands sold, and that exchange must include Galena."[38]

The land exchange that Harriet planned to put together solved the problem of the Sierra Club Defense Fund appeal. The "Land Exchange Agreement between the Bureau of Land Management and American Land Conservancy for the Equalization of Values" signed in late September specifically identified Galena along with other nonfederal lands as the real estate that would be exchanged for federal lands within the boundaries of the CNLV. According to the agreement, ALC anticipated entering into a purchase and sale agreement with the CNLV to convey the BLM land to the city at the same time that the Galena acreage was conveyed to the United States. Forwarding the agreement to Harriet for signature, Ed Hastey noted, "This is one piece of the overall land exchange and we hope we will be successful on the balance of the exchange."[39]

The BLM piece of the land exchange was now in place, but the Galena piece was in danger of slipping away. Harriet was running up against the September 30 deadline the Galena Resort Company set for the sale/exchange of the Galena land. The deadline was not just an arbitrary date. As Nick Badami emphasized at the August 13 meeting in Las Vegas, the company had a big sewer and water bond debt payment to Washoe County due on September 30, and the company needed more than $1 million to pay it. The money had to come either from the sale, or from the development of the Galena land. Harriet needed the proceeds from the sale of BLM's seventy-five hundred acres to the CNLV to pay the Galena Resort Company, but the CNLV still did not have firm commitments from developers.[40]

As the deadline approached, Nick Badami said that if a down payment of $1.3 million for Galena had not been deposited into an escrow account by September 30, then Galena Resort Company intended to develop its project. Construction of an access road would continue, and clearing trees for ski runs would begin next spring. Badami said the project "is still a damn good one and we would love to do it. At some point, you have to call a halt.

That has been the deal all along. If they can't make the deal by September 30, they can't make the deal. The deadline was set 2½ years ago. We can't carry it beyond that."[41]

But Badami still wanted to believe that ALC and the government would find the money. He said, "We have the Interior working very hard to get this thing done. I've never been in a deal in my life that's been so optimistic and at the same time so pessimistic."

BLM's Butch Hayes, chief of lands and recreation in Nevada, said, "We're sure going to try hard. After all this work, we would hate to see Galena slip away."

Senator Bryan's aide, Marlene Lockard, said, "Everyone has done super human work in trying to make this project work for everyone. We are working diligently on some means to get the $1.3 million by the end of September."[42]

Where was Harriet going to get the money? When Babbitt first called and asked her to put together the land exchange, the net worth of ALC was less than $200,000. Now the organization was running a substantial tab to pay expenses associated with the land exchange. ALC did not have the money to keep the deal alive on its own.

Time was running out. An editorial in the *Reno Gazette-Journal* pleading for more time reflected the strong community support of the bid to save Galena:

> The Galena deal can't slip away from us when it is this close to fruition. The sudden September 30 deadline creates a new sense of urgency, but surely that cannot be the end, even if it is not met. . . .
>
> Nothing has been easy. But it has not been easy for the people working to buy the property either, not for the representatives of the Sierra Club, nor Senator Richard Bryan's office, nor the American Land Conservancy, nor anyone else. But they have been trying very hard and very consistently. . . .
>
> The conservancy and federal officials are working very hard to raise the money, and we certainly hope the developers will show just a little more patience if the money is not there precisely on September 30. We are very, very close, and it would be a shame to lose this deal now.[43]

A second editorial two days later sent out an appeal for a benefactor to step forward and save the day:

Help! As in dollars. Lots of dollars. . . .

The American Land Conservancy in San Francisco has been trying to raise the money, but apparently is not succeeding. That means another source must be found. Already people are offering small amounts of money to Senator Richard Bryan's office. This is terrific. But what is needed is a large block of money, from one or two corporations or foundations. Bryan's office is feverishly exploring leads, but time is short. A benefactor is needed now. If anyone out there has the money, please contact Bryan immediately. . . .

If there is anyone out there: Help.[44]

Senator Bryan's office was trying desperately to find the money. Marlene Lockard said, "We're pulling out all the stops. We're absolutely turning over every stone." She said Bryan had been on the phone following up on leads for the week before the September 30 deadline. Harriet, too, had been on the phone that week fielding offers of help and updating Nick Badami and other landowners involved in the exchange. Badami said, "Everybody's running around but nothing is happening. They've been in touch with me but there's nothing of consequence. We don't have any option."[45]

But at the last minute, late in the day on September 30, it looked like they had pulled a rabbit out of the hat. Senator Bryan's office had located a potential benefactor. After all-day negotiations with the undisclosed benefactor's attorneys, agreement was reached on a short-term loan to the American Land Conservancy to cover the $1.5 million payment to the Galena Resort Company. Although the agreement had not yet been signed, Badami thought everything was on track for the deal, and the Galena partners extended their deadline to October 6.[46]

Lawyers went to work on drafting the $1.5 million loan agreement between ALC and the benefactor. At the same time, expecting the $1.5 million loan, lawyers prepared an agreement for ALC's purchase of the Galena Resort property. The purchase agreement dated October 15 divided the sale into two phases. For the first phase, ALC agreed to purchase 1,077 acres of the Galena property on or before January 10, 1994, for $1.5 million. For the second phase, ALC agreed to purchase the remaining 2,649 acres on or before September 30, 1994, for the balance of the total sales price of $19,400,000 plus all interest accrued from October 1, 1993, on Galena's indebtedness for water and sewer facilities. The agreement referenced the connection between the Galena purchase and the CNLV land exchange.[47]

The Galena partners had stretched the deadline again, but ALC had to come up with the $1.5 million payment by what Harriet called the "drop-dead date" of January 10. That should have been no problem because the benefactor had agreed to loan ALC that exact amount. But the benefactor already had started waffling on his commitment by October 6 and dropped out altogether on October 14. Without a documented binding loan agreement in place by October 31, the purchase agreement for Galena was set to terminate automatically. The race to raise $1.5 million was on again.[48]

A funding avenue Harriet had begun to consider before the elusive benefactor appeared on the scene was a loan from The Nature Conservancy (TNC). Not long after Harriet began working on the Galena/CNLV land exchange, TNC's director of the Great Basin Field Office, Dave Livermore, had written to the director of BLM, Jim Baca, offering to help with the exchange. He noted that "time is of the essence and the most important goal is to complete the Galena exchange as soon as possible." Livermore said that TNC had supported efforts made by Senator Bryan, Senator Reid, and Alpine Meadows to protect the Galena acreage for some time. Harriet, Bryan, Reid, Babbitt, Badami, and others were copied on the letter.[49]

As the September 30 deadline approached, Livermore called Senator Bryan's office again to offer TNC's assistance. Following up on that offer, Harriet and Marlene Lockard called Livermore on September 28. Working late on September 29, Harriet faxed a memo to Livermore and Lockard listing the milestones of the Galena/CNLV exchange. She concluded the memo by suggesting how TNC might facilitate the exchange:

The Nature Conservancy could help by giving a note (to be held in escrow) for $1.5M secured by land (175 acres) and water rights (285 acre feet) already identified and agreed to by the land owner and both the Forest Service and BLM review appraisers. The note would sit in escrow until the project closes at which time it would be extinguished.

Harriet scrawled "a late nite effort—I'm no good at computers—call for help!" on the fax transmittal sheet and signed it H2, her usual sign-off. H2, or H², as she often wrote it—was an abbreviation of Harriet Hunt, her name from her first marriage. I do not know why she continued to use her last name from her first marriage to Bob Hunt. She also used Harriet Hunt Burgess on many of her credit cards. Perhaps it was a way of maintaining her connection with her five children. Perhaps it was a way of avoiding using her middle name, Gertrude, a name she disliked. Perhaps it was habit. Whatever the reason, the sign-off fit her perfectly—Harriet was always moving at twice the speed of most everybody else.[50]

Harriet took off the next day to attend the Land Trust Alliance rally in Montana but still spent three hours on the Galena acquisition including phone conversations with her attorney, Badami, and Livermore about the possibility of a TNC loan. When the benefactor withdrew the offer of a $1.5 million bridge loan, TNC was waiting in the wings. After Livermore's discussion with Harriet and Marlene Lockard in September, he had broached the possibility of the loan at TNC's annual meeting in early October. Livermore reported to Harriet and Marlene that TNC would be open to making the loan if certain conditions were met, including formal approval from the TNC board.[51]

Up against the October 31 deadline for a securing a binding loan agreement, Harriet contacted Livermore soon after she knew the benefactor had backed out, but TNC could not act quickly enough to meet the deadline. The Galena partners agreed to extend the deadline to November 5, a deadline that all parties seemed to have ignored as the TNC loan process dragged on through November and December.[52]

As Harriet commented later, "If TNC's requirements preliminary to making loans are consistent with regular banking practices—most groups would find it easier and cheaper to deal with local commercial banks!" The myriad requirements included letters confirming commitments, support, and information from five different government offices; maps and legal descriptions; and loan agreement provisions such as the payment of 8½ percent interest and TNC expenses. Twenty-three items were on TNC's first list of demands, and more came later. Harriet said, "Each time we satisfied the list, they came up with an additional demand."[53]

Although TNC's board of directors approved the loan at their December 3 meeting, the approval was subject to certain conditions. TNC had all of the cautionary roadblocks of an established bureaucracy that Harriet had founded ALC to avoid. Harriet began to believe, "We were *never* going to cross the goal line." After TNC made yet another request in late December, Harriet concluded, "they were never really going to make the loan." TNC wanted to dot all the i's and cross all the t's. Harriet wanted to save Galena. If the loan were not in place by January 10, the Galena Resort Company would not be able to make its sewer bond payment to Washoe County and would begin development of the Galena acreage.[54]

It was time to move on.

Once Harriet gave up on TNC, she acted quickly to secure another source for the $1.5 million loan. She followed up an early morning meeting on December 28 with Cole Wilbur, executive director of the David and Lucile Packard Foundation, with a letter summarizing the key elements of the land exchange. She had three more conversations with Wilbur on December 29. She contacted Babbitt, who wrote a letter to Wilbur and David Packard in support of the loan.

Harriet was very persuasive, and her passionate persistence was rewarded. On January 3, only a few days after she first got in touch with Wilbur, she exulted, "We got the loan from Packard!!" The sale of eleven hundred acres of Galena land to the American Land Conservancy closed on January 10.[55]

Harriet had kept Galena in play, but the land exchange was still up in the air. The city of North Las Vegas had yet to finalize a deal with the developers interested in BLM's seventy-five hundred acres.

The developers were not willing to pay the $1,500/acre fee imposed by the city on top of the $7,000/acre cost of the land. When the city refused to reduce or remove the fee, the developers refused to go forward with the deal, and existing development agreements were canceled in February 1994.[56]

From the beginning, the land exchange had been predicated on the sale of seventy-five hundred acres of BLM selected lands valued at $52 million to the CNLV. Because Galena, one of the offered lands on the other side of the exchange, was worth about $32 million less than the BLM acreage, Harriet had to find additional offered lands to make up the difference. By the time the CNLV dropped out, she had assembled a portfolio of more than $50 million of offered lands. The failure of the CNLV deal put ALC in an awkward situation with many of the sellers of the offered lands that Harriet had lined up because she was not able to close by the time she had promised. Some of the sellers were under severe financial distress because of the delay.[57]

Harriet had to change course. She was a master at finding other ways to get things done. If plan A doesn't work, move on to plan B or plan C or plan D. Just as she had done when trying to nail down a loan for the Phase I Galena purchase, Harriet moved on immediately to a different approach for locating other selected BLM lands to include in the Nevada land exchange.

Harriet did not have to look far to find surplus BLM lands in Clark County to substitute for the seventy-five hundred acres no longer available for the Nevada land exchange. Las Vegas was dotted with small BLM inholdings that were difficult to manage and that were ripe for development in a burgeoning city where available land was scarce. Most of the other developable land was owned by Summa, a Howard Hughes company, whose virtual monopoly shut out eager prospective developers such as Pulte Homes and Del Webb Corporation. BLM agreed to the substitution in an amended exchange agreement with ALC signed in early March 1994.[58]

Harriet called on her real estate adviser and friend Lauren Ward to comb through the scattered BLM lands in Las Vegas and pick the tracts best suited for the exchange. Harriet first met Lauren when she was working for TPL on a project to add two hundred acres to what is known as the "Bean Field" portion of the Butte Sink National Wildlife Refuge. The Fish and Wildlife Service didn't have the money to buy the land, but they wanted the property. One of the two owners of the property, Lauren took Harriet on a tour of the "Bean Field" one night, a night made magical because of the full moon that highlighted the ducks and geese wintering in the wetlands.

Convinced of the value of the "Bean Field" for wildlife habitat, Harriet was able to get an earmark on a bill in Congress to secure the necessary funding. Lauren said,

> I was so impressed that this woman put what was an earmark through Congress that I started sending her notes about all these other things. She didn't have any of her staff that was interested in wetlands. They all wanted to deal with old growth forests and stuff like that. Nobody cared about wetlands and so that's when she sent me the note that said, "Why don't you come help me?" [59]

Lauren was a duck hunter and a real estate developer who often alerted Harriet to conservation projects. Once he sent her a message with his idea about buying rice land in California, turning it back into wetlands, then selling it to duck clubs to make money. At that time, the market for rice land in California had collapsed, creating a great opportunity to acquire land cheaply. Over lunch, Harriet and Lauren sketched out the plan for a project on the back of a napkin. Lauren then flew the Sacramento Valley in a rented plane looking at all of the big pieces of land that were available. They decided to purchase the sixty-seven-hundred-acre Schohr Ranch, which was in foreclosure and had been taken back by the federal government. [60]

Lauren and Harriet "got the biggest runaround imaginable" when they tried to buy the Schohr Ranch from the federal land bank representative.

When Harriet, Lauren, and his wife, Mary Margaret, were talking over the problems with the deal one evening in the kitchen of the Wards' home, Harriet said, "Well, I'll go to Washington and see what I can do." According to Lauren, "That's what it took finally to break the thing loose was that Harriet turned her contacts with congressmen and senators loose on this guy." As the seller was getting ready to sign the papers to close the deal, he asked, "If I sign these papers, will I stop getting phone calls from senators and congressmen?" Harriet and Lauren then divided the Schohr Ranch into two parcels: 3,700 acres were turned into a wildlife refuge, and the remaining 3,000 acres were sold for duck clubs.[61]

Talking about his relationship with Harriet only a few months after his heart transplant operation in 2009, Lauren told me:

> I was never an employee of ALC. We were good friends. I'm sure that Harriet used me for a sounding board a lot. We used to spend a lot of time together. First of all, I had an airplane so I could get Harriet in the plane and I had her undistracted attention. We talked about our [spouses], our lives, kids, everything that was going on. We were very close.
>
> There were no words that were ever missed between Harriet and me. On either side. That was one of the great strengths of the relationship that we had enough respect for each other that we could say things exactly as they were. She always knew that I would give her my best advice. She didn't have to take it. She was the boss. But I was still going to give her whatever my best advice was. That was what I did. And that was one of the advantages of getting her alone in the airplane. She couldn't get away from me.[62]

And flying with Lauren in his pressurized, turbo-charged single engine Cessna P210 gave Harriet an opportunity to get a bird's-eye view of ALC's current and potential conservation projects. It was also another way for Harriet to get to the face-to-face meetings that she favored for persuading landowners, government representatives, and others that her projects were the right thing to do.[63]

Lauren asked local real estate broker Jan Bernard to help him select the Las Vegas lands for the exchange. Lauren had concluded that she would be an excellent resource for identifying the lands and helping to sell them after he worked with her when Harriet had been interested in buying land that Jan owned on Mount Charleston in the Spring Mountains. Harriet designated Lauren and Jan as ALC's exclusive agents for the sale of BLM lands in Clark County.[64]

Lauren and Jan rummaged through the hodgepodge of BLM lands in Las Vegas and chose approximately sixteen hundred acres for the exchange. BLM segregated the lands for exchange on March 15 and published the required notice of the impending exchange of the Las Vegas lands in the local newspapers in early April. The acreage comprised parcels between two and a half and five acres interspersed among privately owned properties. Developers jumped at the chance to purchase the newly available vacant land.[65]

Before BLM conveyed the selected lands to ALC for sale to the developers, unpatented mining claims were discovered that clouded title to some of the parcels. Five mining companies that appeared to be acting collaboratively had filed twelve claims. These mining claims were suspect because they appeared at about the same time the notice of the exchange was published, suggesting that the motivation for filing them was to collect a payment from BLM or ALC to have the claims removed and thereby permit the process of conveying the lands to go forward. Such opportunistic claims had been made before in the rough-and-tumble world of Las Vegas real estate in the 1990s.[66]

To check out the claims, ALC hired an engineer to determine whether they were properly staked and noticed according to Nevada law. The engineer reported they were properly staked with the bottom halves of Pepsi Cola cans screwed to the stakes with the required notices in the cans. Lauren Ward told the engineer to go back out and record the expiration dates on the cans. Then he asked the local Pepsi bottler when the cans were manufactured based on the expiration dates. In what Russell Austin called "a great gotcha," it turned out that the cans had been manufactured six months after the date of the mining claim.

Clearing the claims was a long process masterminded by ALC attorney Al Jahns. At one point, Harriet called Al at home on a Friday night because she was tempted to capitulate to the demands of the claimants, make a settlement payment, and get on with the land exchange. Time was short. But Al told her, "I think we're very close. We have the winning poker hand. We should stay the course. We have other transactions and don't want to set a precedent." Harriet agreed. Al succeeded in convincing the title company to insure around the claims, and the claimants finally settled for a token consideration of $10 instead of the thousands of dollars they had hoped to receive after the lands had been sold.[67]

By May 1994, Harriet was able to report to Bonnie Cohen at the Department of the Interior that the Nevada land exchange was "moving quickly to closing. We are driving for a July 15, 1994 close, at least on the most critical and time urgent projects." It crossed her mind that they might even be able to close on July 16, Senator Bryan's birthday. Not mentioning the problem of the mining claims, she noted:

> The clearance of the newly selected BLM Las Vegas lands is proceeding at a record pace. ALC has paid a premium to contractors to accelerate their schedules. Jack Peterson has been particularly helpful in arranging for immediate BLM reviews. BLM staff changes in Nevada have put particular pressure on the Las Vegas and Reno offices but Jack Peterson, Billy Templeton and Dave McIlnay have arranged for assistance from California and Arizona BLM offices.

Harriet—and everyone involved—was continuing to make an all-out effort to get the land exchange done. As Jack Peterson commented, "This is an action-packed activity with frequent unpredictable surprises—but it's fun and we are making progress."[68]

Yet another surprise came in the form of protests from the Las Vegas Flood Control District, the Nevada Department of Transportation, and the Clark County Department of Comprehensive Planning. The Flood Control District protested against all of the selected lands, claiming that flood channels ran through all of the parcels. The Nevada Department of Transportation worried that the selected lands included parcels where they planned to construct a beltway. The planning department feared that development of the selected lands would be a problem because the area lacked public services and infrastructure. The Clark County Board of Commissioners adopted a resolution in early July opposing and protesting the land exchange.[69]

Negotiations with the Flood Control District led to the reservation of rights-of-way and construction corridors for flood control channels. The Flood Control District also received deeds to certain parcels that were conveyed to ALC by BLM. Negotiations with the Department of Transportation led to the reservation of a right-of-way corridor for the future Las Vegas Beltway. Harriet told Senator Bryan, "All these negotiations were challenging but successfully concluded to the satisfaction of the Regional Flood Control District, the Nevada Department of Transportation, BLM, and ALC." ALC also worked with the Clark County planning department to reserve lands that the county identified for recreation and other public purposes such as rights of way for roads, school sites, and parks. The legal descriptions of the lands conveyed to Clark County covered two hundred pages.[70]

Settlement of the flood control, transportation, and infrastructure issues delayed the anticipated closing of the Nevada land exchange. Appraisals of the selected lands, still not completed by the middle of July, also slowed the process. But on August 12, 1994, all was in place to close what Harriet told Senator Bryan was "by far the most complicated and challenging project I have ever undertaken."[71]

Eight escrows and numerous sub-escrows closed simultaneously on August 12 in the first phase of the Nevada land exchange. Galena, the linchpin of the assembled land exchange, and three other properties encompassing 12,743 acres of private lands became part of the Humboldt-Toiyabe National Forest or Indian Trust lands. Scattered tracts totaling 1,602 acres of public lands in the Las Vegas area were conveyed to ALC and then sold to six development companies. The total value of the lands exchanged was close to $60 million.[72]

The Nevada land exchange was the largest and most complex exchange ever attempted by the Department of the Interior. Although many individuals contributed to making the enormously complicated exchange happen, Harriet Burgess was the driving force behind its success. She said, "I take pride that ALC was founded to do the difficult projects that others could not or would not undertake and that continues to be our purpose. Clearly this exchange fits that description." As she promised in the first ALC newsletter, she took the risks and dared the impossible.[73]

When Harriet first got the call from Secretary Babbitt and agreed to facilitate the Nevada land exchange, ALC's net worth was less than $200,000. ALC had to borrow $1.5 million at 6 percent interest from the Packard Foundation to pay for a portion of Galena. ALC had to guarantee payment of $500,000 in sewer bonds and property taxes to Washoe County. ALC had to borrow $600,000 at 9 percent interest from the owners of one of the offered properties (Peavine Granite) to prevent a foreclosure sale of another of the offered properties (Peavine Venture) and to pay $80,000 in past due taxes. ALC had to persuade both its law firm and its real estate brokers to accept payment for services related to the exchange after the exchange was completed. Without that agreement, ALC would not have been able to make payroll. If Harriet had failed to complete the exchange successfully, ALC would have been forced out of business. Instead, she succeeded, and ALC emerged from the exchange with money in the bank for future projects.[74]

Jubilation! Harriet's joy, relief, and gratitude after the closing of the Nevada land exchange poured forth in more than eighty heartfelt thank-you letters to Bruce Babbitt, Nick Badami, and everyone else who had played a part in getting the deal done. Some are at least partly form letters, but many include handwritten personal notes and many are individualized. To a few Harriet admitted, "At the time I knew it would come together, but looking back is really scary." To others she said, "It was impossible—but with your help, expertise and support we overcame the impossible." She appreciated the "hand holding, arm twisting and the loan of your shoulder." She exclaimed, "It's done, Galena is ours—all of ours!," but then also recognized,

"Of course we're not done yet!" All of the letters are full of the energy and dedication that Harriet brought to the complicated land exchange.[75]

Celebration! The invitations to a mountainside celebration to recognize the public acquisition of Galena went out soon after the closing. On a sunny day in late August, many who had made important contributions to the successful acquisition gathered in a grassy Galena meadow for champagne, lunch, music, and a brief ceremony.

Harriet was there, of course, dressed in jeans and a T-shirt with her auburn hair blowing in the light breeze, looking nothing like the mover and shaker that she was. I was there, too, though I didn't know then what I know now of the magnitude of the achievement. My interactions with Harriet had yet to go beyond answering early morning and late evening phone calls from her.

Me: "Hello."

Harriet: "It's Harriet. I need to talk to Russell."

Me: "OK. I'll get him."

That was about it. She may not always have said, "It's Harriet." All business. I was busy driving carpools, taking kids to soccer games and piano lessons, doing lots of laundry, going to back-to-school nights, remodeling our house, and so on, as a stay-at-home mom when not pursuing my passion for horses, working as a reference librarian at U.C. Davis, or trying to figure out what to do with the rest of my life. And Harriet was just another demanding client—though the only one who called Russell at home in the era before cell phones.

Harriet laughed with delight when she and Senator Bryan each were presented with an almost eight-foot two-man crosscut saw emblazoned with "A Toothful History of Galena Preserve and Enjoy!" That saw graced the wall of her ALC office for the rest of her career.[76]

The first phase of the Nevada land exchange was behind her, but as Harriet said in several of her thank-you letters, she was not finished. Harriet was particularly concerned that the first phase only preserved environmentally sensitive lands in northern Nevada whereas all of the privatized lands were located in southern Nevada. She said,

> I will continue to work in the Las Vegas area until I have fulfilled my commitment to the community to do exchanges which bring land conservation parcels into public ownership close to home for the Las Vegas community. I feel a very strong obligation to fulfill that promise. Getting appraisals approved may not be easy, but I've always been known for my stubbornness, and we will achieve that goal.

Harriet had promised the Nevada congressional delegation and Clark County officials that she would find lands in southern Nevada for conservation. That almost proved to be her undoing.[77]

Harriet had been working on finding offered lands in southern Nevada before Galena and the first phase of the Nevada land exchange closed. She had located the Deer Creek properties in the Spring Mountains less than an hour from downtown Las Vegas that, like Galena before its acquisition and transfer to the U.S. Forest Service, were inholdings in the Toiyabe National Forest. Described as "an island of green in the middle of the desert," the Spring Mountains offered an escape from the city into a rugged mountain landscape fostering more than fifty ecologically sensitive plants and animals—twenty-five found nowhere else in the world—for more than one million people every year. Harriet knew that private inholdings in the Spring Mountains had been high on the list of priority acquisitions for the Forest Service for many years.[78]

What Harriet found in the Spring Mountains was a number of small lots and a 375-acre parcel that were owned by Jan Bernard, the Las Vegas real estate broker, and other investors in a company called Pine Development. The properties were just a few miles from Mount Charleston and adjacent to or within the Mount Charleston Wilderness. Stands of old Douglas fir, ponderosa pine, white fir, and bristlecone pine grew there. The north and south forks of Deer Creek meandered beneath their branches. ALC bought the thirty-four-acre Deer Creek lots from Pine Development and optioned the remaining 375 acres. Harriet had hoped to transfer these lands to the federal government in the first phase of the exchange, but appraisal difficulties prevented their inclusion.[79]

The appraisals for the Deer Creek properties were wildly divergent. I find it hard to believe that the appraisers all were looking at the same real estate. The differences reflected a surging Las Vegas real estate market with values moving rapidly upward and the varied perspectives of the appraisers on technical issues such as absorption and discount rates, the relevance of the original purchase price of the Deer Creek properties, and on debt load in the context of a development approach appraisal.[80]

The first appraisal, prepared by the same appraiser hired by BLM to appraise the Las Vegas selected lands in phase I of the Nevada land exchange and approved by the Forest Service, valued the Deer Creek lots and acreage at $12.2 million. The Forest Service rejected the first appraisal, having concluded that it was too high.

The second appraisal, prepared by an appraiser hired by the Forest Service, valued the Deer Creek lots and acreage at $4.7 million. Harriet and ALC rejected the second appraisal because it was too low and requested a meeting with the Forest Service to resolve the value differences. The March 1995 meeting did not result in a resolution.

BLM hired a third appraiser to reconcile the values determined by the first two appraisers. Jan Bernard's company, Pine Development, rejected that appraiser's $5.16 million valuation of the Deer Creek acreage. The third appraisal valued the Deer Creek lots at $2.25 million. The Forest Service did not want to buy the Deer Creek lots from ALC without the Deer Creek acreage. If push came to shove, Harriet figured she could sell the lots for $4.25 million—for a profit of slightly more than $1 million—but then she would have failed to fulfill her pledge to find conservation lands in southern Nevada. And as she said, "If I sell the lots, I'll just be crucified by the people who are my supporters."[81]

With development planning for the Deer Creek acreage already underway, Senator Bryan convened a Saturday meeting in July with ALC, Pine Development, BLM, and the Forest Service to develop a strategy to resolve the valuation issues. Deer Creek was a special place for Senator Bryan, who remembered picnicking and camping there as a child away from the heat of Las Vegas. Bryan was so determined to save Deer Creek that two of the federal employees in attendance later said he pounded his fist on the table and said he didn't care what the government had to pay, he wanted them to make the trade work. Harriet didn't remember any fist pounding, but she was not optimistic after the meeting. She believed the appraisers used assumptions that included factual errors. She also believed that the Forest Service was placing unmerited emphasis on the original price of $2 million that Jan Bernard had paid for the properties in 1992. Because all three of the first appraisers had dismissed that sale as irrelevant to the current value of the properties, Harriet felt that making the original price an issue was a political rather than an appraisal concern. She said, "We are in trouble. It is not a pretty picture."

Unilaterally and contrary to understandings with ALC and Pine Development, BLM arranged for a fourth appraisal conducted by the BLM and Forest Service appraisal staffs. Their number was lower than the third appraiser, putting the acreage at $4.7 million and the lots at $2 million.[82]

The government and the landowners had reached an impasse. Disillusioned by the appraisal process, Jan Bernard withdrew Pine Development's Deer Creek acreage from any further consideration as an exchange property and intended to proceed with plans to develop the land. Advising Senator Bryan of her decision, Jan wrote, "For nearly two years Pine Development has held back from active development in order to attempt a reasonable trade situation through the Forest Service and BLM. It has been an arduous and disappointing experience that could not be recommended to any land owner."[83]

With the Deer Creek exchange on the verge of collapsing, Harriet was hit with another setback. She and Joe were working in San Francisco when they received the call that fire was racing toward the nearly finished home that they had been building in Inverness for the past three years. As soon as they got the word, they rushed to Inverness but were only able to get as far as Point Reyes Station. They looked up and saw an inferno consuming the ridge where their house was under construction.

Harriet and Joe had planned to move in on Thanksgiving and had invited scores of friends to celebrate the completion of their new home.

Stacks of cherry wood for roof trim were piled neatly in the garage next to gleaming stainless steel kitchen appliances still in their cardboard shipping boxes awaiting last-minute installation. Designed by Jim Campe, an architect and Inverness Ridge neighbor, with lots of input from Harriet and Joe who planned the interior and chose the interior finishes, the reddish brown clapboard house with deep green trim grew out of the side of the ridge surrounded by a forest of bishop pines.

When they were finally able to hike up the hill two days later, all that remained in the midst of scorched rubble were two chimneys and the shop building. A nearby house was untouched by the fire that had sped south from Mount Vision to engulf the Paradise Ranch subdivision on Inverness Ridge, an inholding of 130 homes surrounded by the more than seventy thousand acres of Point Reyes National Seashore. By the time it reached Paradise Ranch, the wall of fire was three hundred feet high with temperatures ranging up to three thousand degrees Fahrenheit. Cinders an inch and a half in diameter rained down on the houses. The sap in the decadent, overgrown, turpentine-infused bishop pines became hot so quickly that the trees exploded like they had been dynamited. By the time the fire was completely contained on October 6, it had burned twelve thousand acres and consumed more than forty homes.

Harriet and Joe soon began looking for a new place to build their home. But no other lots were like their lot on Inverness Ridge, the lot that overlooked stands of bishop pine and Douglas fir; the lot that was surrounded by a national seashore and near a trail that led to the coast; the lot that had been in the path of a firestorm; the lot that can only be reached by driving a narrow, steep, twisting road with a 20 percent grade. So bolstered by Harriet's "we can do this" certainty, Harriet and Joe decided to rebuild on the land left bare by the fire.

Finished in 1998, the second incarnation of Harriet and Joe's dream house hugs the side of Inverness Ridge. It is an exact replica of the first house except for the addition of an interior bridge connecting two upper-story wings. Like the new trees that grew from the seeds of the bishop pines that burst open in the fire, the house rose from the ashes. Now only a few pine skeletons break through the rejuvenated bishop pine forest that cradles the house, reminders of the fire and the sharp edge of vulnerability.

The fire had been extinguished, and Harriet's house was in ashes, but there was still life in the Deer Creek exchange. Jan Bernard had withdrawn Pine Development's Deer Creek acreage, but Jim Nelson was not ready to give up on acquiring the Deer Creek inholdings. Nelson, supervisor of Humboldt-Toiyabe National Forest, asked Harriet to persuade Jan to meet with the two of them to discuss the appraisal issue. At the October 18 meeting, Nelson asked Jan to reconsider the withdrawal of the Deer Creek acreage from the exchange. He suggested that both Jan and Harriet try to resolve the problem through arbitration with the Forest Service. After the meeting, Harriet told Nelson, "I think Jan will consider arbitration but is understandably worried about dealing with the Forest Service." And she kept her congressional contacts advised of the situation.[84]

Instead of arbitration, the Forest Service suggested using a new and untried bargaining process authorized by the land exchange act. ALC and Pine Development agreed. The six-member bargaining team met for two days on December 6 and 7, 1995. Three members of the team were from the Forest Service and the other three were Harriet, Jan Bernard, and Lauren Ward. The entire meeting was recorded.

After negotiations that covered the history of the multiple appraisals of the Deer Creek properties and the technical appraisal issues involved, the team agreed to have a qualified appraiser from Las Vegas review the appraisal reports, the reviews of the appraisal reports, and additional documentation made available by the bargaining team. The new appraiser established values of $2.84 million for the Deer Creek lots and $7.63 million for the Deer Creek acreage. The bargaining team agreed to accept these values and to proceed with the land exchange. The team signed their bargaining agreement on March 13, 1996.[85]

Harriet walked away from the bargaining session believing that the Deer Creek properties were fairly appraised and ready for transfer to the federal government. The Forest Service accepted the lands and they became part of the Humboldt-Toiyabe National Forest. But not everybody in the Forest Service was pleased with the outcome, especially not Paul Tittman, chief appraiser for the Forest Service in Washington, D.C.

Tittman filed a complaint with the Office of the Inspector General for the U.S. Department of Agriculture. His complaint accused the Forest Service staff in Nevada of "'appraisal shopping' in an effort to meet the expectations of the property owners, regardless of the values found in the market." He concluded that the Deer Creek transaction "has all the makings of either scandal or incompetence in managing the public's resources." Before Tittman filed the complaint, he took Harriet out to lunch and told her exactly what he was going to do and how it would go down.[86]

Explaining why Tittman would go after Harriet and the Deer Creek exchange, Lauren Ward said, "Because Harriet did difficult projects, she ended up rolling over a lot of people in the government. When you roll them, they will get even with you eventually. They'll get their retribution and they did [with the Office of the Inspector General (OIG) investigation]. It was simply vindictiveness on the part of Paul Tittman." Harriet's habit of going around government bureaucrats either to their superiors or to power-wielding politicians, what Lauren called rolling people, created resentment. She would start with agency staff, politely explain her position and what she wanted to accomplish. If the staff told her no, she didn't get angry, she just found other ways to get the job done—and that often meant going up the food chain.[87]

Tittman's complaint triggered an audit of land exchanges involving the Humboldt-Toiyabe National Forest from 1990 to 1997 by the OIG of the U.S. Department of Agriculture. Harriet and her attorneys cooperated fully with the OIG investigation. They met with the OIG auditors and responded to all of their questions, even when it was evident that the auditors were unfamiliar with both the basic structure of land exchange transactions and basic concepts of real estate development and appraisal. Boxes and boxes of ALC files were copied and provided to the government.

Russell Austin called Lauren Ward one day during the investigation choking with laughter after one of the auditors told him that the problem they had with the bargaining session was that their people simply weren't as smart as ALC's people. Russell said, "My god, how would you like to work for an institution that backs you up by saying that the problem is that you're not as smart as the people you're dealing with on the other side?"

Harriet later said that a member of the Forest Service's National Landownership Adjustment Team formed to oversee land exchanges confessed to her that "one of their primary concerns was that I had been in the land acquisition business longer than most Forest Service employees, and they felt that I probably knew more about how to do these transactions than most of them did, and thus I could control the process. He said they wanted to take control back." Sometimes it just doesn't pay to be smarter than the other guy.[88]

The OIG's report was published in August 1998. It criticized the Forest Service's land exchanges in Nevada—especially the Deer Creek exchange with ALC. The OIG claimed that the acquisition cost to the Forest Service exceeded the OIG's determination of appraised value by approximately $5.9 million. The OIG concluded that the bargaining process followed by the Forest Service and ALC that established the appraised value for the exchange did not strictly adhere to published regulations and unpublished internal guidelines. The OIG also contended that Forest Service employees had accepted improper gratuities from ALC and other land exchange proponents.[89]

The audit report hit national news media in September 1998, and the *Seattle Times* published a four-part series on land exchanges. The third part, "Environmental Groups Profit from Land Trades," focused on Harriet, ALC, and Deer Creek. The *Seattle Times* claimed that "the story of Burgess and ALC is the story of how third parties—and in particular, environmental groups—can manipulate the business of federal land trading for their own benefit." It reported the OIG allegation that the taxpayers lost nearly $6 million on the Deer Creek deal while Harriet and ALC made $2 million. It described Harriet as a woman with "brains, experience and a blowtorch personality" who "is indefatigable when the going gets rough."

In the photo at the top of the *Seattle Times* story, Harriet sits pensively at her desk resting her chin on clasped hands. The walls of her office are covered with framed acknowledgments of her conservation achievements. Her famous Rolodex—two large wheels of cards with each card listing the name and contact information for one of her many connections—sits on a table near her desk. Her attorney, Russell Austin, stands nearby with his back to the camera. He is on the phone facing the window that overlooks the Transamerica pyramid. Another day at the office saving land.

Harriet told the *Seattle Times*, "It's an uncomfortable situation when you feel you are doing all these virtuous things."[90]

The *New York Times* joined the fray with its early October feature story on the front page of the business section, "Trading This ↑ Even Up for That ↓ An Exchange for the General Good was Better for Some Than Others." The up arrow pointed to a photo of Lauren Ward and Jan Bernard standing on a dirt road overlooking the Deer Creek land. The down arrow pointed to a photo of construction in progress on land in Las Vegas that BLM conveyed to ALC for sale to developers. Once again, relying on the OIG report, ALC's Deer Creek deal is highlighted as an example of how land exchanges can go wrong, and the federal government can lose millions of taxpayers' money.[91]

Even before it was completed and released, the audit forced the retirement of one of the Forest Service's most dedicated and effective employees. Jim Nelson, supervisor of Humboldt-Toiyabe National Forest and a good friend of Harriet's, was under intense scrutiny by the OIG for his role in land exchanges facilitated by ALC. They had worked together often because, as Nelson said, "The reason we did 83 percent of our business with ALC is simple. They got the damn job done. They are/were patient, persistent, tenacious, professional and effective." Besides, Nelson only had a part-time lands staff of two, and ALC was one of the few facilitators working in Nevada. Still, the OIG investigators asked Nelson's staff, "Was he having an affair with Burgess?"[92]

When the OIG started its investigation, Nelson was reassigned from the Toiyabe National Forest to a desk job in Utah until the OIG released its report. Nelson thought he could live with that until the Forest Service told him he wouldn't go back to the forest even if he were cleared. And that's when the fifty-seven-year-old Nelson decided to give up the fight and retire in February 1998 after years of working to protect and enlarge the forest.[93]

Nelson was not the only casualty of the OIG investigation. The audit had a chilling effect on ALC's ability to do deals in Nevada. Projects were stalled both during and after the investigation. In August 1998 Harriet wrote, "Unfortunately, the last two years have witnessed a situation where Forest Service personnel are being directed to drop all transactions involving ALC, are being told not to talk to us, and are spreading false statements about us, I believe, in an effort to destroy the organization." After a late December meeting with Senator Bryan, Harriet told him,

> As I said yesterday, Nevada's landscapes are the true victims of this fiasco and regardless of the personal pain and suffering that the last two years has caused me, ALC and Jim, ultimately, the risk of lost opportunities is Nevada's loss. Although it is disconcerting to hear . . . that there have been people in the Forest Service that have wanted to do me in, I know that there are as many, if not more, who genuinely appreciate the good work that I have done both at TPL and at ALC over the years. . . . Clearly, there are personal agendas behind these "whistle blower" allegations that have nothing to do with either Deer Creek, [or] Galena.

Harriet called the effect on land exchanges a tragedy "because these opportunities come and go and once they go they're gone."[94]

The impact of the OIG investigation on ALC's ability to do work in Nevada was felt deeply by Ame Hellman, ALC's Nevada vice president. She told me that

> the OIG just took a toll on all of us. It was just very stressful. It was intense to be a Nevadan and have to go through that. It was very close to home for me. It was just very stressful for people to wonder if there was anything that went on that wasn't above board. And there was a lot of speculation. . . . It was completely unfair but it definitely changed the perception of ALC in Nevada.

Ultimately, Ame left ALC and went to work for The Nature Conservancy.[95]

Harriet and her team of advisers fought long and hard to refute the OIG's allegations. One of the first public salvos was fired by well-known conservationist and member of Harriet's ALC Board of Councillors, David Brower, in response to leaks of the OIG audit report in July 1998. He sent a letter defending Harriet and ALC to the *New York Times*, the *San Francisco Examiner*, the *Las Vegas Review-Journal*, and the *Reno Gazette-Journal*. In it Brower quoted one of Harriet's favorite sayings, "No good deed goes unpunished" in his defense of her work bringing "back into the public domain a treasure-trove of many thousands of acres of magnificent native lands that otherwise would never have been restored to America's future." He said that in most cases, the only way to get the job done was through land exchanges. He applauded the work of Toiyabe National Forest Supervisor Jim Nelson. Brower concluded, "We can't slow down now. After all, there's still a great big world out there to save. And we haven't much time left in which to do it."[96]

I'm sure Harriet agreed with Brower—there was still a great big world out there to save—but I wonder whether she ever was tempted to give up her quest in the face of the OIG investigation. I once asked her husband, Joe, about it as we walked Kehoe Beach near their home. He said, "The OIG investigation was a really difficult time for Harriet. Anybody without Harriet's will of steel would have thrown in the towel." She had been accused of rigging the Deer Creek appraisal process, of bribing government officials, of becoming rich at the expense of the taxpayers. Her integrity had been questioned in major national newspapers. Her work in Nevada was jeopardized. How easy it would have been to give it all up and retreat to a life of leisure at her newly rebuilt home in Inverness. But, as Harriet readily admitted, she was stubborn. She was driven by such a strong sense of mission that she was not deterred even by the misery the OIG investigation created that took time and money away from her primary purpose of saving land.[97]

Harriet faced her accusers and answered their allegations. She debunked the claims in Tittman's complaint one by one in an eight-page letter to the inspector general after she heard about the draft report from the press. Once she had a copy of the full report, Harriet wrote the deputy chief of the Forest Service:

The OIG Report contains a number of factual errors and fails to mention several facts that, from ALC's perspective, have a material bearing on the conclusions reached in the Report. To the OIG's three main criticisms . . . ALC had very direct, simple, and clear responses:

1. The United States received fair value for the Deer Creek lands.
2. The "bargaining" process used to resolve the valuation issues involved in the acquisition of the Deer Creek lands complied fully with the requirements set forth in published regulations, and both the process and the outcome were consistent with the policies underlying bargaining as a means of resolving value disputes in land exchanges.
3. ALC did not provide any improper gratuity to any employee of the United States.

She detailed its errors and omissions in a memo addressed to ALC's executive board members. She briefed Senator Bryan on developments in the OIG investigation and asked for his help. She responded to a grand jury subpoena for documents.[98]

The investigation dragged on. In early 1999, ALC Councillors Stewart Udall and Pete McCloskey coauthored a letter to the secretary of the Interior, Bruce Babbitt, and the secretary of Agriculture, Dan Glickman, asking for their

> intervention to speed the conclusion of protracted investigations that are unfairly damaging the good name of the American Land Conservancy, and consequently are interfering with its important efforts to secure, for public benefit, valuable elements of our natural resource heritage in America. . . . For more than two years now the American Land Conservancy has been kept under the cloud resulting from the unduly slow-paced inquiries of your respective Offices of Inspectors General.

About the same time, Senator Bryan said, "I think we need to come to closure with this. This inspector general's report is a cloud that hangs over us and the bureaucracy is paralyzed." And still it dragged on.[99]

When it appeared that Clifford Rones at the Department of Justice (DOJ) was considering criminal charges against ALC, Harriet engaged

Pete Romatowski, an attorney in Washington, D.C., to work with ALC's attorneys to clear her organization of wrongdoing. For more than a year, at meetings and in phone calls, Romatowski urged Rones to close the criminal investigation. He and Russell Austin advised Harriet chances were good that the investigation would "die on the vine some day." And they were right. The DOJ never notified Harriet and her attorneys that ALC was cleared, but when Romatowski called Rones in April 2001 to ask him about the status of the investigation, Rones told him that they had closed their files four months earlier and no criminal charges would result. Rones said, "I can save us all a lot of trouble. It went away. Like you say, the transaction happened over five years ago, so we're done!"[100]

One year later, Jack Craven, the Forest Service director of lands in the Washington office, formally notified Harriet that the Forest Service ban on doing business with ALC had been lifted. No exoneration or apology, just that ALC and the regional offices of the Forest Service were now allowed to communicate directly to discuss land proposals. On the letter's fax transmittal, Craven wrote, "Harriette [*sic*]—this has been e-mailed to all regions. Thanks for your patience over the past 4-years. What a time. Please drop in on your next visit to D.C. or give us a call."[101]

What a time, indeed. I don't know if Harriet ever dropped in on Jack Craven or gave him a call. I think Harriet was not one to hold a grudge; with an eye to the future, she may very well have visited Craven on one of her D.C. trips or talked with him by phone. If she did, I wonder if he apologized on behalf of the Forest Service for dragging her and her organization through the mud without justification. I wonder if he expressed regret for the premature end to Jim Nelson's career. I wonder if he congratulated her for surviving the ordeal or thanked her for all of the inholdings in national forests that she and ALC had been responsible for transferring from private to public ownership over the years. I wonder whether he learned how to spell her name.

Interlude

Grand Canyon

THE MORNING'S HOT SUN THAT HAD ME DIPPING MY LIFE JACKET IN THE river before I put it on has disappeared. In its place, a thunderhead looms directly in front of us. A strong wind blows our way.

Kerstin calls today's journey the "Day of the Walls." She is not referring to the walls of Blacktail Canyon that had embraced us the day before but to the canyon walls that edge the river and have a tendency to get in the way more than usual on this stretch.

I keep my eyes on the walls—not looking for lurking dangers but for the carved beauty of the rock and its inhabitants. I spot a bighorn ram with his headdress of large curved and ridged horns lazing on a rock ledge. Bighorn sheep thrive in the Grand Canyon, where they have lived for thousands of years.[102]

Roger, rowing our dory, is watching the walls. We are getting close to Bedrock Rapid, so named because of a huge rock parked right in the middle of the river. Hitting the walls—or the rock in the middle of the river—at Bedrock happens often enough that the boatmen are wary. Even Martin called the rapid "deadly."[103]

Going left at Bedrock is a bad idea. It's known to be the most hazardous route. The current pulls left, but Roger pulls against it and heads to the right of the midstream obstacle—a bit too far right. The wall is so close I could reach out and touch it. Hitting it seems inevitable.

Roger leans back into our seat well, pulling on the oars with all of his strength. Gail and I lean out of his way. Roger yells. He groans. He growls. The river gods must be listening, because we are released from the grip of

165

the current and surge away from the wall and beyond the rapid. Kerstin is not so lucky. She hits a rock as she powers through Bedrock that tears a hole in the bottom of *Dark Canyon*.

Though most of the more recently constructed dories are made of more resilient foam and fiberglass, Litton's first fragile dories—and *Dark Canyon* is one of Martin's dories—all were made of wood. Wood meets rock, and something has to give—and it's never the rock. In the early days of Grand Canyon Dories, when all of the boatmen, including Martin, were learning how to navigate the Colorado River in the fragile wooden boats, dory disasters were the rule rather than the exception. The broken boats were fixed for another go in the river with plywood, duct tape, marine putty, and occasionally driftwood.[104]

The dories still are subject to damage as they transit the river, and boatmen still are prepared to fix them. We all make a pit stop at a sand dune just beyond Bedrock to do a temporary repair with duct tape before continuing uneventfully through the rapid at Dubendorff to our camp just beyond at Stone Creek. We remain at Stone Creek for two days to give the boatmen time to make a more durable repair to *Dark Canyon*.

Dories are beautiful. Dories are thrilling. Dories are one with the river. But dories are vulnerable just like the Grand Canyon that so well suits them and other wilderness areas where human incursions often disrupt the delicate ecological balance. Longtime boatman Lew Steiger called it their "unique disadvantage."[105]

I am sitting on a flat rock just behind our tent when the storm foretold by the thunderhead hits. Lightning, thunder, and rain chase me into the tent. The accompanying winds blow showers of sand into the tent after me before I can close the flap. The storm passes quickly, but another arrives as we are getting ready for bed. I am on my way back from brushing my teeth—following protocol by brushing with toothpaste and purified water before spitting into the forgiving river—when the first drops of rain fall.

I fall asleep to the rat-a-tat of raindrops on the tent and awake to silence at 1:30 a.m. I unzip the tent flap and slide out of the tent into a silky nightlight cast by the waxing gibbous moon shining brightly from a spot above the rim of the canyon across the river from our camp. I stand transfixed and alone. I'm not sure how long I stood there in the night air, breathing the vastness, skin tingling, before I returned to the tent.

"What's for breakfast this morning?"

Russell has just returned from his daily trip to the river with our blue pee bucket.

"Grits, I think. Maybe eggs."

Grits are like manna from heaven for a Southern girl like me, and here I am eating them on a sandy beach beneath the mile-high walls of the Grand Canyon. I moved around a lot growing up, so I lost my Southern drawl long ago but never my taste for grits. And we will have time to enjoy them because we have two days at the Stone Creek camp between miles 132 and 133 and are not rushing to get on the river.

The grits are a good send-off for the morning's hike up the side canyon. The hike follows clear-flowing Stone Creek as it stairsteps down to the Colorado River—Stone Creek after Julius Stone who, along with Nathaniel Galloway and Seymour Dubendorff, were the first to run the river for pleasure in 1909. Stone, a wealthy businessman, hired Galloway, a well-known boatman, to take him down the river on a voyage just like John Wesley Powell's 1869 trip. Galloway invited his friend Dubendorff to join them. Their journey was mostly trouble free, though Dubendorff flipped in a wave on the right side of the rapid that now bears his name. I suspect Dubendorff and Litton were kindred spirits. After his flip, wet from his dousing in the river, Dubendorff said, "I'd like to try that again. I know I can run it!" All of our boatmen ran Dubendorff successfully—one of several rapids in the canyon that is essentially the same as it was in 1909. Galloway is remembered, too, in the eponymous canyon that meets the river just before Dubendorff rapid.[106]

The hike is another one of those boulder affairs—lots of big steps up, some down, a few narrow spots, a vertical rise of three feet where I slip on loose dirt and fall. Embarrassing, but no harm done. Not too far into the hike, Kerstin stops and, perched on a boulder in the sun, describes the prehistoric Pueblo who lived in this and other side canyons more than one thousand years ago. The Puebloans, or Anasazi as archaeologists first called them, resided in stacked-stone houses, raised crops on canyon terraces, and produced ceramic pottery. Roger picks up the story by pointing out a mescal oven that was built more than five thousand years ago and used for roasting agave, sheep, or whatever else was available. Then he points to the vertical canyon walls carved with holes that were used to store grain. The granaries look inaccessible—the better to protect their contents in an unforgiving landscape.[107]

A little while later, I stop to relax and enjoy the second waterfall on Stone Creek that spills thirty or forty feet into a small pool before continuing down to the river in a rocky stream. Others, including Michael but not Russell, more ambitious and daring than I, continue to ascend the canyon. I'm sure Harriet would have gone the last mile unfazed by the narrow ledges and steep drops that we've been told await the intrepid hiker. I'm happy to settle on a rock in the shade in full view of the cascading water to await their return.

CHAPTER FIVE

Saving John Muir

The John Muir Gravesite

Like trees in autumn shedding their leaves, going to dust like beautiful days to night, proclaiming as with the tongues of angels the natural beauty of death. —JOHN MUIR, *THE GRAND CAÑON OF THE COLORADO*

Death is a kind nurse saying, "Come, children, to bed and get up in the morning" a gracious mother calling her children home. —JOHN MUIR, *JOHN OF THE MOUNTAINS*

John Muir is an inspiration for all that we strive to accomplish, all the special places we aim to protect. ALC is proud it was able to protect Muir's special place. —HARRIET BURGESS, *JOHN MUIR'S GRAVESITE*[1]

MORE THAN ONE HUNDRED YEARS GONE, JOHN MUIR REMAINS A FIXTURE in the conservation pantheon. Places he loved have been named after him: John Muir Woods and Muir Beach in Marin County; the 211-mile John Muir Trail in the Southern Sierra that passes through the John Muir Wilderness (which includes Mount Muir); and Muir Glacier in Alaska. Two species of aster, a rose, a wren, a pika, a butterfly, and a millipede bear his name. The Sierra Club, the environmental organization Muir cofounded and served as its first president until his death, named its highest award after him. Muir's image has been inscribed on two U.S. stamps and on a California state quarter. The California Historical Society named Muir the greatest Californian. The California legislature designated April 21 of every year as John Muir Day, and Muir was among the first inductees into the California Hall of Fame.

Yet his gravesite, hidden among small ranch houses at the end of a narrow lane, lay neglected and largely forgotten by the late 1950s. The cemetery that had once been a destination for pilgrims honoring the memory of the great conservationist was surrounded by a tall chain-link fence topped with rows of razor wire imprisoning Muir's grave and denying the spirit of the man who had rejoiced in the freedom of walking the Sierra, scaling Alaskan glaciers, climbing mountains. Weeds concealed the granite headstones in the cemetery that had evoked this description by a visitor in 1930:

Myrtle and the seal of Solomon ramble unforbidden over the grave. A rose bush trails along the railing, sending forth a wealth of white blooms as it did fifty years ago. An immense white hawthorn rears itself into a blossoming canopy and far up in the branches nestles the home of a wood rat. Perhaps the little creatures know that this nearness to their friend still brings them protection. For he loved every "wee skelet, cowrin', tim'rous beastie." Throughout his life he sought to bring again into being "Nature's Social Union" which man's blood lust has broken.[2]

The Sierra Club continued to organize pilgrimages to the gravesite until 1974, but the cemetery ceased to be the focus of efforts to honor Muir's memory after Henry and Faire Sax purchased the Muir homestead in 1955 with the express purpose of saving it from destruction by a proposed subdivision "as a Muir memorial for the benefit of future generations." The drive to protect the Muir house culminated in the establishment of the John Muir National Historic Site in 1964. Managed by the National Park Service (NPS), the historic site encompassed the Muir/Strentzel family homestead and 9.2 surrounding acres—where John Muir lived from 1890 until his death and where he wrote many of his essays and books extolling nature and the need to preserve it—but it did not include the nearby cemetery.[3]

The gravesite was not entirely forgotten. An NPS feasibility study completed in 1980 favored its preservation and federal acquisition but noted that neighbors were concerned that more visitors would mean more noise, congestion, crime, and trespassing. Limited parking was another potential problem. No further progress was made until Congress passed a bill in 1988 to expand the boundaries of the historic site by acquiring 330 additional acres that included the small cemetery tract and the hills of Mount Wanda just south of the Muir house.[4]

John Muir often wandered the rolling hills dotted with oaks that rise behind his family homestead in Martinez, California, escaping from the daily cares of ranch management. He walked there with his daughters, Wanda and Helen, teaching them about the trees and wildflowers. He picnicked there with his family. He enjoyed the views of the Alhambra Valley, Carquinez Strait, Mount Diablo, and the distant Sierra.[5]

I walked the same hills with Harriet's daughter Leslie and her husband, Darrel, on a sunny summer day in 2011. The golden hills and green-leafed oaks beckoned to us. They have changed little since John Muir walked there more than one hundred years ago. As part of the John Muir National Historic Site, this quintessential northern California scene is unlikely to be much altered in the future.[6]

As we climbed the wide dirt trail bordered with oaks that leads to the summits of Mount Wanda and Mount Helen, Darrel recalled some of the hikes they took with Harriet. Harriet charging ahead, stopping to wait for everyone to catch up, then asking if you were all right while ignoring the pain in her knees that grew steadily worse over the years. Leslie remembered all of the hikes that Harriet led as they journeyed through the Grand Canyon on a trip in the 1980s. Each of the strenuous hikes was different. Harriet would advise, "Just go at your own pace." Experience the magical.[7]

When death called John Muir on Christmas Eve 1914, his family buried him next to his wife, Louie Strentzel Muir, in a small cemetery at the base of the hills where Muir loved to walk and about a mile south of the Muir homestead. We drove there after our hike and parked in front of a sign that read "No Parking Fire Lane." It was one of the few places to leave the car on the narrow lane leading to the cemetery. Surrounded by a small subdivision, the gravesite was a contrast to the open expanses of the Mount Wanda trail.

The National Park Service manages the gravesite, but at the time of our visit had yet to make provisions for visitors and did not encourage them. When asked, park rangers would acknowledge that Muir is buried in Martinez but would not reveal the exact location of the grave, because neighbors worried that increased visitation might lead to unacceptable noise, congestion, crime, and trespassing. However, Leslie and Darrel knew exactly where to go.[8]

We lingered in the pear orchard that shields the cemetery. Planted by John Muir's father-in-law, John Strentzel, at about the same time he set aside the land for the gravesite in the 1850s, the pear trees are the remains of one of the oldest surviving commercial orchards in central California. Green pears hung from leafy branches on some of the trees while others displayed craggy twisted limbs bereft of fruit and leaves. John Muir is gone, but the trees endure—as they so often do, outlasting us in spite of or perhaps because of our neglect.[9]

Just beyond the rows of pears, a massive eucalyptus towers overhead. As old as the pear trees, its broad trunk measures six to eight feet in diameter and its height more than two hundred feet. At the 1890 burial of John Strentzel in the family cemetery not far from the tree, John Muir remarked on the size of the eucalyptus and suggested that it was like a guardian angel watching over the graves. The guardian angel still stood when Muir's funeral was held beneath its branches in 1914. Since then, the tree has served as a gathering place to commemorate Muir's life.[10]

The nearby gravesite is a small place—a quiet place that perhaps reminded John Muir of the Bonaventure graveyard on the grounds of an abandoned plantation a few miles from Savannah, Georgia, where he camped among the tombs in 1867. Unable to secure lodging elsewhere while he awaited the arrival of funds expressed to him by his brother from Wisconsin, Muir spent several nights in a place

so beautiful that almost any sensible person would choose to dwell here with the dead rather than with the lazy, disorderly living. . . . The rippling of living waters, the song of birds, the joyous confidence of flowers, the calm, undisturbable grandeur of the oaks, mark[ed] this place of graves as one of the Lord's most favored abodes of life and light.

His sojourn there led him to reflect,

> But let children walk with Nature, let them see the beautiful blend-
> ings and communions of death and life, their joyous inseparable
> unity, as taught in woods and meadows, plains and mountains and
> streams of our blessed star, and they will learn that death is stingless
> indeed, and as beautiful as life."[11]

Granite coping frames the graves in the Muir family cemetery. John Muir and his wife lie under identical black granite gravestones off to one side. The gravestones both are delicately carved with the Scottish thistle of Muir's birthplace. A white granite obelisk anchors the center of the cemetery and marks the graves of Louie Muir's parents. A line of five small granite gravestones commemorates the graves of other family members including Muir's daughter, Wanda, and her husband, Tom Hanna, the last to be buried there in the 1940s. Graves are strewn with autumn leaves going to dust.

On that brilliant summer day, sunlight penetrated the overhanging tree canopy of cedars, redwoods, and oaks, dappling the gravestones with light and shade. Alhambra Creek whispered in the background. I peered between the bars of the wrought iron fence with its padlocked gate that surrounds the gravesite and read the words inscribed in black granite from the Sierra foothills:

JOHN MUIR

BORN DUNBAR SCOTLAND

APRIL 21—1838

DIED DEC. 24—1914

Death called the man, but his spirit remains; it pervades the place where he lived and worked and was buried. A place to reflect on the life and legacy of John Muir, a man who made the most of his moment. A place where visitors may react much as Muir did when he laid flowers on the graves of Ralph Waldo Emerson and Henry David Thoreau in 1893. Reflecting on his visit, Muir wrote in a letter to his wife, "I did not imagine I would be so

moved at sight of the resting places of these grand men as I found I was."
A place that Harriet chose to save because it was the right thing to do.[12]

In the early 1990s, it looked like John Muir's gravesite would be preserved
without the help of Harriet and ALC. The NPS purchased Mount Wanda's 326 acres and began the process of acquiring the Muir family gravesite
from the Muir-Hanna Family Trust. The Park Service contacted Ross de
Lipkau, Muir's great-grandson and a trustee of the family trust, to discuss
the purchase of the gravesite and access easement parcels. Residents of the
neighborhood surrounding the gravesite met with NPS to help develop
a plan for the area that would minimize the impact of gravesite visitors
on their neighborhood. The NPS approved the $200,000 gravesite tract
appraisal. But by the end of 1992 when the Park Service had worked its
way through all of the preliminaries, including providing for the cemetery
in the general management plan for the John Muir National Historic Site,
money that had been allocated for the purchase had been spent, and it was
impossible to know when funds again would be available.[13]

The John Muir gravesite was left in limbo. Having tried to sell it
directly to the NPS for more than three years, a frustrated Ross de Lipkau
turned to Harriet and the American Land Conservancy. He agreed to work
with ALC to facilitate the transfer of the property to the government. After
an initial meeting with de Lipkau in January 1993, ALC's Aaron Peskin
followed up with a letter explaining ALC's mission, its willingness to take
on challenging and difficult projects, and its past success in securing federal
funding. Peskin concluded by recommending that the family trust enter
into an agreement with ALC to option the property. An option agreement
would make it clear that there was a willing seller, an exact sales price, and
a deadline for completing the sale. An agreement would give Harriet the
commitment she needed from de Lipkau to convince her contacts in Washington to appropriate funds for the purchase. De Lipkau decided to accept
Peskin's recommendation.[14]

Just as the effort to acquire the gravesite was getting underway, project
manager Aaron Peskin and in-house attorney Nancy Shanahan suddenly
left ALC employment. Their unexpected departure shifted the task of

drafting the bargain sale option agreement to the lawyers at Marron, Reid, and Sheehy. The agreement signed toward the end of June set the sale price at $180,000. The $20,000 difference between the sale price to ALC and the NPS appraised value was ALC's increment to cover the costs involved in transferring the gravesite to public ownership. ALC made a $100 option payment to seal the deal.

ALC now had the right to purchase the gravesite. Harriet's ultimate goal was to sell the gravesite and the access easement to NPS as part of the John Muir National Historic Site, but public ownership was not a requirement of the option agreement, giving ALC the flexibility to dispose of the property "in any manner the Buyer deems appropriate." ALC had six months, until the end of December 1993 when the option expired, to decide whether to buy the gravesite—the same six months when Harriet was under the gun to complete the Nevada land exchange in record time.[15]

The clock started ticking, but preoccupied with the Nevada land exchange and off on her African vacation, Harriet did not devote more time to the gravesite project until early September. Prompted by de Lipkau's request that Harriet call him, Harriet apologized for being "so slow on getting back to you on the John Muir cemetery site. As you know, I played hookie and took some time to vacation in Africa." She added, "I have a meeting with Lynelle Johnson [from Congressman George Miller's office] next Wednesday to tour the site and expect to get a commitment to complete this transaction."[16]

Harriet toured the gravesite with Lynelle Johnson on September 8. She did not receive a firm funding commitment, but Johnson was ready to help. Johnson told Harriet, "It was *wonderful* to finally meet you." She said she thought the project was doable, but Congressman Miller needed more assurances that concerns the neighbors expressed about increased gravesite visitation had been addressed adequately. She worked with Harriet and the NPS to send a letter to neighborhood residents in late December requesting comments on proposed rules governing visitation.[17]

With the expiration date for the option agreement fast approaching, however, they couldn't wait for responses to the latest homeowner survey that might influence Congressman Miller's decision to support the purchase. ALC had to decide whether to go ahead with purchasing the gravesite without the guarantee of federal funding. As the NPS had advised Harriet in late November, "You should understand the risk in choosing to option the property. Funds have not yet been appropriated and as a result, we are not in a position to acquire the property at this time. The National Park Service cannot guarantee that funds will be available to purchase the property. This letter only documents our intent to purchase if sufficient funds do become available." The letter also referred to title issues for the access easement to the gravesite parcel that had to be resolved before conveyance to the federal government.[18]

But risk taking was Harriet's modus operandi, and here's what she told her executive committee:

ALC has a Bargain Sale Option Agreement to purchase the property for $180,000 (90% of fair market value). The Park Service has appraised the site, reviewed and approved an appraisal which established a value of $200,000. Ed Haberlin, head of land acquisition for the California Region of the Park Service, has told Harriet Burgess that the Park Service can reprogram the funds necessary to purchase the property.

The Park Service has delayed this project for the last two years after acquiring the home site. To speed up the second phase of acquisition, the Hanna-Muir Trust asked for ALC's help, giving us an option on the property. We have been working with Congressman Miller's office to resolve public access issues so that the acquisition can go forward.

A potential problem, however, is that after several months delay, Congressman Miller's office has asked the Park Service to send out a letter to the gravesite's neighbors that invites their comments and suggestions. . . . They did not include a specific date by which the neighborhood must respond. . . .

If we choose to exercise our option on or before December 31, 1993, we then have 60 days to close. So, we could wait to see what problems develop before we purchase. If we decided to terminate the purchase because of complications over the neighborhood letter, we will lose our $100 (one hundred dollar) option consideration fee and our $20,000 increment.

No one at the Park Service seems overly concerned whether we lose the option agreement. Perhaps they assume they will be able to buy the land directly from the Hanna-Muir Trust, now that we have set the project rolling. The family trust really wants the Park Service to acquire the site.

ALC's executive committee approved a resolution to purchase the John Muir Gravesite and subsequently convey it to the National Park Service during a conference call on December 29.[19]

ALC's executive committee functioned as the organization's board of directors, acting in ALC's best interests with voting and governance authority. The committee shared Harriet's vision for ALC and wholeheartedly endorsed its mission statement:

> American Land Conservancy (ALC) is dedicated to the preservation of land and water as enduring public resources, and to the protection and enhancement of our nation's natural, ecological, historical, recreational, and scenic heritage. Compelled by the urgent need to conserve intact our remaining natural and wildland resources, ALC seeks to preserve the diversity of native plant, wildlife, and aquatic communities, to guard and restore the natural integrity of ecosystems, and to expand opportunities for public recreation, education, and scientific research. ALC is committed to promoting a national land ethic to achieve responsible stewardship of our public land and waters for the benefit of present and future generations.

Until 1998, when Dr. Joseph Fink joined them, the executive committee members were Harriet, Martin Litton, and Bob Stephens. Martin and Bob always gave Harriet the benefit of their wisdom and expertise, but they rarely disagreed with her final decisions and recommendations. They gave her the freedom to pursue those projects she wanted to do—after all, that's why she left TPL—and she wanted to do the John Muir gravesite project even if it was risky. As she often told her staff, "If you're looking for stability,

ALC's not the place for you. One of these days, I'm going to bet the farm, and we may go under." It was a warning well worth heeding. Once Harriet got behind a project, she was almost as unstoppable as a runaway freight train. With Joe's support backing, Harriet could afford such risks, but she recognized that many of her employees could not.[20]

Unlike the executive committee, ALC's Board of Councillors was not directly involved in the management of Harriet's organization. With Martin Litton's help, Harriet had enlisted the support of some of the biggest names in conservation to serve on the board, giving ALC immediate credibility when it emerged on the conservation scene in 1990. Bruce Babbitt and his wife were among the first members of the Board of Councillors. They were joined by David Brower, Brock Evans, Bill Garrett, Bill Lane, Martin Litton, Helen and Pete McCloskey, Margaret Owings, Wallace Stegner, Robert Stephens, Stewart Udall, and Ardis Manly Walker. Harriet valued their opinions and support but was not accountable to them.[21]

By 1995, Harriet was able to reward her Board of Councillors by inviting them as her guests to annual meetings at Mike Freed's Post Ranch Inn in Big Sur. Mike Freed was an old friend of Harriet's. He credited her with being the primary reason he was able to get the land for the luxury resort that he built on cliffs rising twelve hundred feet above the Pacific Ocean.

In the early 1980s, Freed had found what he thought was the greatest property he'd ever seen. It was in Big Sur behind Ventana, four or five miles up a dirt road, about eight hundred acres owned by William Post, the scion of a family that had staked one of the first homesteads there in the 1850s. At the time, Freed was in his thirties and making $33,000 a year as a lawyer in San Francisco. Still, he decided to try to buy the property and asked Post if they could do a deal. While Freed was looking for money to finance the deal, he connected with Harriet. Neither of them had any money, but that didn't stop them. They started working on the project.

Eventually, Harriet bought most of the eight hundred acres while she was working at TPL and transferred them into federal ownership. Freed acquired the opportunity to build an environmentally sensitive resort on the ninety-eight acres where the Post Ranch Inn stands today on the cliffs of Big Sur. And he offered the rooms at the inn to Harriet at a reduced price in early December every year.[22]

Project reviews were on the agenda of every annual meeting of the Board of Councillors, so the board heard about the John Muir gravesite year after year. Once the executive committee gave its approval and ALC exercised its option to buy the gravesite, escrow was supposed to close in sixty days—sixty days to clear title to the access easement as required by NPS, and the same sixty days to find $200,000 to pay for the purchase by the federal government. It didn't happen. The sixty days stretched into twelve months, the twelve months into more than six years before ALC finally transferred the gravesite to NPS. Leslie told me that sometimes Harriet became so frustrated with the lack of progress that she'd say, "We'll have to dig up his bones and move them."[23]

ALC and its attorneys working with Ross de Lipkau and the members of the Muir-Hanna Family Trust secured clear title to the access easement first, but even that took more than sixty days to obtain and record the necessary documents. Near the end of the sixty days, when it was evident that ALC needed more time, the closing date was extended from February 28 to April 1. When ALC still needed more time, the closing date was extended again, but this time only if ALC agreed to pay 8 percent interest on the $180,000 purchase price until escrow closed.[24]

By the end of April, the title issue had been resolved, but the money issue had not. Harriet had counted on help from Congressman George Miller, whose district included the gravesite and who sponsored the bill to include it in the John Muir National Historic Site. Toward the end of May, she met with Miller, who assured her that he would make a decision soon. She also collaborated on a letter to Miller from NPS Western Regional Director Stanley Albright in an attempt to get the congressman's support for funding. Albright assured Miller that the homeowners had been consulted about the gravesite acquisition and that their concerns would be addressed adequately. He also reported that ALC had resolved the title issue. He concluded, "If you have no further concerns, we plan to proceed with the acquisition of the gravesite parcel and access easement through the American Land Conservancy."[25]

But neither Harriet's meeting nor Albright's letter pushed the congressman to OK the gravesite acquisition. In early June, Harriet wrote de Lipkau:

> I'm sorry for the delay in responding to your inquiry on the status of our effort to convey the John Muir Gravesite to the U.S. Park Service.
>
> We have completed the title work to the satisfaction of the Park Service Solicitor. I met with Congressman George Miller and his local staff, Lynelle Johnson, May 20th. They promised we would have a decision from the Congressman in a very few days. The Park Service needs only his okay before ordering the check. Since that date I have called several times, as has the Park Service, to no avail. Apparently, a close friend of Miller just died and he has been distracted by that event. Lynelle Johnson promised me yesterday we would hear from Miller next week.
>
> We are all awaiting a go ahead from the Congressman!

They waited in vain.[26]

Harriet did not have much time to devote to the John Muir gravesite over the next few months. She had to put the gravesite on a back burner as she wrapped up the first phase of the Nevada land exchange—the most complicated and challenging project she had ever undertaken. The Nevada land exchange closed on August 12. In what seems like a desperate move prompted by an August 23 letter from de Lipkau complaining that it had been several months since he had heard from either Harriet or her attorneys, Harriet started back on the gravesite acquisition on August 31 with a letter to Roger Kennedy, the director of the National Park Service.

Employing a tactic that had worked well for her in the past, Harriet appears to have decided to bypass NPS underlings and go straight to the top. Because she addressed the letter to Kennedy's home in Alexandria, Virginia, instead of his office, it also looks like she may have had some personal connection with him, perhaps from her years of living and working as a community activist nearby. She apologized for imposing on him, then beseeched him for help on the gravesite and a fifteen-acre inholding in Redwood National Park. She explained the problem with title and wrote,

"The title is now clear and we are ready to close, but I am told that the funds are not available. It is my understanding that $39,500 has been reserved in the John Muir National Historic Site account, but the remaining $160,500 needed to complete the transaction is not available from any Park Service funds nationwide." She concluded by lamenting the difference between her expeditious work with BLM on the Nevada land exchange and the delayed NPS effort on John Muir and Redwood National Park: "Working with the Park Service on these two *small* but worthy projects, on the other hand, has basically been a disaster!"[27]

Kennedy's reply almost two months later was sympathetic but largely nonresponsive. Coming off the high of the Galena success, the letter had to be a letdown. Kennedy merely claimed that NPS actively had pursued the gravesite acquisition since 1988 and reviewed the steps taken by NPS to secure it. He stated that NPS intended to finalize the acquisition as soon as funds were available but gave no indication when that would be. He thanked Harriet for her inquiry, for her patience and understanding. Kennedy promised "to set forth our best efforts to bring both these projects to a satisfactory conclusion." The letter was signed by a staff member acting for Kennedy.[28]

Harriet received a similar letter from Stanley Albright—also signed by a member of his staff—in early November following up on her gravesite acquisition discussions with Sondra Humphries, NPS chief of land resources for the Western Region. Harriet probably contacted Humphries after she received Kennedy's response in late October to try again to make headway at the regional level. Albright's letter followed the company line almost verbatim. No, there is no money. Yes, we will acquire the John Muir gravesite for inclusion in the John Muir National Historic Site if funding becomes available. Thank you for your patience and understanding.[29]

Meanwhile, de Lipkau was increasingly and understandably impatient. He had not heard from Harriet or her attorney, Mary Lu Everett, since June, though he had requested a status update. He fired off an ultimatum on October 5 advising Harriet and her attorney that if escrow did not close by December 31, 1994, the agreement to sell the gravesite to ALC would be canceled. He reiterated ALC's obligation to pay 8 percent interest on the sales price from April 1, 1994, regardless of whether ALC bought the property.[30]

One of Harriet's greatest strengths and a cornerstone of her reputation for saving land always had been her ability to develop and maintain good relationships with landowners. Focused on the Nevada land exchange, her relationship with the owners of the gravesite had soured, but examples of Harriet's positive and productive relationships with landowners are plentiful. There's Colonel Rizor and the Columbia River Gorge. There's Nick Badami and Galena. There's Frank Hathaway and Lower Topanga Canyon. There's Alvin Hackathorn and his cabin in the woods that drew Harriet's attention soon after she founded ALC. Like the John Muir gravesite, the Hackathorn property was small and it involved a memorial.[31]

Harriet took the call to protect Alvin Hackathorn's land and his cabin in May 1991. The land was in the middle of Wayne National Forest, the only national forest in Ohio. It was located in a part of the forest classified as a semi-primitive nonmotorized area, the closest you can get to wilderness in those parts. Seventy acres, more or less. Seventy acres of oak, hickory, yellow poplar, and Virginia pine—and not much else, except a dilapidated cabin, a few exhausted oil wells, and one productive oil well. But for Alvin Hackathorn, it was his wilderness sanctuary. When he'd go to the cabin in the woods for a few days off from his job as a used car salesman in Pittsburgh, the whole world was washed away. Like his grandparents and parents before him, he had to carry water to the cabin from a well. He had to use oil lamps for light. He had to heat the cabin with wood stoves. But for Alvin, a deep breath of the air there was like a tonic.[32]

Alvin's grandfather, William Hackathorn, bought the property and the already century-old log cabin in 1887 for $1,075. A veteran of the Civil War, wounded at Gettysburg, William was looking for a place where he could farm and raise a family. Situated at the bottom of a hill between two creeks in southeastern Ohio, the hand-hewn log cabin became the Hackathorn family home. Surrounded by a farm with an apple orchard, fields of tobacco, and a herd of cattle, the Hackathorns were largely self-sufficient.[33]

The rugged terrain of the seventy-acre tract had been densely covered with white oak, hickory, black oak, and beech trees. Some say the forests were so thick back then that squirrels could travel from the Ohio River to

Lake Erie without touching the ground. Native Americans hunted in these forests for hundreds of years before the first arrival of settlers in the 1700s. They flattened trails in the undergrowth. They set fires to force the game from the forest and to open up the thick stands of trees to forage for berries and seeds. Eventually, they established camps or villages and grew corn, beans, and squash beside the rivers.[34]

By the time William Hackathorn and his wife, Jane, arrived, the forests had been logged for homes and firewood. They had been cleared for farming. When William and Jane needed more space for their family of five children—Catherine, Arthur, Charles, Irvin, and John—farmers from all around gathered for a log-raising to add a half story to the Hackathorn cabin to make space for bedrooms. The farmers turned out in droves to raise the roof, then add three logs to the walls. They celebrated with a big picnic when the job was done.[35]

William died intestate in 1909, leaving his wife and five children as his heirs. The children gave Jane a life estate and became the sole heirs when she died intestate in 1923. For $200, Irvin and Charles conveyed their one-fifth interests to Arthur in 1935. John conveyed his one-fifth interest to Arthur for $1 in 1948. Catherine conveyed her one-fifth interest to Arthur for $1 in 1949, making him the sole owner of the Hackathorn homestead. Arthur had two children, Alvin and Clarence. He conveyed the homestead to each of them as joint tenants in 1971. Arthur died in 1977 after living with Alvin for seventeen years. Clarence also died in 1977, leaving Alvin the sole owner of the cabin in the woods.[36]

The Forest Service had approached Alvin Hackathorn in 1988 about selling his property to the government as an addition to the national forest. Dale Newell, then a Forest Service staff appraiser and a lands specialist when Harriet and ALC became involved, had visited the property with Alvin. He had estimated the value of the land to be between $22,000 and $25,000.[37]

No further action had been taken until January 1991 when Dave Hanson, a Forest Service lands officer, made a written offer of $26,000 for the Hackathorn property. But Alvin was reluctant to deal with the Forest Service. Dave hoped that Harriet would be able to convince him that selling to the government was a good idea, but he warned her that Alvin was cranky and distrustful. He also let her know that Alvin had asked if the American Land Conservancy was a front for the Japanese.[38]

By late June, Harriet was on her way to meet with eighty-nine-year-old Alvin Hackathorn at his home in Pittsburgh. She drove straight there from the airport, pulling up promptly at 10 a.m. in front of the narrow, light gray clapboard house next to Veteran Auto Sales. She introduced herself to Alvin, his companion, Emily Wallace, and his attorney, Michael Georgalas. She told Alvin that she was there to help him. Then she listened to his story.[39]

Alvin told Harriet about the two-room, hand-hewn log cabin where his grandparents had lived. He told her that his grandfather had worked on a riverboat before he fought in the Civil War. That his grandmother used to ride sidesaddle to the nearest town to go to church. That the property had been in the family a long time. That the land was part of the 1.5 million acres first sold to the Ohio Company after the Northwest Ordinance of 1787 opened the territory to settlement. That his family had immigrated from Switzerland to the United States in 1737 when they changed their name from Hedgorn to Hackathorn. Harriet took detailed notes on the pad of yellow paper that she always had at the ready to record the essentials of her projects.[40]

When Alvin finished his story, Harriet asked him whether he wanted to sell his land to the Forest Service. Alvin said he would like to sell—the sooner, the better. He had received five bids in excess of $26,000 from logging companies, but he wanted the land and the cabin to be preserved as it was. He wanted his father to be remembered with a memorial of some kind. He was worried about how the Forest Service would manage the land, but he was willing to sell the family homestead to them if his conditions were met. As Harriet was leaving, she said, "I won't let them screw you over. If it looks like they will, I won't do the project."[41]

On a sunny day in July dressed in gray trousers and a light blue T-shirt with her hair pulled back in a ponytail, Harriet walked with Dave and Dale on the tree-shaded dirt road that led to the Hackathorn cabin. The road narrowed, passed through a creek, and almost disappeared before it reached the cabin in a small clearing. From a distance, Harriet could see the sagging rusted brown metal roof with gaping holes that looked like someone had taken scissors to it. Up close, she looked into its dark interior through openings that once may have been windows. She saw the notches chiseled in the logs chinked together with mud and cement and perhaps was reminded of the Lincoln logs her children used to play with. She noticed the brush growing right up to the cabin walls—and sometimes through them. She must have wondered what living there had been like for Alvin's parents and grandparents.[42]

In her letter to Alvin after the trip, Harriet enclosed some photos that she had taken on her visit to the cabin. She wrote, "I took a picture which doesn't show up very well of the waterfall and the spot where, I think, you said your family had a swimming hole in the summer. What a magic place that is. I thought the cabin was a wonderful spot as well. I can see why you love the place. There are a couple of silly pictures of me just to prove that I was really there."[43]

Harriet put her small staff to work on getting the cabin conveyed to the Forest Service. Nancy Shanahan drafted the necessary legal documents. Leslie was given the task of figuring out a way to erect a memorial to Alvin's father near the cabin. Letters and phone calls were exchanged between ALC and Alvin, between ALC and the Forest Service, between the Forest Service and Alvin as they worked out the details of the agreements to sell the Hackathorn property for $28,000. By the end of October, the documents had been signed and the order placed for a monument. The monument read just as Alvin had requested:

HACKATHORN
This memorial is in honor of
the birth and life here of
ARTHUR HACKATHORN
Son of a pioneer family
1875 – 1977

Harriet's friends at Wayne National Forest installed the sign at the end of November. ALC received no support from the sale to the Forest Service and no reimbursement for the $3,365 project cost.[44]

In their last letter to Harriet, Alvin and Emily told her,

We want you to know what a joy and pleasure it was for us to know you and to work with you these past few months. We feel that you fully understand the deep rooted feeling and love that Alvin has had for this little piece of land that has been so much a part of his almost 90 years of living. A place he has always had to retreat to when the growing and going was a little rough. We know you join with us in the knowledge that a precious family heritage has been sacrificed, but now will be a part of a protected area, always available to everyone needing to go out to the woods and enjoy God's glory.[45]

Harriet's relationship with de Lipkau may not have been as cordial as she usually maintained with landowners—when I talked to him, de Lipkau said selling the gravesite was "not a very good story"—but she was determined to keep her promise to preserve John Muir's gravesite. She believed it had "enormous significance since it preserves the final resting place of one of our country's most revered environmental and literary figures."[46]

Harriet bought the gravesite with $180,000 of ALC's money in January 1995 even though she had no immediate prospect of federal funding to transfer the property to NPS. She later explained:

The American Land Conservancy does not acquire land with the intention of holding it for extended periods of time, but if there is a compelling reason we will sometimes hold a property until a public agency is ready to receive it. We felt the long-term protection of the gravesite is a compelling reason, and have therefore been willing to hold the property until private or public funds can be secured.

She told a concerned conservationist, "We have no intention of selling that property on the open market. We bought it to conserve it and to hold it for eventual National Park Service ownership, where I believe it should reside."[47]

ALC held the property and continued to explore funding options including selling it to the city of Martinez and seeking private donations. Lauren Ward made the first overtures to the city of Martinez. He and Harriet met with city officials seeking their support for the NPS acquisition, and Harriet later formally requested that the city itself consider purchasing the site. But the city manager said, "We're not buying it at this point, unless I find $200,000 lying around." Efforts to secure financial support from private funding sources such as the John Muir Memorial Association, the John Muir Trust based in Scotland, and the Martinez Land Trust were not successful either.[48]

Meanwhile, ALC improved the gravesite by tearing down the unsightly old cyclone fence that had surrounded it since the 1960s and replacing it with a wrought iron fence more suitable both to the man and his era. Donated design services and fence materials helped make it happen. ALC also accepted an offer from the local 4-H group to weed and rake the cemetery every month. The 4-H group enhanced the appearance of the gravesite further by volunteering to plant daffodils to replace plastic flowers around the graves. No doubt Harriet agreed with one of her staff who said, "I stopped by the gravesite . . . just in time to see the daffodils in bloom. They looked wonderful, and were a vast improvement over the plastic flowers that were there for some time. It was very thoughtful thing for the club members to do." As Harriet told Ross de Lipkau, "If we are to continue to own the site, we want to care for it in a way that is appropriate for the extraordinary individual buried there."[49]

ALC shared Harriet's thoughts on the John Muir acquisition in a 1994 newsletter article:

> There's another small project that's close to completion: the purchase and conveyance of just 1.27 acres in a quiet residential neighborhood east of San Francisco. A nice piece of land in this high-cost area, no doubt, especially with its sprinkling of redwood, bay, cedar, oak, and eucalyptus trees growing alongside a small pear orchard.
>
> But it's not the handsome trees which lured us into helping convey the land to the National Park Service. It's the grave sites found in their shadows. For here, in a small family plot, one granite headstone bears the name of John Muir.
>
> Just another example of how we're working to do more than just amass acres. We're working to preserve our nation's natural heritage, too, no matter how small the parcel.[50]

ALC still owned the gravesite when the National Association of Women Business Owners selected Harriet to receive the 1999 Woman of the Year/ Community Advocate award, and that's where Harriet chose to be filmed for the April award ceremony video. In the video, Harriet strolls through the gravesite pausing to respond to questions about her philosophy and her organization. She is dressed in a dark pantsuit and a lavender blue sweater with a thin silver chain around her neck and silver hoops hanging from her ears. Her shoulder length auburn hair is highlighted by the sun. A light breeze scatters her bangs over her forehead above thinly drawn mobile eyebrows and blue-gray eyes. Her broad smile radiates her personality captured by the collage of words that flash on the screen at the beginning of the video:

Vision **endurance** strength beauty **INTEGRITY**
inspiration *joy* commitment ***courage*** **intelligence**
creativity **grace** leadership
PERSEVERANCE wisdom *charm* opportunity
guidance **fortitude** enthusiasm *confidence* focus
excellence honor respect success ***imagination*** teamwork
responsibility **moxie** *inspiration* motivation
tenacity **wit** *competence* ***guts***

Harriet concludes the video with these words: "The land we save is our legacy. It's what we give to our children. It's what future generations can cherish, thanks to our perseverance."

It's what Harriet gave her children. When asked in the video how she wanted to be remembered, Harriet fought back tears before saying, "I want to be remembered by my children and my grandchildren. I want them to be proud." Harriet wanted the John Muir gravesite, and all of the other lands protected by ALC, to be there for her children and for all those who inherit what we leave behind.[51]

After several years of being caretaker in chief and several years of searching unsuccessfully for funding that demanded all of the qualities displayed above, Harriet and ALC finally sold the gravesite to the National Park Service, thanks to the Land and Water Conservation Fund (LWCF). Created by Congress in 1964 and fueled largely by federal revenue from offshore oil and gas drilling, the LWCF exists to protect the natural and cultural heritage of the United States through land acquisitions and state grants. Congress authorized $900 million for the LWCF in 1998—the one and only time in its more than fifty-year history that Congress appropriated the maximum allowable for LWCF spending—and some of that money funded the John Muir gravesite purchase. ALC sold the gravesite to the NPS on August 17, 1999, for $200,000 and made it forever a part of the John Muir National Historic Site.[52]

The costs incurred for holding onto the gravesite for more than six years meant that ALC lost more than $20,000 on the John Muir project. It was not the first or the last time that ALC came out on the short end of a deal. Harriet once said, "In our family, there were two themes: one, do the right thing; and two, the Lord will provide." Harriet knew the risks, and she took them. She never gave up. It was the right thing to do—to remember John Muir and the many other conservationists whose perseverance and dedication to saving land remind us and inspire us to do the same—and, whether or not the outcome was influenced by divine intervention, the federal government eventually provided most of the necessary funding.[53]

Researching Harriet's life and work, I have encountered many fascinating people and places, but perhaps none has intrigued me more than John Muir. As I watched a documentary on John Muir, read his biographies, and read his books, I began to realize that Muir and Harriet shared many qualities that shed light on who they were and why they dedicated their lives to conservation. They are similar in ways that may help explain their shared passion for nature, a passion that pushed them to save land, to preserve wild places for nature's sake and for the sake of all who benefit from nature's restorative power.

John Muir and Harriet Burgess both came from families headed by deeply religious patriarchs. Muir's father, Daniel, left Scotland when John was eleven years old to have the freedom to practice his Presbyterian/

Calvinist/Campbellite religion in the United States as he saw fit. Harriet's father, Clair Vaughn McNeel, was a fervent and faithful Presbyterian minister whose strong views on social justice won over many and alienated others. He moved his family every three to five years answering the call of congregations that needed his help. The two fathers ruled their families with a heavy hand.[54]

Both Muir and Harriet found ways to escape restrictive paternal control at an early age. Muir left his rural home for Madison, Wisconsin, to exhibit some of his mechanical inventions and later attend the University of Wisconsin when he was twenty-two. Harriet moved out of her father's household and into her own by dropping out of college and marrying Robert Hunt when she was nineteen. Neither Muir nor Harriet finished college, but that lack never held back either of them.[55]

The two conservationists rejected the religious fervor of their parents in favor of nature and its preservation. They dropped the constraints of conventional religion and did not attend church after making the break with their traditional religious upbringing. Muir often equated natural beauty with God. On one of his first trips to Yosemite, Muir wrote, "I am dead and gone to heaven," confiding that "I have not been at church a single time since leaving home. Yet this glorious valley might well be called a church. . . ."[56]

Harriet, after leaving her commitment to formal religion behind when she left her first husband, only made casual references to her religious background with comments such as, "The Lord will provide," and "We're doing the Lord's work." Like many conservationists of the twentieth century—William O. Douglas, Rachel Carson, Edward Abbey, and David Brower among them—Muir and Harriet were lapsed Presbyterians. Lapsed but still imbued with the religious principles of their youth that drove them to find spiritual sustenance in nature and to do the right thing to preserve it.[57]

Early in my research into Harriet's life, I began to sense the power of her Presbyterian roots. When I asked those who knew her only after she left Virginia and stopped going to church whether Harriet was religious, none answered affirmatively. But still I felt that her Presbyterian upbringing had played a significant part in her drive to save land. My suspicions were confirmed when I read Mark Stoll's book *Inherit the Holy Mountain: Religion and the Rise of American Environmentalism*. Stoll, a lapsed Presbyterian himself, as am I, makes an excellent argument for the connection between Presbyterians and conservation. He writes:

> the example of John Muir alerted me to the significance of religious upbringing, not adult beliefs, of the leading figures in the history of American environmentalism. . . . [The] evidence convinced me that there must be some relationship between religion and environmentalism. A high proportion of leading figures in environmental history had religious childhoods. A surprisingly large contingent had ministers or preachers as close relatives or had even considered the ministry themselves. Curiously, few (and after 1900, hardly any) were churchgoers as adults. . . . Especially before the 1960s, a very large majority of the figures of the standard histories of environmentalism grew up in just two denominations. Congregationalism and Presbyterianism, both in the Calvinist tradition. . . . [T]here was something about being raised Presbyterian, something that stayed behind after creed and dogma fell away, that made excellent environmental leaders. There is an "inner Presbyterian" that has an enduring moral map and an urgent need to right the wrongs of the world . . . A huge proportion of the leaders of environmentalism during its mid-twentieth century heyday were raised Presbyterian. . . . Presbyterians [gave] the movement a moral and political center that no one has replaced.

Muir and Harriet worked from a moral center to protect what we still have of the wild Earth and to remember those who dedicated their lives to the land conservation mission.[58]

I discovered other parallels in the lives of these two committed conservationists. Both found homes and fresh starts in California, and both ventured forth from California on extensive travels around the world. Muir married into the Strentzel family whose business he managed, providing the economic wealth that he otherwise would not have enjoyed. Harriet also married into economic prosperity with her second marriage to Joe Burgess. Both were devoted parents: Muir to his two daughters, Harriet to her three daughters and two sons.

Both were great talkers. They connected easily with people from all walks of life, forming lasting friendships—friendships that served them well in their quests to preserve and protect land. People were drawn to them like bees to flowers. Describing the first time he met Harriet at a 1999 meeting of environmentalists in Reno organized by Carole King, Tim Richardson, ALC's director of government affairs in Washington, D.C., said, "They put a hundred environmentalists in a room. Harriet was there. ... When I entered the room, my friend said, 'Where do you want to sit?' I looked across the room and saw this woman with long auburn hair, back turned to me, at the bar, getting a drink. She turned around and I said, 'I want to sit wherever she's sitting.' And I'd never seen her before. I didn't know who she was. But she had a theatrical presence, a stage presence. ... An actor is able to convey action by presence ... She was like that ... [I had that] impression when I saw her the very first time."[59]

Muir and Harriet were inspired and supported by steadfast mentors who encouraged and promoted them—Jeanne Carr for Muir and Martin Litton for Harriet. But both were willing to pick up and leave family, friends, and civilization behind when the urge struck—Muir often to his beloved Sierra, Harriet to the cathedral of the Grand Canyon. They took risks and pushed themselves to their physical limits, never allowing pain and discomfort to interfere with their experience of nature and the pursuit of what was right.

Muir and Harriet loved the wildflowers of California's Central Valley. Looking out over the valley one shining morning in 1868, John Muir saw a landscape displayed before him that he proclaimed the most beautiful he had ever seen. He exulted, "At my feet lay the Great Central Valley of California, level and flowery, like a lake of pure sunshine, forty or fifty miles wide, five hundred miles long, one rich furred garden of yellow Compositae." In *A Thousand-Mile Walk to the Gulf*, Muir wrote, "The valley of the San Joaquin is the floweriest piece of world I ever walked, one vast level, even flower-bed, a sheet of flowers, a smooth sea ruffled a little by the tree fringing of the river and here and there of smaller cross streams from the mountains."[60]

Harriet shared Muir's enthusiasm, but the glorious swaths of wildflowers that greeted him were almost completely gone by the end of the twentieth century, overtaken by urban sprawl and corporate agriculture, leaving northern California's Bear Valley one of the few places in California where wildflowers still reign. When Bear Valley was threatened by residential and agricultural development at about the same time that Harriet was working to preserve Muir's gravesite, Harriet and ALC intervened to help save its thousands of acres of spectacular wildflowers that paint the valley and its surrounding hills white, purple, orange, and yellow every spring. Like John Muir, there we still can say, "Sauntering in any direction, hundreds of these happy sun plants brushed against my feet at every step, and closed over them as if I were wading in liquid gold."[61]

Their paths diverged, of course. Muir was a rancher; Harriet was not. Muir was a writer; Harriet was not. Harriet enjoyed politics; Muir did not. No memorials were erected to Harriet Burgess. No places or plants are named for her. No coins or stamps bear her image. She has no gravesite. But acres and acres of land—including John Muir's gravesite—have been preserved because she believed that open spaces, habitat, biological diversity, and opportunities simply to experience nature are essential to our existence.

Interlude

Grand Canyon

BATHING IN THE COLORADO RIVER SEEMS COUNTERPRODUCTIVE. NOT only is the river laden with silt, but it is also the repository for urine (which, I grant you, is sterile), spit, and who knows what else. And it's against the rules to use soap. Eventually, I give up on getting clean in the river and resort to the packaged shower cloths that I stashed in my dry bag, but today I'm able to top off the river wash with a dousing under the solar shower that the boatmen have hung for us.

I have just finished drying off when the rain starts, heralded by spectacular flashes of lightning, accompanied by loud claps and rolling roars of thunder. Thunder rolling like a herd of elephants stampeding along the rim of the canyon. The boatmen say we are safe from the lightning on the floor of our cozy canyon because there's too much to attract the electrical strikes at the top of the canyon. I hope they're right.

I hurriedly gather my partially dry clothes and start to stuff them in a dry bag when the wind shifts from a moderate blow to a formidable gale even worse than the day before. I throw the dry bag into the tent, jump in after it, and try to close the flaps. The wind is blowing buckets of sand into the tent and all over me. Blinded by sand, I'm still struggling with the flap zipper when Russell comes running to help.

"Are you OK?"

"Get the zipper, get the zipper. I can't see!"

"I've got it." Russell zips the flap on my side of the tent and shifts over to zip the other side.

Flaps closed, covered in sand from head to toe, we huddle in the tent to wait out the gale and the downpour that swept in with the wind. The tent rocks and rolls as humongous blasts of wind hammer its sides. Our combined weight anchors our fragile shelter but I wonder if it will be enough. Over the roar of the wind, the rain, and the river, I hear voices outside but can see nothing and have no idea what is happening.

"Do you think Michael is okay?"

"I don't know. I left him in his tent to come help you."

"Do you hear those voices?"

"Yeah, can't tell what they're saying though. I can't believe anybody's out there in this."

"Jesus, I hope it stops soon."

The wind stops after blasting us for about a half hour. We don't wait for the rain to stop to crawl out of our hidey-hole. We want to find out what is happening.

"Do you see Michael?"

"Not yet. His tent should be over there."

I look where Russell points and see Michael climb out of his battered tent.

"Are you okay?"

"Yeah, I'm fine. Almost blew into the river though when the tent stakes popped out. How'd you guys do?"

"Pretty good. Sand is everywhere. Somebody anchored our tent stakes with large rocks. Don't know who it was. Probably the same person who tied one of our sleeping bags that had been left outside with several other loose bags. Otherwise the bag would probably be floating in the river somewhere."

I'm grinning and feeling remarkably cheerful. I'm a mess. The tent is a mess. But I don't really care. Perhaps it has something to do with being safely on the other side of potential disaster. Or the thrill of having been in the middle of one of nature's exhilarating displays of power. A sort of euphoria not too different from the thrill of running rapids.

The boatmen take the interruption in their plans for the evening in stride. By the time we work our way over to the kitchen tent—still in place thanks to the eight people who held onto the large tarp during the storm even after one of the oar supports broke—they have put out guacamole and chips.

But Kerstin does say, "That's the biggest wind I've ever seen since I started on the river in 2000." Roger, who's been on the river since the 1970s, adds, "I've only seen winds like that two or three times."

It was a big blow, yet it left everyone and just about everything none the worse for the experience. The only casualty was Tom and Nancy's tent that was hurled into the river. Neither of them was in the tent, but it held their sleeping bags, pads, and other belongings. Amber hurled herself into the river after the tent and rescued it. All of that baggage raft rowing must have given her the strength to grab a loaded tent and drag it out of the rushing river. That, and probably a little adrenaline.

The dories and rafts remained safely tethered to the beach.

A little sand dune has formed against the side of our tent. Sand is in our sleeping bags. Sand is under our sleeping bags. Sand is piled under the mats and in the spaces between the upper part of the tent and the upper zipper flap. Sand is in my hair, my clothes, my ears, my eyes, my nose. Sand is everywhere.

Even without gales of wind, sand tends to get into everything. In the early days, Martin slept on the damp sand near the river to keep cool and avoid having dry sand blow in his ears. Sleeping that close to the river was possible before the significant fluctuations in the water level of the river caused by Glen Canyon Dam releases. Now we camp on dry sand, and it seeps into everything, wind or no wind.[62]

Sand especially adheres to skin coated in sunscreen—which means every inch of my exposed skin. I feel the grit under my fingers when I clean my face although I've already dusted off much of the sand with my bandana. I figure it's like a free dermabrasion. My feet get the same treatment from the silt-laden water that circulates over them when I am in the dory.

More sand used to be along the Colorado River. In the 1950s when Martin made his first runs of the river, before Glen Canyon Dam blocked its flow through the Grand Canyon, "peninsulas of sand came out into the river that overlapped one another with flowers on them, and willows, and never a human footprint on any of them." Roger says the river has 95 percent fewer beaches now because of erosion from dam releases and siltation capture by the dam.[63]

Two motorized raft trips pass our camp, the engines shattering the early morning silence. The contrast is stark: traveling down the river with the constant thrum of an engine versus traveling down the river with the sounds of dipping oars and the calls of canyon wrens. The motorized rafts speed by, and the sound of their engines soon subsides, replaced by the unchanging hum of cicadas that fills the canyon like a chanted mantra.

We move much more slowly than the motorized rafts, passing through the narrowest part of the river, a mere seventy-six feet wide, and navigating Tapeats and several small rapids, but we catch them at Deer Creek. Deer Creek is a popular stop. Framed by greenery, the crystalline water of Deer Creek Falls plunges 180 feet from a narrow crack in the red canyon wall.

Michael and four others go off with all of the boatmen except Kerstin for a two-hour hike that begins with a steep five-hundred-foot ascent to an overlook then continues into Deer Creek Narrows, a slot canyon. Kerstin has advised us that, in addition to the challenging climb, hikers will have to negotiate a ledge with a thirty-foot drop. That was enough to discourage me. I remember Harriet's almost fatal fall from a Grand Canyon ledge and decide to pass on the hike.

I watch Roger bound up the rock-strewn path as surefooted as the bighorn sheep that call the Grand Canyon home. The rest of the hikers are a bit more cautious. I lounge by myself on an accommodating rock at the edge of the river in full view of the spectacular waterfall to write.

I relish the time to be alone. Time alone is a scarce commodity on a trip shared in close proximity with twenty-three people. Even Harriet, a people person if there ever was one, sought solitude in the Grand Canyon. She regularly disappeared from camp for solitary hikes without telling a soul where she was going. Sometimes, she sat by the campfire at night writing like mad about her life. Then the next morning she disappeared to hide what she'd written and put in a bottle in the rocks somewhere. As far as I know, these hidden missives—that no one is ever likely to read and would be a treasure trove for me as her biographer—are the only reflections on Harriet's life that she left behind.[64]

We are a little more than halfway through our Grand Canyon sojourn. I have become adept at erecting our tent. I have a system for organizing all of my stuff in the tent and in the dry bags. I am coping with The Unit. I am grungy and OK with that. Russell says we should take photos of what we look like when we leave the river at Diamond Creek. We surely will be a sight to see.

Modesty has become increasingly rare as we have gone along. Men and women changing clothes in full view, getting in the river to bathe sans clothes, peeing wherever. I have bathed topless but usually change in the tent. I still try to be discreet when peeing, but that is always problematic.

Everyone pitches in to help set up and take down the camp. Loading and unloading the dories. Gathering around the kitchen tent to fold the huge tarp into a small, neat roll that fits easily into a dry bag. Giving the boatmen a hand with The Unit.

I am back to basics, relaxing into the magic of the canyon. The separation from the rest of the world is complete.

Upset Rapid is waiting for us just past mile 150. Upset can be as easy as a 3 and as tough as an 8 on the scale of Grand Canyon rapid ratings. For Emery Kolb in 1923, it was tough enough to capsize his boat and acquire its name. Kolb and his brother, Ellsworth, were photographers. Photographing both the tourists and the rock formations in the early 1900s, they became intimately acquainted with the canyon and often served as guides for Grand Canyon visitors.[65]

Colonel Claude Birdseye hired Emery Kolb as the head boatman for his 1923 U.S. Geological Survey expedition that was tasked with finding the best places to dam the Colorado River. Rowing the pilot boat, *Marble*, Emery's job was to be the first to go through any rapids that he had not already decided should be lined or portaged instead. The Birdseye Expedition left Lees Ferry on August 1 with five boats and ten men. By the time the USGS team finished their work on October 13, they had made the first accurate survey of the Grand Canyon.[66]

Unlike the Austin Expedition, or the Harriet Expeditions, I expect, the Birdseye Expedition maintained contact with the outside world. Birdseye, ignoring warnings that the Grand Canyon was too deep to receive a signal, brought along a radio. On the first night of the trip, after laying out the antenna on a rock, the ten men heard Los Angeles station KHJ clearly. The second night, they listened again and heard the news that President Harding had died. The USGS party paused a day at mile 44 in memory of Harding and named the rapid there President Harding Rapid. During their journey through the canyon, they kept abreast of the latest news as the radio picked up stations from as far away as San Francisco.[67]

On September 12, Emery Kolb looked at the rapid at mile 150 and decided it was safe to run, but he was concerned enough to take the precaution of removing and portaging the boats' cargos. Leigh Lint, a twenty-one-year-old boatman on the trip, recorded Emery's run of the rapid in his journal:

> Emery started in the center and tried to cut across to the north side but he didn't quite make it and went over the edge of the boulder and upset. Luckily the boat was carried out of the hole and on down stream. As the boat went over, Emery grabbed an oar but that pulled loose and he kept his hand on the hatch cover until a wave knocked him back into the cockpit. He was under the boat and under water for about one hundred yards (the rest of the crew were on shore but helpless to do any good) before he could get out and crawl out on top of the upturned boat. . . . Dodge swam out and grabbed his painter [a rope tied to the bow used for tying up or towing]. I pulled into Dodge and he tied the painter onto the stern lifeline of my boat and then climbed aboard . . . and I went to see if Emery was injured. He had gotten a lot of water in his lungs and strangled but he was soon over that. We righted his boat and bailed it out and then lined them both about one hundred yards upstream . . . The only damage done was the loss of one oar and a pail of lard which was smeared all over inside the rear hold.[68]

And that's how Upset Rapid got its name.

Exactly eighty-eight years later on September 12, 2011, Upset wasn't tough enough to flip *Escalante*, but the waves were huge. I had to bite my tongue not to say, "Don't do it!" when Duffy asked Michael if he'd like to ride through the rapid on the bow of the boat. Michael didn't hesitate and, perched on the point of *Escalante*'s prow like a figurehead, flew through the rapid as Duffy skillfully navigated the chaos. I sat in my usual seat in the stern, worrying and being soaked to the skin by the waves that filled our seat well within inches of the seat even though the *Escalante* was supposed to be self-bailing.

When we stopped for lunch with the sun shining beatifically upon us after a morning rain, I peeled off my rain pants—worn that day for the first time after a serious dousing in a rapid the day before—and turned them inside out to dry on a rock. The pants label proclaimed, "Gore Tex Extreme Weather." I guess running rapids goes beyond extreme weather. Rain pants are not rapids pants.

The rain returns after lunch, but it does not disrupt our tranquil drift and paddle down the river. Duffy tells a story about rescuing a rattlesnake from the river. Two Park Service motorized rafts pass us. The river widens enough for all four dories to make a line and perform a synchronized pirouette.

We hover at the mouth of Havasu Creek where the water runs aquamarine into the milk chocolate brown of the Colorado River. With all of the rain, we do not hike up the creek into Havasu Canyon. The volatile weather has increased the likelihood of a flash flood with the power to destroy us and the dories. Remnants of equipment wedged in the rocks offer proof of the destructive power of flash floods.

I see architecture everywhere in the Grand Canyon. Rocks in columns like a loggia. Massive, rounded, regularly spaced niches in the canyon wall like the niches in a cathedral displaying saints. Castles on cliffs.

The peaceful afternoon is like the quiet before a storm. Tomorrow is Lava Falls.

CHAPTER SIX

Magnificent Obsession

Thunderbird Lodge

A lake is the landscape's most beautiful feature. It is Earth's eye; looking into which the beholder measures the depth of his own nature. —HENRY DAVID THOREAU, *WALDEN*, 1854

[A]t last the Lake burst upon us—a noble sheet of blue water lifted six thousand three hundred feet above the level of the sea, and walled in by a rim of snow-clad mountain peaks that towered aloft full three thousand feet higher still! . . . As [Lake Tahoe] lay there with the shadows of the mountains brilliantly photographed upon its still surface I thought it must surely be the fairest picture the whole earth affords. —MARK TWAIN, *ROUGHING IT*, 1872

[A]s I sauntered through the piney woods, pausing countless times to absorb the blue glimpses of the lake . . . The soul of Indian summer is brooding this blue water, and it enters one's being as nothing else does. Tahoe is surely not one but many. As I curve around its heads and bays and look far out on its level sky fairly tinted and fading in pensive air, I am reminded of all the mountain lakes I ever knew, as if this were a kind of water heaven to which they all had come. —JOHN MUIR, LETTER TO JEANNE CARR, 1873[1]

JUST DOWN THE MOUNTAIN FROM GALENA AND NOT LONG AFTER THE celebration of its preservation, Harriet discovered a stretch of Lake Tahoe coastline that amazed and delighted her. She had conveyed a lot of land around Lake Tahoe into public ownership, so she really thought she knew the lake. But nobody had ever told her about the Thunderbird Lodge and the 140 acres that surround it. When Harriet saw the property for the first time in April 1995, she believed she had found "the most beautiful spot on the lake. The property provides panoramic views of the whole lake. You can see all the way down to the south shore and in the opposite direction to Incline." Harriet later told a *Reno Gazette-Journal* reporter, "I knew instantly: what a gem. Wait till you see it."[2]

I had visited Lake Tahoe only a few times before I made the trip to see Thunderbird Lodge with its panoramic views in late May 2016. The lake is just two hours from where I live in Sacramento, but—perhaps because it is so close and accessible and does not offer the lure of the unfamiliar and remote that travels afar afford—its beauty had only drawn me occasionally and then for short visits that did not focus on the lake itself. Until I began to ferret out the particulars of Harriet's story, I knew little about the splendid alpine lake that has been called the "crown jewel" of the Sierra.

Lake Tahoe is 1,645 feet deep, twenty-two miles long, and twelve miles wide with seventy-two miles of shoreline. It holds enough water to flood the state of California to a depth of fourteen inches and is the second deepest lake in North America after Crater Lake in Oregon. If drained, it would take seven hundred years to refill. On the border between California and Nevada at an elevation of more than six thousand feet, Lake Tahoe attracts three million visitors every year. Its fragile beauty has been threatened many times by logging, mining, damming, and myriad other often destructive uses that inventive humans have found for it and its environs. Efforts to protect it began in the late nineteenth century and have continued to the present day with varying degrees of success.[3]

Standing in the sun's warm brilliance above the massive boulders that line the lake's edge at Thunderbird Lodge, looking across the expanse of deep blue water to the snow-capped mountains beyond, Harriet's magnificent obsession to protect a singular slice of Lake Tahoe shoreline and the surrounding land became even more compelling. It was her dedication and perseverance that had put me there.

Jack Dreyfus Jr., the mutual fund tycoon whose primary residence was in New York, jointly owned the secluded Thunderbird Lodge with the Dreyfus Charitable Foundation and William P. Rogers when Harriet first saw it. No wonder she never before had seen it and its magnificent views of Lake Tahoe. Nor had many others. Jack Dreyfus himself rarely stayed there.[4]

Dreyfus had purchased the lodge and approximately 11,298 acres of land in the Lake Tahoe basin in 1970 from the estate of multimillionaire George Whittell Jr. The land was the remainder of what once had been an estate of more than forty thousand acres, with more than twenty miles of lake shoreline stretching from Crystal Bay in the north to Zephyr Cove in the south, that Whittell had acquired in the 1930s. Whittell had intended to develop his Tahoe property—nearly one-quarter of the Tahoe basin—beginning with a casino and hotel at Sand Harbor and a summer retreat for himself on a rocky promontory just south of Sand Harbor.[5]

George Whittell never went forward with his casino and hotel plans. Instead, the self-indulgent eccentric devoted himself to the creation of his castle on the lake. He hired well-known Nevada architect Frederick J. DeLongchamps to design the Thunderbird Lodge, a three-story stone-clad mansion, along with a lighthouse, a boathouse, and cottages for guests and a caretaker. Native American stonemasons, Italian ironworkers, and Norwegian woodworkers all contributed to the construction of the lodge and its outbuildings. By the time it was finished in 1939, Whittell had decided that he wanted to protect his privacy and keep his Tahoe property to himself.[6]

When he died in 1969, Whittell left behind a legacy of undeveloped land. Although he had sold nine thousand acres in 1959 that soon were developed as the new community of Incline Village, most of his original holdings were still open space. Whittell had leased nine acres to the state of Nevada for Sand Harbor State Park in 1958. A condemnation action brought by the state forced him to sell another fifty-three hundred acres to the state in 1967 as part of Lake Tahoe Nevada State Park. More of the eccentric millionaire's land legacy was transferred to the public when the Forest Service purchased 4,732 acres from the Whittell estate in 1970 and another 10,000 acres from Dreyfus in 1972.[7]

But Dreyfus still owned the Thunderbird Lodge and its 140 acres. He also owned another former Whittell property at Zephyr Cove. These two remnants of Whittell's vast estate were put up for sale in late 1994 to raise funds for the Dreyfus Charitable Foundation. Dreyfus and his partner, William Rogers, wanted to sell the Thunderbird Lodge and Zephyr Cove quickly and for as much money as possible. Development or continued exclusive private ownership seemed the most likely fate for the two pristine properties.

Thunderbird Lodge first appeared on Harriet's radar screen courtesy of her longtime friend, attorney Peter "Mick" Laxalt and his wife, Liz. For more than ten years, Mick Laxalt had joined attorney Ron Alling and environmental consultant Phil Caterino in representing Jack Dreyfus in matters related to his Tahoe properties. Along with his brother, Paul Laxalt, Mick also had represented George Whittell before his death.

As a Nevada native and the son of a sheepherder who immigrated to the United States from the Basque country, Mick Laxalt's passion for Lake Tahoe and the Sierra ran deep. The Laxalt family connection to the Dreyfus/Whittell properties went back to the 1930s when Mick's father used to have coffee with Whittell over a campfire. Mick Laxalt had nothing but praise for Whittell and Dreyfus for their contributions to the pristine preservation of Thunderbird Lodge and Zephyr Cove. A long stretch of the Nevada side of Lake Tahoe was undeveloped because of their stewardship.[8]

By listing his Tahoe properties for sale with Shari Chase of Chase International Real Estate, Dreyfus raised the specter of development where little or none had been before. The Laxalts met the challenge of preserving the Dreyfus lands "with something akin to 'missionary zeal.'" They figured that Harriet was the perfect choice to spearhead the effort to bring the Dreyfus lands into public ownership. In the eyes of Mick Laxalt—having worked with her on several land exchanges while she was at TPL and later at ALC, and having witnessed her many other conservation achievements—Harriet was a miracle worker. Liz Laxalt, a Reno realtor, presented the opportunity to Harriet in January 1995, emphasizing the necessity of saving these last remnants of undeveloped Tahoe shoreline.[9]

I can't imagine Harriet needed much convincing. It was a once-in-a-lifetime opportunity she could not let slip through her fingers. She took on the task of bringing the "jewels of Lake Tahoe" into public ownership, even though she already was in the middle of projects in California such as the John Muir Gravesite, Bear Valley, and additions to the San Bernardino National Forest; projects in Nevada to wrap up the Nevada land exchange; projects in Oregon in the Klamath River Basin and at Siletz Bay; and the Inahgeh Wetlands project in Illinois. Before she finished what became an extremely complicated project for the Dreyfus lands—as she once said, "All of our projects are pretty challenging, but Dreyfus is in a league of its own"—she would be slammed with the OIG investigation.[10]

Harriet signed up Liz Laxalt as ALC's broker for the purpose of securing an option or purchase agreement with the owners of the Dreyfus/Whittell property in February 1995 and went to work. Following initial conversations with Liz and Shari Chase that included the possibility of doing a land exchange, Harriet wrote directly to Jack Dreyfus to introduce herself and detail her qualifications. She met with him and, according to Ame Hellman, "in her wonderfully engaging way, really won him over. Just like with of all of these landowners . . . Harriet's biggest asset . . . was the respect that she gave to the landowner. She would engage them in the possibility of turning their property into a conservation project in a way I've never seen done in my life."[11]

Dreyfus gave Harriet the OK to start an appraisal. He also gave her permission to stay overnight at the Thunderbird Lodge with her husband, her daughter Leslie, and Leslie's boyfriend. Together, they sipped champagne while watching the sun slip below the mountains that ring the lake in a blaze of reds and pinks. They viewed the spectacular display through the expansive windows of a large room that was part of an addition to the original lodge that Dreyfus completed in 1984.[12]

After thanking Dreyfus for their late-April visit to a "truly magnificent place . . . with its incredible views," Harriet added, "I hope we can put together a transaction which meets your needs and allows public acquisition." In return, Harriet received a note from Dreyfus thanking her for her lovely letter. He wrote, "I'm glad you like the place. It really is extraordinary. Give yourself my warmest regards." In the spidery handwriting of an eighty-three-year-old man, he signed it "Jack."[13]

Putting together a land exchange deal with Jack Dreyfus and William Rogers, however, was complicated by their lack of experience with that kind of transaction and their desire to sell their property as expeditiously as possible. To help them understand how exchanges worked, ALC diagrammed "The Anatomy of a Land Exchange." The diagram placed ALC at the center of the transaction by which the federal government traded public lands selected for disposal in southern Nevada with private lands offered for sale by Dreyfus. By arranging the sale of the selected public lands to developers, ALC generated the cash proceeds necessary to acquire the Dreyfus lands for the public. Harriet journeyed to New York two or three times to explain the land exchange process to Dreyfus in person.[14]

Russell Austin also talked to William Rogers several times to explain the land exchange process in an attempt to convince him that the time and effort required to complete a land exchange were worth it. Russell's phone conversations with the man who had been President Eisenhower's secretary of Commerce and President Nixon's secretary of State were an exhilarating challenge. Whenever Rogers called him, Russell would go on full alert because he fully expected Rogers to be "forceful [and] demanding." Russell knew he'd "better have an answer to every question that he was going to ask at my fingertips." He said, "It's like being . . . a staffer in front of the president of the United States, and you're being grilled one snap question after the other. You needed to be prepared with answers to keep the dialogue going."[15]

In October, Russell followed up one of his phone conversations with a letter designed to answer Rogers's questions about "the ALC's ability to effect land acquisition projects in a timely manner." He outlined the steps taken to execute the exchange for the Galena property as an example of ALC's work and concluded:

Only a portion of the lands identified for the first phase of this exchange were used. Substantial additional federal lands in the Las

Vegas area have been identified for disposal and there is a strong market for them. The availability of these lands to ALC, and ALC's track record in marketing federal lands in this same area for the first phase of the Nevada Land Exchange, put ALC in the best position to expedite acquisition of the Dreyfus and Zephyr Cove properties.[16]

Meanwhile, to pave the way for the Dreyfus exchange, Harriet had submitted a "supplemental notice of exchange proposal" to the BLM's Las Vegas district office in June. ALC proposed "to make additional conveyances of private lands to the Bureau of Land Management (the 'BLM') in exchange for public lands located in the vicinity of the City of North Las Vegas." The exchange for the city of North Las Vegas lands hadn't worked before, but perhaps it would now. Thunderbird Lodge and Zephyr Cove were among the offered lands listed in the ALC proposal.[17]

Harriet had submitted her proposal, but BLM and the Forest Service were reluctant to commit to an exchange until ALC had a firm commitment from the landowners to sell, which they were not inclined to provide until the government had committed to the exchange. Surrounded on three sides by ten thousand acres of national forest and featuring old-growth incense cedar and sugar pine, Thunderbird Lodge had long been at the top of the Forest Service's wish list of lands for public acquisition. Acquisition of the property would protect the fragile watershed of Marlette Creek, enhance Lake Tahoe fisheries, protect highly sensitive Washoe Tribe prehistoric cultural resources, and provide additional recreation opportunities.

Notwithstanding these values, the BLM did not want to designate public lands for disposal in an exchange unless it was certain that a deal to acquire the private lands for the Forest Service was in place. Both BLM and the Forest Service were also adamant that they were not interested in acquiring any of the property's structures.[18]

Getting the exchange underway was crucial. Equally important was generating widespread support for the public acquisition of Thunderbird Lodge.[19] While Harriet and her team were negotiating an agreement with Dreyfus and Rogers to purchase the lodge property, she and the Laxalts concentrated their lobbying efforts on elected officials and staff at the Forest Service and the BLM. Harriet made telephone calls, attended meetings in Nevada and Washington, D.C., and wrote letters. Joining Harriet and Liz Laxalt at a July tour of Thunderbird Lodge were representatives from the Forest Service and the BLM, Congresswoman Barbara Vucanovich's office, and Senator Bryan's office. Representatives from the Nevada governor's office and other state offices, Senator Reid's office, and the Forest Service toured the property in October.[20]

Harriet met with Frankie Sue Del Papa, Nevada's attorney general, who then wrote Robert Armstrong assistant secretary for land minerals management, Department of the Interior. Del Papa urged Armstrong to support the proposal to exchange BLM lands in the Las Vegas area for "two premier properties at Lake Tahoe which have long been targeted for public ownership." Noting her agreement with Mark Twain's assessment of Lake Tahoe's beauty, she hoped that serious consideration would be given to the land exchange proposal. Harriet, too, wrote the assistant secretary and enclosed briefing materials.[21]

Harriet also encouraged Bob Harris, the forest supervisor of the Lake Tahoe Basin management unit, to write Jack Dreyfus and emphasize the importance of having a commitment from him to sell Thunderbird Lodge to ALC. Harris told Dreyfus that he and his staff, along with representatives from the regional and national offices of the Forest Service, had toured Thunderbird Lodge and were extremely impressed. He explained:

> Energetic efforts have been underway by many parties for some time now to solidify underlying funding commitments for acquisition, no small task in the current atmosphere of cutbacks and across-the-board austerity measures. These efforts involved the American Land Conservancy and the Office of the Governor of Nevada. Great momentum has been created and . . . I am of the opinion that the funding opportunities exist.
>
> We understand your position that you'd like to know the funds are there before you sign even a conditional commitment to sell, but I'm sure you understand that this has increased the difficulty to carve out this particular funding from competing demands when no acquisition contract exists.

Harris expressed his belief that selling Thunderbird Lodge to ALC for transfer to the U.S. Forest Service would prevent the loss of the property to buyers who "may or may not have the same sense of public interest as you."[22]

Mick Laxalt continued his advocacy for the public acquisition of Thunderbird Lodge and Zephyr Cove by sending a long letter to Senators Bryan and Reid, Congresswoman Vucanovich, and Congressman John Ensign. Laxalt had cleared the letter with Harriet first, and no doubt she was in complete agreement with his intense conviction that "these magnificent parcels in their pristine, natural, park-like status" must be preserved. Laxalt acknowledged that the asking price for the two properties was high, but he argued, "*they are two of the most unique properties in the world.*" He maintained that "it would be one of the most disastrous events in the history of our state if the Dreyfus lands were to escape capture for want of funding, and thereafter become despoiled by private development." He insisted that something heroic had to be done, and done soon, because he had "worked too long and hard in assisting Mr. Dreyfus, and before him (with Paul) with Captain Whittel [*sic*] and the Blisses and others for the preservation of these lands simply to sit by idly and see this grand opportunity be wasted." And as Laxalt noted in his letter, "the enthusiasm for acquisition of the Dreyfus lands is, without exception, extremely high."[23]

The enthusiasm of the many people who advocated for public acquisition of Thunderbird Lodge was not matched by the property's owners. It took nine months of negotiations, but Russell Austin at last was able to write Rogers at the end of November, "ALC is finalizing a transactional structure that it believes will meet your client's objectives for disposition of the Dreyfus estate property." It took another month of back-and-forth on the telephone and in written proposals before ALC reached an agreement with Dreyfus and Rogers for the purchase of Thunderbird Lodge.[24]

Making her case for the deal to Dreyfus and Rogers at the beginning of January 1996, Harriet again argued for the merits of moving the Thunderbird Lodge into public ownership with the assistance of ALC. In a three-page letter, she again explained how the land exchange for the Dreyfus estate would work. This time she wrote that funding would be available from the sale of scattered parcels of land in and around the city of Las Vegas rather than the large block of land near the city of North Las Vegas that seems to have been dropped in favor of other surplus BLM lands. She discussed the merits of completing the exchange through ALC rather than working directly with BLM. She wrote, "Most developers would prefer to work with ALC which has the experience and the technical know how to complete exchanges with BLM, making these lands available to developers with less 'pain and suffering' on their part." She emphasized ALC's experience in working with landowners in similar situations and cited the Galena exchange as one example. Wrapping up her pitch, Harriet wrote,

> The Thunderbird Lodge is an extraordinary property, celebrated in Nevada and renowned for its beauty and remarkable setting throughout the Tahoe Basin. Moving the property into public ownership will complete an effort begun many years ago. The acquisition has wide support throughout Nevada as well as in the Lake Tahoe community and will provide a world class amenity for the public at Lake Tahoe.[25]

The next day, Harriet sent a letter of intent to Dreyfus and Rogers. It summarized the essential terms of ALC's third formal attempt to make an offer for the Thunderbird Lodge that was acceptable to its owners. Harriet was determined to persuade Dreyfus and Rogers to do a deal with ALC even though she told Martin Litton that over the past year "they have had considerable difficulty understanding how the American Land Conservancy operates and how it is possible to do a land exchange that would facilitate the purchase of this property."

Harriet's persistence reminds me of Bob Hunt's comment about his relationship with Harriet—an irresistible force of nature (Harriet) meeting an immovable object (Bob). In this case, the object (Dreyfus and Rogers) moved but the terms of the deal were tough.[26]

The purchase price was set at 97 percent of the fair market value of $50 million established by the ALC appraisal, with the 3 percent difference to be considered a charitable contribution by the seller. ALC's due diligence period was divided into two phases:

First, sixty days to identify additional public lands beyond those that ALC currently had ready for an ALC/federal land exchange sufficient to complete the Thunderbird transaction, complete the federal review of ALC's appraisal, complete the federally required environmental assessment, and review title; and

Second, thirty days following the end of the first phase to complete the preparation of additional exchange lands and finalize sales agreements with the buyers of these lands to fund ALC's acquisition of Thunderbird Lodge.

ALC had to make a deposit of $100,000 when the sale agreement was signed. ALC had to make another deposit of $400,000 at the end of the due diligence period. Closing had to occur on or before 180 days from the date of the sale agreement. If ALC needed additional time, a ninety-day extension would be granted after ALC paid a third deposit of $1.5 million. All deposits were to be credited toward the purchase price, but were non-refundable unless the seller breached the sale agreement.[27]

The initial deposit of $100,000 was far beyond ALC's usual option payment of $100 or less. The necessity of additional deposits further increased ALC's potential exposure to loss. Given the sums at risk, Harriet decided it would be prudent to advise her executive committee/board of directors of ALC's offer. She asked them to call her if they had reservations, concerns, or needed more information. They may have contacted her, but if they did, their counsel did not impede the deal. The sellers agreed to the terms in ALC's letter of intent on January 5 and executed the sale agreement with ALC on January 29.[28]

Harriet really had bet the farm this time. She had no firm commitment from federal agencies for the land exchange essential to securing funding for the Thunderbird Lodge purchase. With all of her experience with land exchanges, she had to know that ninety days would not be long enough to set up the exchange she needed. Even with a ninety-day $1.5 million extension on top of nonrefundable deposits totaling $500,000, it would take nothing short of a miracle to identify and prepare enough public lands to sell to buyers with finalized sales agreements by the deadline. She had no firm commitments from any other funding sources. And she still had to find a solution for taking care of the buildings the Forest Service didn't want.

I can't ask Harriet what she was thinking as she continued to bankroll a project that seemed likely to fail with money that her organization really didn't have, but I can easily imagine what she might have told me: I'm taking a big chance, but that's what I founded ALC to do. The Dreyfus estate is worth the risk. Once it's gone, it's gone, and we can never get it back. If you don't do it, you can only talk about how it could have been. I have to try. I am confident that I'll find a way.

Harriet often said her approach was "like the camel's nose under a tent. You keep trying until you find a way in. It's obviously most often not through the front door. But once you get your nose under, you're there." This time the camel's nose was going to be rubbed raw before the camel finally managed to get under the tent.[29]

Having persuaded Dreyfus and Rogers to sell Thunderbird Lodge to ALC for conveyance into public ownership, Harriet pressed forward with her initiatives to make the deal work. At the conclusion of the first sixty days of the due diligence period, she was able to inform Dreyfus and Rogers that both the environmental assessment and the appraisal of the Thunderbird Lodge property had been completed. The Forest Service accepted the findings of the environmental assessment but called attention to several minor concerns that ALC quickly took steps to address and remedy. The Forest Service expected to approve the appraisal after final review by the end of April but noted that final approval was contingent on a land exchange proposal that included an acceptable management strategy for the improvements on the property. The Forest Service also accepted the preliminary title report subject to the removal of an exception that stated the land may only be used for private residential purposes.[30]

A lot had been achieved in a short time, but the problem of the Thunderbird Lodge improvements loomed large. The Forest Service agreed that the lands have "National Forest character and value to the public." The Forest Service acknowledged that "public acquisition of these properties represents a 'once in a lifetime' opportunity to acquire lands that are considered important for watershed purposes, recreational values, interpretation, and other public opportunities." But—and it was a huge but—the Forest Service would only endorse public acquisition if the agency had no responsibility for the improvements. The Forest Service wanted to have nothing to do with the historic Thunderbird Lodge structures. The BLM had similar objections to selling surplus land to fund the acquisition of improved land.[31]

In her report to Dreyfus and Rogers at the end of March, Harriet addressed the question of ALC's progress toward putting a land exchange in place by detailing her numerous meetings with public officials. Many of those meetings took place during frequent trips to Washington, D.C., Harriet's old stomping ground from her days as a volunteer for the Sierra Club and as TPL's Washington liaison.

Whenever Harriet believed that an ALC project would benefit from visits to members of Congress or federal agency administrators in Washington, she hopped on a plane and headed east. Washington, D.C., is about as far from the wilderness as you can get. What open space remains of the original sixty-four thousand acres set aside for the capital of the United States is neatly groomed, a sort of developed nature. But the fate of hundreds of thousands of acres of undeveloped land is decided in the halls of Congress and the offices of bureaucrats. Harriet's Washington contacts often were crucial to the success of ALC's conservation quests.

Harriet usually boarded a late-night flight in San Francisco, taking a window seat to catch some sleep, landed at Dulles in the early morning hours, then stopped by a friend's house or a hotel for a quick shower before diving into a full day of appointments. On her two-day whirlwind visit in March 1996 to advocate for the Thunderbird Lodge acquisition, she kept this fast-paced schedule:

Day One

8:00 a.m.	Jack Ward Thomas, chief, U.S. Forest Service
8:30 a.m.	Paul Tittman, chief appraiser, U.S. Forest Service
9:00 a.m.	Ken Meyers, director of land acquisition management, U.S. Forest Service

10:00 a.m.	Nevada Senator Harry Reid
11:30 a.m.	Nevada Senator Richard Bryan
1:00 p.m.	Ron Gastelum hearing
3:30 p.m.	Bruce Babbitt, secretary of the Interior
4:30 p.m.	Jay Ziegler, special assistant to Bruce Babbitt
5:30 p.m.	Bob Hunt (drinks)
6:30 p.m.	Allen McReynolds (dinner)

Day Two

9:00 a.m.	Mick Laxalt
10:00 a.m.	Nevada Congressman John Ensign and his assistant, Windsor Laing
11:00 a.m.	Nevada Congresswoman Barbara Vucanovich, her assistant, Dennis Parobek, and Mick Laxalt
1:30 p.m.	Matt Millenbach, assistant director, BLM
2:00 p.m.	John Garamendi, deputy secretary of the Interior
5:15 p.m.	Dulles to SFO

She recorded ten hours on her time sheet for Thunderbird the first day and another eleven hours the second day.

To make it through the labyrinth of government offices and arrive at her appointments on time, Harriet changed from heels into flats when she left one office, ran to the next office, changed back into heels, then calmly walked into her next meeting and delivered her conservation message, usually offering what she called a "pretty book" filled with information and photographs of the project she was promoting. On some trips she squeezed in an early morning swim in the hotel pool, breakfast with a congressional staffer, and lunch with a lobbyist.[32]

By the end of the first phase of the due diligence period, ALC still had a long way to go before achieving the goal of completing the preparations for a land exchange that was set for the end of the second due diligence phase thirty days later. Harriet had submitted a land exchange proposal for Thunderbird to the BLM in February and an agreement to initiate a land

exchange between BLM and ALC in March. Jan Bernard had identified
BLM lands in Las Vegas for inclusion in the exchange and forwarded a list
of developers interested in some of the tracts to Harriet. Harriet also had
taken Jack Peterson, Interior's coordinator for the Galena exchange, on a
tour of Thunderbird Lodge.[33]

Harriet decided to add even more weight to her in-person entreaties
for the exchange that she made during her early March trip to D.C. She
called on her Board of Councillors to send letters or make phone calls to
Secretary Babbitt encouraging him to support the project. Harriet first sent
a brief note to the board with a Thunderbird "pretty book" and her request
for help, then followed it with a longer version based on a draft provided
by Martin Litton that reveals both the unusual nature of her request and
ALC's urgent need for assistance:

> No doubt you remember the promise those of us here in the front
> office made when you agreed to be on our Advisory Board—that it
> would cost you neither money nor advice to be a valued councillor.
>
> We didn't say anything about time, though, and now your
> Conservancy urgently needs a little of yours, to meet a serious time
> problem with respect to the acquisition of the Thunderbird Lodge
> property at Lake Tahoe.
>
> Our $100,000 option on the purchase of the fifty million dollar
> property (for eventual conveyance to the Forest Service) will expire
> at the end of this month: that's *March 31, 1996.* If we don't effect
> the transfer by then, the place goes up for grabs—to go into new
> private ownership for subdivision or other development.
>
> The unusual but not unprecedented situation is that for the
> transfer to occur, the Interior Department's Bureau of Land Man-
> agement must give up some surplus BLM land for the "benefit"
> of an agency of the Department of Agriculture—something the
> Nevada office of the BLM is thus far reluctant to do.
>
> The problem will be solved quickly if BLM's boss, Secretary of
> the Interior Bruce Babbitt, merely instructs the agency to consider
> the interests of the American people and assist in this transaction.
> I have spoken with him at some length, and although he expresses
> no objection to the process, he still has taken no action.

Some of you enjoy Bruce's personal friendship, but whether you know him personally or not, will you help give him the push needed to make this Tahoe dream a reality? All he has to do is tell his Nevada BLM director that he wants this project done. And I believe you know how to help persuade him to take that simple step.

Harriet concluded by suggesting that the Councillors call Babbitt at his office and send a letter to him "where he'll really get it, to his home"—an approach that Harriet had used on other projects when bureaucratic layers blocked access to the official decision makers—then signed off with "your Conservancy and the quality of America's future really need you on this one!"[34]

Martin answered his own call to action and wrote Babbitt on the same day that he sent the draft to Harriet. He encouraged Babbitt to spend at least an overnight at the lodge, believing that Babbitt would be inspired by a stay. He offered to arrange everything. He suggested that Babbitt bring his wife and anyone else he cared to bring. He said no one would be there to bug him as he relaxed and enjoyed his surroundings. All Babbitt had to do was "just tell us where to send the plane/car(s)/chopper/weasel/etc." It sounded like an offer Babbitt could not refuse, but he never made the visit Martin believed would make all the difference, even when he was only a few miles away participating in the run-up to President Clinton's September 1996 Tahoe Summit.[35]

Councillors Galen Rowell and Bill Garrett also wrote letters. Renowned wilderness landscape photographer Rowell penned his missive in cursive. He urged Babbitt to act to procure the Thunderbird Lodge by March 31 "or the opportunity arranged by the American Land Conservancy will expire and the most beautiful, least developed chunk of the Nevada side will be up for private grabs." Rowell had photographed the lodge for *National Geographic* some years before, and one of his shots had been used to describe Thunderbird as a Lake Tahoe icon.[36]

Garrett, former editor of *National Geographic* who had served on the ALC Board of Councillors with Babbitt in the early 1990s, argued for getting Thunderbird Lodge "off the auction block and under the protection of public ownership. There are few pieces of property so worthy of protection and so well placed to be protected." He reminded Babbitt that Harriet was named Professional Conservationist of the Year in 1995, claiming that "no one is better qualified to make an exchange which will make almost everyone happy—especially generations to come who will be able to enjoy the property in perpetuity and the shoreline around it which would be enhanced by preventing commercial development of this jewel."[37]

Other strong letters of support descended on the Interior secretary. The Washoe tribal chairman, the executive director of the League to Save Lake Tahoe, and the governor of Nevada all tried to convince Babbitt to put his stamp of approval on the Thunderbird acquisition, to no avail.[38]

Babbitt may have been reluctant to become involved in an exchange at a time when questions about BLM exchanges were beginning to be raised. He may have hoped that a bill recently introduced by Nevada Senators Richard Bryan and Harry Reid that designated half of the proceeds from BLM land sales for the purchase of environmentally sensitive lands such as the Thunderbird Lodge would eliminate the need for a land exchange. He told Harriet that he only wanted land that was not encumbered with improvements such as the historic structures on the Thunderbird property.[39]

As a *Reno Gazette-Journal* editorial recommending that every effort be made to acquire the Dreyfus land noted, it was "always a tricky enterprise" to get money for an exchange by selling BLM land in Las Vegas. Secretary and former ALC Councillor Babbitt did not throw his weight behind a land exchange for Thunderbird Lodge, and the Nevada BLM was not on track for a swap. BLM's Nevada State Director Ann Morgan responded to Harriet's February land exchange proposal for Thunderbird Lodge by pleading that the BLM was too busy with more than fifty pending land exchange proposals to process yet another one. Morgan recommended that "care be exercised to ensure that commitments are not made on individual private properties in advance of proposed acquisitions being examined and approved by BLM." It was a little late for that advice.[40]

Still, Harriet told a *Reno Gazette-Journal* reporter, "It's coming along just fine. We're working with the government. That's a deliberate process for us. For them, it is an accelerated transaction."[41]

Harriet had long been aware of the problem presented by the Thunderbird Lodge improvements that deterred Babbitt from endorsing the public acquisition of the property. Shortly after she returned from her August 1995 vacation in Fiji and Tonga, memorable for her swims with Joe in the warm, nonstop rain, Harriet had contacted Mike Freed about the possibility of transforming the Thunderbird Lodge into a resort similar to the Post Ranch Inn. It is probably no coincidence that she had stayed at Mike Freed's Jean-Michel Cousteau Fiji Islands Resort just before coming up with the idea.[42]

After visiting the Dreyfus property several times, Freed's Resort Design Group (RDG) told Harriet that "the historic uses and unique setting make it possible to undertake a joint public/private development that would enhance public access and education in conjunction with providing a unique resort experience." RDG suggested a lease/concession arrangement "where RDG would manage the existing structures and construct additional improvements to enhance public access and provide a financially viable high-end resort." Harriet asked her staff to get to work with RDG on their proposal for an environmentally sensitive public/private partnership as soon as possible.[43]

The letter of intent for the sale of Thunderbird Lodge to ALC had just been signed by Harriet, Dreyfus, and Rogers when Loring Sagan, one of RDG's three owners along with Mike Freed and Herb McLauglin and the principal of Sagan Design Group based at Lake Tahoe, called a meeting with Ron Alling, Phil Caterino, and the Design Group's Gary Furumoto to "officially get the ball rolling." Sagan's memo to Harriet, Freed, and others after the meeting outlined what had to be done within 180 days to get the project off the ground. The tasks were many and included a list of people to contact for support, the need to address development issues such as getting permits from the Tahoe Regional Planning Agency (TRPA) and the state of the Thunderbird Lodge sewage system, and the preparation of a proposal to present to the Forest Service.[44]

The proposal made jointly by RDG and ALC that Harriet sent to Bob Harris at the U.S. Forest Service (USFS) in early May 1996 made the case for converting the Dreyfus/Whittell estate into a commercial resort operated by a private concessionaire. The existing structures would be redeveloped into "a unique lodging experience taking full advantage of their original character and craftsmanship." Some of the revenues from the for-profit lodge would be used to preserve the site and provide access for the general public to the lakefront and to an educational/interpretive center. It was a public/private partnership designed to address the USFS objections to owning and managing the buildings. In the likely event that the acquisition of the Thunderbird Lodge property occurred in advance of the completion of USFS planning procedures and contracting requirements for implementing a public/private partnership, ALC offered to post a bond of at least $1 million to pay for the costs of managing the facilities until the USFS reached an agreement with a private partner.[45]

On the same day that Harriet forwarded the RDG/ALC proposal to the Forest Service, she wrote Dreyfus and Rogers to advise them of ALC's progress at the end of the second phase of due diligence toward completing the land exchange to fund the purchase of Thunderbird Lodge. She explained that she hoped to add the Thunderbird property to ALC's already existing assembled land exchange agreement. That approach would sidestep BLM's refusal to accept a new exchange proposal. She also reported that she had contracts with four developers for BLM lands in Las Vegas, that the issues raised by the environmental assessment were being addressed, and that a title company might have a solution for eliminating the title exception limiting use of the Thunderbird Lodge property to private residential purposes. ALC had made the $400,000 deposit due at the end of the second phase a few days previously.

Harriet ended her letter to Dreyfus and Rogers by asserting, "I am confident that we will be successful in completing this transaction." She had to be confident. ALC now had $500,000 riding on the successful completion of the Thunderbird Lodge transaction.[46]

Harriet and ALC had three months until the closing date mandated by the sale agreement to resolve all of the issues impeding the Thunderbird deal. Harriet's conviction that she could—that she must—do the Thunderbird deal powered her through the next few months, but confidence had to be backed by results. She had to deliver what she promised by July 29 or pay $1.5 million to keep trying.

Harriet kept moving forward. She made more trips to D.C. and Las Vegas to promote the land exchange that continued to be hung up on the problem of the buildings. Responding to a letter from ALC director Joseph Fink to Secretary Babbitt, an underling in BLM's Washington office reiterated the "concern about the significant investment that would be required to make the facilities accessible to the public and to provide for the long-term management, operation, and maintenance of the lodge and other improvements on the estate" and stated that Harriet was "very much aware of the agencies' concerns in this regard."[47]

Joe Fink, who retired as president of Dominican University in 2011, had been a member of ALC's executive committee for about a year when he wrote to Babbitt. A longtime client of Harriet's husband, he was introduced to ALC when Joe Burgess said, "I want you to come talk to Harriet about coming on the board of the American Land Conservancy."

Fink asked, "What is that?"

Burgess answered, "Harriet will explain it to you, but it has people on it like Martin Litton and David Brower and Stuart Udall and Brock Evans."

Fink felt that the ALC board was "not his crowd," but he agreed to talk to Harriet anyway. They went out to dinner, and some time after the second glass of wine, Joe Fink asked Harriet why she was interested in having him on the board. His management skills, she said. ALC was growing and needed structure and organization.

"How do you get your revenue?" was his next question. Harriet mentioned a number of sources: land exchanges, fund-raising, the Department of the Interior, borrowing from nonprofits or banks. Fink and Harriet went round and round about funding sources for about half an hour, then Harriet said, "I'll tell you more about this, but I have to get a red-eye to Washington now" and left.

Joe Fink turned to Joe Burgess and asked, "How do you get your revenue?"

Burgess answered, "Well, Harriet explained it to you, didn't she?"

After she left, Fink told Burgess that he wasn't sure the board was for him, but then Joe Burgess told him that the annual board meetings were at the Post Ranch Inn. Joe Fink said he would join.[48]

The land exchange for Thunderbird hit another snag when a draft audit by the Department of the Interior suggested that BLM land exchanges may have cost taxpayers $12.2 million. Nevada Congressman John Ensign then called for a halt to all exchanges in Nevada. Harriet referred to the audit as a bump in the road that would not stop the exchange for Thunderbird, but she was "not going to sit around and see what happens." She said the property "is a treasure, and we should get on with it." For her, that meant looking for interim financing until the exchange was approved. ALC had a deadline to make the payment to Dreyfus and Rogers. Harriet had to find the money.[49]

Looking for funding, Harriet wrote one potential donor, "Everybody has an agenda for the buildings but nobody wants to pay for anything. It's going to be dicey to pull this off but we're doing the best we can." She continued, "as a result of discussion with Secretary Babbitt, we have agreed to also raise the funds for the purchase of the buildings themselves from private sources, thus the federal government will not pay for the cost of the buildings. Nor will they be responsible for the maintenance and management of the buildings." Harriet—writing perhaps in jest but still showing her growing frustration—admitted that she "may consider retirement from this business or maybe I'll run for office" once the Thunderbird acquisition was completed.[50]

With the RDG proposal on the table, ALC explored another possible option for the buildings. Phil Caterino arranged a tour of Thunderbird Lodge in mid-July for Ron James, Nevada's state historic preservation officer (SHPO), and a member of his staff along with the director and a board member of

Nevada's Cultural Affairs Commission. Phil, Harriet, and Liz Laxalt joined them for the tour and provided them with background information.

Nevada's SHPO was impressed. He enclosed the draft of a proposal for having the Nevada Department of Museums, Library and Arts (MLA) assume responsibility for managing the Thunderbird Lodge buildings with his thank-you letter to Harriet for a great tour. According to the MLA, "there are obvious advantages to running the Thunderbird Lodge as a historic/public facility." Besides protecting environmentally sensitive lands, "the historical and architectural significance of the complex makes it one of the most important cultural resources in the Tahoe Basin. It will rival the famed Vikingsholm in Emerald Bay and will exceed that facility for accessibility."

The SHPO and MLA were enthusiastic, but their efforts never seemed to have gotten any traction. They went no further than what Harriet might have called "happy talk." Phil Caterino told me that Ron James—a stalwart historic preservationist and coauthor with Susan James of *Castle in the Sky: George Whittell Jr. and the Thunderbird Lodge*—later said that he would tear down the buildings in a heartbeat if it meant saving the land.[51]

Harriet had called on Phil Caterino to help with her projects ever since her days at Trust for Public Land. Phil first met Harriet when he did a study for the Friends of Hope Valley—an organization that Harriet had helped the Sierra Club and two individual supporters found in 1986—that convinced Alpine County to support the purchase of Hope Valley's high mountain meadows. Harriet worked on Hope Valley for ten years while she was at TPL and conveyed more than twenty-six thousand acres into public ownership, funded mostly with LWCF monies and some small exchanges.[52]

Phil helped again when Harriet was having a problem getting a rancher to agree to an option on his land. Harriet couldn't figure out why. When Phil saw the "hippy guys" she was sending out in a VW van to talk to the rancher, he knew what had to be done. He offered to go talk to the rancher himself. Harriet agreed and gave him a $100 bill to pay for the option. Phil put on his cowboy boots, drove to the ranch in a pick-up truck, and made a deal on a handshake.

Phil got another insight into how Harriet operated the first time he picked her up at the airport when she arrived on one of her whirlwind visits to Las Vegas. He parked his car and went inside to meet her and help carry whatever she had brought with her. When they connected and he explained what he was doing, she exclaimed, "I don't have anything to carry. Never come in. Just come by and grab me." Her message was clear: we have lots to do and no time to fool around. Phil trailed her as she raced out of the airport. He said he never could keep up with her, even wearing running shoes.

Phil Caterino's work as president of the nonprofit environmental planning and design firm Alpengroup, which he founded in 1981, had connected him with Jack Dreyfus and other wealthy clients. He became the project manager for all of the Dreyfus lands at Lake Tahoe. He oversaw the restoration and the construction of an addition to the Thunderbird Lodge after the Dreyfus purchase. Money made from people such as Dreyfus who could afford to pay him financed his passion for protecting natural resources such as Lake Tahoe through land acquisitions, surveys, environmental impact reports and feasibility studies, studies of aquatic invasives and submerged trees, and even the design of the Lake Tahoe California license plate.

Over the years, Harriet called on Phil often, especially for help with projects in Nevada. When she needed someone deeply involved in the Lake Tahoe community to strive valiantly for the preservation of the Thunderbird Lodge and its nearly mile-long stretch of pristine shoreline, Harriet enlisted Phil Caterino in her crusade.[53]

During the run-up to the closing deadline of July 29, Harriet kept in close touch with Martin Litton. Martin picked her up in his plane at the Oakland airport for a quick trip to Lake Tahoe in late May for one of the many tours of the Thunderbird Lodge conducted to gain support for its acquisition. The guests for the Memorial Day tour were Senator Harry Reid and his staff. After his tour, Senator Reid said, "It would be a shame if this window of opportunity that we have to preserve this for the public were lost. I don't know how we are going to do it. We are going to try to be inventive."[54]

A glider pilot in World War II, Martin had been flying Harriet on conservation missions for years. He piloted a vintage Cessna 195. Martin called it "a perfect flying machine." He used his shoulder to rotate the propeller blades once or twice before hopping in and starting the engine. Smoke always rose from the engine as it roared to life—just a little oil burning off—before Martin headed down the runway. Once in flight, the engine had a habit of "burping"—quitting for a moment before restarting.

One rainy day when Harriet was flying to Oregon with Martin, an oil line blew and sprayed oil all over the windshield. Martin landed the plane on a muddy grass strip with his head hanging out of the window to see where he was going. They hiked into town, found someone to patch the oil line, and took off again. After that, Joe told Harriet, "That's it. You're not going to fly with Martin anymore." But Joe later acknowledged that forbidding Harriet to do something didn't mean she wouldn't do it.[55]

Just before meeting Russell on July 20 to work on ALC's request to extend the closing date, Harriet met Martin for lunch at Sinbad's, their favorite place in San Francisco to convene for the midday meal. Sinbad's wasn't far from Harriet's office, and Martin could park there easily at no charge after driving from his home in Portola Valley. Their regular lunches at Sinbad's usually were at least two-martini affairs, but with the possible collapse of the Thunderbird deal hanging over their heads, they may have abstained that day in favor of brainstorming strategies for keeping the deal alive. As Senator Reid had commented, they needed to be inventive.[56]

They also needed time to be inventive. ALC paid a steep price for that time. Harriet's nonprofit made an additional nonrefundable deposit of $1.5 million on July 29 and agreed to nonrefundable monthly payments of $310,000 (8 percent of the purchase price) due January 1, February 1, and March 1, 1997, for an extension of the closing date to March 31, 1997. ALC also agreed to provide Dreyfus and Rogers with clear evidence that BLM was committed to proceed with the land exchange by December 31, 1996, and that the exchange would be completed by March 31, 1997. Writing to Thunderbird's owners, Harriet reiterated her "firm belief that we can successfully complete this project" and stated, "ALC's willingness to continue to invest substantial resources in this project is evidenced by our work to date and our financial commitment."[57]

Harriet believed and put money that she didn't have yet behind her belief, even though Russell advised against it. Russell said, "Harriet did not accept my counsel on Dreyfus. She kept going on Dreyfus. My job, as a lawyer, was to say, 'Here are your choices. Okay, that's your choice, now I have to saddle up and try to make that choice work for you.'"[58]

Harriet later said, "There are a lot of zeroes out there. I bet the store on it." Perhaps one of her favorite phrases, "the Lord will provide," crossed her mind as she signed the amendment to the agreement of sale documenting ALC's commitment to pay hundreds of thousands of dollars to Dreyfus and Rogers.[59]

With the purchase of more time, the fight to save Thunderbird Lodge continued. The League to Save Lake Tahoe (LSLT) held its annual luncheon on the grounds of the Dreyfus estate in early August, giving 357 prospective supporters the opportunity to visit the property that previously they only had been able to glimpse from a boat. Commenting on the newspaper write-up of the event, Harriet said, "That will probably be the only time ALC appears in the society column in the *San Francisco Chronicle!*"[60]

Ame Hellman, who had recently joined ALC as Nevada project manager, took advantage of the relaxed atmosphere at the 1996 Democratic National Convention to talk at length with the Nevada delegation about the Thunderbird Lodge acquisition. She reported that Senator Bryan was very positive, and Senator Reid was cautiously optimistic. Governor Miller assured Ame that no action would be taken on the acquisition until after the November election. She also talked with Secretary Babbitt, who insisted that the BLM was not in the business of acquiring buildings.[61]

ALC invited the press to tour Thunderbird Lodge at the end of September. With the spectacular views of Lake Tahoe as a backdrop, Harriet stood in the Dreyfus living room where she had sipped champagne with her family more than a year before and told the reporters that she was really worried about the deal. She said, "Dreyfus is sympathetic. I think he genuinely wants it to happen," but time was running out, and he wasn't likely to grant ALC any more extensions. Harriet said, "I think I've pushed that string about as far as I can push it."[62]

Harriet said the land exchange that ALC needed to make the deal work had been delayed because BLM was reviewing its land exchange process. She did not expect any progress on the land exchange until after the November elections. Although the delay reduced the time that ALC had to complete the deal even further, Harriet said that ALC had already identified surplus BLM lands around Las Vegas that were available for an exchange. She said, "We can move very quickly. We've done five or six months work in one day." As an editorial in the *Reno Gazette-Journal* declared, "if anybody can swing a deal, it's the American Land Conservancy."[63]

Harriet and her ALC team pushed the deal forward, taking advantage of opportunities whenever, however, wherever they arose. The camel's nose kept nudging under the tent. Phil Caterino organized many more tours to showcase the Thunderbird Lodge property and connected with many in the Lake Tahoe community to promote the project. Harriet met frequently with BLM and Forest Service staff. She talked with potential financial partners about purchasing Thunderbird Lodge and holding it until ALC completed the land exchange. Ame pursued the possibility of a Friends of Thunderbird Lodge group to fund-raise for the acquisition. Harriet kept her finger on the political pulse by calling and meeting with the Nevada senators and their staffs.[64]

But ALC seemed to be getting nowhere. Babbitt persisted in his opposition to the Thunderbird exchange. BLM's Ann Morgan insisted that she was too busy and needed to complete ongoing exchanges before taking on new exchanges. She also said she wanted to wait for a decision on the bill Senators Bryan and Reid introduced regarding the sale of Nevada's public lands before considering the Thunderbird Lodge proposal. None of the investors contacted about a financial partnership were willing to join with ALC to save Thunderbird Lodge.

Then Fritzi Huntington, a past president and current member of the League to Save Lake Tahoe who had cochaired the LSLT August luncheon at Thunderbird Lodge, contacted ALC to suggest a possible solution to the difficulties that the buildings on the Dreyfus estate presented. She called Harriet in early November to tell her that Charles Goldman, director of the Tahoe Research Group at UC Davis, was interested in using the buildings as a research site in partnership with the University of Nevada, Reno (UNR). Three days after her call, Harriet contacted Goldman and started the process that led to an agreement with UNR to assist in the acquisition and management of the Thunderbird Lodge buildings.[65]

UNR's participation in the Thunderbird project offered a way out of the problem that had plagued the effort to do a land exchange for the property from the beginning: what to do with the buildings that the federal government did not want. Support for UNR's involvement developed quickly. Mick Laxalt wrote Senator Reid a few weeks after Fritzi Huntington's first conversation with Harriet about "the new and logjam-breaking developments. The ALC itself, at great risk, is willing to buy the structures at fair market value. Next, President Joe Crowley and the University of Nevada, Reno, are willing to lease them with an option to buy within three years. ...THIS IS A PERFECT SOLUTION TO THE DILEMMA."[66]

Dennis Murphy, president of the Center for Conservation Biology and Society for Conservation Biology at Stanford University and a close personal friend of Secretary Babbitt's, added his voice to the growing support. Murphy reminded Babbitt of how he had championed land exchanges over the years. He described the property as "a Lake Tahoe waterfront parcel of incomparable scenic and biotic values." He applauded the solution to the vexing problem of the Thunderbird Lodge structures that the offer of the University of Nevada to manage the buildings as a biological field station promised.[67]

In a letter to Babbitt, UNR President Joseph Crowley confirmed the university's willingness to take over the buildings. He laid out a three-pronged plan for the use of the Thunderbird Lodge buildings: supervised public access including tours and a conference center, development of a field research station to explore the Lake Tahoe environment, and instruction of undergraduate and graduate students in ecology and conservation biology.[68]

Harriet presented Babbitt with the UNR solution in person. She took the red-eye to D.C. arriving on December 20, met with the secretary at 5 p.m. then immediately flew back to California. On Christmas Eve, she reported to Dreyfus and Rogers that Babbitt had committed to supporting the exchange given ALC's new concept for handling the structures on the property. Babbitt agreed "that it would be a shame to miss this opportunity for public ownership, and a greater shame to see the property end up in the hands of those who might want to use it for subdivision or gaming purposes." Harriet ended her report by saying, "I hope you understand that I am doing everything humanly possible to meet t[he] demands of the acquisition and reach the goal which is so earnestly desired by so many."[69]

And with that, ALC wire transferred $310,000 to Dreyfus and Rogers on January 1, 1997, advising them that ALC did not have written evidence of the status of the land exchange for Thunderbird but expected to have it by February 1, the date of the next deposit payment. ALC used $100,000 of its funds to make the payment and borrowed the rest.[70]

No sooner were hopes for the Thunderbird acquisition raised than they were dashed again. By January 10, Babbitt was backpedaling on his commitment to Harriet. Babbitt's spokesman said that the Interior secretary liked the general outline of the UNR plan but had decided that he would rather continue to work with the Nevada congressional delegation on proposed legislation for selling instead of exchanging public lands. Perhaps Harriet had taken away more from her December conversation with Babbitt than he intended, but I think it more likely that he agreed to the exchange in Harriet's persuasive presence, then later reconsidered. Harriet didn't mention Babbitt's late-December commitment to the exchange publicly, but said, "It breaks my heart to lose this opportunity."[71]

Still Harriet persevered. She spent more than seventy-five hours in January working the Thunderbird deal, but by the end of the month, with another $310,000 payment due on February 1, Phil Caterino sensed that she was about ready to give up. When he returned to Lake Tahoe after meeting with Harriet in San Francisco on January 28, he serendipitously found a cartoon on his desk that he sent to her immediately with the news that TRPA had just designated the acquisition of Thunderbird a priority project. The cartoon portrayed a pelican attempting to devour a frog. The small frog, trapped in the bird's mouth and about to be swallowed, was desperately squeezing his captor's throat with his hands to avoid his imminent destruction. The caption inscribed below the drawing: Don't *EVER* give up. Even though it was late at night when she picked up the fax, Harriet got on the phone to Phil. Laughing, she thanked him and admitted, "I was on the verge of quitting."[72]

Harriet didn't quit, but she did ask Dreyfus and Rogers to give her an extension until February 17 to make the next $310,000 deposit payment. Her request was granted. Harriet hoped to secure another loan, but she had to write Dreyfus and Rogers on February 18, one day after the deposit payment was due, that even though she had the full support of the Nevada congressional delegation for the acquisition of the Thunderbird Lodge estate by a public land exchange, it was unlikely that ALC would be able to complete the acquisition by the March 31 closing date and so ALC would not make the February deposit payment.[73]

Back in September, Harriet had predicted that Dreyfus and Rogers would not be willing to push the closing date beyond March 31. She was right. Time had run out. Jack Dreyfus answered Harriet's letter immediately. He wrote, "Unfortunately, because of ALC's failure to make the February Payment, together with its inability to give appropriate assurances concerning a definite closing date (the original closing date, prior to extension, was July 29, 1996), we are terminating the Agreement of Sale between myself, the Dreyfus Charitable Foundation, and Bill [Rogers], as seller and ALC, as buyer." Terminated but with a small ray of hope. Dreyfus and Rogers had not completely closed the door on selling the Thunderbird Lodge to ALC. Dreyfus suggested that Harriet contact him if she would like to arrange a meeting to discuss the property.[74]

No surprise that Harriet wrote Dreyfus one week later that they were working on a proposal to reinstate the sale agreement, and she hoped to be able to meet with him in New York as soon as it was ready. Mick Laxalt also wrote Dreyfus to implore him to give ALC another chance to close the deal for the public acquisition of the Thunderbird Lodge because

> it is warranted and justified by the immense and heroic . . . effort put into this transaction by Harriet, Liz and Phil Catarino [sic] and many, many other people, the vast majority of whom want nothing but a good outcome for the people, not themselves, and the transaction can and will close, given your patience and tolerance and an appropriate extension which will allow things to fall into place, and—not to allow Harriet the time to close when she has fought tooth and nail and at great personal risk to bring this matter to the proverbial "five yard line" would simply not be fair.[75]

Moved by the threat—indeed, the likelihood—that the opportunity to acquire the Thunderbird Lodge for the public would slip away, UNR's Joe Crowley and his good friend and supporter, Senator Harry Reid, stepped into the breach. Crowley flew to D.C. in early March to meet with Reid and the rest of the Nevada delegation—Senator Richard Bryan, Congressmen John Ensign, and Joe Gibbons—to explore alternative strategies for purchasing the estate. Afterward, a Reid spokeswoman said, "We're exploring all avenues," including adding the property to the current public lands bill.[76]

But with no time to wait for government action, Reid contacted Jack Dreyfus and persuaded him to come to D.C. to meet with Secretary Babbitt and the Nevada delegation on March 20. Before the meeting, Reid told Paul Laxalt, "We have a real good shot at making the acquisition happen." His optimism was well placed. Dreyfus agreed to give ALC until the end of the year to acquire Thunderbird but said, "I probably will not extend the option again." He wanted to use the sale proceeds to finance medical research into the drug Dilantin that was approved for treating epilepsy but that Dreyfus also claimed was effective for more than seventy disease symptoms. For Dreyfus, "this medicine is more important than preserving one hundred forty acres." Besides, having already sold ten thousand acres to the Forest Service, he said, "I think I've done my duty to Lake Tahoe more than anyone else."[77]

Harriet, Dreyfus, and Rogers signed the reinstatement of and third amendment to agreement of sale for the Thunderbird Lodge property on April 17 and 18. The February 20 termination notice was rescinded, and the closing date was extended to not later than December 31, 1997. The extension carried a price tag of $1 million, to be paid in nonrefundable bimonthly deposits of $200,000. ALC already was into the deal for $2,310,000 and was now obliged to pay another $1 million just to stay in the game.[78]

On the same day that Jack Dreyfus had written Harriet to terminate the sale agreement, the White House had made an announcement that highlighted Lake Tahoe and offered a ray of hope for the ultimate purchase of Thunderbird Lodge for the public. President Clinton had decided to convene a summit at Lake Tahoe to discuss the challenges of restoring and protecting the environmental and economic health of the lake and its communities. A White House spokesperson said that the president agreed that Tahoe was an issue of national importance worthy of his time, a place where "the environment is the heart of a healthy economy."[79]

Senators Reid and Bryan had pushed for the summit. When Reid informed the Nevada legislature that it would take place, he said, "The lake is in real trouble. About half the trees up there are dead. Water quality is going downhill, literally, every year." The Forest Service estimated that 30 percent of the Tahoe Basin's two hundred thousand acres of forest were dead. The chances of a devastating forest fire were high. The lake's clarity was decreasing at the rate of more than one foot every year. A ten-inch white disc visible at a depth of 105 feet in 1968 was only visible at a depth of 64.1 feet in 1997. Bryan included the acquisition of Thunderbird Lodge on his list of issues that needed to be considered at the summit, though Reid later said that the estate was not likely to be a priority. Some speculated about the possibility of the president spending the night at Thunderbird during the event.[80]

The summit was scheduled for late July, preceded by June workshops hosted by high-level officials including secretary of the interior Bruce Babbitt and secretary of agriculture Dan Glickman. Workshop topics included Lake Tahoe water quality, forest ecosystem restoration, recreation and tourism, and transportation. As an invitation sent to Harriet for one of the preliminary meetings leading up to the summit noted, "You have a rare, and brief, opportunity to focus the highest level of federal attention on your needs at Lake Tahoe."[81]

Attention was focused on Lake Tahoe, but it did not directly affect the public acquisition of Thunderbird. The president issued an executive order on July 26 that established a federal interagency partnership to promote the well-being of the Lake Tahoe Basin. Forest health, water quality, and research were among the items on the partnership's to-do list—all of which the Thunderbird acquisition would facilitate.[82]

The president further directed his administration to begin acting on the recommendations that came out of the June workshops, including having the Forest Service "continue efforts to acquire environmentally sensitive and valuable parcels of land in the Lake Tahoe Basin. . . ." Nothing specific for Thunderbird but at least a stamp of approval for its acquisition if circumstances permitted.[83]

ALC hoped to increase awareness of the merits of Thunderbird Lodge during the summit by hosting a party there on the evening of July 25. As the sun set, the governor of Nevada, the assistant secretary of Interior, UNR's president, and staff from congressional and federal agency offices munched crudités, smoked salmon pate on cucumber slices, and pinwheel sandwiches with bay shrimp while sipping wine and mineral water with other guests invited to enjoy the views of Lake Tahoe.[84]

Another glimmer of hope surfaced with the successful passage by the House of Representatives on April 23 of a bill introduced by Nevada's Congressman Ensign to authorize the auction to private developers of roughly twenty-seven thousand acres of federally owned land in the Las Vegas area. The bill, which eventually became known as the Southern Nevada Public Land Management Act, designated most of the proceeds from the sale of the federal lands for the purchase of environmentally sensitive lands in Nevada. It still had to be approved by the Senate, where Senator Bryan had introduced similar legislation, but the news boosted ALC's chances of securing funding for Thunderbird. The Forest Service's Dave Marlow, a strong supporter of the Thunderbird purchase, said, "If it goes through, the Dreyfus property may be one of the first to be acquired." Testifying before a Nevada Assembly committee about the bill, Bryan agreed that some of the proceeds could be used to help acquire the Dreyfus property.[85]

Harriet believed that Thunderbird was high on the list of the government's priorities for land purchases if the legislation passed, but she also knew that she had to continue searching for other funding. She couldn't wait for the bill to work its way through Congress with a closing date for Thunderbird set for the end of 1997.

As summer slid into fall, and the deadline for closing Thunderbird approached, Harriet logged more than four hundred hours on the acquisition at her usual breakneck pace interspersed with occasional diversions

such as going to the opera—she had always been an avid fan of opera—
and a one-week vacation in early August. Other interruptions included
her six-hour interview with the office of the inspector general as part of
the investigation into possible improprieties connected with the Deer
Creek land exchange, a Land Trust Rally in Savannah, and the annual
Board of Councillors retreat at Post Ranch Inn, not to mention the other
ALC projects she was juggling.[86]

With the land exchange that was crucial to the public acquisition of
Thunderbird Lodge moving at a snail's pace—the ongoing OIG investigation made staff in the BLM and Forest Service field offices exceptionally
cautious, slowing down an already ponderous process—ALC explored
several avenues to facilitate completion of the exchange. One possibility
involved the Del Webb Corporation.[87]

Like other developers in the Las Vegas area, Del Webb wanted land
owned by BLM to build new housing for the rapidly growing city. Del
Webb hoped to do a land exchange to acquire the necessary land but was
about $50 million short of having enough privately owned property to
offer the federal government. One day in the spring of 1997, as Del Webb
vice president Scott Higginson sat in a rental car during a visit to the Lake
Tahoe area, he told Phil Caterino how critical it was for him to find enough
offered lands to make Del Webb's Las Vegas exchange work. When Phil
told him that ALC had one property—Thunderbird—that would meet Del
Webb's exchange needs, Higginson leapt out of the car so fast he hit his
head on the door in his eagerness to hear what Phil had to say. Higginson
called Del Webb's president right after talking to Phil, and negotiations
with ALC soon began.[88]

The dialogue between ALC and Del Webb went on for months. In the
meantime, Harriet tested the waters with other potential investors by suggesting a bridge loan to finance the purchase of Thunderbird by the deadline of December 31, 1997, that would be repaid once the land exchange
was completed. She also held discussions with the city of North Las Vegas
to consider reactivating the exchange that originally had figured in the discussions for the Galena acquisition.[89]

Like Nevada congressmen Ensign and Gibbons who wrote Interior
Appropriations Subcommittee Chairman Ralph Regula to ask for Land

and Water Conservation Fund monies to make the purchase, Harriet may have hoped for federal funding, but I suspect she agreed with Senator Reid, a member of the Senate Appropriations Committee, that "there are going to be about five hundred other parcels and forty-nine other states competing for this money. When you ask the committee for $50 million for a Nevada project—I don't see this happening." And knowing the congressional process as well as she did, I imagine she was not counting on help from the Southern Nevada Land Management Act that was working its way through the Senate after House passage.[90]

In the end, it came down to making a deal with Del Webb. At first, Harriet had welcomed the Del Webb opportunity. Adding Thunderbird to an exchange that Del Webb already had in the BLM pipeline avoided the moratorium on new exchanges and expedited the process. But reaching an agreement on their partnership was not easy, especially when Del Webb once suggested buying out ALC and removing the organization from the deal altogether. One of ALC's attorneys didn't even want to mention that proposal to Harriet. Harriet also was concerned about Del Webb's commitment to UNR and to getting the land into public ownership. At one point, she wrote "Bad Deal" on one of the memos outlining the essential elements of a cooperative agreement between ALC and Del Webb.[91]

Harriet may not have been entirely happy about it but by mid-November, with the end-of-the-year deadline fast approaching, ALC and Del Webb had worked out the terms of their agreement and signed a memorandum of understanding (MOU) for the acquisition of the Thunderbird Lodge property. According to the MOU, ALC and Del Webb planned to work together to acquire the property in a way that allowed them to close pending exchanges and allowed ALC to acquire the improvements for eventual UNR ownership.

The MOU also spelled out the terms of a restructured purchase agreement with Dreyfus and Rogers necessary to accommodate the ALC/Del Webb agreement. The restructured agreement provided for the deposit of the balance of the purchase price (the purchase price less the $3,110,000 already paid by ALC and the $200,000 payment that ALC had to make on or before December 15, 1997) into escrow to be released in phases by

July 1, 1998. ALC and Del Webb had until December 1, 1997, to convince Dreyfus and Rogers to go along with the new plan.[92]

Dreyfus and Rogers were not interested in the new plan. They wanted to close by year end and did not want any contingencies to interfere with full payment of the purchase price. Harriet, Mick Laxalt, and Phil Caterino made a last-minute trip in December to snowy New York to try to persuade them to change their minds. Harriet told them that ALC would get the money. Bill Rogers didn't believe ALC had the money.

Jack Dreyfus asked Phil, "What do you think?"

Phil said, "Harriet has never let me down."

That was enough to keep the deal alive, though not as restructured in the MOU. ALC and Del Webb then proposed a new financing structure that was acceptable to all parties.[93]

Before the final deal was fully in place—ALC had yet to sign an agreement with Del Webb for the acquisition of Thunderbird Lodge and did not have a firm commitment from Dreyfus and Rogers for the new financing structure—ALC had to pay the last $200,000 deposit due on December 15. ALC's financial manager, Chris Jehle, was not at all sure that making the payment was a good idea.

Harriet had hired Chris in August 1995. After he had talked to ALC's accounting consultant, John Kerns, Harriet interviewed him. She didn't ask him a single question during their hour together. Instead, she told him her life story, including how ALC started and her beginnings at TPL.

At the end, Harriet said, "So John Kerns seems to think you're the one. Have I scared you off?"

Chris said, "No," and he was hired.

Chris went into Harriet's office just before the $200,000 deposit was due and said, "This last payment to Dreyfus is going to deplete the line of credit. Why are we doing this? Is there no other way? Do you really want to give this guy the last $200,000 knowing that you don't have a deal in place?" Harriet sat Chris down, laid out all the maps and documents, explained to him why the property was important, why ALC had to do the deal. She explained the game plan and detailed the steps she was going to take.

She said, "We can do this."

Chris wasn't completely convinced, but he made the payment.[94]

Harriet sent a revised and extended resolution to her board on December 19 requesting approval of ALC's purchase of the Thunderbird/Dreyfus property under the new terms of the transaction. She summarized the revised transaction in her letter to Martin Litton:

> Our expectation is that we will acquire the property on or before December 31st, reconveying it to the Del Webb Corporation in a back to back closing. Our contract with Del Webb provides that they will put up $12,000,000 as a down payment on the acquisition. That $12,000,000 payment, in addition to the $3,310,000 payment that ALC has already made to Jack Dreyfus brings the down payment to $15,310,000.
>
> Dreyfus will give a non-recourse purchase money loan for the balance owed him for the balance of the purchase price. ALC will sell the Dreyfus property to the Del Webb Corporation, who will use this land in pending federal land exchanges. ALC is conveying the property to Del Webb for $50,400,000. We are acquiring the property from Jack Dreyfus for $48,500,000.
>
> In addition, we will have an agreement with Del Webb that protects ALC's increment, our payments to date and the $3,400,000 we need to complete the PermaBilt exchange. Further we will have a provision that protects our expected arrangements with the University of Nevada for the conveyance of the buildings and the rights of use associated with the buildings.

Harriet went on, "This is a complicated transaction." Martin, Bob Stephens, and Joseph Fink approved the resolution the day after Christmas.[95]

Harriet signed an agreement of purchase and sale with Del Webb on December 31, 1997, that incorporated the terms of the transaction as outlined for ALC's board. Escrow closed on January 5, 1998.[96]

Announcing the sale in ALC's press release, Harriet said,

> This property is the largest single, privately-owned [*sic*] parcel of land with lake shore frontage in the Tahoe Basin. Its preservation was extremely important not only for its scenic and historic beauty but to allow the University of Nevada, Reno, to develop an important research facility that will even further ensure the environmental viability of the region.

She acknowledged the critical importance of working with Del Webb as part of their ongoing land exchange then concluded, "I'm extremely excited and pleased that we've been able to meet our goal of preserving and protecting for future generations this wonderful, valuable asset."[97]

Kudos came pouring in. Bob Harris expressed the gratitude of many, with his card picturing an upstanding lion pushing his fist into the air and exclaiming, "y-y-e-s-s-s-s-s!" He wrote, "Wow, whoopee, the grandkids are un-ransomed!! What a credit you and your staff are to serving the public so well. How much I appreciate your perseverance, patience, energy, excitement, and all those wonderful attributes you demonstrated in making this happen." Jack Dreyfus wrote, "I am glad that the Thunderbird Lodge and the beautiful addition to it will be in your hands."[98]

Harriet sent thank-yous to her many supporters writing, "We have made the first important step toward completing this transaction. I think at least we are off life-support now."

She also acknowledged, "This has been a hard project and we really had to hang in there and push. It seems that nothing I work on is a slam dunk." And she made it clear, "We have a lot more work to do before it is in public ownership." Or as she put it in another note, "It ain't finished until the fat lady sings."[99]

Harriet summarized what remained to be done to finalize the Thunderbird Lodge transaction in a letter to Martin Litton:

On April 1st we will begin a series of transactions to convey the property to the Forest Service and the University of Nevada, Reno.…

BLM is acquiring Thunderbird by exchange, and will subsequently convey it to the Forest Service. The University of Nevada will acquire the buildings for a research and conference center. The property will be conveyed in phases throughout 1998.…

We still have a number of hurdles to pass, including working with BLM and Del Webb to complete the approval process for disposal of the BLM lands, and with the University of Nevada to raise the funds for them to acquire the buildings. But this first step ensures that the property will not be lost to the public.[100]

There were, indeed, hurdles to be passed, and not all of them were overcome successfully. UNR never did establish its research center at the Thunderbird property. ALC was excluded from "any of the substantive discussions among Del Webb, UNR, and the U.S. Forest Service regarding ownership and use of the Thunderbird Lodge." Del Webb eventually sold the Thunderbird buildings to a newly created nonprofit foundation, the Thunderbird Lodge Preservation Society (TLPS), established to operate for the benefit of UNR. The reported sales price of $9,897,000 was financed by Del Webb.[101]

When TLPS failed to raise the funds to pay off Del Webb after three years, the debt was forgiven. TLPS no longer is affiliated with UNR. Its stated mission is to preserve and protect the Thunderbird Lodge; promote public appreciation and education through public tours, conferences, and forums; and support and participate in programs for the protection of the Lake Tahoe environment.[102]

The phased exchanges for the land did go forward. The first phase, including 86.55 unimproved acres, was completed in July 1998. At the end of the second phase in October 1999, the 140 acres of the Thunderbird/ Dreyfus estate were under the control of the Forest Service. The public now has unobstructed access to all 140 acres except for the area controlled by TLPS, which can be visited on tours by anyone who buys a ticket or reserved for weddings and similar functions by those who have made a significant contribution to the TLPS charitable programs. It was not exactly the outcome that Harriet intended, but it was close enough.[103]

Harriet and ALC had saved nearly one mile of Lake Tahoe shoreline and 140 acres of adjacent land for the public's enjoyment in perpetuity. The erstwhile Dreyfus estate with its spectacular views of Lake Tahoe now welcomes visitors. The surrounding acres are available to hikers. Like the wide-open vistas along the Mount Rose Highway to the north and the breathtaking beauty of Hope Valley to the south, Thunderbird Lodge joined the long list of projects Harriet spearheaded to preserve magnificent landscapes for posterity.

Russell waves on the trail to Parker Mesa Overlook in Topanga State Park, January 2016.
AUTHOR'S COLLECTION

View of downtown Los Angeles from Topanga State Park.
AUTHOR'S COLLECTION

Elizabeth at Parker Mesa Overlook in Topanga State Park, January 2016

Harriet speaking at the August 28, 1994, Galena celebration
ESTHER LITTON

The 8-foot two-man crosscut saw presented to Harriet at the Galena celebration on August 28, 1994
ESTHER LITTON

Looking toward Lake Tahoe from the trail up Mt. Rose, August 2011
AUTHOR'S COLLECTION

The trail up Mt. Wanda at the John Muir Historic Site in Martinez, CA. Elizabeth hiked this way with Leslie and Darrel in July 2011.
AUTHOR'S COLLECTION

John Muir's gravestone

View of Lake Tahoe from Thunderbird Lodge, May 2016
AUTHOR'S COLLECTION

Touring Thunderbird Lodge, May 2016
AUTHOR'S COLLECTION

View of Lake Tahoe from Thunderbird Lodge, May 2016

David Brower, Harriet Burgess, and Martin Litton together at the Thunderbird Lodge

Thunderbird Lodge
AUTHOR'S COLLECTION

Interlude

Grand Canyon

WE ARE IN LAVA COUNTRY NOW. SWIRLING FAN PATTERNS OF LAVA DECO-
rate the canyon walls—the slower it cooled, the darker the lava. Seeing the
lava in 1869, John Wesley Powell wrote, "What a conflict of water and fire
there must have been here! Just imagine a river of molten rock running
down into a river of melted snow. What a seething and boiling of waters;
what clouds of steam rolled into the heavens!"[104]

About a mile upriver from Lava Falls, Vulcan's Anvil protrudes fifty feet
out of the river like an iron fist. A sacred site for Native Americans, the lava
plug is all that's left of a volcano that erupted in the Colorado River about
two hundred thousand years ago. Like the rock all along the edges of the
river, a white skirt rims the bottom of the Anvil where the black lava has
been scoured by high water.

Vulcan's Throne, a cinder cone volcano looming over Lava Falls on
the North Rim, is one of many volcanoes that spewed lava flows around
and into the Grand Canyon within the past million years. Streams of lava
solidified and formed dams as high as fifteen hundred feet in the area of
Lava Falls, creating a lake that may have reached as far back as Lee's Ferry.
Eventually the lake overflowed the dams and carved a path for the Colorado River, leaving Lava Falls as a daunting reminder of volcanic activity to
test the skills of those who dare to run it.[105]

Lava Falls is arguably the most difficult rapid on a river of difficult rapids. A
ten on the difficulty scale of one to ten. The Big Daddy. A combination of

the huge waves of Granite and the chaos of Hermit. In the 1950s, Martin Litton always walked around and lined his boats through the rapid.

By the time he was rowing dories in the 1960s, Martin had figured out how to run Lava. The first time he was on a trip with his son John and author François Leydet. They wanted to run Lava. Martin said, "No, we can't run that. That's a rapid you can't run." But then a group of young guys showed up, gave Martin a hand lining his boat, and told him they were planning to run Lava in rafts. And Martin changed his mind. François ran the rapid over the fall in the middle. From then on, Martin and his boatmen ran Lava. And Martin was still running Lava Falls in one of his beloved dories at age eighty-seven.[106]

Martin ran Lava on Harriet's first river trip through the Grand Canyon in 1973. All of the other passengers were going to walk around—including Harriet's daughter Julie—but Harriet wanted to run the rapid. Martin said, "Sure, come with me." Harriet climbed into Martin's dory without telling Julie, who watched from the top of a nearby hill as the dory sliced into the rapid and flipped. Harriet tucked her head between her knees and wrapped her arms around her ankles. She took a deep breath and went through the rapid like a tennis ball in a washing machine. She ended up on the other side of the river part way through Lava Rapid. The next boatman, a trainee rowing a raft, went after the dory, tied it to his leg, and pulled it out of the rapid. The dory's paint was scratched where Harriet had tried to hang on. The next boatman cut out of the rapid to retrieve Harriet, then finished his run through Lava. Afterward Harriet told everyone, "It was the most exhilarating experience I ever had in my life."[107]

"Holy shit." The words slip out unbidden after I take my first look at the Lava Falls Rapid. A short stretch of churning, muddy water. Waves tripping over each other. The roar of the roiling rapid like heavy rain pounding a metal roof. Water speeding by at 17,200 cubic feet per second. And, because of changes in the shoreline, it's now more dangerous to walk around it than to go through it.

The night before Lava, we all ate a special "Last Supper." Roger grilled a marinated pork loin and served it with chutney and applesauce. Sides of garlic mashed potatoes, broccoli, and carrots. Salad. No dessert. The night before, Kerstin shaved her legs and armpits—a pre-Lava tradition that she learned from the first women to row the rapid. Today she dresses in her brightest and newest color, this time hot pink. And she washes her boat. All part of her Lava "procedure." Roger washes his boat, too. Signs of respect for the Colorado River and its most dangerous rapid. Go into the river clean. The night before, the group decided to run Lava before lunch. That way the boatmen will be able to eat. The night before, I woke at 2:30 a.m. thinking about Lava. My first time, and no reassuring rituals. The bees are swarming.

Roger is our boatman for the day. Russell asked to ride in his dory days before figuring the veteran boatman would be our best bet for a successful run through wild and crazy Lava Falls. Roger is chatty as he rows the twelve miles to Lava Falls under cloudy skies. He tells us that two-thirds of the boatmen are men, one-third are women, that some boatmen are too chauvinistic to lead trips that include women rowing the dories, that no motors are allowed on the river after September 15. That he usually rows *Roaring Springs*, but it's getting a new paint job so he's in *Paria*. That photographer John Blaustein—Harriet's old friend, a boatman on her first trip—is rowing a baggage raft on the trip behind us because Blaustein thinks the light is best in September. But as soon as we reach Lava Falls, he is all business.

It's 12:04 p.m. when we stop to scout the rapid. According to the astrological forecast that Nancy, one of the doctors on our trip, shared with us, it is important to run Lava after noon. Our timing is good. All of the boatmen go over the plan for running the rapid. It is the first time through Lava for three of them—Morgan in *Lost Creek*, and both baggage raft rowers—so Duffy takes some extra time with them to discuss today's rapid conditions and the best approach.

Roger, more serious and focused than I have ever seen him, looks intently at the rapid and considers the best route through. Left. Left to avoid the Ledge Hole. The Ledge Hole, formed by four large basalt boulders during a flood in 1957, is just waiting to suck you in and (eventually) spit you out. The entry point is narrow, about two feet wider than our dory, which is a little over six feet wide and sixteen feet long. If Roger hits it just right, the run through Lava will be relatively easy. If he misses it, the dory may flip, and somebody may die.

We are going in two groups of three, two dories and one baggage raft in each group. Duffy in *Escalante* first. Rumor has it that Duffy flipped his last time through Lava. Then we will go next in Roger's *Paria* and serve as Duffy's rescue boat if needed. (With the second group watching us from shore, the big question is: where is our rescue boat?) Brian's baggage raft is the last of the first group.

Roger and Duffy take off their shirts and strap on their life jackets and helmets. We are already settled into our usual seats in Roger's dory—Russell and Michael in the bow, Gail and I in the stern—life jackets and helmets fixed in place. Duffy glides into the racing river. Roger starts the camera attached to a post at the rear of his dory, jumps into the rower's seat in the middle of the dory, and follows.

Looking ahead, I can't see the rapid. What I see is the river disappearing in front of me. Duffy's dory disappears. I try to remember what I am supposed to do if the dory flips and we are dumped into middle of the maelstrom. Roger gave us instructions just before the lookout: get back to the boat if you can; press the release on the line that runs around the boat's stern; climb on the bottom of the boat and grab the flip line; flip the boat right side up. All of this in forty-five seconds or less before the dory drops into Lower Lava. Right. If you can't get back to the boat, go down the rapid in the defensive swimming position: on your back, feet first, head resting on the life jacket's pillow. Then either get picked up by a boat or get to shore before you are swept into Lower Lava. OK. I grab the strap in front of me with my left hand and the gunwale with my right.

Roger rows for the edge, points the bow at the waves. We are drawn quickly into the rapid. Waves are coming at us from all sides. Roger rows, and we high side the waves, pushing our weight against the force of the water. Frothing waves, way over my head, threaten to swamp us, but the dory's bow rises high in the air, then lands gracefully in a wave's trough before taking another hit. We smash through the waves or ride high over them like riding a horse over a jump. For fourteen seconds. And then we're on the other side. Alive below Lava!

No time for more than a few celebratory yells. Roger heads for the shore where Duffy has already pulled in and unloaded all of his passengers but one. He jumps out, stakes the boat, asks Russell to watch it, then jumps in

Duffy's boat. They take off and position themselves just below the rapid to wait for the next two dories, Kerstin's *Dark Canyon* and Morgan's *Lost Creek*, and Amber's baggage raft. Brian's baggage raft also has negotiated Lava successfully—just barely; a big wave nearly pushed him over in the middle of the rapid—and is standing ready to help on the other side of the river.

I stand on the shore, peering at the rapid. Kerstin's dory appears, a small speck in the distance. It dips into the rapid, is clearly visible for a few seconds, then is obscured by waves and spray until the bright aqua-blue prow of the boat pokes through the water to announce its progress. Sometimes only the prow is visible; sometimes only the occupants of the dory are visible in their bright orange life jackets and yellow helmets; sometimes nothing is visible. Then they're through! And Morgan's dory only a few seconds behind. And Amber's baggage raft behind Morgan.

At lunch, after Lava, my fellow passengers and I are smiling, laughing, reliving the excitement. The crew is more subdued. Duffy hugs his wife, Kerstin. Roger, Duffy's uncle, looks quietly satisfied. Morgan sits on a sand ledge, elbows on his knees, head down.

There's one last Lava ritual just before dinner. Amber invites Lava newbies to pick a costume from her supply. She already is dressed for the occasion: sky blue and white knee-length tights overlaid with cutaway chaps and topped with a jeans vest, bikini top, and hoodie. Amber quickly outfits everyone else. A long pink polyester dress for Jim, her assistant. Green snakeskin pants and a multicolored print halter top for Michael. Striped shorts, Hawaiian shirt, and green baseball cap for Russell. A fuzzy elephant head for Steve. A superhero outfit for Bill with blue tights and red cape. A pink and green nightgown for Liz, the oldest in our group in her mid-seventies. A crayon sheath for her granddaughter, Marguerite. A blond wig for Brian. A pirate getup for Roger (even though it is his 166th trip through Lava). An orange gauze wrap with lots of silver, dangly, jingly decorations for me.

We Lava survivors relax into the lazy rhythm of the river on our penultimate day in the Grand Canyon.

Ocotillo backlit by the rising sun. Barrel cacti like sentinels perching on a rock edge. Silvery brittle bush growing out of a rock ledge like flowers in a vase. Invasive tamarisk; unwanted immigrant. Round sprays of yucca like silvery green porcupine quills. A great blue heron gliding by, settling on an offshore rock, flying away, a blue blur. An audience of egrets. A peregrine falcon killing a bird overhead, its feathers drifting into the river. Canyon walls etched and chiseled by the Colorado River. Images to remember.

Stopping at mile 202, we eat lunch and then hike through boulders and up a canyon, past a mescal pit, to take a close look at pictographs painted red on rosy rock walls by Native Americans thousands of years ago.

Kerstin lets our dory slide into 209 Mile Rapid. Slipping past a hole and an eddy, we emerge dry on the other side. A little farther on, Little Bastard bares its fangs—small sharp rocks jutting from the river's surface—on both sides of the river but doesn't bite. Farther on still, an orange travertine bowl shaped like a pumpkin filled with bitter green, arsenic-laced water.

In camp that night, we share e-mail addresses.

Chapter Seven

Crown Jewel of the Coast

Hearst Ranch

I love this ranch. It is wonderful. I love the sea and I love the moun-
tains and the hollows in the hills and the shady places in the creeks and
the fine old oaks and even the hot brushy hillsides—full of quail—and
the canyons—full of deer. It is a wonderful place. I would rather spend
a month at the ranch than anyplace in the world. —WILLIAM RAN-
DOLPH HEARST, 1917[1]

Remember the greatest triumph in the world, Hearst Ranch.
—MARTIN LITTON, 2008[2]

NOT FAR FROM THE ENTRANCE TO HEARST CASTLE, ABOUT A MILE NORTH
on Highway 1 and directly across from Old San Simeon Village, Russell
and I turned right onto the road that leads to Hearst Ranch. As we pulled
up to the closed gate flanked by stone walls, I saw a long-standing sign that
confirmed our arrival at Piedra Blanca Rancho—the name first given to the
ranch because of the large rocks bleached white by seabird guano lining the
nearby shoreline of San Simeon Bay. Crafted with cutouts of cattle, trees,
and a cowboy riding the range, the open wrought iron sign framed a view of
the rolling golden hills of the ranch that the Hearst family has called home
for seven generations.

The ranch covers more than eighty-two thousand acres. That's about
128 square miles. Five times the size of Manhattan. Two and a half
times the size of the city and county of San Francisco. Bigger than all of

Sacramento. George Hearst purchased the first 50,000 acres of the Piedra Blanca Rancho from Jose de Jesus Pico in 1865. His son, William Randolph Hearst, added 154,000 acres to the ranch in 1925. At its peak in the 1930s, Hearst Ranch spread over 250,000 acres until debt forced the sale of 153,865 acres to the federal government for Hunter Liggett Military Reservation in 1940. It always has been a cattle ranch, using the same methods for producing grass-fed beef for more than 150 years.[3]

But the Hearst Ranch is much more than a cattle-raising operation. Stretching inland thirteen miles east from the rugged coastline over the Santa Lucia Mountains to Lake Nacimiento and eighteen miles south to Pico Cove from the northern border at the Monterey County line, the ranch is a scenic wonderland boasting extraordinary natural resources and abundant habitat fostered by the stewardship of one family for one and a half centuries. Its biological diversity is an environmentalist's dream. Almost every habitat type present in California exists on the ranch. Grasslands, chaparral, oak woodlands, pine forests, marsh, and riparian habitats harbor more than one thousand different species of plants and wildlife. Steelhead trout, the California red-legged frog, and the western pond turtle are there. Eagles, hawks, and snowy plovers are there. The cobweb thistle, Santa Lucia fir, and multiple species of oak and ceanothus are there.

I am there in the spring of 2011 to get my first glimpse of the ranch and its many resources. We had been waiting at the gate to the ranch only a few minutes when Cliff Garrison, the ranch manager for the last eleven of the twenty-five years he has worked there, pulled up in his four-door white pickup. He opened the gate, then came over to our car to introduce himself. A big man with a white mustache and friendly eyes under his tan cowboy hat, Cliff confirmed our identity and asked us to follow him for about a half mile to the ranch office. We parked our car and joined Cliff in his truck for a tour of the ranch that Stephen T. Hearst, William Randolph Hearst's great-grandson, had asked Harriet and ALC in partnership with the California Rangeland Trust (CRT) to help him preserve forever.

Harriet took Steve Hearst's call on the day before Thanksgiving in late November 2002. Their conversation was brief and to the point.

"Hi, Harriet, it's Steve Hearst."

"Hi, Steve, how's the deal going?"

"Harriet, do you want to play varsity? I have just ended negotiations with The Nature Conservancy. Since you have taken on controversial deals in the past and completed them, would you like to talk?"

"Yes, sure I'd like to talk."

Steve had just walked out of the conference room of the Hearst Corporation's offices in San Francisco where he had informed Henry Little and Bill Hunter of The Nature Conservancy (TNC) and Tom Macy of The Conservation Fund (TCF) at 9:15 a.m. on November 27 of his decision to end their negotiations to conserve Hearst Ranch. He had then walked straight into his office where he already had Harriet's phone number on a Post-it. Within fifteen minutes of Steve's call, Harriet had joined him. Steve handed her an exclusive negotiating agreement with her name above his on the signature page.

Attached to the negotiating agreement was the Hearst Ranch Conservation Framework that listed the Hearst Corporation's five must-have items for any conservation deal. Harriet read the list, then she raised her hand, snapped her fingers, and said, "May I have a pen, please? All the things that you are asking for are not going to negatively affect the conservation values." Back in her office after signing the agreement, Harriet called an all-hands-on-deck meeting to announce what clearly would be the biggest project ALC had ever done.[4]

ALC had been one of five organizations Steve Hearst originally considered as potential "conservation partners" for Hearst Ranch. Steve had been the head of the Hearst Corporation's Sunical Land and Livestock Division, responsible for ranch operations since his uncle, Jack Cooke, had retired from the position in 1998. When Steve took charge after twenty-four years in the newspaper division, the Hearst Corporation had just suffered a major setback in its development plans for the ranch in the face of fierce local opposition.

The idea of developing at least part of the ranch had been floated several times, beginning with the Hearst Corporation's 1964 announcement of plans for a $340 million project with eight villages along fifteen miles of coastline. The proposal was development on a grand scale: a city of sixty-five thousand served by a yacht harbor, convention center, airport, hospital, eighteen-hole golf course, twenty churches, eleven elementary schools, three junior highs, three high schools, and a college. The county planning commission granted tentative approval despite concerns about an adequate water supply, but the corporation decided not to proceed with the project.[5]

The Hearst Corporation changed its approach with its next development proposal. Instead of a small city, the corporation envisioned the creation of "the next Pebble Beach" with its 1983 introduction of a resort plan for San Simeon that had been in the works since 1977. The plan featured three hotels offering 650 rooms accompanied by restaurants and shops on three hundred coastal acres. One of the hotels and an 18- to 27-hole golf course were slated for construction on San Simeon Point, where groves of Monterey pines, eucalyptus, and Monterey cypress planted by William Randolph Hearst thrive and thousands of monarch butterflies shelter every year.[6]

By this time, any development on the coast was subject to approval by the California Coastal Commission. Established temporarily by California voters in 1972 and permanently by the California Coastal Act of 1976, the commission controls land use in the coastal zone—which varies from several hundred feet inland in urban areas to five miles inland for the Hearst Ranch—through permits issued either directly or through commission-certified local coastal programs (LCPs). The Hearst development fell under the jurisdiction of the San Luis Obispo LCP, which incorporated it into its 1988 plan for the area. But, after reviewing the plan, the Coastal Commission insisted that Hearst agree to place an easement on the remaining acres of the ranch—a restriction the corporation refused to accept.[7]

Progress on obtaining approval for the resort development was slow, but by the mid-1990s the Hearst Corporation's plans for development had moved closer to realization. In June 1997, a newly elected pro-growth San Luis Obispo County Board of Supervisors voted to amend the LCP to permit the Hearst development, including the highly controversial hotel and golf course just north of San Simeon Point. The vote set the stage for the "coastal fight of the decade" when the amended plan came up for consideration by the California Coastal Commission in January 1998. It was a crucial test of the California Coastal Act. As Coastal Commission executive director Peter Douglas said, "This is the crown jewel of California's undeveloped coast. What we do in this case is going to make a lasting mark on a place beloved to many, many people."[8]

An overflow crowd of more than one thousand people gathered at the Embassy Suites Hotel in San Luis Obispo for the January 15 Coastal Commission hearing on the Hearst Ranch resort development. Rusty Areias, chairman of the commission, opened the meeting at 9 a.m. with a request for mutual respect and courtesy. He reminded the audience, "This is not a battle between good and evil."[9]

Both sides testified. Environmentalists, ranchers, local residents, and even two members of the Hearst family argued for protecting the agricultural and scenic values of the pristine coastline property. The Hearst Corporation, supported by organized labor and business groups, argued for developing an economic asset that would bring jobs and tax revenues to the county. Finally, after twelve hours of debate, the commission voted 12-0 to reject the LCP amendment and 9-3 to support its staff recommendation for approving a significantly reduced development project that would bring the LCP into compliance with the Coastal Act. A standing ovation greeted the decision.[10]

Developing the ranch was not the way Steve Hearst wanted to go when he took over the Hearst Corporation's real estate division in November 1998. For Steve, and for many members of the Hearst family, the ranch is home. Steve had grown up vacationing there on land that was little changed from the time George Hearst first laid eyes on it in the 1860s. Family picnics, horseback rides, and hunting trips all contributed to making him intimately familiar with the ranch that he has called "my favorite place on the planet."[11]

Meeting with Hearst CEO Frank A. Bennack Jr. in the Hearst Corporation's New York office just after he assumed his new position, Steve told him, "I want to put all the development plans for San Simeon on hold, and I want to place the property under a conservation easement." He later told a *New York Times* reporter, "When you look at having this big dark cloud over the Hearsts in this area, it drove a lot of us to frustration. I thought I can continue down this road and fight to develop or I can find a way to meet the needs of the community, meet our fiduciary responsibilities to the [Hearst family] trust and everybody wins."[12]

It was a tall order. Steve Hearst first had to convince the fifty-six heirs who were part of the Hearst family trust that it was possible both to move forward on conservation and preserve the value of the Hearst Ranch as an asset of the corporation. He had to persuade the local community that the Hearst family and its corporation were not the enemy. He had to find a conservation partner to make it all happen. It was not an undertaking for sissies, as Steve said after it was done, and he relied on Marty Cepkauskas, the Hearst Corporation's director of Western real estate, to handle many of the conservation project details.[13]

It took two years to persuade the Hearst family heirs to support Steve's new approach. The corporation board was skeptical at first.

The board told Steve, "It sounds like smoke and mirrors."

He told the board, "Absolutely not, it's real."

In the end, a member of both the family trust and the corporation boards said, "All the family members I've talked to are right behind Steve."[14]

With the backing of the family and the corporation, Steve Hearst announced his new plan for the ranch in February 2001. While one headline read, "Hearst Renews Bid for Resort at San Simeon," another questioned, "Conservation Easement for Hearst?" The new proposal had elements of both: the development of 257 coastal acres with "some level of compatible, visitor-serving project" in return for the preservation of the remaining 82,000 acres as open space.[15]

Steve Hearst told reporters, "We are looking for a conservation solution." A key component of that solution: a conservation organization to buy the development rights and place a conservation easement on the 82,000 acres of undeveloped ranchland. Hearst already had started looking for the right conservation partner to help assemble a conservation and development package. He was in talks with ALC, CRT, TNC, TCF, and TPL. He said, "These are the largest ones and ones with the most proven track record of putting together these types of deals."[16]

ALC and CRT put together a joint proposal for Hearst's consideration, explaining,

ALC and CRT share the philosophy that landowners should be fairly compensated for their property rights and that conservation easements, to work successfully over the long term, must allow the landowner flexibility to remain profitable while at the same time protecting the resources. We believe the partnership of ALC and CRT offers the best opportunity to meet the financial and ownership objectives for the Hearst Ranch while preserving the unique resources of the ranch in an environmentally responsible manner.

With ALC's history of completing difficult, controversial, and complex land preservation transactions and CRT's established reputation for protecting ranchland through conservation easements, it must have seemed like an unbeatable combination to Harriet and Nita Vail, CRT's executive director.[17]

Hearst responded to the ALC/CRT proposal with an invitation to join him and his advisers at the ranch on April 24, 2001, for a full-day strategy session facilitated by Bruce Babbitt. Babbitt, a member of Harriet's Board of Councillors before he became Interior secretary in 1993, had recently left Interior and joined the Los Angeles office of the Latham and Watkins law firm that was representing the Hearst Corporation. TPL was invited for the same day as ALC. TNC and TCF were invited for the following day. Accepting Hearst's invitation, Harriet reiterated ALC's qualifications and added, "ALC is prepared to 'take the heat' and defend rational solutions that satisfy a broad community of interests—a strategy that has proved successful time and again."[18]

As it turned out, the unbeatable combination of ALC and CRT had to wait until after Steve Hearst and his team had spent fourteen months negotiating with TNC and TCF. Given the size, resources, local reputation, national standing, and financial strength of TNC and TCF, these two organizations had been Hearst's first choice. By September 2002, after passing the six-month deadline set by their initial August 2001 agreement and several extensions beyond that, TNC/TCF and Hearst were close to signing an agreement. They had developed a conservation framework that laid out the general approach for the conservation of the ranch, had negotiated many of the terms of the conservation easement, and had agreed to a total value of $95 million ($80 million in cash and

$15 million in California state tax credits) for the purchase of the development rights. Then TNC dropped a bombshell.

At a meeting held at the ranch on September 18, TNC's Henry Little told Steve Hearst that TNC was ready to do the deal but only at a significantly lower price tag than the $95 million offer that TNC and TCF had made on August 28. The cash amount in the new offer was reduced from $80 million to $72.7 million, with the $15 million in tax credits still subject to the approval of the state of California. Little also said that TNC wanted changes to other key terms of the August 28 offer.

Steve was infuriated at what he considered a broken promise. As he pushed back from the meeting table, excused himself, and walked away, Steve said, "Today's my birthday. What a great birthday present." The meeting was over. Steve contacted TNC president and CEO Steve McCormick to tell him that the TNC deal was in jeopardy. McCormick called the TNC Hearst Ranch negotiators, but the valuation and other problems remained. After more phone calls and meetings, it was clear that TNC was not going to support the terms in the August 28 offer. Steve Hearst decided to end the negotiations.

But Hearst did not give up on his plan to conserve the ranch. Instead, he called Harriet. Steve said, "We selected Harriet because she wasn't like the rest. ALC set itself apart because of its win-win attitude in making a bridge between conservation and the property owner." Harriet said, "The Hearst Ranch is one of this country's rare jewels and represents an important conservation project for not only the American Land Conservancy but for the state. Our goal is to protect the beauty of the ranch for all generations."

Harriet was willing to take a risk that TNC with its thousands of employees, tremendous financial resources, and methodical approach preferred to avoid. She felt the terms and the $95 million price tag were reasonable. She had no funding guarantee, but she had faith that she would find the money. Failure was not an option. Like David taking on Goliath, Harriet was ready to step in with ALC's small staff to dare the impossible and get the deal done—all in full view of the public—much to the chagrin of TNC and other conservation organizations that often were uncomfortable with her unorthodox approach. Harriet signed an exclusive negotiating agreement with Hearst at their meeting on November 27, 2002.[19]

ALC was in a good position to take over the Hearst Ranch conservation project. As Steve Hearst commented when making the announcement of the switch from TNC, "We're working with a local hero." ALC's local hero status stemmed largely from its success in protecting the East West Ranch in Cambria. Spreading over four hundred acres with more than a mile of coastline, the East West Ranch was just a few miles south of Hearst Ranch.[20]

The East West Ranch had been owned by the Fiscalini family for close to one hundred years. Known locally as the Fiscalini Town Ranch, it always had been generously shared with the community of Cambria that surrounded it. When the family was unable to pay the property taxes on the ranch—which soared in the 1980s as the surrounding land was developed—they sold the land to Rancho Pacifica Developments. Much like the Hearst Corporation from the 1960s to the 1990s, Rancho Pacifica dreamed of building thousands of homes, a hotel, and a golf course right on the coast.

Rancho Pacifica's plans were thwarted by local opposition that mobilized as Friends of the RanchLand to protest the intensive development of open space in the heart of Cambria. Rancho Pacifica went bankrupt, and the property was sold at auction to a Hong Kong partnership for $2.95 million. The Hong Kong partnership's development plans did not fare any better than its predecessor's. But Friends of the RanchLand had been unable to find a way to preserve the Fiscalini Ranch permanently until they reached out to ALC. Unlike TPL and other organizations the Friends approached, ALC responded to their request for help in early 1998.[21]

Harriet began working her magic. She contacted the landowner. She met with members of Congress in Washington, D.C. She supported the efforts of her project manager, Glen Williams, who told Ame Hellman, "I think Harriet is being very generous in letting me run with this a ways. . . . With Harriet's experience, record with Packard and congressional relationships, we can help a motivated community a long ways." Still, it was not a slam dunk by any means. Ame told Russell, "The project is extremely controversial within the community [with regard to how the ranch should be acquired, owned, and managed], and unless we can succeed at communicating to the East West folks that we are an asset to them, we need to walk away."[22]

ALC did not walk away but convinced the community that the conservancy was the right organization to facilitate preservation of the ranch, then persevered through a difficult appraisal process and lengthy negotiations with the landowner. ALC secured a matching grant from the California Coastal Conservancy to purchase the property, then worked to find the matching funds from the Cambria Community Services District, a community bank, and local fund-raising. ALC subsidized a local office that took responsibility for directing the fund-raising campaign. Rummage sales, bike rides, and direct contributions generated $1 million for the purchase. ALC also worked with two state legislators to include funding for East West Ranch in the state budget.[23]

Harriet flew down to one meeting in Cambria with Martin and Esther Litton. After landing, Martin accidentally backed their car into Harriet, gently knocking into her. That didn't stop Harriet. She still went to the meeting—looking like she'd been in a war zone, according to one eyewitness, but uninjured, according to another—and was rewarded with a donation of $10,000 from a Cambria resident for the preservation of the ranch.[24]

Escrow on the East West Ranch sale for $11.1 million closed in November 2000 and was almost immediately followed by a jubilant dedication ceremony with more than four hundred people holding a mile-long ribbon and joining "Hands Across the Ranch." Harriet attended the celebration and said, "I've never seen a community rise up to support a project like this town has." Waving a hand at the spectacular view, she added, "It has been an awesome treat to work with you, and I congratulate you on this [land] you've helped save for the whole state and the world to share." Harriet then joined State Senator Jack O'Connell and San Luis Obispo County Supervisor Shirley Bianchi at the gate to the ranch, where they pulled down the private property signs.[25]

The rolling hills of what is now the Fiscalini Ranch Preserve rise from the rocky coast to a four-hundred-foot ridge. Red-tipped ice plant hugs the coastal bluff. A rare stand of Monterey pines line the ridge. The preserve habitat nurtures red-legged frogs, tidewater gobies, western pond turtles, steelhead, monarch butterflies, great blue herons, burrowing owls, Cooper's hawks, coyotes, and black-tailed deer. Otters play in tide pools. Egrets walk through tall grasses waving in the breeze.

Many residents and visitors roam the preserve's wide-open spaces, walking the trails that meander along the coast and across meadows and up to the ridge. Driftwood benches just off the main trail offer a place for all who walk there to take in the views of the coast and the ocean beyond. The brass marker on one of those benches reads, "In Memory of our Angels.... Honoring Those Whose Work Saved the Ranch Forever." Angels and heroes.

Harriet did not waste any time getting to work on the challenge of negotiating a conservation solution for the Hearst Ranch. She quickly added a key member to her team with a call to Kara Blakeslee. Kara had been TNC's local project manager for the Hearst Ranch and had been deeply involved in the negotiations. Still recovering from jet lag after cutting short her Thanksgiving trip to Florida with her family, Kara met Harriet at the airport in San Luis Obispo.

Kara adored Harriet from the first moment she met her. Harriet's warmth, fearless personality, and passionate commitment to conservation won her over completely. Harriet's understanding of the challenges working moms faced—Kara was then pregnant with her second daughter—was icing on the cake. Dedicated to preserving the ranch, Kara promptly accepted Harriet's offer to go to work for ALC. Kara told reporters, "This is a once-in-a-lifetime opportunity to protect the Hearst Ranch and all its resources. I'm thrilled to be with the American Land Conservancy. They're the right team."[26]

Building on the foundation laid during the Hearst/TNC negotiations, the new Hearst/ALC partnership was able to release the conservation framework that set the stage for the agreement to preserve the Hearst Ranch just a few days after signing their agreement to negotiate. The one-page framework issued in early December confirmed the new direction taken by the Hearst Corporation. Its terms were exactly the same as the terms of the framework negotiated with TNC. Having met with more than one thousand state and local groups and leaders, Steve Hearst said, "I think we've got a framework . . . that includes almost everything people have been clamoring for."[27]

What had people been clamoring for? No golf course or resort at San Simeon Point. No hotel at the Hearst Castle Visitor Center. No equestrian center at Pico Creek. No new areas for resort development. Permanent public access to the coastline on the west side of Highway 1, including the addition of eighteen miles to the California Coastal Trail. Preservation of the ranching/agricultural operations east of Highway 1. Restricted development in Old San Simeon Village in keeping with architect Julia Morgan's original vision. Reduction of new residential development to twenty-seven homes for Hearst family members from the potential four hundred allowed for the 271 certified Hearst lots. These key elements contributed to the fulfillment of the overall goals of the framework to protect the natural resources, habitat, ranching operations, pristine beaches, and rugged coastline of the Hearst Ranch using conservation easements and other means with fair compensation to the landowner for development restrictions.[28]

Reaction to the framework was swift and mostly very positive. Shirley Bianchi, San Luis Obispo County supervisor for the district that included the Hearst Ranch, said, "Happy birthday to me, and happy holidays to us all." Bianchi had fought long and hard against the earlier Hearst Ranch development proposals. She was one of the first local leaders Steve Hearst contacted after he decided to pursue a new conservation plan for the ranch. He invited her to the ranch to talk. Reluctant to confront Hearst alone—many local environmentalists had refused to talk to him at all—Bianchi insisted on having her legislative assistant come with her to that first meeting.

Not long after their initial discussion, Bianchi invited Hearst to her house for an "information-exchange" meeting with about a dozen community leaders and activists. She later recalled, "Steve and I danced around each other for about two years. I didn't trust him, and he didn't trust me." But when Steve Hearst and his local attorney, Roger Lyon, met with Bianchi to tell her about the conservation framework, she was impressed. She said, "I'm basically a very paranoid person. But if this framework goes through, I, for one, am ecstatic."[29]

Bianchi made a public service announcement a short time after the release of the conservation framework. Steve Hearst was driving across the ranch with Marty Cepkauskas and Cliff Garrison to see the sunset when he heard Shirley Bianchi's comments on the radio. She asked for patience. She said she'd met with Hearst, liked his ideas, and was "cautiously supportive." Hearst turned to Cepkauskas and said, "Marty, did you just hear what I heard?" Years later, Steve said, "It was a turning point for us."[30]

Kara Blakeslee, Roger Lyon, and other members of the ALC/Hearst team lost no time in reaching out to the community. They met with hundreds of local groups and individuals to explain the framework and ask for their support. The need to demonstrate public support for the conservation framework was especially urgent, because money from recently approved Proposition 50 that might be crucial for the purchase of the Hearst Ranch development rights was up for grabs in Sacramento. As CRT's Steve Sinton said, "There's a feeding frenzy going on in Sacramento. If we don't get in there with the rest of the sharks, we'll lose this opportunity."[31]

Within weeks of its release, endorsements of the conservation framework came pouring in. The San Luis Obispo County Board of Supervisors unanimously declared its approval. The Cambria Community Services District added its endorsement. The San Luis Obispo Council of Governments voted in favor of the framework. By early April, ALC and Hearst had received more than twenty endorsements from public officials, environmental organizations, local governments, and business groups.[32]

Not everyone greeted the framework with enthusiasm. Some criticized the proposed construction of a one hundred–room hotel in Old San Simeon Village based on a Julia Morgan design that Roger Lyon had recently discovered in the attic of Hearst's San Francisco office. Others worried about the location and size of the twenty-seven homes specified in the framework. Still others believed that supporting the framework now before the determination of the final plan was premature. A few insisted on the purchase of the Hearst Ranch even though it wasn't for sale. Sam Schuchat, executive director of the California Coastal Conservancy, asked, "I wonder what the ALC is going to be able to do that TNC hasn't been able to do?"[33]

The first thing ALC was able to do was to reach an agreement with Hearst to conserve the ranch. Money, as is so often the case, generated the most back-and-forth between Hearst's and ALC's attorneys as they worked out the terms of the agreement. How much should ALC pay to secure the option on the Hearst Ranch? How much would Hearst pay ALC in the form of a contribution to ALC to complete this extremely complex conservation transaction successfully? To what extent would Hearst reimburse ALC for the conservancy's project expenses?

All of these questions and others were answered in the conservation option agreement signed on February 19, 2003. All of the answers were cloaked in confidentiality, but Steve Hearst clarified the conservation agreement in a letter to the editor of *The Tribune*, a San Luis Obispo County newspaper, and the ALC press release announcing the agreement revealed its general provisions. Calling the agreement a "key milestone in efforts to preserve the historic 82,000-acre Hearst Ranch," ALC said it was authorized to begin implementation of the conservation framework as outlined in December. ALC had one year with the possibility of extensions to work out the details for translating the framework into reality, including establishing the value of the development rights and finding funding sources for their purchase. Harriet told the *New York Times*, "It's a fabulous deal. I really view this as a golden opportunity for the Golden State." With her usual confident élan, she said, "This will happen."[34]

Making it happen took two more years. Appraisals had to be completed to determine the value of the ranch and its development rights. An environmental assessment had to be conducted to identify any potential or existing environmental contamination. Funding sources had to be located. Baseline studies inventorying the cultural, water, botanical, range, wildlife, and fishery resources on the eighty thousand acres of the ranch that would be subject to the conservation easement had to be undertaken to document current conditions. The specifics of the conservation easement had to be determined, including the location of the twenty-seven reserved future home sites for the Hearst family that had to be positioned outside of the viewshed from Hearst Castle and Highway 1. Local and statewide endorsements had to be gathered. Agreements with state agencies had to be negotiated. Tours and site inspections of the ranch had to be arranged.

Making it happen was a long, grueling process that taxed the skills, resources, and patience of the ALC and Hearst teams and their consultants to the limit. Harriet Burgess, Steve Hearst, and Roger Lyon all had moments when the temptation to quit was almost irresistible. Harriet's moment came during a three-hour meeting at the Hearst's San Francisco office in March 2003.

The Hearst team insisted on having the Hearst law firm of Latham and Watkins take the lead in negotiations with state agencies on the key elements of the transaction. Harriet was furious because she felt that her usual leadership role where her expertise and connections would be vital—the role that she had played so successfully in completing conservation projects throughout her career—had been usurped.

Russell asked if they could have the room. He knew Harriet was ready to explode. He said, "Harriet, if you want to exit, then now's the time to do it." Torn between wanting to do the deal and wanting to do the deal her usual way, Harriet sat silently for a few minutes staring across the table at her lawyer. Then jaw set, eyes blazing, she said, "All right, we'll let them do it their way."

Harriet followed the advice that she often gave to others to "get over it." She kept abreast of all project developments and participated in all high-level discussions. She was ALC's ultimate decision maker and the driving force behind ALC's mission to save the ranch despite having a role that she did not consider commensurate with her skills, experience, and standing in the conservation community. Harriet stepped back and let her very capable staff—primarily Kara Blakeslee, Jeff Stump, and Kerry O'Toole—handle the bulk of the work in concert with ALC's legal counsel and outside consultants.[35]

Steve Hearst had more than one moment when he considered walking away from a conservation solution for the ranch. He admitted, "If it weren't for Roger Lyon's level-headed and wise counsel, I would have thought about throwing in the towel several times." Steve had known Roger for decades, having first met him when he visited the offices of the Hearst Corporation's Los Angeles law firm as an eighteen year old. Roger was now a land use attorney and rancher in Cayucos, a town a little more than twenty miles south of San Simeon. He often served as local counsel for the Hearst Corporation on ranch matters and had been instrumental in creating the Cayucos Land Conservancy that protected four miles of coastline just north of Cayucos by preventing the development of Estero Bluffs.[36]

Not long after Steve took over responsibility for the Hearst Ranch, he called Roger to talk about its future. Roger asked him, "Have you considered a conservation easement?" Under a conservation easement, the Hearst Corporation would continue ranching operations but would be paid to give up most of its rights to develop the property.

Once Hearst agreed to a conservation solution for the ranch, Roger worked tirelessly to make it happen, but he too was tempted to quit after months of wrangling with the Hearst Corporation's longtime and valued attorneys at Latham and Watkins over the most effective means to achieve the conservation goal. When Roger's advice on an aspect of the negotiations with the state conflicted with the Latham and Watkins recommendation, that was the last straw. Roger told Steve that if he wanted to go with the law firm's recommendation, he would have to quit. It was a question of trust. Steve Hearst followed Roger's advice, and Roger emerged as the first among equals.[37]

Harriet didn't quit. Steve didn't quit. Roger didn't quit. Working together with the teams from ALC, Hearst, and CRT in cooperation with state agencies, they achieved what the *New York Times* called "one of the biggest and most complex land-conservation deals in the nation's history."[38]

By July 2004, ALC, Hearst, and the state of California were ready to share the fruits of their prodigious and occasionally contentious labors with the public. Some details had been disclosed as negotiations went forward. A letter to the editor of *The Tribune* in February, written mostly by Kara Blakeslee but signed by Harriet, served as an update on the conservation partners' progress:

To begin, ALC and Hearst have completed our substantive negotiations, and conservation easement documents covering the entire Ranch are being finalized. The terms of the deal are consistent with the published Conservation Framework. . . .

Many rumors have circulated regarding the cost of conserving the Hearst Ranch, including media reports of $250 million. I am pleased to report that the ALC's agreed-upon price is actually $80 million in cash, and $15 million in state tax credits. . . . The difference between the price that ALC will pay and the approved fair market value represents a very large charitable contribution by the Hearst Corp. . . .

More than 1,100 acres west of Highway 1 will be purchased outright—a hard-fought term of the negotiations, pursued in large part because of the will of the community. . . .

The baseline [inventory to document the existing resources of the Ranch for monitoring and enforcement of the easement] is nearly complete, created by experts hired by ALC . . .

In short, in concert with the community and the landowner, ALC has reached agreement on a conservation transaction that meets and often exceeds industry standards, for a price that will be well-below market value. . . . The process has been long, intense, sometimes contentious, and always challenging as ALC and Hearst have hammered out one of the most significant deals in history.

The letter let the public in on key provisions of the Hearst Ranch conservation deal while also focusing attention on ALC's role as Hearst's conservation partner—and not Hearst's agent, as some opponents of the deal had suggested.[39]

Hearst and ALC made further concessions and refinements to the proposed easement documents before the June announcement of a tentative agreement with the state disclosed additional details. Leading up to the late May meetings that finalized the agreement—which had been far from a sure thing—Kara Blakeslee said, "If we don't do this . . . you can say good-bye to Hearst Ranch as it is today. Anybody who doesn't believe it, take a drive along the California coastline." Steve Hearst, who had to recommend a position on the agreement to the Hearst Corporation's board of directors, said, "I can't sit out here forever." The tentative agreement set the stage for the final steps on the long road to the preservation of the Hearst Ranch.[40]

All terms of the conservation agreement for Hearst Ranch were released by the California Resources Agency on July 12. Available online, the more than five hundred pages of public review documents laid out the specifics of the deal. Never before had the public been given so much information about a state-funded conservation project.

Three days after the documents were released, a crowd of about four hundred packed into the Veteran's Hall in Cayucos and spilled over onto the town's pier to view maps, hear presentations, and ask more than 130 questions about the plan. They heard from the state agencies that had participated in shaping the deal—the Coastal Conservancy, State Parks, the Wildlife Conservation Board, and Caltrans—along with representatives from the Hearst Corporation, ALC, and CRT. Local officials added their input. Encouraging ALC staff to attend and reflecting the importance of public support, Kara Blakeslee had called it " probably the single most important date in the history of the project."[41]

Given a chance to ask questions and share their views, the people in favor of the deal outnumbered those against. The crowd roared approval when rancher Ralph Covell said, "This is probably the biggest bargain ever put before the people of California. If they [environmental activists] are too blind to see it, they're brain dead." Speakers against the plan included eleven Sierra Club members whose coastal programs director had said before the meeting, "If we don't get access to the east side, then this deal lacks a long-term public benefit." But as Sam Schuchat, executive director of the Coastal Conservancy, who led the meeting said, "We may not get everything we want, but if you get enough, then you have to say, 'This is a big opportunity.'"[42]

The Hearst Ranch conservation transaction was a big opportunity, but would the state of California take advantage of it? On May 5, the San Luis Obispo Council of Governments (SLOCOG) unanimously had approved an amendment to its Federal Transportation Improvement Program to include the Hearst project. SLOCOG's approval paved the way for the California Transportation Commission's May 13 grant of $23 million of transportation enhancement funds to purchase the development rights for 1,202 acres of the Hearst Ranch located on the west side of Highway 1, but the two highest hurdles to success remained. Although the state tentatively had approved the deal in June, both the Wildlife Conservation Board (WCB) and the State Coastal Conservancy (SCC) had to agree to fund the transaction to make it a reality.[43]

The WCB met in Sacramento on August 12 to consider the Hearst Ranch proposal. The meeting room in the state capitol was crowded with officials, WCB staff, and members of the public, including a busload of supporters from San Luis Obispo County. Steve Hearst was thrilled to see the supporters—many of whom were wearing cowboy hats—and greeted them enthusiastically as they disembarked from the bus. He hadn't planned to be there originally, but he returned early from a trip to Italy after he saw an article in the *International Herald Tribune* that suggested the Hearst deal was falling apart.

Thirty-five items were on the WCB agenda that day. The Hearst Ranch Conservation Area was number thirty-five and was scheduled for consideration at 2 p.m. Going into the meeting, the Hearst/ALC/CRT teams knew they had no guarantee of a favorable vote, though the Schwarzenegger administration had put its weight behind getting the conservation deal approved.[44]

Al Wright, the WCB executive director, introduced and explained the proposal. He reported on the many letters of support the WCB received, but he also said many letters had suggested changes and requested that the WCB postpone its decision. Eight assembly members and one senator signed one of the postponement requests. Elected officials expounded at length on their views of the proposal. Then the floor was open to comments from the audience.[45]

Kara Blakeslee, Jeff Stump, and Kerry O'Toole spoke for ALC, but Harriet, on a three-week vacation in Canada, did not attend the meeting. Lauren Ward also spoke, though not as a representative of ALC. He had listened to the many passionate speakers who had preceded him—the majority in favor of the deal—and realized that their often lengthy remarks were losing their effectiveness. He shortened his prepared speech, saying that the Hearst Ranch was the holy grail of conservation, that many people had tried to get it done and all had failed. The WCB had a chance to succeed, and they should not allow "the perfect to be the enemy of the good." His brief words were rewarded with a round of applause. Nita Vail and Steve Sinton championed the proposal on behalf of CRT.[46]

Among the other members of the audience at the WCB meeting who spoke in favor of the conservation of Hearst Ranch were many of the supporters who had taken the long bus ride to Sacramento that morning. Elizabeth Scott-Graham and Bruce Gibson voiced their strong approval as representatives of Hearst Ranch Conservation NOW, an organization whose effective advocacy for the conservation of the ranch had included lobbying and a website that detailed the history of the project, monitored its status, provided links to press coverage, and responded to critics' objections.[47]

Some four hours after the WCB began consideration of the Hearst Ranch proposal, a member of the board asked the executive director for his recommendation. Al Wright, who had been directly involved in ranch negotiations and who had toured the ranch earlier in the year but had expressed reservations about the deal in the past, recommended that the board approve the project by allocating $34.5 million of Proposition 50 money to fund the WCB grant subject to three conditions.[48]

Supporters greeted the unanimous vote of the three-member board in favor of the recommendation with a standing ovation. A delighted Steve Hearst, who expected the WCB conditions would be resolved quickly, said, "On to the Coastal Conservancy!"[49]

One month later, the SCC convened in the town of Windsor just north of Santa Rosa to consider the Hearst Ranch project. The SCC had been the lead agency in the state's negotiating process with Hearst and ALC. As executive director Sam Schuchat said early in the negotiations,

The Coastal Conservancy, with its extensive experience in buying land and easements, as well as restoring land and aquatic habitats, protection of valuable coastal agricultural land, and developing low-impact public access trails where appropriate, is well suited to take the lead in this endeavor, representing the interests of and in close cooperation with all relevant state agencies.

But he acknowledged that the deal was "mind-numbingly complicated."[50]

Like the WCB, the SCC had received many letters both for and against the Hearst Ranch transaction. Letters in favor outnumbered those opposed. The California Transportation Commission and the Bureau of Land Management urged approval. Bill Garrett, former editor of the *National Geographic* magazine and still a member of ALC's Board of Councillors, advised, "Never will you have a conservation project for the Hearst Ranch as good as this one. You probably will never get a Hearst family member as good as Stephen Hearst in favor of a conservation project." Harriet and Nita Vail, CRT's executive director, wrote the SCC board to refute assertions made by the Environmental Defense Center in opposition to the Hearst deal. Their letter concluded, "We are proud to be a part of this historic conservation transaction . . . that, with your support, will benefit the State of California now and for future generations by preserving in perpetuity the unique legacy, beauty, and resources of the Hearst Ranch." The letters of support buttressed the SCC staff recommendation of approval.[51]

But some members of the SCC board still had reservations. After all, TNC, the Sierra Club, some local environmental activists, and the Coastal Commission had expressed serious concerns about the Hearst Ranch transaction. Knowing that the deal was dead without SCC approval, Harriet, Jeff Stump, and ALC lobbyist Phil Isenberg met with SCC board member Doug Bosco at his Santa Rosa home the day before the meeting. Both sides, including the Sierra Club, had been lobbying Bosco, who was concerned about the location of the coastal trail.

Jeff Stump took the lead in the conversation with Bosco. Jeff had worked for Harriet since leaving his position as legislative coordinator at the Coastal Commission in 1999. Following her usual sink-or-swim approach with new employees, Harriet had thrown Jeff into the deep end of the pool and waited to see what he could do. Jeff likes to say that Harriet gave him enough rope to either hang himself or tie a lasso around a project to get it done. She was not a hands-on manager but empowered him to do his job. Having proven himself with his work on East West Ranch and other projects, Harriet gave him the opportunity to play a significant role in the day-to-day tasks of getting the Hearst deal over the goal line.

Jeff went through the project, explaining the issues to Bosco and emphasizing coastal access. He acknowledged that the deal wasn't perfect but still was an amazing accomplishment. A calm and thoughtful discussion followed. Jeff believes that was the conversation that swung the agency. During the six-hour meeting the next day, Doug Bosco said he would support the Hearst Ranch project. He and the seven-member board voted unanimously—with a few changes to increase public access to the coast—in favor of granting $34.5 million to the WCB as part of the funding for the acquisition of the Hearst Ranch conservation easement.[52]

Dressed all in white like a beneficent angel, Harriet sat in the audience next to Kara during the SCC hearing. A member of the Sierra Club sporting a blue "Save the Coast" sticker asked Harriet if she were the president of ALC, then asked why she supported the Hearst Ranch conservation transaction. Harriet talked quietly to the woman. She said, "We're doing the Lord's work." She explained that the beauty of the ranch needed to be protected. She said she understood that the Sierra Club wanted more access but that ALC had negotiated the best deal possible. Putting her hand on Harriet's shoulder, the woman thanked her and left feeling that perhaps she too should support the project. When Kara later spoke at the hearing, she wore the green "Hearst Ranch Conservation Now" sticker that Hearst Ranch supporters wore—and the blue Sierra Club "Save the Coast" sticker given to her by Harriet's visitor.[53]

After the meeting, Karen Scarborough, Governor Schwarzenegger's appointee to the SCC board who had been a very effective behind-the-scenes force for getting the deal done, said, "This is a very carefully balanced win-win. Not everybody's happy, but fifty years from now when our grandkids are here, they'll be glad we did what we did." Harriet, along with the more than seventy supporters from San Luis Obispo County who had traveled to the meeting in buses ALC and CRT chartered, surely agreed.[54]

The final pieces of the Hearst Ranch conservation deal fell into place over the next few months. The Public Works Board—the last state agency to sign off on the transaction—unanimously agreed to accept Hearst's 832-acre donation of land along the coast to California State Parks in November 2004, calling it "one of the most valuable transactions in the history of California." The WCB conditionally approved the Hearst donation of land for inclusion in the National Heritage Preservation Tax Credit Program in February 2005 to provide the $15 million in tax credits essential for reaching the $95 million total payment for the conservation of Hearst Ranch.[55]

The ALC and Hearst teams laboriously worked out the last details of the deal. With each taking the care of a painter applying the final brushstrokes to his masterpiece, Roger, Al, and Russell put the transaction documents under the microscope to ensure that they were exactly correct. They could not afford mistakes because, once officially approved, conservation easements are difficult if not impossible to alter. Sending Al and Russell a very minor change to the east side easement in early February, Roger said, "I want all of you to share the proposed award and therefore suggest that this change be suggested only with the concurrence of the esteemed group of nit pickers [sic]." It was only one of many nitpicks before the documents met the high standards set by the Hearst and ALC lawyers. The terms of the purchase and sale agreement and the contribution agreement between Hearst and ALC were subjected to equally close scrutiny before they were signed on February 8.[56]

It was time to close the deal. Harriet Burgess, Steve Hearst, and Nita Vail gathered at the office of Russell Austin's law firm in Sacramento to sign documents on February 10, 2005. Kathy Hustrei, Russell's paralegal, had organized stacks of documents in the main conference room with color-coded signature lines to ensure that each document was signed by the right person in the right place: green for Harriet, blue for Steve, and yellow for Nita.[57]

When the ink had dried on the last signature and the documents had been boxed for delivery to the First American Title Company in San Luis

Obispo, the three signatories posed with Jeff Stump, Al Jahns, Russell Austin, Kathy Hustrei, Julie Ehly, Roger Lyon, and Marty Cepkauskus in front of J. T. Ravize's photograph of Lake Tahoe's Emerald Bay in the law firm's conference room. Three cameras clicked to preserve the moment. Their smiles say it all. Satisfaction, exultation, and perhaps a bit of "I can't believe we did it."

Eight days later, on February 18, Harriet and Jeff flew to San Luis Obispo to witness the recording of the documents at the County Record-er's office. Escrow had closed just before noon that morning. Over the past week, the state agencies had completed all reviews and signed all remaining documents. The WCB's John Donnelly had hand delivered the state warrants for $80 million to First American Title in Sacramento. Joined by Steve Hearst, George Hearst, Kara Blakeslee, Shirley Bianchi, and many local supporters, they popped champagne corks and celebrated in the parking lot outside the County Recorder's office.[58]

They had done it: one of the biggest and most complex land-conservation deals in the nation's history.[59]

Driving All-American Highway 1 north from Cambria in May 2017, Russell and I left the motels of San Simeon Acres behind as we crossed San Simeon Creek and entered the realm of the Hearst Ranch. The rocky coast west of the highway includes fifteen hundred acres that Hearst donated to the state of California. Thirty beaches and eighteen miles of coastline. Eighteen miles added to the California Coastal Trail. Room for a realignment of the highway to reduce erosion. A little more than seven hundred acres still belong to Hearst at San Simeon Point, San Simeon Village, San Carpoforo Creek, and Pico Point, but public access is permitted.

Waves rose from the blue-green Pacific Ocean and spread over sandy beaches. Hordes of elephant seals sunbathed. Hikers and windsurfers took advantage of the clear, windy day with its blue skies that subsided to a white glow at the horizon. Occasional breaks in the barbed wire running along the road enticed visitors to enter and linger. The hundred-room inn based on Julia Morgan's design has yet to be built in Old San Simeon Village, and perhaps it never will be. The California coast undeveloped and glorious as perhaps no other place on Earth can be.

Still, I felt an undeniable affinity for the rolling green hills spreading up from the coast to meet the Santa Lucia Mountains. The hills that we navigated in Cliff Garrison's truck six years before. Thousands and thousands of acres preserved as a working ranch and harboring an extraordinary biological diversity. Plant and wildlife habitat fostered by 24,000 acres of grassland and coastal prairie; 15,000 acres of chaparral; 27,000 acres of oak and other woodlands; and 5,500 acres of forests. Seven major watersheds. Twenty-eight endangered, threatened, or rare plant and wildlife species. All monitored regularly by CRT to ensure compliance with the terms of the conservation easement that protects the ranch forever.

I have been to Hearst Castle and understand its fascinating appeal, but it is the open land that draws me. And I do not have to walk on it or ride on it to appreciate its magnificent existence. It is enough to know that it is there and always will be there.

The ALC and Hearst Ranch teams gathered at Hearst Ranch in February 2004 to discuss fundraising. Participants from left to right: Kara Woodruff, Jerry Meral, Harriet Burgess, Robert Glenn Ketchum, Steve Hearst, Martin Litton, Cynthia Berg, Marty Cepkauskas, and Kerry O'Toole.
KARA WOODRUFF

Hearst Ranch
HEARST CORPORATION

The coast at Hearst Ranch, May 2017
AUTHOR'S COLLECTION

Hearst Ranch
HEARST CORPORATION

The ALC, CRT, and Hearst Ranch teams gathered for a celebratory dinner after the Coastal Conservancy meeting in Windsor, CA in September 2004. Left to right: Jeff Stump, Cynthia Berg, Nita Vail, Kara Woodruff, Steve Hearst, Roger Lyon, Harriet Burgess, Al Jahns, Kerry O'Toole, Shawn Connolly, and Daniel Waggoner.

KARA WOODRUFF

Steve Hearst and Harriet at the bunkhouse on Hearst Ranch for an ALC/CRT fund-raiser in April 2005

KARA WOODRUFF

Everyone gathered in the conference room of Russell's Sacramento office after the document signing for the conservation of Hearst Ranch on February 10, 2005. Back row, left to right: Marty Cepkauskas, Kathy Hustrei, Julie Ehly, Al Jahns, Roger Lyon, Jeff Stump, and Russell Austin. Front row, left to right: Nita Vail, Steve Hearst, and Harriet Burgess.
MARTY CEPKAUSKAS

The Austins and friends at Hearst Ranch, April 2019
AUTHOR'S COLLECTION

Hearst Ranch
HEARST CORPORATION

Finale

Grand Canyon

IN DUFFY'S *ESCALANTE* THE LAST MORNING IN THE GRAND CANYON under a bright sun and blue skies, I am granted one final thrill in Rapid 217. The dory shoots into the air as we go through the milk chocolate waves. Duffy says, "That really stood us up!"

Diamond Peak, rising thirty-five hundred feet near mile 225, announces the imminent end of my run down the Colorado River. In my mind, I have already made the trip out: lists of what I have to do, who needs to be called, and where I need to go have replaced my immersion in the canyon, the river, and camp. The separation is confirmed by the stop at the Seligman A&W Root Beer mini-mart on the drive back to Flagstaff. The bright lights, the chattering customers, the gaudy souvenirs, the noise, the bathrooms hit me like a blast of cold air and shock me into the twenty-first century.

But I take many memories with me and a little bit of the canyon itself—a necklace of clay beads that Roger fired from Colorado River sediment as a parting gift for each of the women on the trip. I sense all of the rocks of the Grand Canyon around my neck carrying the magical power of the canyon and its river that pulled Harriet back again and again.

Epilogue

Grand Canyon Reprise

This is the true joy in life, the being used for a purpose recognized by your-self as a mighty one; the being thoroughly worn out before you are thrown on the scrap heap; the being a force of nature instead of a feverish selfish little clod of ailments and grievances complaining that the world will not devote itself to making you happy. —GEORGE BERNARD SHAW, 1903[1]

The land we save is our legacy. It's what we give to our children. It's what future generations can cherish thanks to our perseverance. —HARRIET BURGESS, 1999[2]

HARRIET LIVED HER LIFE AS IF THERE WOULD BE NO TOMORROW. SHE HAD long feared that she would succumb to Alzheimer's memory-sucking scourge like her father and sister before her. As early as the 1980s, she told a TPL colleague that she figured she would die young, so she had to make the most of the time that she had. She knew her tomorrows were limited—as they ultimately are for all of us—and embraced those that were given to her to leave a legacy of tomorrows for the places she loved. She devoted her one wild and precious life to saving those places for generations to come.

Alzheimer's crept into Harriet's life like the fog that often obscures the San Francisco skyline in the summer. Only, for Harriet, the fog never burned off. It slowly erased her ability to recall the past and comprehend the present. She fought hard to keep her independence—telling her "no" was not easy, even in the later stages of the disease—but she gradually had to cede control over her daily activities to her family, friends, and colleagues.

Harriet joined the more than five million Americans age sixty-five and over—two-thirds are women—who suffer from Alzheimer's. In the United States, a new case of Alzheimer's is diagnosed every minute. Neither cure nor treatment delays the progress of the disease.

In the beginning, Harriet's friends thought her occasional memory lapses were just the normal result of her busy and stressful life. Ame Hellman noticed that Harriet began to seem a little lost in airports when they took one of their frequent trips to Washington, D.C. She figured Harriet was just tired. Harriet's daughter Leslie accompanied Harriet on her last ALC trip to Washington, D.C., in 2004 to assist her in getting to appointments and other tasks.

Lauren Ward noticed that Harriet began making lists and writing information on notepads that she used to keep in her head. At some meetings, he saw her writing the same thing in her notes three times, but he didn't think anything of it. Only later did he realize that the alterations in Harriet's behavior were signs of encroaching Alzheimer's.

Then Harriet's memory lapses became more obvious. She asked her project managers repeatedly for project updates. They had to keep Harriet constantly updated—and re-updated. Lauren heard Harriet tell the same stories repeatedly. After asking, "Did I tell you this before?" she'd launch into another account of the same story.

When she gave up driving to work in San Francisco and began taking the bus, she often struggled to find her way to the ALC office after it moved to a new location on Montgomery Street.

Harriet always had had a great memory for facts and figures, names, and places. She had been really sharp, a very quick study of complex real estate deals. But not anymore.

As Harriet slid into the confusion of Alzheimer's, her judgment was affected. Instead of her customary well-groomed appearance, Harriet began to look a little unkempt. She arrived at meetings pulling up her stockings.

Instead of waiting until she had healed, Harriet came to the office the day after a surgery with visible bruising and incision scars. The first person who saw her asked, "Who beat you up?" It was one of the first big tip-offs for her staff that something was not right.

Instead of her usual strategic use of the telephone to move deals forward, Harriet tried to call contacts on current projects so many times that her staff hid her Rolodex. During her last year as ALC's president, Jeff and Kerry had to make sure they were with her when she took calls or attended a meeting. Shawn Connolly, Harriet's assistant, took notes during conference calls for Harriet to review later.

By the spring of 2005, ALC's board of directors realized that Harriet's decision-making abilities were seriously impaired. The board, always Harriet's fan club, had been slow to recognize the changes in her behavior. ALC staff finally had to insist on a meeting with the board to disclose the brutal facts of Harriet's challenges at the office.

Harriet retired from ALC in the fall of 2005. Under her leadership over fifteen years, ALC completed 360 projects that protected more than two hundred thousand acres. A complete list of her ALC projects with brief descriptions of many of them is included in appendix 1.

In 2006, Brock and Linda Evans visited Harriet and Joe at their Inverness home. While Joe was preparing dinner, Harriet asked him, "What are you doing?" every five minutes. Brock said Harriet was "just charming. Just asked the same question fifty-nine times."

Harriet and Joe joined other family members on a sailing trip in the Adriatic in 2007. By the time they reached Chicago on their way home, Harriet had no memory of the three-week adventure.

In June 2008, Harriet sat with me on the curved deck of her home overlooking the forested ridges of Point Reyes National Seashore. She was very chatty. She told stories about how her children would run off in the surrounding forested areas and disappear. How she then needed her dog, Simba, to find them. She repeated the story several times, once including an embellishment of two old men that lived nearby who helped her keep an eye on the kids. None of her children, all of whom are now adults, grew up there. Simba was a young dog that joined Harriet and Joe long after her children were grown.

At a lunch at Sinbad's in December 2008, Harriet introduced herself to Russell as if she had never met her longtime friend and attorney.

Joe took care of Harriet at home for as long as he could. He kept her at home with him even when she took a wrong turn into the step-down shower on the way from the bathroom to the bedroom and fell, breaking her elbow. He listened patiently to her repeated questions. He dressed her. He cooked for her. He watched her dwindle into a frail ghost of her former self.

Finally, in late 2009, Joe recognized that he was no longer able to take care of Harriet in their home. He moved her to a care facility a few miles away in Point Reyes Station. He visited often.

Now working nearby for the Marin Agricultural Land Trust, Jeff Stump occasionally saw Harriet walking the town's main street. Sometimes she recognized him. Sometimes she didn't.

Harriet Hunt Burgess died on April 19, 2010, just a few days shy of ALC's twentieth anniversary. Death had called Harriet home. Her death was unexpected—Joe told Russell the previous week that Harriet was doing fine—but not a surprise. Alzheimer's is always fatal. Most suffering from the disease live four to eight years after the initial diagnosis. Harriet had worsened over the last year of her life, then she had stabilized, then she was gone.

On a sunny day in May 2010, Russell and I gathered with many of Harriet's family and friends at the Inverness home she had shared with Joe. We were all there to remember Harriet. After a few opening remarks by Bob Stephens, who noted that it was not a memorial service but a celebration of Harriet's life, Joe was the next to speak.

Looking out at the crowded room, Joe said that one of Harriet's pet phrases was, "Don't feel any pressure." He continued, "The only pressure I feel is how we could possibly do justice to Harriet, such an incredible person." He shared many happy memories including falling down in the snow and laughing like children when they were skiing in Yellowstone and swimming in the rain in Tonga. He called Harriet "our prime mover and our inspiration." After he read a note from Senator Harry Reid that called Harriet "a gracious woman who brightened everybody's life around her," Joe said, "That was the truth. That was Harriet."

Mike Freed described his amazing friendship with Harriet, praising her integrity and energy. Then he said, "Harriet's not gone. Her spirit stays with us."

Dick Anderson's comments were echoed by many who were there that day. "Harriet accepted no limits. She crackled with energy. She just didn't have any stop in her. She didn't like boundaries. She saw what the possibilities were when we saw the impossible."

Jeff Stump emphasized that it was always about personal relationships for Harriet.

Kerry O'Toole, who became president of ALC in 2008, said, "I think of her daily, twice daily, three times daily. WWHD. What would Harriet do?"

Russell recalled Harriet's "magic" that had two essential elements. The first was incredible hard work and determination. The second was incredible courage, "the courage always to try, and the courage to fail sometimes, to tackle the hardest projects and, more often than not, to succeed."

Martin Litton was one of the last to speak. He concluded, "What Harriet wanted done was always the right thing."

I listened and wondered, like Joe, whether it would be possible to do justice to Harriet.

Some months later, Joe spread Harriet's ashes in her beloved Grand Canyon, where she will forever be a part of the land that inspired and sustained her.

After Harriet's retirement, the American Land Conservancy continued to fight the good fight for another eight years, but without Harriet and in a different economic and political environment, the organization founded to dare the impossible took on no new projects after 2013 and dissolved in 2016. Cash generated by the liquidation of ALC's remaining assets funded generous donations to the Grand Canyon Trust, Wildlife Forever, California Rangeland Trust, and the California Council of Land Trusts.

Harriet was driven to save land wherever and whenever the opportunity arose. Once she decided that the land was worth saving, she put all of her energy, skills, and resources behind getting it done. Obstacles were distractions but not deal killers. She focused on undeveloped land—finding it, figuring out how to fund its purchase, and transferring it to a public agency or protecting it with a conservation easement. She often responded to desperate community members who were trying to protect the land they loved. Harriet did not have a specific strategy for choosing her projects. She did what had to be done to secure the land before it was bulldozed or clear-cut or denied to the public.

Harriet's opportunistic model worked well for her and for conservation in the 1980s and 1990s but became less effective in the 2000s. Its success hinged on Harriet's relationships with landowners and with authorities in state and federal government. She knew the right people to help her identify the places that needed to be saved and the right people to find the necessary funding. She knew the government agency priorities. She knew the financial gatekeepers. For many years she was able to sit down with a staff member of the House Appropriations Committee, convince that staff member of the merits of her project, and walk away with an earmark to fund the project. Or she might go to lunch with the director of a state agency, talk about her project, and leave lunch with a promise that the project would be funded. As time went by, Harriet lost many of her connections to retirement or new jobs. And the rules of the game changed: the informal process based on personal relationships that had worked so well for Harriet was replaced by strict rules and procedures.

Finding funding for conservation projects was never easy, but it is even more difficult now. Although California voters passed a proposition in 2014 that addressed water issues and a proposition in 2018 that authorized $4 billion in general obligation bonds for state and local parks, environmental protection and restoration projects, water infrastructure projects, and flood protection projects, the LWCF expired in 2018 and only will continue if it is reauthorized by Congress. Land exchanges are limited by increased regulatory requirements and public scrutiny. Bargain sales are rare, given the high cost of real estate.[3]

Priorities for environmental funding have changed, too. Instead of inholdings in national forests or large tracts of land threatened by development, urban parks are often at the top of the list. The cover of a recent issue of TPL's magazine demonstrates the shift in emphasis from open spaces far from cities to urban land accessible to more people, especially those that have been designated "disadvantaged communities." It proclaims, "Everyone Deserves a Park," and TPL has launched a nationwide campaign to put a park in every neighborhood within a ten-minute walk of home. The proposition California voters passed in 2018 requires the expenditure of 15 to 20 percent of the bond's funds on projects in communities with median household incomes less than 60 percent of the statewide average (about $39,980 in 2016).[4]

I believe Harriet would have welcomed the emphasis on connecting all people with nature, just as I believe she would have adjusted her strategy to succeed in the new conservation context while still working with fierce determination to save threatened land that fosters biodiversity and sustains the intrinsic value of nature. After all, it's the only Earth we will ever have.

Acknowledgments

THERE ARE TWO PEOPLE WITHOUT WHOM THIS BOOK WOULD NEVER have been written. The first, of course, is Harriet Hunt Burgess, who dared the impossible to leave a legacy of land for us all to enjoy. The second is Russell Austin, my husband and one of the principal attorneys for Harriet's American Land Conservancy (ALC). He fully supported my work on a book about Harriet and her achievements from the time I first suggested the idea at 4 o'clock one morning more than ten years ago until he read the final manuscript.

I owe a tremendous debt of gratitude to Harriet's family, particularly to Leslie King Cowan, whose contributions were many. She saved and gave me access to all of ALC's project files and other documents, from Harriet's time sheets to the ALC newsletters. Leslie freely shared her stories of growing up with and working for her mother. She paved the way for me to talk with other members of her family and with Harriet's friends and staff. Harriet's daughter Julie was an excellent source for details on Harriet's first trip through the Grand Canyon. Harriet's son John was especially helpful in providing photos of Harriet's family and details about growing up. Harriet's first husband, Robert Hunt, shared his memories and photos. Harriet's second husband, Joe Burgess, provided invaluable insights into Harriet and their life together.

Many thanks also go to Harriet's friends, staff, and advisers. Martin Litton, Harriet's inspiration and mentor, and his wife, Esther Litton, graciously responded to my inquiries and gave me excellent advice on how to get the most out of our trip through the Grand Canyon in a dory. It was a privilege to get to know them both. Lauren Ward, Harriet's real estate adviser and flying buddy, gave generously of his time and knowledge. Phil

Caterino's enthusiasm for the book helped keep me going—never *ever* give up! His knowledge of the details of the Thunderbird Lodge project enhanced the chapter on Harriet's magnificent obsession. Ame Hellman welcomed Russell and me into her Virginia home for a weekend of ALC talk, with some dressage digressions. Kara Woodruff answered all of my questions about the Hearst Ranch project and made her files available to me. Kerry O'Toole, Jeff Stump, Tim Richardson, and Chris Jehle all offered their perspectives on Harriet, both as a friend and as a boss. Ralph Benson and Steve Costa opened windows into Harriet's work at the Trust for Public Land. Al Jahns shared his Harriet stories and helped choose the five quintessential American Land Conservancy projects chronicled here. John Blaustein generously shared his photographs.

Harriet was well known for her ability to work well with landowners. My thanks to Stephen Hearst, both for his contributions to the chapter on Hearst Ranch and for the foreword. Thanks to Marty Cepkauskas and Ben Higgins for our spectacular tour of the ranch. I also would like to thank Ross de Lipkau, who answered my questions about the gravesite of his great-grandfather, John Muir, and the effort that he and ALC made to convey the gravesite to the federal government.

My research, especially into the context of Harriet's life and activities, was greatly facilitated by libraries and archives. The Sacramento Public Library provided many books that I needed and served as a conduit for essential books in the collections of other public and university libraries through LINK+. The digital archives of Northern Arizona University's Cline Library provided easy online access to their invaluable collection of oral histories. The oral histories collected by the Bancroft Library of the University of California, Berkeley, and made available online also made an important contribution to my work.

Writing is largely a solitary endeavor. I was very fortunate to have poet and writing coach extraordinaire Rae Gouirand reading and responding to the words I wrote during the last two years of my work on the book. Rae also shared her expertise with me in her creative nonfiction workshops and online Scribe lab. She has an uncanny ability to go straight to the heart of a piece and offer just the right suggestion or ask just the right question to move the writing to the next level. I would also like to thank all of my fellow participants in Rae's workshops and online sessions. I appreciated both their encouragement and constructive suggestions.

The Grand Canyon is at the heart of Harriet's story. A big thank you to O.A.R.S. and the boatmen who showed us the Grand Canyon in the same way that Harriet experienced it. My trip on the Colorado River was a once-in-a-lifetime journey that would not have been possible without Kerstin, Duffy, and Roger Dale; Morgan Holpuch; Amber Shannon; and Brian Rudd. The journey would not have been the same without the company of my husband, Russell, and our son Michael. Our son, Peter, was there in spirit if not in person. His dedication to his writing is an inspiring example. The presence of my family was essential both to my survival in the Grand Canyon and to my happiness there and always.

Appendix 1

American Land Conservancy Projects 1990–2005

THE PROJECT DESCRIPTIONS WERE EXCERPTED FROM ALC DOCUMENTA-tion with some additions and revisions. If the project information is marked with a single asterisk, it is one of the five projects featured in the book. If the project information is marked with a double asterisk, it is described within featured projects with additional information included here. The remaining projects are described for the first time.

Projects followed by (E) indicate easements. All other projects were owned or conveyed in fee. At the end of 2005 when Harriet retired, ALC owned eleven properties that had yet to be conveyed to a public agency or sold to a private buyer.

BLM: Bureau of Land Management
CCSD: Cambria Community Services District
CDFG: California Department of Fish and Game
CRT: California Rangeland Trust
DPR: California Department of Parks and Recreation
NPS: National Park Service
NRCS: Natural Resources Conservation Service of the USDA
ODOT: Oregon Department of Transportation
SMMC: Santa Monica Mountains Conservancy
USFS: United States Forest Service
USFWS: United States Fish and Wildlife Service
WCB: Wildlife Conservation Board

ALASKA

Year	Project Name	Acres	FMV ($)	Agency/Owner
2001	Denali National Park	43.49	580,000	NPS

ALC facilitated the federal acquisition of a 43.49-acre inholding located in the center of Alaska's Denali National Park and Preserve. Denali is home to North America's highest mountain, Mount McKinley (renamed Denali in 2015), at 20,320 feet and countless other spectacular mountains and glaciers. Covering six million acres, the park encompasses a complete subarctic ecosystem inhabited by grizzly bears, wolves, Dall sheep, and moose. The inholding was the largest remaining private property suitable for development in the historic Kantishna Mining District. Tied up for more than ten years in complex legal proceedings, the parcel suddenly was placed on the auction block in June 2001. In a live auction by telephone with Russell in Sacramento and Harriet in San Francisco using an instant messenger protocol to coordinate their bidding strategy, ALC bid against competing development interests and won the right to purchase the inholding. Within a few months after its acquisition, ALC successfully cleared title to the land and transferred it to the National Park Service. Project manager: Glen Williams.

Year	Project Name	Acres	FMV ($)	Agency/Owner
2005	Afognak (Waterfall)	2,185.20	1,036,200	Alaska
2005	Afognak (5B: Timber Rights)	873.00	363,000	Alaska

ALC joined with the Rocky Mountain Elk Foundation and the Kodiak Brown Bear Trust to protect more than twenty thousand acres on Afognak Island, the second largest island in the Kodiak Archipelago off the southern coast of Alaska. The first forty-four hundred acres of the project were preserved by 2005. The island's rocky coasts, streams, lakes, and forests provide habitat for more than 160 bird species, the Kodiak brown bear, Roosevelt elk, Sitka black-tailed deer, and four salmon species. Fourteen marine mammal species, including seals, porpoises, sea lions, and eight species of whales, migrate through the bay. Timber harvesting and habitat degradation from property subdivision threatened the Afognak Island environment. Project managers: Tim Richardson, Cynthia Berg, Kerry O'Toole, and Glen Williams.

CALIFORNIA
Bay Area

Year	Project Name	Acres	FMV ($)	Agency/Owner
1992	Burdell Ranch	582.00	1,455,000	CDFG

In 1992, only 5 percent of San Francisco Bay's tidal marshlands remained, the rest buried under landfill or drained for agriculture. Marshland once bordered the Petaluma River, twenty-five miles north of San Francisco.

ALC purchased 582 acres of the Burdell Ranch just north of the bay and adjacent to the Petaluma River, then conveyed it to a partnership of public agencies—the California Wildlife Conservation Board (representing the Department of Fish and Game), the California Coastal Conservancy, and the Marin Open Space District—to oversee the restoration of marshland acreage that for decades was drained of life-giving waters.

Restoring and preserving this acreage was especially significant because the land lies in the middle of hundreds of acres of already protected marshland and uplands, part of the extensive Petaluma Marsh. The land also is important historically because it was the site of a rare land grant from the Spanish to a Native American, a Miwok named Camillo Ynitia.

Lauren Ward first alerted Harriet to the Burdell Ranch project. Not long after ALC began working on the acquisition of the ranch, Lauren planned to give a tour of the project area to a representative from the Department of Fish and Game. Harriet decided to go along accompanied by Leslie and another staff member. Dressed in jeans and tennis shoes, Leslie was prepared for the trip that took them through marshland that kept getting muddier and muddier. Harriet was wearing a skirt, stockings, and sling-back high heels, but she was determined to make the walk. She did, though eventually she took off her shoes and finished the walk barefooted. Project manager: Harriet Burgess.

Year	Project Name	Acres	FMV ($)	Agency/Owner
1996	Black Point	63.70	5,400,000	ALC
1999	Pleasanton Ridge Mitigation Bank	601.72	3,310,311	Shea Homes
1999	Pleasanton Ridge Mitigation Bank	52.82	304,181	Shea Homes

Overlooking San Francisco Bay to the west, the Livermore Valley to the east, and Mount Diablo to the north, steeply sloping Pleasanton Ridge is a critical piece of the open space greenbelt surrounding San Francisco Bay. Under constant threat of development before ALC's intervention, it serves as a buffer between the rapidly growing cities in the Livermore Valley and the densely populated communities along San Francisco Bay. The property is surrounded on three sides by the Pleasanton Ridge East Bay Regional Park (EBRPD).

Working with the U.S. Fish and Wildlife Service and the California Department of Fish and Game, ALC established the property as a mitigation/conservation bank. The bank assists those who have approved development projects that disturb specific types of habitat by providing an opportunity for the permanent protection of the same type of habitat on a larger scale in another location. Those who have responsibility for mitigation can purchase credits at the bank. Habitat credit buyers provide the funds necessary for the purchase of private land and the creation of an endowment to manage and protect the property in perpetuity. The Pleasanton Ridge Conservation Bank can market its credits within a forty-mile radius.

ALC worked with Wildlands, Inc., a for-profit mitigation development firm, to complete a restoration plan and secure final approval for the establishment of the mitigation bank. As the bank was nearing completion at the end of 1998, ALC was approached by Shea Homes, a developer who needed a large number of credits. ALC sold the entire property to Shea Homes predicated on their legal obligation to finish the bank and an assurance that once the bank was completed, the property would be donated to the EBRPD. The sale to Shea Homes netted ALC a gain of $1.58 million—one of a few "home runs" that kept ALC going financially. Project manager: Glen Williams.

Year	Project Name	Acres	FMV ($)	Agency/Owner
1999	*John Muir Gravesite	1.27	200,000	NPS
1999	Cascade Ranch (E)	96.00	6,410,000	ALC
2002	Purisima Farms (E)	534.00	3,540,000	ALC

Big Sur/Central Coast

Year	Project Name	Acres	FMV ($)	Agency/Owner
1994	Limekiln	636.00	3,642,372	DPR

On one end of this spectacular property located fifty-two miles south of Carmel, Pacific Ocean waves crash against rocky headlands and spread on a sandy beach. Moving inland, coast redwoods and tanoak shade a narrow canyon leading to a hundred-foot waterfall framed by ancient redwoods. When the privately owned property, managed for many years as a public campground, went up for sale, Harriet Burgess knew she had to find a way to transfer it into public ownership.

With assistance from the Save-the-Redwoods League, the Packard Foundation, and others, ALC added Limekiln to the California State Park system giving the public access to sorrel-carpeted forest with pockets of old-growth redwoods, year-round creeks, the beach, and the campground. The Packard Foundation made a grant that allowed ALC to option the property; then, funding for the purchase was provided equally by a grant from Save-the-Redwoods and by the state of California using tax dollars earmarked by Proposition 117, a state bond measure passed in 1990. The seller, S. H. Cowell Foundation, sold the property at a significant discount.

Robert Glenn Ketchum contributed some of his photographs of Limekiln as part of the campaign to add the privately owned property to the California state park system. Ketchum had been exploring and photographing Limekiln for many years. He joined ALC's Board of Councillors in 1994.

The Limekiln State Park brochure available on the State Parks website (www.parks.ca.gov/page_id=577 as of September 11, 2017) includes details about the park such as its history and a map.

Year	Project Name	Acres	FMV ($)	Agency/Owner
1996	Limekiln	80.00	457,628	DPR
2000	Kutcher	100.71	1,800,000	DPR

The Kutcher property, part of Rancho Ventano, lies southeast of Pfeiffer Big Sur State Park and encompasses most of the ridge line seen from Highway 1. It offers spectacular views of the Big Sur coast, magnificent old-growth redwood forests intermingled with tanoak, bay, and madrone, and sweeping vistas of the surrounding mountains. The property is accessible from Coast Ridge Road, which is heavily used as a hiking, biking, and equestrian trail into the mountains. The property also has easy access to the Pine Ridge Trail, one of the most popular portals into the Ventana Wilderness. Most of the property slopes to the Big Sur River, and residential development would adversely affect water quality.

ALC originally optioned the property in 1997. The option was extended until the landowner faced possible foreclosure and bankruptcy in 1999. ALC secured bridge financing to hold the property until funding was available for public acquisition. Passage of a $2.1 billion park bond initiative in March 2000 (Safe Neighborhood Parks, Clean Water, Clean Air, and Coastal Protection Bond Act of 2000) permitted the purchase of the property by the California Department of Parks and Recreation in December 2000. Project manager: Glen Williams.

Year	Project Name	Acres	FMV ($)	Agency/Owner
2000	**East West Ranch	406.57	11,064,913	CCSD
2002	Coast Ridge (E)	4.87	110,000	ALC
2003	**Sea West/Ormsby	748.39	17,500,000	DPR
2005	*Hearst Ranch (E)	82,000.00	230,000,000	CRT
2005	**Molinari	175.50	1,950,000	DPR

The Molinari Ranch property is located near the town of San Simeon, wedged between San Simeon State Park and the Hearst Ranch. Van Gordon Creek abuts the property and provides important habitat for a run of the federally threatened central coast steelhead as well as the threatened California red-legged frog and the Southwestern pond turtle. Coastal prairie, which comprises approximately 65 percent of the property, is grazed regularly by flocks of snow and Ross's geese during the winter. The area also is known as a foraging site for the American peregrine falcon and the California condor. Burrowing owls roost there during the winter. Adding Molinari Ranch to San Simeon State Park increased recreational trail opportunities and offered the possibility of additional affordable camp facilities.

ALC optioned the property in 2001. After a six-month extension to the original one-year option term expired in November 2002, ALC secured a bank loan to purchase the property. ALC held the property until May 2005, when it was sold to the California Department of Parks and Recreation as an enhancement to San Simeon State Park. Project managers: Glen Williams, Beth Valkenburgh, and Jeff Stump.

Blue Ridge Berryessa

Year	Project Name	Acres	FMV ($)	Agency/Owner
1998	McCloskey (E)	30.00	74,000	ALC
1999	Sulphur Creek/ Homestake (E)	120.00	240,000	ALC
2000	Walters	116.00	520,000	WCB
2000	Walker Ridge	480.00	145,000	BLM
2001	**Bear Valley/ Gabrielsen (E)	12,893.00	2,290,000	CRT

Located two hours north of the San Francisco Bay Area, Bear Valley is home to one of the most spectacular displays of wildflowers in California. Largely undisturbed and managed for limited cattle grazing, the valley is habitat for many rare native wildflowers, including the star-tulip, adobe lily, and serpentine butterweed. The California Native Plant Society considers it one of the foremost wildflower displays in the world. The wildflower area comprises approximately five thousand acres on the valley floor; the remaining acreage is oak woodlands on the surrounding hills. In 1996/97, as part of an awareness campaign, ALC published a field guide to the wildflowers at Bear Valley with fifty color photographs. Bear Valley also hosts the bald eagle and species of special concern, including the prairie falcon, golden eagle, Coopers hawk, and Pacific pond turtle. Project managers: Nancy Stryble, Glen Williams, and Kerry O'Toole.

Year	Project Name	Acres	FMV ($)	Agency/Owner
2002	Otis	617.43	242,000	Yolo County

Lassen County/Bizz Johnson Trail

The Bizz Johnson Trail follows the old Fernley and Lassen branch line of the Southern Pacific Railroad, winding 25.4 miles from Susanville to Mason Station. The trail then runs along existing roads an additional 4.5 miles into Westwood where a railroad station type kiosk marks the Westwood trailhead.

Horseback riders, hikers, joggers, and mountain bicyclists use the trail. In the snowy winter months, cross-country skiers and snowmobilers can be seen traveling its length. Most of the trail traverses the rugged Susan River Canyon with beautiful views of the surrounding mountains and reminders of the railroad and logging days of the past.

The trail is named in honor of former Congressman Harold T. "Bizz" Johnson, who served in the U.S. House of Representatives from 1958 to 1980. Congressman Johnson was instrumental in the success of this rails-to-trails project.

Harriet began working on the Bizz Johnson Trail project in 1980 while at TPL. At that time, the Southern Pacific Railroad right-of-way was acquired as well as a trailhead parcel near downtown Susanville. BLM asked ALC to complete this project by acquiring private properties along the trail that, if developed, would significantly diminish the trail's scenic beauty. The private properties acquired by ALC for BLM are listed below. Project manager: Lesley Rosselli.

Year	Project Name	Acres	FMV ($)	Agency/Owner
1997	Britt	25.00	36,000	BLM
1997	Ferguson	100.00	110,000	BLM
1998	Lasick	16.37	30,000	BLM
1998	Skelton	4.70	15,000	BLM
1999	Ervin	5.00	15,000	BLM
1999	Kalker	5.00	15,000	BLM
1999	Henner	24.00	65,000	BLM
2000	Bronson's Corner	.48	30,000	BLM

Year	Project Name	Acres	FMV ($)	Agency/Owner
2000	Korver	13.33	45,000	BLM
2000	Grunauer	67.69	95,000	BLM
2000	Tierney	3.35	15,000	BLM
2000	Mignone	3.35	15,000	BLM
2000	Fannin	4.70	15,000	BLM
2001	Brown	20.00	65,000	BLM

Los Angeles County

Year	Project Name	Acres	FMV ($)	Agency/Owner
2000	Vista Pacifica	68.00	41,100,000	SMMC

Located in the northeast corner of the Baldwin Hills, a small mountain range rising from the heart of the Los Angeles Basin in Culver City, Vista Pacifica provides sweeping views of the Pacific Ocean, Hollywood Hills, the San Bernardino Mountains, and the Palos Verde Peninsula.

Vista Pacifica is an example of a public/private agency partnership. Community and park planning work completed by Community Conservation International and funded by grants from the Packard Foundation and Environment Now laid the foundation for broad governmental support at the state and local levels. Passage of Proposition 12, the Kelley-Villagarosa "Safe Neighborhood Parks, Clean Water, Clean Air and Coastal Protection Bond Act of 2000," subsequent legislative appropriations engineered by Senator Kevin Murray and Assemblyman Herb Wesson, and Los Angeles County Proposition A funds secured by Supervisor Yvonne Brathwaite Burke made the $41.1 million project possible. An innovative acquisition team made up of staff and consultants from ALC, SMMC, California Department of Parks and Recreation, and the Baldwin Hills Recreation and Conservation Authority worked around the clock for four months to make the acquisition a reality.

ALC purchased the sixty-eight-acre property from Vista Pacifica LLC. As Harriet often did, she had kept in touch with the landowner for years trying to acquire the land, but funding and support for the purchase only became available after the landowner had successfully entitled the land and had permits to start grading and building a 294-unit upscale residential subdivision. The bulldozers were on site and beginning work when ALC intervened. The landowner was not willing to work with government agencies but was willing to work with Harriet. ALC transferred fifty-eight acres to SMMC, acting on behalf of the California Department of Parks and Recreation, and ten acres to SMMC, acting on behalf of the Baldwin Hills Regional Conservation Authority.

The acquisition of Vista Pacifica was a critical first step in the expansion of state park land in the Baldwin Hills with the expectation of creating a new "Central Park" in urban Los Angeles for millions of residents. Project manager: Jeff Stump.

Year	Project Name	Acres	FMV ($)	Agency/Owner
2001	Avatar	328.00	8,110,500	SMMC

North Central

Year	Project Name	Acres	FMV ($)	Agency/Owner
1996	Pit River Canyon	358.00	51,000	BLM
1998	Adair Brown (Modoc National Wildlife Refuge)	325.00	550,000	USFWS
1998	Justeson (Gray Lodge)	750.00	1,760,000	WCB

North Coast/King Range

Year	Project Name	Acres	FMV ($)	Agency/Owner
1996	Arcata Mill B Site	15.00	50,000	NPS
1997	Mill Creek (I)	133.98	908,339	BLM
1997	Mill Creek (II) 2	20.02	1,491,661	BLM
1997	Scheinman	160.00	136,000	BLM
1998	Morreale	40.00	400,000	BLM
1998	Habashi	40.00	240,000	BLM
1998	Dienhart	1.02	100,000	BLM
1998	Reuter	42.96	315,000	BLM
1998	De la Cruz	.19	45,000	BLM
1998	Fairbanks	34.00	160,000	BLM

Year	Project Name	Acres	FMV ($)	Agency/Owner
1998	Russell	49.00	232,750	BLM
1999	McCoy Creek	160.00	45,004	ALC

Sacramento County

Year	Project Name	Acres	FMV ($)	Agency/Owner
2000	Stone Lakes	537.35	2,200,000	USFWS

The Stone Lakes property was privately owned wetland located within the boundaries of the Stone Lakes National Wildlife Refuge created in 1994. When the U.S. Fish and Wildlife Service approached the landowner to acquire the property for inclusion in the refuge, their offer was rejected because the owner did not approve of the refuge and was not willing to deal with USFWS. Wildlands, Inc., a habitat development and land management company, secured an option on the property and assigned the option to ALC. The landowner agreed to this arrangement as long as he did not have to deal directly with USFWS. After acquiring the property, ALC leased the land to Wildlands, Inc., for restoration. On completion of the restoration, ALC transferred ownership of the property to the USFWS for incorporation in the refuge. Project manager: Harriet Burgess.

Sacramento River

Willows and cottonwoods once lined the shores of California's Sacramento River, which wends its way south from the Cascade Range, across the broad Sacramento Valley, and then empties into the delta on the east side of San Francisco Bay. In 1992, less than 2 percent of the river's riparian habitat remained. Often the river's naturally dense vegetation was replaced by riprap, tons of crushed rock that retards erosion but also almost eliminates habitat. ALC, in conjunction with the BLM, worked to acquire acreage along the river for restoration and protection of important salmon and steelhead fisheries, riparian wildlife habitat, and recreational opportunities such as boating, fishing, hiking, and wildlife-watching. The private properties acquired by ALC for BLM are listed below.

Year	Project Name	Acres	FMV ($)	Agency/Owner
1992	Amen (I)	225.24	656,490	BLM
1993	Amen (II)	288.72	999,371	BLM
1993	Horseshoe (III)	432.57	1,278,135	BLM
1996	Osbon—Avilla Estates Lot #5	54.90	225,000	BLM
1996	Schoer—Avilla Estates Lot #4	46.70	220,000	BLM
1996	Bullert—Avilla Estates Lot #6	58.90	225,000	BLM
1999	Parker—Avilla Estates Lot #3	42.30	230,000	BLM
2000	Vacek	419.39	754,574	BLM
2002	Storch—Avilla Estates Lot #2	48.30	315,000	ALC
2002	Ash Creek	140.00	98,000	BLM

San Bernardino National Forest

Beginning in 1993, ALC worked with the USFS to acquire Garner Ranch, one of the largest inholdings in the San Bernardino National Forest (SBNF). The Garner Ranch is a historic landmark in the rugged mountains east of Los Angeles. Formerly part of one of the largest working cattle ranches in the United States, it had been owned by the Garner family since 1905.

The grassy meadows and forested mountain slopes of Garner Ranch are located just south of the popular tourist town of Idyllwild and at the foot of the San Jacinto Mountains and San Jacinto Wilderness within the SBNF. Magnificent pine-, fir-, and oak-covered hills surround the two spring-fed meadows of upper and lower May Valley on the Garner Ranch. The area is within the viewshed of the Pacific Crest Trail and on the migratory-bird Pacific Flyway.

With its spectacular beauty and proximity to the Los Angeles metropolitan area and its susceptibility to development, every acre that ALC has acquired from the Garner family has been a welcome addition to SBNF, one of the most frequently visited national forests. Between 1993 and

1999, ALC conveyed approximately 1,275 acres of the Garner Ranch for a total value of more than $5.6 million. It took seven different transactions to achieve this transfer (see 1993–1999 entries for Garner Ranch below). The land acquired in the eighth transaction in 2003 was part of the Garner Home Ranch, the most developable portion of the ranch given its gentle terrain and frontage along the Pines to Palms Highway.

Year	Project Name	Acres	FMV ($)	Agency/Owner
1993	Garner Ranch (I)	229.75	986,050	USFS
1994	Garner Ranch (II)	281.75	1,211,525	USFS
1995	Garner Ranch (III)	307.50	1,322,250	USFS
1996	Deep Creek	299.28	1,705,000	USFS
1996	Garner Ranch (IV)	40.00	172,000	USFS
1996	Garner Ranch (V)	131.25	564,375	USFS
1996	Garner Ranch (VI)	26.25	114,950	USFS
1997	Garner Ranch	50.00	214,536	USFS
1997	Garner Ranch	188.49	808,759	USFS
1997	Garner School Site (I)	13.83	186,705	USFS
1997	Lombardi	97.60	580,000	USFS
1998	Boy Scouts of America	124.50	657,000	USFS
1998	Calvary Chapel	100.63	503,000	USFS
1998	Garner School Site (II)	6.17	83,295	USFS
1998	Grenzow	640.00	700,000	USFS
1999	Garner Home Ranch (II)	78.11	471,000	USFS
2000	Grenzow	80.00	184,000	USFS
2001	Healy	320.00	240,000	USFS
2001	Sontag	240.69	960,000	USFS
2002	Healy	674.83	510,000	USFS
2003	Aeneas	504.80	910,000	USFS
2003	Garner Ranch	477.00	3,340,000	USFS

South Coast

Year	Project Name
1995	Bolsa Chica

The largest saltwater marsh between Monterey Bay and the Tijuana River, the Bolsa Chica wetlands cover 1,449 acres along the coast in Orange County. For a full description of Bolsa Chica and its resources, visit the website of the Bolsa Chica Conservancy, www.bolsachica.org.

ALC began working to preserve the Bolsa Chica wetlands in 1992 at the request of Huntington Beach residents after years of public preservation efforts sparked by the 1970 purchase of the wetlands by the Signal Landmark Corporation with plans for a huge waterfront development. Negotiations for the conservation of the wetlands that were valued at $60 million by the landowner involved agencies of the federal government (Fish and Wildlife, the Environmental Protection Agency, and the Army Corps of Engineers); agencies of the California state government (Fish and Game, Coastal Conservancy, Coastal Commission, Resources, State Lands Commission); and local agencies (the Ports of Los Angeles and Long Beach, the city of Huntington Beach and Orange County).

Three major issues had to be resolved: funding; toxic problems (active oil wells had been on the wetlands since the 1930s), and ultimate ownership of the property. ALC devoted several years to finding a conservation solution for Bolsa Chica that had to be approved by all of the agencies listed above.

The solution involved the purchase of the wetlands by the State Lands Commission for the benefit of the Ports of Los Angeles and Long Beach in the form of mitigation credits that permitted substantial port expansion. When the Lands Commission refused to deal with ALC and insisted on dealing directly with the landowner, ALC withdrew from the transaction to ensure that conservation of the wetlands was achieved.

The landowner made a contribution to ALC after closing to reimburse ALC's expenses for the project. Project manager: Harriet Burgess.

Year	Project Name	Acres	FMV ($)	Agency/Owner
2001	*Topanga Canyon	1,655.00	43,000,000	DPR

Tahoe/Sierras

Year	Project Name	Acres	FMV ($)	Agency/Owner
1991	West Fork Carson—North	102.78	120,000	USFS

Year	Project Name	Acres	FMV ($)	Agency/Owner
1993	Red Lake (acre-feet of water)	426.53		CDFG
1993	Red Lake (land)	85.00	1,048,730	CDFG

Red Lake overlooks Hope Valley on the east side of the Sierra Nevada, south of Lake Tahoe. From the 1800s, the lake was used to store irrigation water for farmers in Nevada's Carson Valley, twenty miles to the east. When the water rights were offered for sale in 1989, they were snapped up by a water development partnership. That group planned to sell the water to fast-growing Carson Valley cities. Instead, ALC purchased the water rights and preserved the lake. ALC also purchased acreage around and under the lake.

Year	Project Name	Acres	FMV ($)	Agency/Owner
1994	Red Lake (acre-feet of water)	400.72	1,001,769	CDFG
1994	West Fork Carson	10.65	67,005	USFS
1996	West Fork Carson— Middle	31.47	200,000	USFS
1998	Bodie (I) Mining Claims		1,000,000	BLM
1998	Bodie (II) Mining Claims		1,500,000	BLM

Located east of Bridgeport, California, near the Nevada border, Bodie was once a major gold mining area and is now a ghost town preserved in a state of "arrested decay" as Bodie State Historic Park. ALC worked with BLM and the California Department of Parks and Recreation to acquire land and mineral rights within the Bodie Bowl, a BLM designated Area of Critical Environmental Concern in California's Mojave Desert. ALC purchased a 40 percent undivided interest in the mining claims on 430.69 acres in and around Bodie State Historic Park. The project assured the preservation of the scenic viewshed and the quiet, stark beauty of Bodie State Historic Park, eliminated the threat of mining under the park, and eliminated the additional threat of open pit mining adjacent to the park. Acquisition of the mineral rights was authorized under the 1994 federal California Desert Protection Act. Project manager: Harriet Burgess.

Year	Project Name	Acres	FMV ($)	Agency/Owner
1999	Sunset Stables	189.55	3,000,000	CTC

Working in partnership with the California Tahoe Conservancy (CTC) and the David and Lucile Packard Foundation, ALC transferred 190 acres within the Lake Tahoe Basin to public ownership. Acquisition of the Sunset Stables parcel, one of the largest remaining private parcels along the Upper Truckee River, was a priority for CTC. The property boasts a large meadow supporting native grassland vegetation, wetland and bog communities, scattered stands of mixed conifers, 1.5 miles of river frontage, and recreational opportunities including perhaps the best quality stream fishing in the entire Tahoe Basin, hiking, and wildlife viewing. The Packard Foundation awarded ALC a $200,000 challenge grant to acquire this spectacular property, which subsequently was conveyed to the CTC for management and restoration. ALC lost $175,000 on this transaction. Project manager: Phil Caterino.

Year	Project Name	Acres	FMV ($)	Agency/Owner
2003	High Meadows	1,789.33	29,500,000	USFS

Owned by the Trimmer-Giovacchini family since 1905, High Meadows was used only for summer cattle pasture and annual fall harvesting of Christmas trees. Spreading over almost eighteen hundred acres, the pristine property was the largest single-owner private holding in the Lake Tahoe Basin. Conveying High Meadows to the Forest Service provided public access to some of the most beautiful recreational land in the United States and protected the watershed from development. The property lies two miles from the city of South Lake Tahoe in a valley between Heavenly Valley ski resort and Freel Peak, the tallest mountain in the Lake Tahoe Basin. Home to the headwaters of Cold Creek, High Meadows boasts emerald meadows, spring waterfalls, and summer wildflowers including red columbine, blue monkshood, purple delphinium, white Sierra angelica, and many variations of Indian paintbrush. Project managers: Jacques Etchegoyhen and Jeff Stump.

Year	Project Name	Acres	FMV ($)	Agency/Owner
2003	Canyon View	50.00	1,313,000	PLT
2003	Centennial/ Dressler (E)	6,350.00	4,200,000	CRT

The Centennial/Dressler Ranch includes nearly half of the irrigated acreage in the Bridgeport Valley located on the east slope of the Central Sierra Valley. Bridgeport Valley is one of the last remaining undeveloped mountain valleys in California and home to the largest wetland complex along the Eastern Sierra created almost entirely through irrigation. The ranch has been a working agricultural operation for 143 years.

ALC acquired a conservation easement on the property that it donated to the California Rangeland Trust to hold and monitor. Protection of this property begins the creation of a habitat "system" that links a national park, wilderness area, and private lands. By permanently preserving the ranch as rangeland and ensuring continued irrigation, the conservation easement will protect tens of miles of riparian areas/primary fish-rearing habitat for the Walker River system, one of the greatest trout fisheries in the West. This project also preserves habitat for Mono sage grouse, raptors, and the endangered wolverine while protecting a critical deer migration corridor between Yosemite National Park (only ten miles from the ranch) and the Hoover Wilderness. Project managers: Glen Williams and Jacques Etchegoyhen.

CANADA

Year	Project Name	Acres	FMV ($)	Agency/Owner
2002	Mayne Island	1.33	131,712	Island Trust

ILLINOIS

Year	Project Name	Acres	FMV ($)	Agency/Owner
2001	Bartels Farm	887.60	1,327,000	TNT Land Trust
2001	Randolph County	472.40	736,000	TNT Land Trust
2002	Witz Landing	1.26	85,000	Village of Thebes
2003	Devils Island	2,749.96	1,781,624	Illinois Department of Resources (IDR)

Year	Project Name	Acres	FMV ($)	Agency/Owner
2003	Devils Island	1.36	3,400	Private
2003	Kaskaskia (E)	2,110.00	3,587,000	NRCS

In the 1950s, much of the Mississippi River floodplain was cleared for soybean production. A substantial portion of the 16,000 acres on Kaskaskia Island was farmed, despite frequent flooding and crop destruction. ALC acquired a 3,200-acre farm there and enrolled 2,110 flood-prone acres into a conservation easement program that provided funds for wetlands restoration and tree planting. By reducing runoff of nutrient-rich fertilizer, the project benefits the ecology of the Gulf of Mexico and the endangered pallid sturgeon, a native big-river fish. ALC donated the property to the Middle Mississippi River National Wildlife Refuge. ALC sold the conservation easement to the Natural Resources Conservation Service for $3,587,000 on December 22, 2003, netting an increment of $2,675,800, which was crucial to keeping ALC afloat financially during the Hearst Ranch conservation project. Project manager: Jenny Frazier.

Year	Project Name	Acres	FMV ($)	Agency/Owner
2004	Beaver Island	245.00	118,800	Wetlands America Trust
2005	Jones (II)	105.00	210,000	Ducks Unlimited
2005	Rockwood Island (Shelton)	147.46	276,500	Ducks Unlimited
2005	Rockwood Island (Surman)	20.30	30,450	Private
2005	Rockwood Island (Vasquez)	66.20	132,000	Ducks Unlimited

Inahgeh

Inahgeh is the Cherokee word for desolate wilderness. The Cherokee gave the area that name when they first saw it during their forced relocation along the Trail of Tears in 1838. Originally hardwood bottomland, the Inahgeh wetlands lie along the Mississippi River below the bluffs of the Shawnee National Forest in southern Illinois.

ALC worked with landowners to convey permanent conservation easements on approximately five thousand acres of unproductive farmland in the

Inahgeh wetlands to the Natural Resources Conservation Service. The farmland was inundated eight out of every ten years; and after the floods of 1993, many of the submarginal farms were rendered useless for farming.

The project goal was to restore the hardwood cypress bottomland once extensive on this stretch of the Mississippi River; re-create essential habitat for waterfowl and songbirds migrating along the Mississippi flyway; and allow reintroduction of rare and endangered species. Additional benefits included the elimination of ongoing farm subsidies and disaster payments on the acquired lands and the need to make costly repairs to portions of the levee system. The private properties ALC acquired and conveyed are listed below. ALC purchased a 40 percent undivided interest in the mining claims on 430.69 acres in and around Bodie State Historic Park.

Year	Project Name	Acres	FMV ($)	Agency/Owner
1996	Abernathy (E)	47.00	27,155	NRCS
1996	Atkins/McBride (E)	94.00	96,750	NRCS
1996	Browder (E)	114.96	131,704	NRCS
1996	Browder	113.96	18,200	USFS
1996	Browder (house)	1.00	21,500	Private
1996	Five Brothers Farm (E)	1,015.84	930,416	NRCS
1996	Five Brothers Farm	1,015.84	147,000	USFS
1996	Lambdin Farm (E)	81.00	43,900	NRCS
1996	Lambdin Farm	81.00	12,400	USFS
1996	McCrate (E)	1,025.00	688,123	NRCS
1996	Morgan (E)	145.30	160,870	NRCS
1996	Morgan	145.30	25,400	USFS
1996	MTM Farm (E)	473.97	283,303	NRCS
1996	MTM Farm	473.97	94,000	USFS
1996	Munz Farm (E)	124.02	93,698	NRCS
1996	Munz Farm	124.02	21,100	USFS
1996	Myers Farm (E)	348.50	354,150	NRCS
1996	Myers Farm	348.50	59,000	USFS
1996	Rendleman Farm (E)	163.75	147,425	NRCS
1996	Rendleman Farm	163.75	25,000	USFS
1996	Russell Hill (E)	141.49	129,151	NRCS
1996	Russell Hill	141.49	23,300	USFS
1996	Seesing (E)	68.00	72,569	NRCS

Year	Project Name	Acres	FMV ($)	Agency/Owner
1996	Williams (E)	226.25	226,275	NRCS
1996	Williams	226.25	36,300	USFS
1996	Wilson (E)	89.00	51,950	NRCS
1996	Wilson	89.00	12,100	USFS
1997	Aldridge (E)	487.00	311,613	NRCS
1997	Mills (E)	203.00	177,750	NRCS
1998	Reimann (E)	199.00	288,500	NRCS
2001	Aldridge	487.00	48,695	Private
2002	Abernathy	47.00	7,755	Private
2002	Atkins/McBride	96.00	15,510	Private
2002	Baugher	44.49		IDR
2002	McCrate	1069.00		IDR
2002	Reimann	199.00		IDR
2002	Seesing	68.00		IDR
2004	Mills	185.70	20,284	Wetlands America Trust

Midewin National Tallgrass Prairie

Year	Project Name	Acres	FMV ($)	Agency/Owner
2004	Barr	13.77	100,000	USFS

INDIANA

Year	Project Name	Acres	FMV ($)	Agency/Owner
1995	Cummins (Hoosier National Forest)	108.00	84,000	USFS
1995	Cummins	11.00	4,000	Private

MICHIGAN

Year	Project Name	Acres	FMV ($)	Agency/Owner
1994	Shaw Estate/Huron National Forest	220.00	143,000	USFS

The Zeta Shaw property, in Michigan's lower peninsula, was an inholding in the Huron National Forest. One border of the 220-acre, heavily wooded land lies near the AuSable River, one of the nation's premier trout-fishing streams and a federally designated Wild and Scenic River. On the property itself, Loud Creek runs clean and clear. Supporting brook, brown, and rainbow trout populations, the locals have dubbed the creek a "trout factory" for the AuSable. But perhaps the most notable feature on the Shaw acreage is its ancient pines, reds and whites, with some three hundred growth rings wrapping their impressive girths. The trees stand as ancient relics of once vast forests in the Midwest, where today only remnants of old-growth forest remain.

The owners of the Shaw property wanted to sell it to the USFS for incorporation in the national forest. When the USFS did not have funds available for the purchase, ALC bought the property and traded it for other acreage in the forest system that had been designated as available for exchange. ALC then sold the exchange lands to finance the Shaw purchase.

Harriet commented, "People seem to think that, in terms of land preservation across the U.S., there are coastlines, mountains, lakes, and not much in between but corn and wheat. We like to remember that there's more that than in the Midwest, and that a lot of it is worth protecting." Project manager: Don Hanson.

Year	Project Name	Acres	FMV ($)	Agency/Owner
1995	Haney	40.00	23,500	USFS
1996	Seelye	36.00	31,300	USFS
1998	Azschuetz	41.76	36,000	Private
1998	Balczo	40.00	27,500	USFS
1998	Holmes (Huron-Manistee National Forest)	40.92	41,200	USFS
1999	Leknius	5.00	2,000	USFS

The Leknius family donated its five-acre inholding in the Huron-Manistee National Forest to ALC when negotiations between the family and the USFS stalled because of complex title issues. Containing significant populations of wild lupine plants, habitat crucial to the survival of the endangered Karner blue butterfly, whose larvae eat only wild lupine leaves, the Leknius family felt the property should become part of the national forest, but the USFS did not have the legal and financial resources necessary to resolve the title issues. ALC resolved the title issues, then conveyed the property to the Forest Service. Project managers: Don Hanson and Lesley Roselli.

Year	Project Name	Acres	FMV ($)	Agency/Owner
2000	Bolton & Landgraf (Huron-Manistee National Forest)	90.00	144,000	USFS

MISSOURI

Year	Project Name	Acres	FMV ($)	Agency/Owner
2001	Wilder (I), North Tract	942.00	1,064,050	Missouri Conservation Commission (MCC)
2001	Wilder (II), South Tract	1,959.00	2,359,975	MCC

MONTANA

Year	Project Name	Acres	FMV ($)	Agency/Owner
2004	Crow Creek Falls	19.90	150,000	USFS

NEVADA

Year	Project Name	Acres	FMV ($)	Agency/Owner
1991	Truckee River Canyon (Lands of Sierra)	93.78	30,000	USFS

Just ten miles southwest of Reno, Nevada, black bears lumber through stands of lodgepole and sugar pine and splash after endangered Lahontan trout in snowmelt-filled streams. Mountain lions cross granite ridges at eight thousand feet, and deer bound across lowland meadows.

Much of this rugged area known as the Carson Range lay within the Toiyabe National Forest, but thousands of acres still were privately owned by Fibreboard, a timber company, until ALC purchased their forest inholdings as listed below and conveyed them to the USFS over a period of several years from 1992 to 1994. The addition of the Fiberboard lands to the Toiyabe National Forest and Mount Rose Wilderness enhanced the habitat for wildlife and offered new opportunities for hiking and fishing.

Year	Project Name	Acres	FMV ($)	Agency/Owner
1992	Farrington Ranch	31.28	80,000	USFS
1992	Fibreboard (I)	3,681.17	2,003,863	USFS
1992	Fibreboard (II)	1,918.45	999,326	USFS
1992	Fibreboard (III)	372.46	194,204	USFS
1992	Water Canyon	1,025.71	180,000	BLM
1993	Fibreboard (IV)	3,552.46	1,981,472	USFS
1993	Fibreboard (V)	3,859.97	1,931,225	USFS
1993	Fibreboard (VI)	308.50	290,000	USFS
1993	Pole Canyon/Iveson/ High Rock Canyon	160.00	32,000	BLM

ALC transferred 160 acres of privately owned high-desert wilderness, practically unchanged since pioneers passed through 150 years before, to the BLM. The property, named Pole Canyon for the aspen poles homesteaders collected there, is a side canyon of High Rock Canyon. The Lassen-Applegate portion of the California Trail, used by thousands of pioneers and gold-digging forty-niners as they headed west, is located in High Rock Canyon.

In the shadow of the Warner Mountains, twenty-four-thousand-acre High Rock Canyon is a BLM-designated Area of Critical Environmental Concern. The land is managed to maintain its natural condition: cold creeks at the base of black cliffs of volcanic rock that rise nearly a thousand feet to sagebrush-topped mesas. Golden eagles, prairie falcons, and other raptors nest here. Native bighorn sheep were reintroduced in 1996 after an absence of fifty years.

Year	Project Name	Acres	FMV ($)	Agency/Owner
1994	Fibreboard (VII) Last Chance	360.00	230,027	USFS
1994	Fibreboard (VII) USFS land	88.00	222,000	Private

Year	Project Name	Acres	FMV ($)	Agency/Owner
1995	Harris Heights	7.60	1,820,000	USFS
1996	Cafferata (I)	12.50	9,375	USFS
1996	**Durkee Donation (Hunter Creek)	33.00	375,000	USFS

Contiguous with the Toiyabe National Forest in Washoe County, the Durkee donation fronts on the Truckee River and includes a segment of Steamboat Ditch, a favorite hiking and jogging path on the lower shoulders of Mount Rose overlooking Reno and Truckee Meadows. The property provides access to the Hunter Creek watershed, a popular recreation area on the east side of Toiyabe National Forest above Reno.

Sierra Power Company donated the property to ALC. The company previously had completed a number of transactions with Harriet Burgess when she was at TPL and later at ALC. When ALC and Sierra Power first discussed conveying the property to the USFS in 1991, the Forest Service agreed that it was an opportunity to expand public access to Toiyabe National Forest. ALC worked with the USFS for five years to process the donation, and the deed was recorded in 1996. Then the USFS regional office claimed that the deed was recorded without their approval. When Jim Nelson, supervisor of Toiyabe National Forest resigned in 1998, the USFS quitclaimed the property back to ALC. After years of discussions, the USFS finally agreed to accept the property, and ALC made the donation for a second time in September 2004. Project managers: Harriet Burgess and Jeff Stump.

Year	Project Name	Acres	FMV ($)	Agency/Owner
1996	Harris Heights	30.47	5,155,000	Del Webb
1998	Cafferata (II)	12.50	9,375	USFS
1998	*Thunderbird Lodge	140.00	50,400,000	Del Webb
1998	*Thunderbird Lodge	18.34	3,410,585	USFS
1999	Cafferata (III)	15.00	11,250	USFS
2001	Laborde	11,816.00	1,740,000	BLM

ALC first optioned the property owned by Gloria Laborde and her family in 1994, intending to trade it to BLM for federal parcels in the Reno area.

For six years, Gloria and her family were patient as the BLM slowly worked through the exchange process. In September 2000, however, the Laborde family informed ALC that they no longer could delay the sale of their $1.74 million property. ALC made the purchase several weeks later even though the BLM was not in a position to acquire the property immediately, nor was a close date in sight.

For ALC, the Laborde property's open space and habitat values made it worth taking the risk. Located between Reno and Carson City just east of Washoe Lake, it offers spectacular views of the lake below and the Sierra range across the valley. It is critical winter mule deer habitat for the herd that migrates out of the snowy Sierra. It is also home throughout the year for a herd of wild horses. Large groves of aspen, with anthropologically significant Basque carvings, overlook thousands of acres of piñon-juniper forests and tall sage. At the very highest elevations of the property sits a crown of remnant Western white pines most likely established during a "little ice age" 150 years before.

ALC worked closely with Washoe County and the Citizen's Advisory Board representing the area to facilitate this land exchange with the BLM. Both groups voted unanimously to support the exchange. Eight months after ALC acquired the Laborde property, and after a lengthy appeal process, ALC conveyed it to the BLM. BLM acquisition not only prevented further development in an area popular because of the views but also filled in gaps in BLM's checkerboard pattern of ownership. It created more than twenty thousand continuous acres of public land stretching east from the shores of Washoe Lake. Project managers: Harriet Burgess, Ame Hellman, Lesley Rosselli, and Kerry O'Toole.

Year	Project Name	Acres	FMV ($)	Agency/Owner
2001	Red Hill (Donation)	404.69	366,714	Washoe County
2001	Red Hill (West Peak)	12.63	327,444	Private
2002	Spanish Springs	229.44	100,000	BLM
2003	Red Hill (Chocolate Drive)	41.11	125,286	Private
2004	Hunter Creek	32.00	375,000	Washoe County

Year	Project Name	Acres	FMV ($)	Agency/Owner
2004	Red Hill (Communications Site)	10.27	372,555	Private
2005	Deer Creek (Olive)	.50	119,000	USFS
2005	Deer Creek (Rittenhouse)	.50	108,000	USFS
2005	Urrutia (Tank Site #1)	4.64	5,969	Washoe County

Nevada Land Exchange I

Year	Project Name	Acres	FMV ($)	Agency/Owner
1994	* BLM Las Vegas Lands:			
	*Appraisal 1 (Laub)	1,042.50	13,880,000	Private
	*Appraisal 2 (Pacific Southwest)	110.00	4,610,000	Private
	*Appraisal 3 (Pine Development)	355.62	3,865,000	Private
	*Appraisal 4 (Aleman)	205.00	2,460,000	Private
	*Appraisal 5 (Perma-Bilt)	110.00	3,960,000	Private
	*Appraisal 6 (Lewis Homes, Section 18)	40.00	2,051,000	Private
	*Appraisal 6 (Flangas, Tract 3)	25.00	1,167,000	Private
	*Appraisal 6 (David Argier, Tract 2)	15.00	288,000	Private
	*Appraisal 6 (Plon, Tract II)	25.00	480,000	Private
	*Appraisal 6 (Davis, Tract 2)	10.00	192,000	Private
	*Appraisal 6 (Scarpelli, Tract 2)	5.00	96,000	Private
	*Appraisal 6 (Doris Argier, Tract 2)	10.00	192,000	Private

Year	Project Name	Acres	FMV ($)	Agency/ Owner
	*Appraisal 6 (Secchiaroli, Tract 2)	5.00	96,000	Private
	*Appraisal 6 (Integrity Homes, Tract 2)	35.00	672,000	Private
	*Appraisal 7 (Halco, Tract 2)	95.00	1,311,000	Private
	*Appraisal 7 (Shearling, Tract 3)	262.63	4,739,000	Private
	*Depaoli I Home Ranch (Washoe and Storey Counties)	493.00	4,132,525	BLM/ BIA
		2,103.20 acre-feet of water		
	*Galena	3,726.00	19,868,696	BLM/ USFS
		778.39 acre-feet of water		
	*Peavine/Granite	5,404.00	3,475,000	BLM/ USFS
		71.20 acre-feet of water		
	*Peavine/Venture	3,120.00	2,150,000	BLM/ USFS
		110.00 acre-feet of water		
	*Pyramid Lake (Comer)	1.12	17,000	BLM/ BIA
	*Pyramid Lake (Crean/ Big Bend Ranch)	244.15	2,115,750	BLM/ BIA

Year	Project Name	Acres	FMV ($)	Agency/ Owner
	659.32 acre-feet of water			
	Pyramid Lake (Pulver)	1.06	45,500	BLM/ BIA
	Urrutia	116.28	1,292,000	BLM/ BIA
		84.83 acre-feet of water		
1995	*BLM Las Vegas Lands:			
	*Appraisal 6 (Brown, Tract 2)	5.00	96,000	Private
	*Appraisal 6 (Johnson, Tract 4)	10.00	432,000	Private
	*Appraisal 6 (Gamma, Tract 4)	5.00	216,000	Private
	*Appraisal 7 (Falcon Homes, Tract 1)	255.00	3,480,000	Private
	*Appraisal 8 (Perma- Bilt, Section 6)	105.00	1,810,000	Private
	Bitner Ranch (Coops)	3,296.53	692,000	BLM
	Depaoli (Pah Rah Mountains)	10,542.23	752,475	BLM
		359.77 acre-feet of water		
	Harris Springs (Red Rock Conservation Area)	32.50	339,000	BLM
	Massacre Ranch (Bunyard)	4,194.09	836,200	BLM
	Rosaschi (I)	1,370.00	2,090,000	USFS

Year	Project Name	Acres	FMV ($)	Agency/ Owner
	Rosaschi (II)	1,013.49 3,419.16 acre-feet of water	1,600,000	USFS
1996	*Deer Creek Acreage	383.21	7,630,000	USFS
1996	*Deer Creek Lots	75.77	2,890,000	USFS
1996	Washoe County	20.00	230,000	Washoe County
1996	Washoe County	200.00	234,000	USFS

Nevada Land Exchange II

Year	Project Name	Acres	FMV ($)	Agency/ Owner
1997	BLM Las Vegas Lands:			
	Lewis Homes	5.00	550,000	Private
	Nevada Bighorns Unlimited	4,300.02	335,000	BLM
	Perma-Bilt I	83.75	5,450,000	Private
	Silver Saddle	703.00	5,350,000	BLM
	Urrutia (Poeville I & II, Peavine Mountain)	407.50	213,354	USFS
	Urrutia (Poeville III, Peavine Mountain)	102.49	53,661	USFS
	Urrutia (Poeville IV, Peavine Mountain)	91.65	47,985	USFS
1998	BLM Las Vegas Lands:			
	**Faye-Luther Canyon	2.35	40,000	USFS
	Perma-Bilt IIa	45.00	2,600,797	Private
	Perma-Bilt IIb	60.00	3,467,730	Private
	RO Ranch	1,838.74	1,200,000	USFS/ BLM
2000	Ash Meadows	353.68	447,000	USFWS

Approximately 90 miles northwest of Las Vegas, the 353.68-acre Trenary property in Nye County, Nevada, was the largest private inholding within the Ash Meadows National Wildlife Refuge. The spring-fed wetlands and the alkaline desert uplands of this oasis—one of only a few desert oases remaining in the southwestern United States—provide habitat for at least twenty-six plants and animals found nowhere else in the world. The Ash Meadows refuge contains the greatest localized concentration of endemic species in the United States and the second greatest concentration in all of North America. The addition of the Trenary property to Ash Meadows ensured continued protection of these sensitive lands as well as the consolidation of public ownership in the area.

ALC purchased the property in 1997. In early 2000, the BLM auctioned public lands in Nevada for $12 million, with the cash proceeds designated for the purchase of environmentally sensitive lands in and around Clark County (as specified by the Southern Nevada Public Land Management Act). Using funds generated by the BLM public land sales, the USFWS purchased the property from ALC for addition to the Ash Meadows National Wildlife Refuge.

OHIO

Year	Project Name	Acres	FMV ($)	Agency/Owner
1991	**Hackathorn	70.00	28,000	USFS
1991	Jones Estate / Wayne National Forest	863.52	250,000	USFS

OREGON

Siletz Bay

Located approximately 128 miles south of the mouth of the Columbia River, Siletz Bay contains some of the last private wetlands habitat along the Oregon coast. The area provides breeding grounds for fish and a stopover feeding ground along the Pacific Flyway for migratory waterfowl. It was identified by the U.S. Fish and Wildlife Service (USFWS) as crucial to the future integrity of many endangered bird populations, including the bald eagle, peregrine falcon, brown pelican, and Canada goose. The open water of the bay supports Dungeness crab and ghost shrimp. It is critical to the Siletz Bay fishery. At the request of the USFWS, ALC participated in the establishment of Siletz Bay as a new wildlife refuge and conveyed the four parcels to augment lands already in the public domain.

Year	Project Name	Acres	FMV ($)	Agency/Owner
1993	Siletz Bay (Gray)	151.04	150,000	USFWS
1993	Wood River (I)— South	1,540.51	860,000	BLM
1994	Siletz Bay (ODOT)	27.36	19,400	ODOT
1994	Wood River (Parcel 2) BLM land	10.00	45,456	Private
1994	Wood River (Parcel 3) BLM land	56.50	71,820	Private
1994	Wood River (IV)	1,680.00	1,182,850	BLM
1995	Siletz Bay (Jackson)	43.90	220,000	USFWS
1995	Wood River (Parcel 1, Lot 1) BLM land	13.91	20,932	Private
1995	Wood River (Parcel 1, Lot 2) BLM land	21.34	28,511	Private
1995	Wood River (Parcel 1, Lot 3) BLM land	19.63	25,191	Private
1997	Siletz Bay (Shaffer)	26.00	145,000	USFWS
1998	BLM Land	1,600.00	625,450	Jeld-Wen

WISCONSIN

Year	Project Name	Acres	FMV ($)	Agency/Owner
1999	Whittlesey Creek	40.00	32,000	USFS
2002	Glacial Springs	320.00	245,000	USFWS

Appendix 2

ALC Board of Directors/Councillors
1990–2005

DIRECTORS/EXECUTIVE COMMITTEE
Harriet Burgess, 1990–2005
Joseph Fink, 1995–2005
Gary Giacomini, 2004–2016
Martin Litton, 1990–2005
Robert Stephens, 1990–2016

COUNCILLORS
Bruce Babbitt, 1990–1992
    United States Secretary of the Interior, 1993–2001
    Governor of Arizona, 1978–1987
    Attorney General of Arizona, 1975–1978

Harriet C. Babbitt, 1990–1992
    Deputy Administrator, United States Agency for International Development, 1997–2001
    United States Ambassador to the Organization of American States, 1993–1997

Edward J. Blakely, 1998–2001
    University of Southern California, School of Urban and Regional Planning, Dean, 1994–2001

University of California, Berkeley, Department of City and Regional Planning, Chair, 1986–1994
Member of task forces and commissions at the local, state, national, and international levels

David Brower, 1990–2000
Earth Island Institute, Founder, 1982
Friends of the Earth, Founder, 1969
League of Conservation Voters, Founder, 1969
Sierra Club, Executive Director, 1952–1969

Brock Evans, 1990–2006
Endangered Species Coalition, 1997–
National Audubon Society, Vice President for National Issues, 1981–1996
Sierra Club, Washington D.C., Director, 1973–1981
Sierra Club, Northwest Representative, 1967–1973

W. E. "Bill" Garrett, 1990–2003
National Geographic, Editor, 1980–1990

Gary Giacomini, 2003–2016
California Coastal Commission, 1989–1999
Marin County, Board of Supervisors, 1972–1996

Robert Glenn Ketchum, 1994–2006
International League of Conservation Photographers, Founding Fellow, 2005
Outstanding Photographer of the Year, North American Nature Photography Association, 2001
United Nations, Global 500 Outstanding Environmental Achievement Award, 1991
Ansel Adams Award for Conservation Photography (Sierra Club), 1990

L. W. "Bill" Lane Jr., 1990–2003
Lane Publishing Co., Cochairman

Sunset Magazine, Publisher, 1959–1990
United States, Secretary of the Interior, Advisory Board and Council on National Parks
Ambassador to Australia and Nauru, 1985–1989
First International Ocean Exposition in Japan, Ambassador-at-large and Commissioner General, 1975–1976
National Parks Centennial Commission, Chair, 1971

Paul Laxalt, 2001–2003
The Paul Laxalt Group (Washington, D.C., lobbying firm), 1998–2015
U.S. Senator, Nevada, 1974–1987
Governor of Nevada, 1967–1971
Lieutenant Governor of Nevada, 1963–1967

Orville Magoon, 2001–2006
Guenoc Winery and Guenoc Ranch, Manager, 1969–2003
U.S. Army Corps of Engineers, South Pacific Division, 1953–1983 (retired as Chief of the Coastal Engineering Branch of the Planning Division)
Coastal Zone Foundation, President (forty years)
Coastal Engineering Research Council, Vice Chair (forty years)
American Shore and Beach Preservation Association, President (ten years)

Floyd J. Marita, 1998–2006
U.S. Forest Service, Eastern Region, Regional Forester

Helen McCloskey, 1990–2006

Paul N. "Pete" McCloskey, 1990–2006
U.S. House of Representatives, Member, 1967–1983

Jerry Meral, 2003–2006
Natural Heritage Institute, California Water Program, Director
California Natural Resources Agency, Deputy Secretary, 2011–2013
Planning and Conservation League, Executive Director, 1983–2003

California Department of Water Resources, Deputy Director, 1975–1983
Environmental Defense Fund, Western Water Resources, Director, 1971–1975

Margaret W. Owings, 1990–1999
Environmental Defense Fund, Trustee, 1972–1982
Friends of the Sea Otter, Founder and first President, 1968–early 1990s
California Parks Commission, 1963–1969
National Audubon Society Medal
United Nations Environmental Program Gold Medal
U.S. Department of the Interior, Conservation Service Award

E. Lewis Reid, 1998–2006
Buck Institute for Age Research, Trustee
The California Endowment, President and Chief Executive Officer, 1998–2000
Marron Reid and Sheehy, LLP, Founding Partner, 1980–1998
U.S. Senate, Interior Committee, Minority Counsel, 1966–1968
Principal author of Proposition 20, the 1972 initiative that created California's coastal program and the Coastal Commission

Galen Rowell, 1992–2002
Internationally known landscape photographer and author of *Bay Area Wild*, *North America the Beautiful*, *Poles Apart*, and other books
Ansel Adams Award

Wallace Stegner, 1990–1993
Author of thirty books including *The Big Rock Candy Mountain*, *Angle of Repose* (Pulitzer Prize), and *Beyond the Hundredth Meridian: John Wesley Powell and the Second Opening of the West*
Environmentalist who wrote "The Wilderness Letter" in 1960
Stanford University, Professor, 1945–1971

Stewart Udall, 1990–2003
U.S. Department of the Interior, Secretary 1961–1969
Author of *The Quiet Crisis* (1963, rev. 1988) and other books on the West

National Audubon Society Medal
Ansel Adams Award

Ardis Manley Walker, 1990–1991
Poet and environmentalist

Colburn Wilbur, 2000–2006
David and Lucile Packard Foundation, Trustee, 1999–2014
David and Lucile Packard Foundation, President, 1976–1999
Sierra Club Foundation, Executive Director and CEO, 1969–1976

Appendix 3

ALC Staff
1990–2005

Staff and positions are included as listed in periodic ALC newsletters and on ALC letterhead.

Fall 1990
  Harriet Burgess, President
  Aaron Peskin, Project Manager
  Serena Herr, Grants Writer
  Wendy Shuken, News Editor

Fall 1992
  Harriet Burgess, President
  Nancy Shanahan, General Counsel
  Aaron Peskin, Western Conservation Program
  Leslie King, Staff Assistant
  Carrie Knopf, Legal Assistant
  Harriot Manley, Editor and Writer
  Lucy I. Sargeant, Designer and Illustrator

August 1993
  Harriet Burgess, President
  Bucky Mace, Project Manager
  Leslie King, Office Manager
  Lesley Coffin, Paralegal

Pam Kay, Receptionist
Harriot Manley, Editor and Writer
Lucy I. Sargeant, Designer and Illustrator

Winter 1994
Harriet Burgess, President
Leslie King, Office Manager
Lesley Coffin, Paralegal
Pam Kay, Receptionist
Kimberly Moses, Staff Assistant
Chuck East, Donald P. Hanson, Midwest Consultants
Harriot Manley, Editor and Writer
Lucy I. Sargeant, Designer and Illustrator
Stephanie Pressman, Production Coordinator

Winter/Spring 1995
Harriet Burgess, President
Lesley Coffin, Paralegal
Leslie King, Office Manager
Thomas Jordan, Attorney
Nancy Stryble, Director of Development
Kimberly Moses, Ted Reid, Bradley Schabert, Project Assistants
Cynthia Cole, Financial Manager
Lisa Kitchen, Receptionist
Chuck East, Donald Hanson, Midwest Consultants
Harriot Manley, Editor and Writer
Lucy I. Sargeant, Designer and Illustrator
Stephanie Pressman/Frog on the Moon, Production Coordinator

December 1996
Harriet Burgess, President
Lesley Rosselli, Project Director
Leslie King, Office Manager
Joshua A. Bloom, Ame Hellman, Bill Livermore, Project Managers
Nancy Stryble, Director of Development

Ted Reid, Project Assistant
Chris Jehle, Financial Manager
James Bromberg, Receptionist
Grant Barbour, Nevada Consultant
Donald Hanson, Midwest Consultant
Harriot Manley, Editor
Pam Cullen, Designer

January 14, 1997
Harriet Burgess, President
Grant Barbour, Nevada Consultant
Jim Bromberg, Receptionist
Phil Caterino, Project Manager
Don Hanson, Midwest Consultant
Ame Hellman, Project Manager
Chris Jehle, Financial Manager
Ted Reid, Project Manager
Lesley Rosselli, Project Director
Nancy Stryble, Director of Development

Summer/Fall 1998
Harriet Burgess, President
Ame Hellman, Vice President
Melvin B. Shaw, Executive Director of Development
Grant Barbour, Western Consultant
Phil Caterino, Project Associate
Kristin Coates, Executive Assistant to the President
Nicole Dooskin, Project Assistant
Esther Feldman, Southern California Consultant
Donald Hanson, Midwest Consultant
Chris Jehle, Financial Manager
Kaija Jones, Development Assistant
Ted Reid, Project Manager
Lesley Rosselli, Project Manager
Glen Williams, Project Manager

Fall 1999

Harriet Burgess, President
Ame Hellman, Vice President
Melvin B. Shaw, Executive Director of Development
Kristin Coates, Project Manager
Nicole Dooskin, Project Associate
Donald Hanson, Midwest Consultant
Chris Jehle, Financial Officer
Kerry O'Toole, Assistant to the President
Lesley Rosselli, Project Manager
Jeff Stump, Project Manager
Glen Williams, Project Manager

Winter 2000

Harriet Burgess, President
Shawn Connolly, Assistant to the President
Nicole Dooskin, Project Consultant
Jacques Etchegoyhen, Project Manager, Nevada
Jennifer Frazier, Project Manager, Missouri
Donald Hanson, Midwest Consultant
Chris Jehle, Vice President of Finance
Kerry O'Toole, Project Manager
Pamela Rey, Project Associate
Jeff Stump, Project Manager
Beth Van Valkenburgh, Project Manager
Daniel Waggoner, Assistant to the Vice President of Finance
Glen Williams, Vice President

Summer 2001

Harriet Burgess, President
Glen Williams, Vice President
Chris Jehle, Senior Vice President of Finance
Shawn Connolly, Executive Assistant
Jacques Etchegoyhen, Project Manager, Nevada
Jennifer Frazier, Project Manager, Missouri
Kerry O'Toole, Project Manager

Pamela Rey, Project Associate
Jeff Stump, Project Manager
Beth Van Valkenburgh, Project Manager, California Central Coast
Daniel Waggoner, Finance Assistant

Winter 2003
Harriet Burgess, President
Chris Jehle, Senior Vice President of Finance
Glen Williams, Vice President
Cynthia Berg, Development Associate
Kara Blakeslee, Project Manager
Shawn Connolly, Assistant to the President
Jacques Etchegoyhen, Project Manager
Jenny Frazier, Project Manager
Kerry O'Toole, Project Manager
Jeff Stump, Project Manager
Beth Van Valkenburgh, Project Manager
Daniel Waggoner, Project Associate
Patrick Ward, Project Associate

Winter 2006
Mark Bergstrom, President
Cynthia Berg, Development Director
Shawn Connolly, Communications Director
Steve Dettman, Stewardship Director
Mike Dwyer, GIS Specialist
Jennifer Frazier, Director, Mississippi River Program
Chris Jehle, Senior Vice President of Finance
Kerry O'Toole, Director, Central Valley Program
Tim Richardson, Director of Government Affairs
Jeff Stump, Director, Coastal Program
Elisa Royce, Mississippi River Project Coordinator

Notes

Introduction

1. Reynold Thomas, telephone conversation with author, February 25, 2013.

2. Betty Friedan, *The Feminine Mystique* (New York: Norton, 2013, 1963), 1; Harriet Burgess, "Woman Entrepreneur of the Year 1999," video, https://www.youtube.com/watch?v=4n6w9KMc43g, April 22, 2010.

3. Sheryl Sandberg, *Lean In: Women, Work, and the Will to Lead* (New York: Alfred A. Knopf, 2013).

4. Elizabeth Barham Austin, *To Be the Change You Wish to See: A History of the Assembly, Executive, Judicial Administration & Senate Fellowship Programs*, 2nd ed. (Berkeley: University of California, Berkeley Public Policy Press, 2017).

5. Edward Abbey, *Beyond the Wall* (New York: Holt, Rinehart and Winston, 1984), xvi.

6. George Bernard Shaw, epistle dedicatory to *Man and Superman; a Comedy and a Philosophy* (New York: Penguin, 2004; New York: Brentano's, 1904), 32.

7. Harriet Hunt Burgess, letter to Peter Stein, May 18, 1993.

8. Theodore Roosevelt's remarks were delivered on May 6, 1903, during his first visit to the Grand Canyon. "Mr. Roosevelt Sees the Grand Canyon," *New York Times*, May 7, 1903; Address of President Roosevelt at Grand Canyon, Arizona, May 6, 1903. Theodore Roosevelt Papers. Library of Congress Manuscript Division. https://www.theodorerooseveltcenter.org/Research/Digital-Library/Record?libID=o289796. Theodore Roosevelt Digital Library. Dickinson State University.

9. Between 1903 and 2014, thirty-six people died while hiking the Bright Angel Trail. Michael P. Ghiglieri and Thomas M. Myers, *Over the Edge: Death in the Grand Canyon*, rev. and expanded 2nd ed. (Flagstaff, AZ: Puma, 2012), 151–63.

10. Martin Litton, interview by Lew Steiger, Flagstaff, Arizona, October 10, 1992, *Grand Canyon River Guides Oral History Collection*, interview no. 53.32A, Northern Arizona University, Cline Library, archive.library.nau.edu/cdm/fullbrowser/collection/cpa/id/63428/rv/singleitem/rec/1, May 16, 2016; Brad Dimock, "Articulate Outrage, Righteous Wrath—Martin Litton," *Boatman's Quarterly Review: Journal of the Grand Canyon River Guides* (Winter 2014/2015): 26–46, www.gcrg.org/bqr/pdf/28-1.pdf, November 23, 2015; Kevin Fedarko, "Ain't It Just Grand," *Outside Magazine*, June 2005, www.outsideonline.com/1927766/aint-it-just-grand, March 30, 2016.

11. Brad Dimock, "Articulate Outrage, Righteous Wrath," 34; Martin Litton, interview by Lew Steiger, Flagstaff, Arizona, October 10, 1992.

12. The two boatmen who first added fliplines were Regan Dale and Kenton Grua. Regan Dale, interview by Lewis Steiger, Flagstaff, Arizona, November 6, 1998, Grand Canyon

River Guides Oral History Collection, interview no. 53.15, Northern Arizona University, Cline Library, archive.library.nau.edu/cdm/singleitem/collection/cpa/id/63443/rec/13, January 7, 2016; Kenton Grua, interview by Lewis Steiger, Flagstaff, Arizona, December 30, 1997, Grand Canyon River Guides Oral History Collection, interview no. 53.23C, Northern Arizona University, Cline Library, archive.library.nau.edu/cdm/singleitem/collection/cpa/id/63423/rec/8, January 7, 2016.

13. Marion Softky, "Crusader for Nature," *The Almanac*, September 13, 2000.

14. All river guides usually are called boatmen regardless of sex.

15. Robert G. Hunt and Julie Walsh, interview by the author, June 29, 2010.

Chapter 1: Two Husbands and Five Children: Beginnings

1. Friedan, *Feminine Mystique*, 22.

2. John Muir, *A Thousand-Mile Walk to the Gulf* (Boston: Houghton Mifflin, 1916; San Francisco: Sierra Club Books, 1991), 70.

3. Construction on the house began in November 1962. The house was completed by the end of May 1963. Personal files of Leslie King Cowan, reviewed November 17, 2015.

4. Robert G. Hunt, telephone interview by the author, April 28, 2010.

5. Cedarville College was a Presbyterian college until McNeel's last year there when it became a Baptist institution. Western Theological Seminary still is affiliated with the Presbyterian Church. It became known as the Pittsburgh Theological Seminary when it joined with the Pittsburgh-Xenia Theological Seminary in 1959 after the 1958 merger between the Presbyterian Church in the United States and the United Presbyterian Church of North America. Clair Vaughn McNeel, "Minister's Information Form," The Presbyterian Church in the United States of America, Department of Ministerial Relations, May 23, 1957, www.pts.edu/History and www.cedarville.edu/About, April 4, 2016.

6. McNeel, "Minister's Information Form."

7. Ibid.

8. Ibid.

9. Ibid.; Leonard J. Moore, *Citizen Klansmen: The Ku Klux Klan in Indiana, 1921–1928* (Chapel Hill: University of North Carolina Press, 1991); Tim Richardson, interview by the author, June 29, 2010.

10. Session is the governing body of a local Presbyterian Church whose members are elders elected from the congregation. McNeel, "Minister's Information Form," www.sharoncpc.com/detailed-history.html, April 4, 2016.

11. Hunt, telephone interview, April 28, 2010.

12. McNeel, "Minister's Information Form"; Hunt, telephone interview, April 28, 2010.

13. Hunt, telephone interview, April 28, 2010; Harriet Burgess, oral history interview by Carol McLaughlin, January 12, 2006.

14. Ibid.

15. Ibid.; Hunt, telephone interview, April 28, 2010; Robert G. Hunt, interview by the author, June 29, 2010.

16. Hunt, telephone interview, April 28, 2010; Robert G. Hunt, e-mail to the author, September 5, 2012; Eugenia Kaledin, *Daily Life in the United States, 1940–1959, Shifting Worlds* (Westport, CN: Greenwood Press, 2000), 108; James T. Patterson, *The Dread Disease: Cancer and Modern American Culture* (Cambridge, MA: Harvard University Press, 1987), 176.

17. Online images of 1950s advertisements; David Halberstam, *The Fifties* (New York: Villard, 1993), 590–92; Loveland Burial Park, www
.cityofloveland.org/departments/parks-recreation/burial-park-cemetery, April 5, 2016.

18. Friedan, *Feminine Mystique*, 36–37; Hunt, telephone interview, April 28, 2010; Kaledin, *Daily Life*; Brett Harvey, *The Fifties: A Women's Oral History* (New York: HarperCollins, 1993), 75.

19. Hunt, telephone interview, April 28, 2010; Kaledin, *Daily Life*, 106.

20. The Department of Housing and Urban Development was created in 1965. Hunt, telephone interview, April 28, 2010.

21. Hunt, telephone interview, April 28, 2010; Leslie King Cowan, conversation with the author, November 17, 2015.

22. Harvey, *The Fifties*, 88–89, 91–92.

23. Brian Ward, ed., *The 1960s: A Documentary Reader* (Hoboken, NJ: Wiley-Blackwell, 2010), 13; Harvey, *The Fifties*, 226–27; Stephanie Coontz, *A Strange Stirring: The Feminine Mystique and American Women at the Dawn of the 1960s* (New York: Basic Books, 2011), 25, 32; Friedan, *Feminine Mystique*, 22.

24. Membership in the League of Women Voters increased 44 percent in the 1950s and provided a springboard for many women into the world of politics. Cowan, conversation, November 17, 2015; Fairfax County Federation of Citizen Associations, 19th Annual Awards Dinner and Washington Star Citizenship Trophy Presentation Program, February 27, 1969; Kaledin, *Daily Life*, 104.

25. Hunt, e-mail, August 16, 2012; Fairfax County Federation of Citizen Associations, 19th Annual Awards Dinner; Leslie King Cowan, personal files; Robert G. Hunt and Julie Walsh, interview by the author, June 29, 2010.

26. Fairfax County Federation of Citizen Associations, 19th Annual Awards Dinner; Hunt, e-mail, August 16, 2012.

27. Hunt, e-mail, August 16, 2012; Fairfax County Federation of Citizen Associations, 19th Annual Awards Dinner; Hunt and Walsh, interview, June 29, 2010.

28. Fairfax County Federation of Citizen Associations, 19th Annual Awards Dinner; Hunt, telephone interview, April 28, 2010; Glenda Riley, *Women and Nature: Saving the "Wild" West* (Lincoln: University of Nebraska Press, 1999), 91, 181; Harriet Burgess, "Biographical Data," 198? (prepared while Harriet Burgess was employed by Trust for Public Land per Leslie King Cowan, February 23, 2016).

29. Sarah [surname not given], letter to Harriet Hunt, April 18, 1968.

30. Thomas, telephone interview, February 25, 2013; Harriet Burgess, "Biographical Data"; Hunt, telephone interview, April 28, 2010; *The Comprehensive Plan for Fairfax County, Virginia* (1986), www.fairfaxcounty.gov/dpz/comprehensiveplan/planhistoric/1986_doc uments/1986_countywide.pdf, February 15, 2016; Betsy Hinkle, ed., *Fairfax County Newsletter*, 20 February 20, 1975.

31. Robert G. Hunt, e-mails to the author, March 15 and 30, 2013.

32. Hunt, telephone interview, April 28, 2010; Leslie King Cowan, interview by the author, November 17, 2008.

33. Robert G. Hunt, e-mail to the author, September 5, 2012; Cowan, interview, November 17, 2008; Rachel Carson, *The Sense of Wonder* (New York: Harper & Row, 1965; New York: HarperCollins, 1998), 26, 55, and 67.

34. Hunt, telephone interview, April 28, 2010; Harriet Hunt Burgess, *Curriculum Vitae*, August 20, 1996.

35. Hunt and Walsh, interview, June 29, 2010; John Hunt, conversation with the author, March 24, 2019.

36. Harriet Hunt, letter (handwritten draft) to Mr. Campbell, n.d..

37. A. H. Maslow, "Dominance, Personality and Social Behavior in Women," *Journal of Social Psychology* 10 (1939): 3–39, and "Self Esteem (Dominance-Feeling) and Sexuality in Women," *Journal of Social Psychology* 16 (1942): 259–94, quoted in Friedan, *Feminine Mystique*, 382–95; William E. Black, "Busy Mother of Five Thrives on Schedule," *Alexandria Gazette*, October 19, 1974.

38. Friedan, *Feminine Mystique*, 8–9, 15.

39. Friedan, *Feminine Mystique*, 369–70.

40. National Association of Women Business Owners, "Harriet Burgess, Woman Entrepreneur of the Year, Community Advocate, 1999," video uploaded to YouTube April 22, 2010, www.youtube.com/watch?v=4n6w9KMc43g.

41. Brock Evans, interview by the author, June 29, 2010.

42. Ibid.

43. Harriet coordinated women's activities for Northern Virginia for the William Battle for Governor campaign in 1969; she was cochair of the Omer Hirst for Virginia Senate campaign in 1971; and she was treasurer of the Packard for Chairman campaign in 1975.

44. Hunt, telephone interview, April 28, 2010; Harriet Burgess, oral history interview by Carol McLaughlin, January 12, 2006; Dan Gunderson, "Coya's Story," Minnesota Public Radio, May 3, 2004, http://news.minnesota.publicradio.org/features/2004/05/16_gunder sond_coya/, May 13, 2016.

45. Hunt, telephone interview, April 28, 2010; Evans, interview, June 29, 2010.

46. Hunt, e-mail, March 15, 2013.

47. Tom Turner, *David Brower: The Making of the Environmental Movement* (Oakland: University of California Press, 201), 118; Kevin Fedarko, *The Emerald Mile* (New York: Scribner, 2013), 78–79; Buzz Belknap and Loie Belknap Evans, *Grand Canyon River Guide* (Evergreen, CO: Westwater, 2007), 32, 61; U.S. Bureau of Reclamation, *Pacific Southwest Water Plan, Report* (January 1964).

48. Sierra Club, minutes of the annual organization meeting of the board of directors, Oakland, California, May 4, 1963, http://content.cdlib.org/ark:/28722/bk000795z3j/ ?order=30&brand=calisphere, May 16, 2016.

49. Fedarko, *Emerald Mile*, 83–84; Address of President Roosevelt at Grand Canyon, Arizona, May 6, 1903. Theodore Roosevelt Papers. Library of Congress Manuscript Division. https://www.theodorerooseveltcenter.org/Research/Digital-Library/Record?li bID=o289796. Theodore Roosevelt Digital Library. Dickinson State University.

50. Philip L. Fradkin, *A River No More: the Colorado River and the West*, expanded and updated (Berkeley: University of California Press, 1995), 230; Art Buchwald, "Down the Rapids with Bobby," *Milwaukee Sentinel*, July 11, 1967 (originally published in the *Washington Post*); Fedarko, *Emerald Mile*, 91.

51. David Brower, *For Earth's Sake: The Life and Times of David Brower* (Salt Lake City: Peregrine Smith, 1990), 364–68; Marc Reisner, *Cadillac Desert: The American West and Its Disappearing Water*, rev. and updated (New York: Penguin, 1993), 286.

52. Brower, *For Earth's Sake*, 364–65.

53. David Brower quoted in Turner, *David Brower*, 127; Colorado River Basin Project Act, P.L. 90-537 signed by President Johnson on September 30, 1968, Title III, Sec. 303 (a) "*Provided,* That nothing in this section or in this Act contained shall be construed to authorize the study or construction of any dams on the main stream of the Colorado River between Hoover Dam and Glen Canyon Dam," http://www.usbr.gov/lc/region/pao/pdfiles/crbproj.pdf, May 18, 2016.

54. Approximately five hundred people went through the Grand Canyon on the Colorado River in 1965; more than sixteen thousand people made the trip in 1972. Fedarko, *Emerald Mile*, 91; Jeff Ingram, *Hijacking a River: A Political History of the Colorado River in the Grand Canyon* (Flagstaff, Arizona: Vishnu Temple Press, 2003), iii.

55. Lew Steiger, "My God, It's Waltenberg!" *The News (Grand Canyon River Guides)* 6, no. 1 (Winter 1992/1993), www.gcrg.org/bqr/6-1/waltenberg.htm, April 20, 2009; François Leydet, *Time and the River Flowing: Grand Canyon* (abridged) (San Francisco: Sierra Club and New York: Ballantine, 1964 and 1968).

56. Fedarko, *Emerald Mile*, 98; Martin Litton, interview by Lewis Steiger, Mile 196 camp in the Grand Canyon, September 18, 1994, Northern Arizona University, Cline Library, Tape Number 1994.100.37.

57. Daniel Luten, a successful chemist, then a lecturer in geography at the University of California, Berkeley, served on the Sierra Club's board of directors and as president of Friends of the Earth. Dimock, "Articulate Outrage, Righteous Wrath," 28; Martin Litton, interview, September 18, 1994.

58. Steiger, "My God, It's Waltenberg!"; Thomas, telephone interview, February 25, 2013.

59. Robert H. Keller and Michael F. Turek, *American Indians & National Parks* (Tucson: University of Arizona Press, 1998), 157–61.

60. S. 1296 introduced in March 1973 and enacted January 3, 1975, as the Grand Canyon National Park Enlargement Act (P.L. 93-620). Keller and Turek, *American Indians & National Parks*, 164.

61. The other environmental groups included the Audubon Society, the Wilderness Society, the Isaak Walton League, the National Parks and Conservation Organization, the Federation of Western Outdoor Clubs, the Western River Guides Association, and the National Wildlife Federation. Keller and Turek, *American Indians & National Parks*, 163–65.

62. Harriet Burgess, letter to Martin Litton, July 2 and 3, 1974.

63. Martin Litton shared his memories of Harriet at the celebration of her life on May 8, 2010, at her home in Inverness, California. He also told this story to the author by telephone on July 31, 2011.

64. Grand Canyon National Park Enlargement Act, P.L. 93-620, 88 Stat. 2089, 16 USC §228a-228j; Ingram, *Hijacking a River*, 91–94.

65. Martin Litton, interview no. 53.32A; Fedarko, "Ain't It Just Grand."

66. Hunt, telephone interview, April 28, 2010.

67. Hunt, e-mail, May 18, 2013; Commonwealth of Virginia—Report of Divorce or Annulment, State file 78-011832.

68. Robert G. Hunt, e-mail to the author, May 19, 2013; John Hunt, conversation with the author, March 24, 2019.

69. Robert G. Hunt, e-mail to the author, July 18, 2013.

70. Harriet Burgess, oral history interview, January 12, 2006; Evans, interview, June 29, 2010.

71. Harriet Hunt Burgess, *Curriculum Vitae*; Pete Stark, "Honoring Harriet Burgess, President and Foundation [*sic*] of American Land Conservancy, November 15, 2005, in the House of Representatives," *Congressional Record (Extensions of Remarks)*, E2360, https:// www.congress.gov/crec/2005/11/15/modified/CREC-2005-11-15-pt1-PgE2360.htm, January 31, 2016.

72. Commonwealth of Virginia—Report of Divorce or Annulment, State file 78-011832; Hunt, e-mail, July 18, 2013.

73. Hunt, telephone interview, April 28, 2010.

74. Joe Burgess, interview by the author, August 22, 2010.

75. Burgess, interview, August 22, 2010; remarks by Joe Burgess at the gathering to celebrate the life of Harriet Hunt Burgess, Inverness, California, May 8, 2010.

76. Burgess, interview, August 22, 2010.

77. Burgess, interview, August 22, 2010.

78. Kevin Fedarko, "They Call Me Groover Boy," *Outside*, July 7, 2008, https://www.out sideonline.com/1892656/they-call-me-groover-boy, July 18, 2018.

79. Regan Dale, interview by Lewis Steiger, Flagstaff, Arizona, November 6, 1998, *Grand Canyon River Guides Oral History Collection*, interview no. 53.15, Northern Arizona University, Cline Library, archive.library.nau.edu/cdm/singleitem/collection/cpa/id/63443/ rec/13, January 7, 2016.

80. Hunt and Walsh, interview, June 29, 2010.

Chapter 2: Another Canyon: Topanga Canyon

1. Michele Johnson, ed., *The Topanga Story*, expanded ed. (Topanga, CA: Topanga Historical Society, 2012), 13.

2. Martin Litton quoted in Brad Dimock, "Articulate Outrage, Righteous Wrath," 30.

3. Litton said, "Topanga Canyon was pretty wild then, and it had a perennial stream where you could swim and do all of these things. It was a great wilderness then."Martin Litton, "Miss Swish-to-Malibu," *Los Angeles Times*, July 1, 1952; Martin Litton, oral history interview, "Sierra Club Director and Uncompromising Preservationist, 1950s–1970s," by Ann Lage, December 10, 1980 (Regional Oral History Office, The Bancroft Library, University of California, Berkeley, 1982), 6.

4. Betty Lou Young, *Our First Century: The Los Angeles Athletic Club, 1880–1980* (Los Angeles: LAAC Press, 1979), 55–56, 120.

5. Young, *Our First Century*, 149; Frank Garbutt, letter to William Randolph Hearst, February 12, 1927.

6. William Randolph Hearst sold his five-ninths interest to the Provident Investment Trust in 1944; the trust assigned its rights to the five-ninths interest to LAAC in 1946. Young, *Our First Century*, 144, 149.

7. The Coastal Commission controls land use in the coastal zone through permits issued either directly or through commission-certified Local Coastal Programs. Malibu Local Coastal Program, Land Use Plan, 12/86, 60–61.

8. Tom Furlong, "Investment Group Weighs Sale of 1,600 Topanga Canyon Acres," *Los Angeles Times*, September 9, 1989, http://articles.latimes.com/1989-09-09/business/ fi-1507_1_topanga-canyon-boulevard, March 3, 2016; Tom Byrnes, "Mini-Malls & Motels at Mouth of Canyon," *Topanga Messenger*, September 21, 1989.

9. Byrnes, "Mini-Malls and Motels at Mouth of Canyon."

10. Joe Burgess, conversation with the author, June 26, 2016.

11. Harriet Burgess to Martin Rosen, memorandum, March 5, 1990.

12. Frank Hathaway, LAACO, letter to Harriet Burgess, January 1, 1990.

13. Burgess to Rosen, memorandum, March 5, 1990.

14. Huey Johnson's replacement as president was Joel Kuperberg. Martin J. Rosen, oral history interview, "Trust for Public Land Founding Member and President, 1972–1997: The Ethics and Practice of Land Conservation," by Carl Wilmsen, October 19, 1998 (Regional Oral History Office, The Bancroft Library, University of California, Berkeley, 2000), 39; Ralph Benson, interview by the author, August 14, 2011.

15. Benson, interview, August 14, 2011.

16. Steve Costa, interview by the author, March 9, 2017; Steve Costa, interview by Huey Johnson, December 16, 2014, http://theforcesofnature.com/movies/steve-costa, February 12, 2016.

17. Cowan, interview, November 17, 2008.

18. Cowan, interview, November 17, 2008; Harriet Burgess, oral history interview, 18; Jennie Gerard, interview by the author, March 14, 2017.

19. Montchalin v. Skamania County, Skamania County Wash., Superior Court Case No. 6931 (1981) cited in Bowen Blair Jr., "The Columbia River Gorge National Scenic Area, Its Genesis and Legislative History," *Environmental Law* 17 (1986–1987): 863. On its website, Friends of the Columbia Gorge lists the Friends' lawsuit in 1981 to block 21-lot Rizor subdivision across from Multnomah Falls as one of its major accomplishments, http://gorgefriends.org/section.php?id=10, March 2, 2016.

20. Carl Abbot, Sy Adler, and Margery Post Abbot, *Planning a New West: The Columbia River Gorge National Scenic Area* (Corvallis: Oregon State University Press, 1997), 70–71, 82, 84.

21. Benson, interview, August 14, 2011.

22. According to an article by John Harrison, "List of Properties," in *The Columbian*, March 11, 1985, the price for the Rizor property was "apparently between $350,000 and $500,000." Benson, interview, August 14, 2011.

23. "Campaign for Cape Horn," narrated by Jack McGowan; written and produced by Kevin Gorman at the beginning of the Friends of the Columbia Gorge's two-year fund-raising campaign to protect Cape Horn permanently. The campaign successfully concluded after raising $4.11 million. Video uploaded to YouTube August 28, 2009. https://www.youtube.com/watch?v=65bI_7aIr0s, March 4, 2016.

24. Figures as of 2012; https://www.tpl.org/media-room/scenic-columbia-gorge-property -protected, January 30, 2016.

25. For a detailed discussion of the background and legislative history of the Columbia River Gorge National Scenic Area, see Bowen Blair Jr., "The Columbia River Gorge National Scenic Area."

26. The $100,000 was designated for the option payment ($50,000), the appraisal ($45,000), and project site photography ($5,000). Martin J. Rosen to Ralph Benson (cc: Harriet Burgess, Woody Robertshaw), memorandum, March 28, 1990; Ralph Benson to Harriet Burgess (cc: Woody Robertshaw, Marty Rosen), memorandum, March 13, 1990.

27. Harriet was hospitalized for a few days at the beginning of April, which probably explains her not responding to Marty Rosen's March 28, 1990, memo until April 5, 1990. Hospitalization is mentioned in Nancy Shanahan's April 4, 1990, letter to Karen Hathaway.

28. Harriet Burgess to Martin J. Rosen (cc: Ralph Benson, Woody Robertshaw), memorandum, April 5, 1990.

29. Martin J. Rosen to Harriet Burgess (cc: Ralph Benson), memorandum, April 18, 1990.

30. Benson, interview, August 14, 2011.

31. "The American Land Conservancy is Born," *American Land Conservancy* 1, no. 1 (Fall 1990): 1.

32. "The American Land Conservancy is Born"; Joe Burgess, interview, August 22, 2010; Martin J. Rosen, "Trust for Public Land Founding Member and President, 1972–1997," 189.

33. Benson, interview, August 14, 2011; Martin J. Rosen, "Trust for Public Land Founding Member and President, 1972–1997," 189; Merle Haggard, "This Town's Not Big Enough," 1966.

34. Marian Stephens first suggested the name, American Land Conservancy, for the new organization. Harriet Burgess, oral history, January 12, 2006, 46; Bob Stephens's remarks at the celebration of Harriet Burgess's life, May 8, 2010; Martin and Esther Litton, interview by the author, September 20, 2008.

35. The terms of the settlement are confidential. Joseph Burgess, interview, August 22, 2010.

36. Harriet Burgess to Ruth Kilday, memorandum, April 23, 1990.

37. Joseph T. Edmiston, executive director, Santa Monica Mountains Conservancy, letter to Harriet Burgess, senior vice president, Trust for Public Land, December 20, 1989.

38. Harriet Burgess, letter to Karen Hathaway, vice president and general counsel, LAACO, April 27, 1990; expense report, Harriet Hunt Burgess—Topanga, 4/20–5/30/90.

39. LAACO, Ltd., "LAACO Announces Agreement to Sell Topanga Property to Mountains Conservancy Foundation," May 4, 1990.

40. Ruth Kilday confirmed that she was acting strictly as a fiscal agent for SMMC during our February 13, 2016, telephone interview. Pete Larsen, "Conservancy Land Purchase Near; Board to Vote on Property for Park," *Daily News*, May 5, 1990; Kate Poss, "Foundation to Buy 1,600 Topanga Acres," *Country & Canyon Times*, May 10, 1990; Burgess, letter to Karen Hathaway, April 27, 1990; Kilday, telephone interview, February 13, 2016.

41. Harriet Burgess, handwritten notes, April 27, 1990; May 1, 2, 10, 27, and 31, 1990; June 5, 6, 11, 15, 25, and 28, 1990; expense report, Harriet Hunt Burgess—Topanga, 4/20–5/30/90; expense report, Harriet Burgess—Topanga, 5/31–6/15/90; expense report, Harriet Burgess—Topanga, 6/16–7/25/90; expense report, Harriet Burgess—Topanga, 7/26–8/29/90; Nancy C. Shanahan, Western regional counsel, letter to Robert H. Flavell, MAI, Favell, Tennenbaum & Associates, April 23, 1990; Ruth Kilday to MCF board of directors, memorandum, May 3, 1990; Flavell, Tennenbaum & Associates and MCF, contract, May 8, 1990; Harriet Burgess and Marc Litchman, professional services agreement, May 31, 1990; Robert Glenn Ketchum, letter to Marc Litchman, June 1, 1990; Harriet Burgess, letter to Neil Sigmon, June 13, 1990; Lewis "Pete" Douglas, letter to Harriet Burgess, July 27, 1990.

42. Harriet Burgess, letter [draft] to Ruth Kilday and Fred Zepeda, July 30, 1990; Ruth Kilday, letter to Harriet Burgess, August 13, 1990.

43. Santa Monica Mountains Conservancy, news release, August 13, 1990; LAACO, press release [draft], August 8, 1990.

44. "Saving Topanga Canyon," *American Land Conservancy* [newsletter] (Fall 1990): 3.

45. Marian Hollon, "The River of the Canyon—the Colorado Has Solitude and Thundering Excitement," *Huntsville Times*, July 28, 1986.

46. Martin Litton, interview no. 53.32A.

47. Regan Dale, interview no. 53.15.

48. John Noble Wilford, "Lure of the White Water," *New York Times Magazine*, July 22, 1979.

49. Dick Brown, "William Wallace Bass (1849–1933)," *The Ol' Pioneer: Newsletter of the Grand Canyon Pioneers Society* (1999), kaibab.org/kaibab.org/gcps/bass_bio.htm, August 8, 2016; Arizona Historical Society, *William Wallace Bass Collection, 1848–1976, Biographical Note*, http://www.azarchivesonline.org/xtf/view?docld=ead/nau/ahs_bass.sml&doc .view=print;chunk.id=0, August 8, 2016; Sarah Bohl Gerke, "South Bass Trail," *Nature, Culture, and History at the Grand Canyon* (Arizona State University and Grand Canyon Association), grandcanyonhistory.clas.asu.edu/sites_rimtoriverandinnercanyon_southbass trail.html, August 8, 2016.

50. "Ross Wheeler," http://www.gcrivermuseum.org/river-heritage/the-boats/ross-wheeler/, August 8, 2016.

Chapter 3: It's Still There: Topanga Canyon

1. Elden Hughes, letter to Harriet Burgess, December 29, 1996; Harriet Burgess, letter to Elden Hughes, January 3, 1997.

2. Harriet Burgess, letter to Elden Hughes, October 22, 1991; Elden Hughes, letter to Harriet Burgess, May 17, 1993.

3. "Topanga Canyon: 15-Year Fight for Parkland Ends as Escrow Closes," *Los Angeles Times*, April 2, 1994, articles.latimes.com/print/1994-04-02/local/me-41196_1_topanga -canyon-boulevard, May 30, 2016; Aaron Curtiss, "Local Elections: Prop. 180's Defeat Puts the Squeeze on Park Agency: Santa Monicas: Conservancy Faces Layoffs. Purchase of land in Topanga Canyon Is Now in Doubt," *Los Angeles Times*, June 9, 1994, articles.latimes .com/print/1994-06-09/local/me-2226_1_santa-monica-mountains-conservancy, May 30, 2016; "Disneys to Sell Disputed Land," *Variety*, March 10, 1994, variety.com/1994/biz/ news/disneys-to-sell-disputed-land-119127/, May 31, 2016.

4. Proposition 180, "Park Lands, Historic Sites, Wildlife and Forest Conservation Bond Act," would have authorized a bond issue of almost $2 billion for the acquisition, development, restoration, and conservation of park lands, historic sites, wildlife areas, and forests throughout California. It was defeated by a vote of 56.7 percent opposed and 43.3 percent in favor on June 7, 1994. "California Proposition 180, Bonds to Acquire Park Lands (1994)," *Ballotpedia*, https://ballotpedia.org/California_Proposition_180,_Bonds_ to_Acquire_Park_Lands_(1994), May 30, 2016; "Proposition 180 'Park Lands, Historic Sites, Wildlife and Forest Conservation Bond Act'" [text], repository.uchastings.edu/cgi/ viewcontent.cgi?article=2097&context=ca_ballot_props, May 30, 2016; Harriet Burgess, telephone conversation with Jerry Meral, notes, April 26, 1994; Jerry Meral, fax to Harriet Burgess, April 26, 1994; Joe Edmiston, telephone message to Harriet Burgess, January 5, 1993. SMMC made the final payment on the Disney property on October 20, 1995.

5. Harriet Burgess, notes, May 4 and 6, 1994; Karen Hathaway, letter to LAACO Limited Partners, May 9, 1994; Karen Hathaway, letter to Harriet Burgess, June 2, 1994; Harriet Burgess, letter to Karen Hathaway, June 8, 1994.

6. Joe Burgess, telephone conversation with the author, June 2, 2016.

7. See chapter 6 for further information on the Thunderbird Lodge project. Ame Hellman, interview by the author, June 30, 2010.

8. Hellman, interview, June 30, 2010; www.blm.gov/nv/st/en/fo/carson_city_field/blm_programs/recreation/faye-luther-luther_trail.html, June 2, 2016.

9. Hellman, interview, June 30, 2010.

10. Hellman, interview, June 30, 2010; Ame Hellman, "Guestbook—Post Your Memories," alcnet.org, May 3, 2010.

11. Ame Hellman, interviews by the author, June 30 and July 1, 2010; minutes of the [American Land Conservancy] executive committee meeting of the board of directors, March 17, 1998.

12. Use of the trail doubled after the trailhead was constructed in 2000 from approximately twenty-five hundred annual visits to approximately fifty-five hundred annual visits in 2006. Hellman, interview, June 30, 2010; Bureau of Land Management, "Fay-Luther Trail System: Environmental Assessment" (2006): 9, https://eplanning.blm.gov/epl-front-office/projects/nepa/57652/72271/79290/FinalEA.pdf.

13. The new California governor was Gray Davis, elected November 3, 1998. The new legislative initiative was Proposition 12, the Safe Neighborhood Parks, Clean Water, Clean Air and Coastal Protection Bond Act of 2000. Harriet Burgess, letter to Karen Hathaway, December 16, 1998.

14. Ame Hellman, notes, n.d., but the location of the notes in the ALC files strongly suggests after October 22 but before December 9, 1998. Rents ranged from $427 to $1,280 per month for the LAACO properties compared to $724 to $3,250 per month in nearby residential areas, according to Pacific Relocation Consultants, Topanga Canyon Relocation Issues (July 2000), 3.

15. ALC's finances were improved in large part by the successful completion of the Nevada Land Exchange discussed in chapter 4. Burgess, letter to Hathaway, December 16, 1998.

16. Nonexclusive options exist but are rare. Trust for Public Land, *Doing Deals: A Guide to Buying Land for Conservation* (San Francisco: TPL, and Washington, D.C: Land Trust Alliance, 1995), 54–55.

17. Trust for Public Land, *Annual Report* (San Francisco: TPL, 1976–1977, 1977–1978, 1979).

18. ALC file notes of telephone conversations between Harriet Burgess and Russell Austin, Ame Hellman, Karen Hathaway, and Fred Zepeda.

19. Charles Michaels was LAACO's general counsel. Fred Zepeda, LAACO Real Estate Division vice president, was responsible for property management. Ibid.; bargain sale option agreement between LAACO and ALC dated January 6, 2000; Harriet Burgess, notes, September 3, 1999; Kauttu valuation, appraisal report for the Topanga Canyon property (in two parts: undeveloped property and commercial residential component) (Newport Beach, CA, October 31, 1999).

20. Julie Turrini, fax to Harriet Burgess, October 12, 1999.

21. Bargain sale option agreement between LAACO and ALC dated January 6, 2000; Kauttu valuation, appraisal report for the Topanga Canyon property; undeveloped property, 9.

22. First amendment to the bargain sale option agreement between ALC and LAACO, dated March 15, 2000; Harriet Burgess and Karen Hathaway, letter agreement, January 4, 2001.

23. Proposition 12 was approved by 63.2 percent of the voters March 7, 2000. It allocated $1.364 billion to California State Parks, with $519 million designated for additions and

improvements to the State Park system and the remaining $845 million for local park grants, www.parks.ca.gov/?page_id=24975, June 14, 2016; Sheila Kuehl, Assemblymember 41st District, letter to Governor Gray Davis, April 4, 2000.

24. Sylvie Belmond, "Lower Topanga Canyon Optioned for Sale," *Malibu Times*, September 7, 2000; *Southern Sierran* 6, no. 11 (November 2000).

25. Greg DeYoung, letter to Harriet Burgess, February 17, 2000.

26. Jeffrey Kauttu, letter to Fred Zepeda, March 14, 2000; Kendall Thurston, Mason & Mason, letter to Harriet Burgess, appraisal review, July 27, 2000.

27. Mason & Mason, self-contained appraisal report, LAACO ownership of 1,659± acres of land, prepared for Harriet Burgess and Jeff Stump, American Land Conservancy, date of value, February 19, 2001; Mason & Mason, invoices submitted to ALC, January 16 and March 5, 2001. The cost of the appraisal was $51,718.72.

28. Russell Austin, e-mail to Harriet Burgess and Jeff Stump, February 22, 2001; Thomas Crandall, Department of General Services, to David L. Wrightsman, Department of Parks and Recreation, memorandum, May 1, 2001.

29. Harriet Burgess, notes of telephone calls with Russell Austin, Karen Hathaway, and Fred Zepeda, February 23 and 26, 2001; Harriet Burgess, letter to Karen Hathaway, March 14, 2001; Fred Zepeda, letter to LAACO tenants, March 12, 2001.

30. Burgess, letter to Hathaway, March 14, 2001.

31. Mason & Mason, self-contained appraisal report, 22; Erler & Kalinowski, Inc., Phase 1 environmental site assessment, Topanga Canyon site, Los Angeles, California, draft, prepared for ALC, July 7, 2000; Sonja Magdevski, "The Disappearing Bamboo Grove," *Malibu Magazine* (August/September 2005).

32. LAACO, Topanga historical summary, n.d.; Fred Grassle, senior land agent, letter to John H. Brooks, senior land agent, August 10, 1978; Harriet Burgess, notes, December 21, 1989, March 20, 1990 and May 10, 1990; Kate Poss, "Foundation to Buy 1,600 Topanga Acres," *Country & Canyon Times* 1, no. 13 (May 10, 1990).

33. See California Health and Safety Code §7260, et seq., for the California Relocation Assistance Law. The first step in the relocation process is the development of a relocation plan. The plan must be completed before the "displacing agency" may proceed with any phase of the project. Harriet Burgess, letter to Karen Hathaway, December 16, 1998; Ame Hellman, undated notes; Harriet Burgess, notes, March 5 and 30, 2000, and April 11, 2000.

34. Pacific Relocation Consultants, Topanga Canyon relocation issues, prepared for LAACO, July 2000.

35. Sylvie Belmond, "Tenants Fearful They Will Be Ousted in Sale," *Malibu Times*, September 7, 2000.

36. Susan Chasen, "A New Park in Our Future?" *Topanga Messenger* 24, no. 11 (June 1–14, 2000), http://www.topangamessengercom/archives/V24NO11.htm, February 6, 2012.

37. Belmond, "Tenants Fearful They Will Be Ousted in Sale."

38. Susan Chasen, "Half a Park Better Than None?" *Topanga Messenger* 25, no. 7 (April 5–18, 2001), http://www.topangamessenger.com/Archives/v25n07/news.shtml#N2, June 20, 2016.

39. Fred Zepeda, letter to LAACO tenants, March 12, 2001.

40. ALC signed the relocation services agreement with PRC on April 20, 2001. The maximum cost of the contract was set at $34,000. Pacific Relocation Consultants, Topanga

Canyon relocation issues; Susan Chasen, "Tenants Say Wait! It's Too Soon to Relocate," *Topanga Messenger Online* 25, no. 9 (May 3–16, 2001), http://www.topangamessenger.com/ Current/News/shtm, May 21, 2001; Susan Chasen, "Relocation Plan on Fast Track," *Topanga Messenger Online* 25, no. 10 (May 17–31, 2001), http://www.topangamessenger .com/Current/News/shtm, May 21, 2001.

41. ALC Message Points, April 9, 2001; Pacific Relocation Consultants, Topanga Canyon relocation issues; Pacific Relocation Consultants, letter to LAACO residential tenant, April 17, 2001; Pacific Relocation Consultants, letter to commercial tenant, April 18, 2001; Chasen, "Relocation Plan on Fast Track"; Barry McDaniel (PRC), e-mail to Charles Michaels, Fred Zepeda, Harriet Burgess, and Jeff Stump, April 18, 2001; Julie Benson, e-mail to Fred Zepeda, April 12, 2001; California Relocation Assistance Law, §6046(a)(1).

42. Two business owners and five residential tenants attended the three meetings. Two representatives from the Topanga Association for a Scenic Community and Supervisor Zev Yaroslavsky's planning deputy also attended the meetings, as did PRC's David Richman. ALC Message Points, April 9, 2001; David Richman, e-mail to Julie Benson, Charles Michaels, Fred Zepeda, Barry McDaniel, and Harriet Burgess, April 23, 2001; Chasen, "Tenants Say Wait!," and "Relocation Plan on Fast Track."

43. Chasen, "Tenants Say Wait!"; Susan Chasen, "Malibu Feed Bin: Going, Going . . . ," *Topanga Messenger Online* 25, no. 9 (May 3–16, 2001), http://www.topangamessenger .com/Current/News/shtm; Marcelas Rojas, "Losing the Place They Call Home," *Westside Weekly News*, May 4, 2001; Annette Kondo, "Acreage from Mountains to Sea to Become Parkland," *Los Angeles Times*, March 15, 2001; Sylvie Belmond, "Simple Topanga Lifestyle Threatened," *Malibu Times*, May 17, 2001.

44. Frank Angel's client was the Lower Topanga Community Association, formerly the Topanga Ranch Residents Association. He did not represent all of the tenants nor did he represent tenants individually. PRC, letter to Russell Austin, May 9, 2001; Sylvie Belmond, "Lower Topanga Tenants Told to Go," *Malibu Times*, May 9, 2001; Curtis M. Horton (law offices of Frank P. Angel), letter to David Richman, PRC, April 23, 2001; Curtis M. Horton (law offices of Frank P. Angel), letter to Fred Zepeda, April 11, 2001; Fred Zepeda, letter to Russell Austin, May 7, 2001; Fred Zepeda, letter to Curtis M. Horton, April 19, 2001; David Richman, e-mail to Julie Benson, May 1, 2001; Frank Angel, letter to Jeff Stump, September 26, 2000; Frank Angel, fax to Assemblywoman Fran Pavley (attn.: Susan Little), May 10, 2001; Frank Angel, letter to Russell Austin, May 10, 2001; Harriet Burgess, handwritten notes, telephone call to Barry McDaniel, David Richman, Roy Ableson, Fred Zepeda, Celeste Brady, Charles Michaels, Karen Hathaway, Jeff Stump, and Mary Taylor, May 14, 2001.

45. Chasen, "Relocation Plan on Fast Track"; Harriet Burgess quoted in *Southern Sierran* 56, no. 11 (November 2000).

46. Rojas, "Losing the Place They Call Home"; Chasen, "Tenants Say Wait!"

47. Chasen, "Tenants Say Wait!"

48. Harriet Burgess, handwritten notes, telephone call to Barry McDaniel, David Richman, Roy Ableson, Fred Zepeda, Celeste Brady, Charles Michaels, Karen Hathaway, Jeff Stump, and Mary Taylor, May 14, 2001; Susan Chasen, "Lower Canyon Park: Kuehl to the Rescue," *Topanga Messenger Online* 25, no. 11 (May 31–June 13, 2001), www.topangames senger.com/Archives/v25n11/news.shtm.

49. Lower Topanga Community Association, letter to neighbors, May 16, 2001; Harriet Burgess, handwritten notes, meeting with Frank Angel, May 15, 2001; Ken Gale, "Lower Topanga Acquisition Delayed," *Malibu Times*, May 30, 2001.

50. Fred Zepeda, letter to individual tenants, May 15, 2001; Fred Zepeda, letter to Mark Sherman, May 24, 2001.

51. David Richman, Pacific Relocation Consultants, letter to business tenants, May 15, 2001.

52. Harriet Burgess, "Aid for Topanga Tenants," *Malibu Times*, May 17, 2001. The letter is in response to the article "Lower Topanga Tenants Told to Go" by Sylvie Belmond that was published in the *Malibu Times* on May 9, 2001.

53. Topanga briefing, 9 a.m., June 4, 2001, Assemblywoman Fran Pavley's office, agenda; Harriet Burgess, notes for her talk at the meeting with Pavley, Kuehl, and Yaroslavsky.

54. Gale, "Lower Topanga Acquisition Delayed"; "State Adds Funds to Buy 1,600-Acre Park Site," *Los Angeles Times*, May 17, 2001; Chasen, "Lower Canyon Park."

55. Chasen, "Lower Canyon Park"; Clara Sturak, "Paradise Lost, or Found? Depends Who You Ask," *Santa Monica Mirror* 2, no. 51 (June 6–12, 2001); donation of relocation assistance planning contracted services; acknowledgment and consent thereto by and between American Land Conservancy and the State of California, Department of Parks and Recreation, signed by ALC President Harriet Burgess, June 1, 2001; and Department of Parks and Recreation Chief Deputy Director Mary Wright, June 5, 2001.

56. Anne Soble, "Publisher's Notebook, Communication," *Malibu Surfside News*, June 28, 2001.

57. "Meet the new boss / Same as the old boss" are lines originally penned by Pete Townshend of The Who as the conclusion of his 1971 song "Won't Get Fooled Again." The lines since have passed into common usage. Ken Gale, "State Takes Charge in Lower Topanga Canyon Tenant Evictions," *Malibu Times*, July 5, 2001; Bonnie McCourt, "Re: location," *Topanga Messenger Online* 25, no. 14 (July 12–25, 2001), http://www.topanga messenger.com/Archives/v25n14/news.shtml.

58. Chris Jehle and Leslie King, letter to Karen Hathaway, July 5, 2001; Harriet Burgess, handwritten notes, June 29, 2001.

59. California Department of Parks and Recreation, "State Parks Announces Public Hearing for Lower Topanga Canyon," June 29, 2001.

60. Kenneth R. Weiss, "State to Buy Topanga Canyon Coastal Acreage for Parkland," *Los Angeles Times*, July 3, 2001.

61. Harriet Burgess, letter to Friends of the Santa Monica Mountains, July 2, 2001; Harriet Burgess, handwritten notes, meeting, July 29, 2001.

62. Harriet Burgess, "Topanga Parkland a True Dream Come True," *Daily News of Los Angeles*, July 9, 2001.

63. Rusty Areias, State Parks director, letter to The Honorable John L. Burton, President Pro Tempore of the Senate, July 11, 2001; Michele Johnson, "Huge Lower Canyon Park Hearing," *Topanga Messenger Online* 25, no. 15 (July26–August 8, 2001), http://www .topangamessenger.com/Archives/v25n15/news.shtml; Libby Motika, "Public Meeting for Topanga Park Draws Acrimonious Debate," *Palisadian-Post*, July 12, 2001.

64. Areias, letter to John L. Burton, July 11, 2001; Johnson, "Huge Lower Canyon Park Hearing."

65. Areias, letter to John L. Burton, July 11, 2001; Johnson, "Huge Lower Canyon Park Hearing"; Frank Angel, transcript of remarks at July 9, 2001, public hearing on the acquisition of Lower Topanga Canyon.

66. Fred Zepeda, "Statement of Fred Zepeda," *Malibu Times*, July 27, 2001.

67. The tenants at Crystal Cove finally were relocated in 2006. Johnson, "Huge Lower Canyon Park Hearing"; Edward Humes, "Paradise Regained: Crystal Cove Looks Like a Blast from the Past as It Hurdles Towards a Secure Future," *Orange County Register*, April 15, 2016, http://www.ocregister.com/articles/davick-712365-cove-cottages.html.

68. Areias, letter to John L. Burton, July 11, 2001. The other elected officials who received the letter were Robert M. Hertzberg, speaker of the assembly; Assemblywoman Fran Pavley; Senator Sheila Kuehl; Supervisor Zev Yaroslavsky; and Los Angeles City Council Member Cindy Miscikowsi.

69. Harriet Burgess, letter to Karen Hathaway, August 27, 2001.

70. Russell Austin, e-mail to Jerry Carlton, August 22, 2001.

71. Harriet Burgess, letter to Karen Hathaway, August 24, 2001; Harriet Burgess, letter to Karen Hathaway, August 27, 2001.

72. Hathaway, letter to Harriet Burgess, August 24, 2001; Harriet Burgess, fax to Russell Austin, August 24, 2001.

73. Harriet Burgess, letter to Karen Hathaway, re: closing of Topanga Canyon Project, August 27, 2001; Harriet Burgess, letter to Karen Hathaway, re: consummation of bargain sale, Topanga Property California, August 27, 2001; State of California, Department of Parks and Recreation Parcel No. A33901; State of California, Department of General Services Parcel No. 10044; Topanga State Park addition, August 27, 2001.

74. Russell Austin, e-mail to Jeff Stump, cc: Harriet Burgess and Kathy Hustrei, August 30, 2001; Julie Ehly to Jeff Stump, memorandum, August 31, 2001; Russell Austin, e-mail to Charles Michaels, August 31, 2001.

75. Kenneth R. Weiss, "Parkland to Extend from Valley to Sea," *Los Angeles Times*, August 31, 2001; Harriet Burgess, letter to ALC Board of Councillors, Board of Councillors retreat, 2001; LAACO press release from Alexander Auerbach, Auerbach & Co. Public Relations, August 30, 2001; California Department of Parks and Recreation, "News Release: Relocation Service Opens Office in Topanga," February 22, 2002.

76. Weiss, "Parkland to Extend from Valley to Sea"; Martha Groves, "Glum Stares Amid Roar of Bulldozers," *Los Angeles Times*, April 17, 2003; Hans Laetz, "Lower Topanga Businesses, Homes Demolished," *Malibu Times*, January 11, 2006.

77. Groves, "Glum Stares Amid Roar of Bulldozers"; Laetz, "Lower Topanga Businesses, Homes Demolished"; Tracy Marcynzsyn, "Lower Topanga Residents Dig in Heels, Resisting Relocation," *Malibu Times*, May 8, 2002, www.malibutimes.com/news/article_b60c9ed2-1068-511a-8ba1-374ee91b667a.html; Martha Groves, "Lower Topanga Tenants Facing Eviction by State," *Los Angeles Times*, March 3, 2002; "Topanga Motel Owner to Vacate Property," *Malibu Times*, March 2, 2005.

78. Topanga State Park general plan, http://www.parks.ca.gov/?page_id=25956, July 5, 2016.

79. Chasen, "A New Park in Our Future?"

80. Rosi Dagit, "Topanga Creek Restoration: Rodeo Berm Removal," *Urban Coast* (November 2009), 37–41, urbancoast.org/wp-content/uploads/2014/10/10-Topanga.pdf, January 19, 2016.

81. Dagit, "Topanga Creek Restoration," 38.
82. Johnson, *Topanga Story*, 35; Rosi Dagit, conversation with the author, March 2016; Rosi Dagit, e-mails to author, March 20 and 21, 2019; Rosi Dagit, Ethan Bell, Krista Adamek, Jennifer Mongolo, Elizabeth Montgomery, Nina Trusso, and Peter Baker, "The Effects of a Prolonged Drought on Southern Steelhead Trout (Oncorhynchus mykiss) in a Coastal Creek, Los Angeles County, California," *Bulletin of the Southern California Academy of Sciences* 116, no. 3 (2017): 162. California Trout produced a fascinating video, "Southern California Steelhead: Against All Odds," that tells the story of the steelhead trout. Rosi Dagit is among those interviewed for the video that can be viewed at https://vimeo.com/79393289.
83. Thomas Dudley, "Invasive plants of California's Wildland, Arundo donax," California Invasive Plant Council, http://www.cal-ipc.org/ip/management/ipcw/pages/detailreport.cfm@usernumber=8&surveynumber=182.php, March 21, 2016; California Invasive Plant Council, "Euphorbia terracina (carnation spurge)," http://www.cal-ipc.org/ip/management/plant_profiles/Euphorbia_terracina.php, March 21, 2016; Christy Brigham, "Euphorbia terracina: Be Afraid, Be Very Afraid," California Invasive Plant Council Symposium, 2006, http://www.cal-ipc.org/symposia/archive/pdf/2006/EDBrigham.pdf, March 21, 2016.
84. Much of the information in this section was gleaned from conversations with Rosi Dagit as we toured the site with her and from the tour itself in March 2016.
85. Stanley S. Beus and Michael Morales, eds., *Grand Canyon Geology*, 2d ed. (New York and Oxford: Oxford University Press, 2003), ix, 6, 8.
86. Unconformities may be observed in layers of rock around the world but the term "Great Unconformity" is reserved either for the Grand Canyon unconformity or the unconformity that is located on the east coast of Scotland. K. E. Karlstrom et al., "Paleoproterozoic Rocks of the Granite Gorges," in Beus and Morales, *Grand Canyon Geology*, 37.

Chapter 4: No Good Deed Goes Unpunished: Galena and the Nevada Land Exchange

1. Aldo Leopold, *A Sand County Almanac and Sketches Here and There* (New York: Oxford University Press, 1949), 204; Wallace Stegner, letter to David E. Pesonen regarding the Outdoor Recreation Resources Review Commission's report, December 3, 1960; Edward Abbey, *Desert Solitaire, A Season in the Wilderness* (New York: Simon & Schuster, 1968), 129, 169, and *Beyond the Wall* (New York: Holt, Rinehart and Winston, 1984): xvi.
2. Just before her trip to Nepal, Harriet needed a restorative trip to the Grand Canyon. She didn't have time for the whole river trip, so she hiked out at Phantom Ranch, took a van to Flagstaff, flew home, and then immediately left for Nepal. Joe Burgess, interview, August 22, 2010; Joe Burgess, conversation with the author, August 13, 2011.
3. Federal land exchanges are governed primarily by the Federal Land Policy and Management Act of 1976 (FLPMA, P.L. 94-579, 43 U.S.C. §§1701-1785) as amended by the Federal Land Exchange Facilitation Act of 1988 (FLEFA, P.L. 100-409, 43 U.S.C. §1701 note and 43 U.S.C. §1716 note).
4. The fund that Babbitt references here is the Land and Water Conservation Fund (LWCF), not the Land and Water Trust Fund. Created by Congress in 1965, the LWCF conserves land and water with the revenue generated by the royalties that energy companies pay to drill for oil and gas on the Outer Continental Shelf. Congress often has diverted funds from the LWCF for purposes other than conservation. Rita Beamish,

"Land Swaps Favored over Purchases as Way to Add to Parks, Babbitt Says," *Phoenix Gazette*, April 9, 1993; Bruce Babbitt, "Testimony before the House Natural Resources Committee, 2/16/93" CSPAN, https://www.c-span.org/video/?38047-1/interior-depart ment-programs, October 18, 2016.

5. Babbitt cites as examples the exchange of state lands in the Agua Fria National Monument for BLM lands near urban areas in Maricopa County and the exchange of state holdings in the Buenos Aires National Wildlife Refuge for BLM lands near Tucson. Beamish, "Land Swaps Favored over Purchases"; Babbitt, testimony before the House Natural Resources Committee; John H. Cushman Jr., "U.S. Using Swaps to Protect Land," *New York Times*, September 30, 1996, www.nytimes.com/1996/09/30/us/us-using-swaps -to-protect-land.html?pagewanted=all&_r=0, October 18, 2016; Bruce Babbitt, remarks, Arizona Town Hall, October 29, 2007, Grand Canyon.

6. Harriet Burgess, list of telephone calls, July 7, 1993; Margaret Eadington, TPL, to Billy Templeton, BLM, memorandum, December 11, 1991; "Thousands of Acres across Nevada Saved," *American Land Conservancy* [newsletter] (Winter/Spring 1995); Harriet Burgess, letter to Bruce Babbitt, September 7, 1994; Harriet Burgess, letter to Ed Hastey, July 26, 1993; Lauren Ward, oral history interview by Carol McLaughlin, June 28, 2006.

7. That was how Harriet recalled responding to Babbitt when asked five years later. At the time, she expressed concerns about taking on the exchange, perhaps in part because two key staff members had left recently. Eric Nalder et al., "American Land Conservancy and Others Who Arrange Deals Can Profit at Taxpayers' Expense," *Seattle Times*, September 29, 1998.

8. Charles Siebert, "Toxic," *New York Times Magazine*, July 5, 1998; Tom Kenworthy, "Babbitt Viewed as Practical, Able," *Washington Post*, December 25, 1992, http://www .washintonpost.com/wp-srv/politics/govt/admin/stories/babbitt122592.htm, February 15, 2016; Harriet Burgess, oral history interview.

9. The original members of Harriet's Board of Councillors were Bruce and Harriet Babbitt, David R. Brower, Brock Evans, W. E. "Bill" Garrett, L. W. Lane, Martin Litton, Helen and Pete McCloskey, Margaret W. Owings, Wallace Stegner, Robert Stephens, Stewart Udall, and Ardis Manley Walker. Harriet Burgess, oral history interview.

10. Harriet Burgess, oral history interview; Kenworthy, "Babbitt Viewed as Practical, Able."

11. When LaVere Redfield, Nell Redfield's husband, died in 1974, his beloved mountain estate included approximately forty thousand acres of land that he showed off to friends by Jeep and truck. A section added to the Tax Reform Act of 1976 allowed for the transfer of twenty-nine thousand acres of that land to the United States as a credit against an esti-mated estate tax of more than $17 million. Robert Frohlich, "California Dreamin' Imagine Skiing from Homewood to Sugar Bowl, with Lifts the Whole Way—This Unfulfilled Dream and More," *Moonshine Ink*, March 13, 2007, http://www.moonshineink.com/moun tain-life/california-dreamin, December 10, 2015; U.S. Senate, Committee on Finance, Hearings on S. 309, April 5, 1981.

12. According to the Hall et al. report, the partnership interests in the Galena Resort Company were divided among the Quadriga Development Company of Nevada (the General Partner, 10.635 percent), Galena Ski Corporation (a subsidiary of AMOT, Inc., 42.380 percent), Nell J. Redfield Trust (29.349 percent), Robert L. Weise (13.490 percent), Kuma Trust (1.20 percent), and four individuals (2.838 percent). Of AMOT's 1,920 acres, 881 acres were resold to the U.S. Forest Service. Robert Frohlich, "California Dreamin'"; Faith Bremner, "Here's a Look at Groups That Made Galena Buyout Possible," *Reno*

Gazette-Journal, August 29, 1994; Steven A. Hall, John T. Widdoss, and John Frome, feasibility study and appraisal report of proposed Galena Resort located southwest of Reno, Nevada, for Galena Resort Partners, September 1992.

13. Hall et al., feasibility study and appraisal report; Susan Voyles, *Reno Gazette Journal*, "Galena Deadline Nears," September 23, 1993.

14. "Friends of Mount Rose," *Toiyabe Trails* 21, no. 11 (September–October 1983): 11.

15. According to information from the Nevada secretary of state (http://nvsos.gov/sosen titysearch/CorpDetails.aspx?lx8nvq=Vb0OsQYaVvrZ7iitri8PJw%253d%253d), Friends of Mount Rose was incorporated October 5, 1983, although the organization was founded earlier that year. Rose Strickland still was listed as treasurer and the legal registered officer as of October 9, 2016. The September–October 1983 issue of *Toiyabe Trails* was addressed by hand to Harriet Burgess at the Trust for Public Land.

16. Hall et al., feasibility study and appraisal report; "RPC Hearing on Galena Resort Approval without Reservation," *Toiyabe Trails* 21, no. 11 (September–October 1983): 1.

17. Bremner, "Here's a Look"; Tom Knudson, "Fireworks of Protest for Tahoe's July 4th— Resort Plan Opponents Line Highway," *Sacramento Bee*, July 5, 1990.

18. Bremner, "Here's a Look."

19. S. 476, "Galena Regional Recreational Development Act of 1991," introduced February 22, 1991; Faith Bremner, "Galena Ski Resort Partner Willing to Listen to Federal Buyout Offer," *Reno Gazette-Journal*, February 25, 1991. Bryan did not remember the bill when I talked to him in 2016.

20. Harriet Burgess, handwritten notes, January 10, 1991; Harriet Burgess, letter to Nick Badami, January 11, 1991.

21. Faith Bremner, "Mediator Backs out of Galena Dealings," *Reno Gazette-Journal*, February 21, 1992; Bremner, "Here's a Look."

22. Margaret Eadington to Billy Templeton, state director (Nevada), BLM, memorandum, December 11, 1991; Bremner, "Mediator Backs Out."

23. American Land Conservancy, fact sheet: Galena property, August 1994; Russell Austin, interview by the author, January 3, 2010.

24. Harriet Burgess, letter to Billy Templeton, June 4, 1993; Harriet Burgess, handwritten notes, June 28, 1993; Harriet Burgess handwritten note on newspaper article by Faith Bremner, "Galena Buyout Imperiled," *Reno Gazette-Journal*, January 31, 1992.

25. Washoe County Special Assessment District #9 (SAD #9) was created to fund the construction of sewer and water facilities for the Galena development. Bonds were sold to pay the assessment for the sewer plant and a lien placed on the property until the Galena Resort Company paid off the bond debt of $8,555,000. Galena Resort Company paid two installments of the assessment, but as of January 31, 1993, it still owed $6,844,148 plus a late payment charge of $184,364. Amended and restated agreement for assessment district payoff and distribution of sewer connection fee revenues; water connections; and assessment district bond fund surplus between Galena Resort Company and Washoe County, January 31, 1993; Ted Farwell and John Bohling, an appraisal review and alternative valuation of the Galena Ski Resort, Mount Rose, Nevada, for U.S. Forest Service, June 7, 1993, 54; Bremner, "Galena Buyout Imperiled."

26. Harriet Burgess to Senators Richard Bryan and Harry Reid, memorandum, July 16, 1993.

27. Harriet Burgess, letter to Ed Hastey, July 26, 1993; Jack Peterson, updated tasks and schedule, Nevada and California land acquisition/exchange, July 28, 1993.

28. Jack Peterson, status report, Nevada land exchange, August 12, 1994; Jack Peterson, background Nevada land exchange, February 11; 1994.

29. Peterson, updated tasks and schedule.

30. Both Aaron Peskin and Nancy Shanahan had worked with Harriet at Trust for Public Land. Peskin followed Harriet to ALC in October 1990 and was joined by Shanahan in March 1991. Peskin and Shanahan quit March 15, 1993, and March 5, 1993, respectively, after Shanahan received a memo from Harriet dated February 19, 1993, that contained suggestions for changes in Shanahan's approach to ALC negotiations. Peskin filed suit for breach of contract on April 23, 1993, against Harriet Burgess and ALC along with past and present members of the ALC Board of Councillors: Bruce and Harriet Babbitt, David Brower, Brock Evans, Bill Garrett, Bill Lane, Martin Litton, Pete and Helen McCloskey, Margaret Owings, Galen Rowell, Robert Stephens, and Stewart Udall, claiming constructive termination. Constructive termination requires actions and conditions of the employer so intolerable or aggravated that a reasonable person would have been compelled to resign. Peskin was dissatisfied at ALC before the Shanahan memo. He complained that Harriet had assigned him a "grossly excessive number of real estate projects." He differed with Harriet on which projects "were important for environmental and political reasons." After almost a year, the parties settled the case without going to trial. The terms of the settlement are confidential. Peskin v. Burgess, San Francisco County Superior Court, Case Number CGC 93 951271.

31. Leslie took a short break during her employment at ALC, but she worked there either full- or part-time for most of its existence. Cowan, interview, November 17, 2008; Leslie King Cowan, e-mail to author, July 29, 2017.

32. Russell Austin, oral history interview by Carol McLaughlin, August 31, 2006; Russell Austin, interview by the author, November 15, 2009. According to Harriet's time sheet, the meeting with Russell and Lew took place March 10, 1993.

33. Joe Burgess, interview, August 22, 2010.

34. Linda Hunt was in a serious automobile accident in Colorado in 1982 that left her a quadriplegic. Harriet waged a long battle to secure a financial settlement from the insurance company and always was involved in making arrangements for Linda's care. Harriet Burgess, time sheets for periods ending July 31, August 15 and 31, 1993; Leslie King Cowan, telephone conversation with the author, October 27, 2016.

35. Billy Templeton, letter to Bob Wells, July 8, 1993; Jim Nelson, letter to Billy Templeton, August 20, 1993.

36. Lauren Ward to Harriet Burgess, memorandum, August 16, 1993; attendance list for NLV Meeting—Las Vegas Airport, August 13, 1993; agenda North Las Vegas land discussion, Las Vegas airport commissioner's conference room, August 13, 1993.

37. City of North Las Vegas, request for developer qualifications for the acquisition and development of up to seventy-five hundred acres located in the city of North Las Vegas, February 16, 1994.

38. Adding to the CNLV's troubles, one of the prospective developers of the BLM land filed a lawsuit against the secretary of the Interior and the Sierra Club Legal Defense Fund in November 1992. Excerpts from chronology of BLM acquisition by the city of North Las Vegas, apparently distributed at the August 13, 1993, Las Vegas meeting at the airport; Laurens H. Silver, Sierra Club Legal Defense Fund, letter to Hugh Hewitt of Pettis, Tester, Kruse & Krinsky [attorney for four of the developers interested in purchasing the land for development from the CNLV once CNLV purchases it from BLM], January 6, 1992.

39. Land exchange agreement between the Bureau of Land Management and American Land Conservancy for the equalization of values, September 20, 1993; Ed Hastey, letter to Harriet Burgess, September 20, 1993.

40. Harriet Burgess to Dave Livermore, Nature Conservancy, memorandum, September 29, 1993; Susan Voyles, "Galena Deadline Nears," *Reno Gazette-Journal*, September 23, 1993.

41. Voyles, "Galena Deadline Nears"; Sevil Omer, "Ski Resort Developers Demanding $1.5 Million," *Reno Gazette-Journal*, September 29, 1993.

42. Voyles, "Galena Deadline Nears"; Omer, "Ski Resort Developers."

43. "Galena Resort Land Purchase Can't Die Now," *Reno Gazette-Journal*, September 27, 1993.

44. "Benefactor Needed to Save Galena Deal," *Reno Gazette-Journal*, September 29, 1993.

45. James Robbins, "On Again, Off Again," *Bonanza Times*, September 29, 1993; Harriet Burgess, handwritten notes, September 22–30, 1993; Tim Anderson, "Galena Deal: Public Land Advocates Race Clock," *Reno Gazette-Journal*, October 1, 1993.

46. Russell Austin, letter to Marlene Lockard, October 1, 1993; Anderson, "Galena Deal"; "Galena Negotiators Near Deal," *Reno Gazette-Journal*, October 7, 1993.

47. Russell Austin, letter to William Davis, October 6, 1993; "Galena Negotiators Near Deal"; agreement to purchase real property by and between Galena Resort Company, Trustees of the Nell J. Redfield Trust (seller) and American Land Conservancy (buyer) made as of October 15, 1993.

48. Harriet Burgess, handwritten notes, September 30, October 6 and 19, 1993; Agreement to Purchase, October 15, 1993.

49. Dave Livermore, TNC, letter to Jim Baca, director BLM, August 20, 1993.

50. Harriet Burgess, letter to Bill Garrett, May 5, 1994; Harriet Burgess, list of telephone calls for 28 September 1993 attached to time sheet for period ending September 30, 1993; Harriet Burgess to Dave Livermore and Marlene Lockard, memorandum, September 29, 1993 [appears to have been written on September 28, 1993]; Harriet Burgess, fax to Dave Livermore, September 28, 1993.

51. Harriet Burgess, schedule attached to time sheet for period ending October 15, 1993; Harriet Burgess, handwritten notes, September 30, 1993; Dave Livermore, letter to Marlene Lockard and Harriet Burgess, October 7, 1993.

52. Amendment number one to agreement to purchase real property by and among ALC, Galena Resort Company, and the Redfield Trust, October 29, 1993; Harriet Burgess, handwritten notes, October 7, 1993.

53. Harriet Burgess to Bill Garrett, memorandum, May 5, 1994; Dave Livermore, letter to Harriet Burgess, November 3, 1993.

54. Harriet Burgess to Bill Garrett, memorandum, May 5, 1994; "Nature Conservancy to Assist with Galena Purchase," TNC draft press release, December 2, 1993.

55. The interest rate for the Packard loan was 6 percent compared with the 8½ percent demanded by TNC. The loan did not mature until December 31, 1994, but ALC paid it in full August 12, 1994. Colburn Wilbur joined ALC's Board of Councillors in 2000. Harriet Burgess, schedule for December 28 and list of phone calls for December 29 attached to time sheet for period ending December 31, 1993; Bruce Babbitt, letter to David Packard and Colburn Wilbur, December 29, 1993; Harriet Burgess, letter to Colburn Wilbur, December 28, 1993; Harriet Burgess, handwritten notes, January 3, 1994.

56. In the mid-1990s, BLM tried to divide its seventy-five hundred acres into smaller one- to five-acre parcels to be sold individually. The CNLV fought this plan because it meant piecemeal rather than planned development. After the 1998 passage of the Southern Nevada Public Lands Management Act mandated the auction of federal lands subject to local approval, 1,905 of the 7,500 acres were auctioned for $47.2 million (approximately $25,000 per acre) to North Valley Enterprises, a partnership of the American Nevada and Del Webb Corporations, in 2001. Construction on the community of Aliante began in 2003. The remaining BLM acreage has yet to be sold and developed. Geoff Schumacher, *Sun, Sin & Suburbia; The History of Modern Las Vegas*, rev. and expanded (Reno: University of Nevada Press, 2015), 212–14; Peterson, update Nevada land exchange, January 23, 1994, February 1, 1994, March 7, 1994.

57. Harriet Burgess, letter to Jack Peterson, August 25, 1994.

58. Russell Austin, conversation with the author, June 27, 2010; Peterson, update Nevada land exchange, February 1 and March 7, 1994; Ward, oral history interview; second amended and restated land exchange agreement between Bureau of Land Management and American Land Conservancy for the equalization of land values, March 8, 1994.

59. Located west of the Sutter Buttes and east of the Sacramento River near the town of Colusa, California, the Butte Sink National Wildlife Refuge has the highest concentration of waterfowl per acre in the world. With the loss of more than 95 percent of California's Central Valley wetlands over the past one hundred years, conserving the remaining wetlands is essential for the survival of waterfowl. Author's interview with Lauren Ward, January 4, 2010; Ward, oral history interview; www.fws.gov/refuge/butte_sink/, November 6, 2016; www.ducks.org/Page2482.aspx, January 26, 2010.

60. Ward, interview, January 4, 2010.

61. Ward, interview, January 4, 2010; Ward, oral history interview.

62. Ward, interview, January 4, 2010.

63. Before the Cessna P210, Harriet flew with Lauren in his Piper Cherokee Six. Lauren Ward, e-mail to the author, May 16, 2017.

64. ALC, Southern Nevada potential acquisitions summary, June 29, 1993; Harriet Burgess, letter to Jan Bernard, July 6, 1993; Lauren Ward, letter to Harriet Burgess, February 17, 1994; letter agreement among ALC, Jan Bernard Realty, and Ward Investments, March 1, 1994; exclusive agent agreement, March 29, 1994; Ward, oral history interview.

65. American Land Conservancy, Nevada land exchange phase I, August 1994; Rachael Conlin, "BLM Sale Creates Dilemma for County Planners," *Las Vegas Sun*, August 21, 1994; Al Jahns, letter to Harriet Burgess, April 7, 1994.

66. Mining claims may be staked on public land whenever someone believes he has discovered a valuable mineral that is worth recovering. National parks, state parks, national wildlife refuges, and certain other public lands are not open to mining claim location. The claim must be marked with corner monuments like wooden posts with a notice of location posted on or in the monument stating the name of the claim, the name and mailing address of the locator, the date of location, and other details. The notice may be in a can, jar, or other device attached to the post. The claim must be recorded with the county recorder and the BLM. The claim is unpatented until the owner of the claim has proven to the federal government that minerals can be extracted from it at a profit and the government issues a patent (or deed) for the claim. More details on mining claims in Nevada may be found in Keith G.

Papke and David A. Davis, *Mining Claim Procedures for Nevada Prospectors and Miners,* 5th ed. (Nevada Bureau of Mines and Geology Special Publication 6), Reno: Nevada Bureau of Mines & Geology, 2002, http://minerals.nv.gov/uploadedFiles/mineralsnvgov/content/Programs/Mining/MiningClaimProceduresSP6.pdf. A sixth edition was published in 2019.

67. Ward, oral history interview; Russell Austin, oral history interview; Russell Austin, letter to Andrew M. Flaherty dba Sedona Mining Company, May 25, 1994; Al Jahns and Russell Austin, conversation with the author, February 17, 2010; Al Jahns, conversation with the author, November 9, 2016.

68. Harriet Burgess to Bonnie Cohen, memorandum, May 5, 1994; Harriet Burgess, handwritten notes, May 3, 1994; Jack Peterson, fax to Ron Wenker [new BLM state director for Nevada], May 11, 1994.

69. Harriet Burgess, handwritten notes, May 11 and 13, 1994; Richard B. Holmes, director, Clark County Department of Comprehensive Planning, letter to Gary Ryan, Las Vegas district manager, BLM, May 25, 1994; Harriet Burgess, fax to Peter Arapis, June 1, 1994; Peterson, Nevada land exchange status, June 3, 1994; Harriet Burgess to Senator Reid, Senator Bryan, Congressman Bilbray, memorandum, July 5, 1994; Clark County Board of Commissioners, resolution opposing and protesting the American Land Conservancy's Nevada land exchange (Case #N-57877), July 5, 1994.

70. Lesley Coffin, ALC, letter to Steve Roberts, Regional Flood Control District, Las Vegas, July 27, 1994; Julie Turrini, letter to Brian Hutchins, Nevada Department of Transportation, August 10, 1994; Harriet Burgess, letter to Senator Richard Bryan, August 25, 1994; Harriet Burgess, letter to Ed Hastey, September 7, 1994.

71. Burgess, letter to Bryan, August 25, 1994.

72. The two private properties that became public land were on Peavine Mountain, 3,120 acres owned by Venture Corporation and 5,404 acres owned by Granite Construction Company. The 493 acres of the DePaoli ranch located south of Pyramid Lake within the Pyramid Lake Indian Reservation were reconveyed to the Bureau of Indian Affairs to be managed for the benefit of the Pyramid Lake Indian Tribe. American Land Conservancy, Nevada land exchange phase I, August 1994. The six development companies purchasing BLM's Las Vegas lands were Federal Land Management, Aleman Development Corporation, Perma-Bilt, Lewis Homes, Evans, and Halco Inc. Russell Austin, oral history interview; Harriet Burgess, letter to Nancy Wilder, National Title Co., August 12, 1994.

73. Jack Peterson, *Status Report, Nevada Land Exchange,* August 12, 1994; American Land Conservancy, "The American Land Conservancy is Born," *Newsletter* 1, no. 1 (Fall 1990); Harriet Burgess, letter to Jack Peterson, August 25, 1994.

74. Peterson, status report, Nevada land exchange, August 1994; Harriet Burgess, letter to Jack Peterson, August 25, 1994.

75. Harriet Burgess, letter to Preston Hale, September 7, 1994; Harriet Burgess, letter to Jack Peterson, September 15, 1994; Harriet Burgess, letter to Marlene Lockard, August 25, 1994; Harriet Burgess, letter to Lauren Ward, September 15, 1994.

76. Invitation to attend the celebration at Galena Meadows, August 28, 1994; program for Galena Meadows celebration, August 28, 1994; photos taken at the Galena celebration, August 28, 1994.

77. Harriet Burgess, letter to James Tallerico, September 7, 1994; Harriet Burgess, letter to Keith Harper, September 8, 1994; Russell Austin, oral history interview; Ame Hellman, interview by the author, July 1, 2010.

78. American Land Conservancy, "Spring Mountains: Cool Relief from Las Vegas," *American Land Conservancy* [newsletter] (Winter/Spring 1995): 5; www.fs.usda.gov/detail/htnf/about-forest/offices/?cid=fsm9_026952, November 13, 2016; Harriet Burgess, letter to Robert Joslin, deputy chief of National Forest System, September 18, 1998; Jim Nelson, letter to Thomas R. C. Wilson, September 29, 1998.

79. ALC purchased the lots September 2, 1994, for $3,060,000 after optioning them November 18, 1993. Jan Bernard and Pine Development originally purchased the 524-acre Deer Creek property in August 1992 for $2 million from the Simpson family. Pine Development subdivided the land into lots and sold fifteen four-acre lots for $1,577,000, leaving the thirty-four two-acre lots that were sold to ALC September 2, 1994, and the 375-acre parcel. Ward, oral history interview; Harriet Burgess, letter to James Tallerico, September 7, 1994; ALC, project summary sheet—Deer Creek Lots—80 acres, Clark County, March 19, 1996; ALC, NVLE II Spring Mountains Deer Creek, February 14, 1996.

80. Harriet Burgess, letter to Roger C. Viadero, inspector general, July 27, 1998; bargaining agreement, March 13, 1996.

81. Eric Nalder, Jim Simon, Deborah Nelson, and Danny Westneat, "Environmental Groups Profit From Land Trades," *Seattle Times*, September 29, 1998.

82. The first appraisal was completed August 2, 1994, by Keith Harper; the second October 13, 1994, by Lee Smith; the third January 13, 1995, by Shelli Lowe; the fourth in early October 1995 by BLM Nevada and Arizona State Review appraisers and a Forest Service appraiser from Utah. ALC, project summary sheet—Deer Creek Lots—80 acres, Clark County, March 19, 1996; ALC, "Deer Creek/Spring Mountains NRA/Las Vegas Nevada," October 20, 1995; Harriet Burgess to Jim Nelson, memorandum, August 2, 1995; Susan Greene, "Federal Land Swap Shelves Deer Creek Development," *Las Vegas Review Journal*, January 12, 1996; Richard Bryan, "Owners Originally Planned to Develop a Subdivision," January 24, 1996.

83. Jan Bernard, letter to Senator Richard Bryan, October 9, 1995.

84. Harriet Burgess, letters to Congresswoman Vucanovich, October 19, 1995; Senator Harry Reid, October 18, 1995; Jim Nelson, October 18, 1995; Congressman Ensign, October 19, 1995.

85. The bargaining process is permitted and described by the Federal Land Exchange Facilitation Act (FLEFA) of 1988 and its regulations. According to Jim Nelson's response to the OIG report, Jack Blackwell (then regional forester, Intermountain Region) directed the regional lands staff to undertake the bargaining process at the suggestion of Gordon Small, director of lands in the U.S. Forest Service Washington office. No appraisers were on the bargaining team. The Forest Service was represented by Robert W. Ross Jr., director of recreation and lands, Intermountain Region; Susan Bybee, lands adjustment officer, recreation and lands, Intermountain Region; and Alan Pinkerton, assistant forest supervisor, Humboldt-Toiyabe National Forest, Intermountain Region. The bargaining team's review appraiser was Gary H. Kent. Kent met the qualifications stated in FLEFA regulations, had done work for the federal government, was familiar with federal guidelines, and was acceptable to all members of the team. Lauren Ward described Kent as the "dean of appraisers in Las Vegas. He was an old guy whose reputation was impeccable." Bargaining agreement, March 13, 1996; Ward, oral history interview; Jim Nelson, letter to Thomas R. C. Wilson, September 29, 1998.

86. Ward, oral history interview; Paul Tittman to director of lands, memorandum, April 4, 1996, that was given to Harriet by Senator Bryan's office as she notes in her July 27, 1998,

letter to Inspector General Roger C. Videro; Ted Williams, "Fallen Forester: Did Whistleblowers Destroy a Fine Public Servant?" *High Country News* (December 21, 1998): 4–5.

87. Ward, oral history interview; Ward, interview, January 4, 2010; Ame Hellman, interviews, June 30 and July 1, 2010.

88. The U.S. Forest Service created the National Landownership Adjustment Team in November 1998 to review land exchanges that were valued over $500,000 or were controversial. Ward, oral history interview; Harriet Burgess, letter to Paul Laxalt, December 23, 1998; U.S. General Accounting Office, BLM and the Forest Service: Land exchanges need to reflect appropriate value and serve the public interest, GAO/RCED-00-73, June 2000, http://www.gao.gov/assets/240/230398.pdf, November 21, 2016; USDA Office of Inspector General Western Region, Audit report: Forest Service National Landownership Adjustment Team Washington, D.C., Report No. 08601-27-SF, March 2002, https://www.usda.gov/oig/webdocs/08601-27-SF.pdf, November 21, 2016.

89. U.S. Department of Agriculture, Office of Inspector General, Forest Service Humboldt-Toiyabe National Forest land adjustment program fiscal years 1990 to 1997, Sparks, Nevada, Audit Report No. 08003-02-SF, August 1998.

90. Nalder, Simon, Nelson, and Westneat, "Environmental Groups Profit from Land Trades."

91. Jon Christensen, "Trading This ↑ Even Up for That ↓ An Exchange for the General Good was Better for Some Than Others," *New York Times*, October 3, 1998.

92. Ted Williams, "A Smear Campaign: Bureaucrats Destroy an Effective Conservationist's Career," *Fly Rod & Reel* (January/February 1999).

93. Jim Nelson and Harriet had been friends since 1983. While she was employed by TPL, they worked together on several projects, including Hope Valley and the East Fork of the Carson River, and continued working together after she founded ALC in 1990. Ted Williams, "A Smear Campaign"; Thomas R. C. Wilson, letter to Russell J. Austin, September 24, 1998.

94. Harriet Burgess, letter [draft] to Secretary Dan Glickman, Department of Agriculture, August 31, 1998; Harriet Burgess, letter to Senator Richard H. Bryan, December 29, 1998; Russell Austin, letter to Roger C. Viadero, inspector general, USDA, December 30, 1997; Jeff DeLong, "Activists See Threat to Sierra Land Deals," *Reno Gazette-Journal*, January 12, 1999.

95. Ame Hellman left ALC in 2000. Hellman, interviews, June 30 and July 1, 2010.

96. David Brower, letter to the *Las Vegas Review-Journal*, August 5, 1998.

97. Joe Burgess, conversation with the author, August 22, 2010.

98. Harriet Burgess, letter to Roger C. Viadero, inspector general, USDA, July 27, 1998; Harriet Burgess, letter to Robert Joslin, September 18, 1998; Harriet Burgess to executive board members, memorandum, October 2, 1998; Harriet Burgess, letter to Senator Richard Bryan, December 29, 1998; Harriet Burgess to ALC staff, memorandum, July 27, 1999.

99. Stewart Udall and Pete McCloskey, letter to Bruce Babbitt and Dan Glickman, January 20, 1999; DeLong, "Activists See Threat to Sierra Land Deals."

100. Harriet Burgess, handwritten notes, September 7 and October 22, 1999, February 8, April 10, and August 15, 2000; Pete Romatowski, letter to Clifford Rones, April 20, 2001; Peter J. Romatowski, e-mail to Russell J. Austin, April 20, 2001; Russell Austin, conversation with the author, June 30, 2010; Russell Austin to ALC board members, memorandum, December 2, 1998; Russell Austin, oral history interview.

101. Jack L. Craven, letter and fax transmittal to Harriet Burgess, March 22, 2002.

102. Bighorn sheep studies, https://www.nature.nps.gov/views/Sites/GRCA/HTML/Big horn/Bighorn_ET.htm, August 11, 2016.

103. Martin Litton, interview no. 53.32A.

104. Kevin Fedarko, "Ain't It Just Grand"; Regan Dale, interview no. 53.15; Kerstin Dale, e-mail to author, September 5, 2017.

105. Steiger, "My God, It's Waltenberg!"

106. Bob Webb, "The Changing Rapids of Grand Canyon—Three Rapids That Haven't Changed," http://www.gcrg.org/bqr/15-1/rapids.html, August 13, 2016.

107. Michael F. Anderson, *Living at the Edge; Explorers, Exploiters and Settlers of the Grand Canyon Region* (Grand Canyon: Grand Canyon Association, 1998): 9.

Chapter 5: Saving John Muir: The John Muir Gravesite

1. John Muir, "The Grand Cañon," in *Steep Trails*, edited by William Frederic Badè (Boston: Houghton Mifflin, 1918; Dunwoody, GA: Norman S. Berg, 1970), 380–81; John Muir, *John of the Mountains: The Unpublished Journals of John Muir*, edited by Linnie Marsh Wolfe (Boston: Houghton Mifflin, 1938), 440; Harriet Burgess, *John Muir's Gravesite*, 1999.

2. The 35- by 27-foot cyclone fence was added by John Hanna, one of John Muir's grandsons, in the early 1960s to prevent vandalism by high-school students who partied there. Jeffrey Killion and Mark Davison, *Cultural Landscape Report for John Muir National Historic Site*, vol. 1 (Boston: National Park Service, 2005), 171–72, 180.

3. Beginning in 1959, the Sierra Club organized John Muir pilgrimage hikes that commenced at the house and passed by the gravesite, where participants joined hands around a giant eucalyptus there and sang "Auld Lang Syne." The hikes ended in 1974. The John Muir Memorial Association, organized in 1956, joined with the Contra Costa County Historical Society to restore the house as a memorial and to campaign for its acquisition by the federal government. Congress designated the John Muir National Historic Site August 31, 1964 (H.R. 439, P.L. 88-547, 78 Stat. 783) and authorized the land acquisition with appropriated funds. Killion and Davison, *Cultural Landscape Report* vol. 1, 172, 180, and 216.

4. National Park Service, *Feasibility Study, John Muir Gravesite, Contra Costa County, Draft* (San Francisco: NPS, Western Regional Office, May 1980) referenced in Killion and Davison, *Cultural Landscape Report*, vol. 1, 227–29. H.R. 4315, "A bill to provide for the inclusion of certain lands [including the gravesite] within the John Muir National Historic Site," sponsored by Representative George Miller of California's 7th District, was added as Section 5 of H.R. 3408, "A bill to increase the amounts authorized for the Colorado River Storage Project," sponsored by three representatives from Utah and then passed by both houses of Congress as H.R. 3408 in October 1988. Signed by President Ronald Reagan October 31, 1988, it became Public Law 100-563. The government's goal for the gravesite was "to preserve the site in its present undeveloped condition and to provide all maintenance of the site."

5. Killion and Davison, *Cultural Landscape Report*, vol. 1, 279, 318.

6. Killion and Davison, *Cultural Landscape Report*, vol. 1, 279.

7. Leslie King Cowan and Darrell Cowan, conversation with the author, July 8, 2011; Cowan, interview, November 17, 2008.

8. The June 2016 NPS environmental assessment of the Strentzel-Muir Gravesite acknowledged that "there has been uncertainty regarding appropriate levels of visitor use and appropriate resource management strategies since the gravesite was set aside sixteen

years ago" (i) and "the NPS has been managing the gravesite without the guidance of a comprehensive plan since acquiring the parcel. (3)" The NPS conducted "public scoping" in 2013 and issued an initial environmental assessment in 2015 that was superseded by the 2016 environmental assessment. The June 2016 assessment presented four gravesite management alternatives for public input and review and a summary of public comments received during the planning process. On October 24, 2017, a press release from the John Muir National Historic Site announced the completion of planning for the Strentzel-Muir Gravesite and released the finding of no significant impact (FONSI) that documents the selected management alternative. According to the FONSI, visitor access will be designed to "encourage a sense of reverence for Muir's life and legacy . . . which will be ensured through the preservation of the historic landscape and through limiting group sizes and duration of stay. . . . [T]he entire 1.27-acre parcel will be fenced, greatly minimizing the ability for people to access the site when closed. Pedestrians and cyclists will have access through a pedestrian gate Monday through Friday from 10:30 a.m.–4:30 p.m., but through regulatory and interpretive signage, they too will be encouraged to respect the solemn, reverential character of the site. The Muir family will continue to have open access, and will also have the right to hold an annual, private, family commemoration at the gravesite—closed to the general public." Private vehicles will not have access, but visitors will be taken to the gravesite in park shuttles for tours. Current funding and staffing is expected to support up to two tours Monday through Friday and two tours on weekends accommodating 24–50 visitors per week. Additional visitation options, for example, at NPS-hosted events during the year, are included in the FONSI. The FONSI also details steps that will be taken to preserve the historic resources and add new facilities (e.g., informational signs); notes that the wrought iron fence installed by ALC will be maintained; addresses natural resources management; and makes provisions for safety. Gretchen Stromberg, chief of planning and administration, John Muir National Historic Site, e-mail to the author, January 25, 2017; Killion and Davison, *Cultural Landscape Report*, vol. 1, 228; U.S. National Park Service, Strentzel-Muir gravesite environmental assessment, June 2016, https://parkplanning.nps.gov/document.cfm?documentID=73215, December 3, 2016; John Muir National Historic Site, "News Release: John Muir NHS Announces Completion of Strentzel-Muir Gravesite Planning and Release of the Finding of No Significant Impact," October 24, 2017; U.S. National Park Service, "Finding of No Significant Impact Strentzel-Muir Gravesite," September 2017.

9. Killion and Davison, *Cultural Landscape Report*, vol. 1, 398.

10. Killion, and Davison, *Cultural Landscape Report*, vol. 1, 399.

11. John Muir, *A Thousand-Mile Walk to the Gulf* (Boston: Houghton Mifflin, 1916; San Francisco: Sierra Club, 1992), 39, 41–42.

12. John Muir, letter to Louie Strentzel Muir, June 12, 1893, Holt-Atherton Special Collections at the University of the Pacific, http://cdm16745.contentdm.oclc.org/cdm/ref/collection/muirlette/rs/id/14608, August 14, 2017.

13. Killion and Davison, *Cultural Landscape Report*, vol. 1, 237; U.S. National Park Service, *General Management Plan and Environmental Assessment, John Muir National Historic Site* (San Francisco: Western Regional Office, January 1991); Phyllis Shaw, letter to Kimberly Moses, February 30, 1993; Edward Haberlin, letters to Ross de Lipkau, April 7, July 14, 1992; Arlen C. Mills, [appraisal report for the John Muir Gravesite], October 28, 1992; Roger Kennedy, letter to Harriet Burgess, October 29, 1994.

14. Ross de Lipkau does not remember exactly how ALC became involved with the John Muir gravesite, but he already knew about the organization because he was working with Harriet on a project in Alpine County at the time (the conveyance of Red Lake water rights—the first conveyance of water rights for conservation purposes in California) and was the Galena Resort Company's water rights attorney at the time of the sale of the Galena property. Ross de Lipkau, interview by the author, December 5, 2016; Ross de Lipkau, letter to Jim Nelson, January 17, 1996; Aaron Peskin, letter to Ross de Lipkau, January 29, 1993; Ross de Lipkau, letter to Harriet Burgess, December 28, 1994.

15. De Lipkau dismissed the first draft of the bargain sale option agreement in his April 29, 1993, letter as a "boiler-plate agreement to be used on a complicated or hard-driven agreement. Such are not the facts here." De Lipkau went on to report that, during his recent visit to Scotland, the John Muir Trust, an organization much like ALC, had "expressed an interest in the Muir gravesite," implying that if ALC didn't accept the conditions of sale specified in his letter, the John Muir Trust might. Lew Reid, fax to Harriet Burgess, March 12, 1993; Harriet Burgess, letter to Ross de Lipkau, April 12, 1993; Ross de Lipkau, letter to Harriet Burgess, April 29, 1993; Mary Lou Everett, letter to Harriet Burgess, June 16, 1993; Ross de Lipkau, letter to Harriet Burgess, June 29, 1993; bargain sale option agreement dated June 16, 1993, and signed by Harriet Burgess June 16, 1993, for ALC and by Ross de Lipkau, trustee, June 16, 1993, and William Hanna, trustee, June 23, 1993, for the Muir-Hanna Family Trust.

16. Ross de Lipkau, letter to Harriet Burgess, August 25, 1993; Harriet Burgess, letter to Ross de Lipkau, September 1, 1993.

17. Lynelle Johnson, fax to Harriet Burgess, September 8, 1993; Lynelle Johnson, telephone message for Harriet Burgess, September 9, 1993; Lynelle Johnson, letter to Harriet Burgess, October 6, 1993; Harriet Burgess to Lynelle Johnson, memorandum, October 11, 1993; Kimberly Moses, ALC project assistant, letter to Ross de Lipkau, November 3, 1993; Kimberly Moses to Harriet Burgess, memorandum, November 17, 1993; Stanley Albright, letter to Congressman George Miller, May 23, 1994.

18. Stanley T. Albright, regional director, Western Region, NPS, letter to Harriet Burgess, November 22, 1993.

19. American Land Conservancy, executive committee fact sheet; Project Name: John Muir Gravesite, National Historic Site, n.d. (but dates in the body of the fact sheet and a December 28, 1993, letter from Kimberly Moses to Robert Stephens point to a date of December 28, 1993); Kimberly Moses, letter to Robert Stephens, December 28, 1993; certified copy of a resolution adopted by the executive committee of the board of directors of American Land Conservancy, December 29, 1993.

20. Now retired, Robert Stephens, in addition to being Harriet's neighbor and best man at her wedding to Joe Burgess, was an internationally recognized expert in toxic waste disposal. Members of the executive committee are listed in the appendix. Kerry O'Toole, interview by the author, November 17, 2008.

21. Members of subsequent Boards of Councillors are listed in appendix 2. When Martin asked everyone to be on ALC's Board of Councillors, he said, "I don't want you to do anything. Just give me your name. Just put your name on the stationery." Martin Litton et al., conversation with the author during lunch at Sinbad's in San Francisco, November 17, 2008.

22. Mike Freed, comments made May 8, 2010, to the group gathered at Harriet's Inverness house for the celebration of her life.

23. American Land Conservancy, Board of Councillors' Retreat, Post Ranch Inn, Big Sur, [meeting information], 1994–1999; Leslie King Cowan, e-mail to the author, March 27, 2017.

24. As of 1973, the access easement parcel was owned in co-tenancy by nine descendants of John Muir. Three of these owners had died by 1993, but none of their estates had been probated in California, so title to the easement parcel never had passed formally to the heirs of the deceased owners. Affidavits signed by the heirs of the deceased owners at the request of ALC attorneys bypassed probate because the real property interest of the decedent named in each affidavit was worth less than $10,000 as confirmed by a probate referee. The affidavits served as deeds from the deceased to the heirs. All of the owners then quitclaimed their ownership of the access parcel to the Muir-Hanna Trust, giving the trust clear title to the parcel and making possible its sale to ALC and subsequently to NPS. Matt Paroly [ALC attorney at Marron Reid & Sheehy] to Mary Lu Everett [ALC attorney at Marron Reid & Sheehy], memorandum, February 4, 1994; Mary Lu Everett, letter to Gary Chulla, NPS, February 8, 1994; Matt Paroly, letter to Ross de Lipkau, February 23, 1994; Mary Lu Everett, fax to Harriet Burgess, March 16, 1994; Matt Paroly, letter to certified probate referee, David Elefant, March 21, 1994; Matt Paroly, letter to Ross de Lipkau, March 23, 1994; Ross de Lipkau, letter to Mary Lu Everett, March 23, 1994; Mary Lu Everett, letter to Gary Chulla, April 28, 1994.

25. Stanley T. Albright, regional director, Western Region, NPS, letter to Congressman George Miller; Harriet Burgess, fax to Lynelle Johnson, May 31, 1994; Burgess, letter to de Lipkau, June 10, 1994.

26. Harriet Burgess, letter to Ross de Lipkau, June 10, 1994.

27. Harriet Burgess, letter to Roger Kennedy, August 31, 1994.

28. Roger Kennedy, letter to Harriet Burgess, October 20, 1994.

29. Stanley Albright, letter to Harriet Burgess, November 10, 1994.

30. Ross de Lipkau, letter to Harriet Burgess and Mary Lu Everett, October 5, 1994.

31. Cowan, interview, November 17, 2008.

32. Dale Newell, letter to Nancy Shanahan, April 23, 1991; David Hanson, letter to Alvin Hackathorn, May 28, 1991; Harriet Burgess, handwritten notes of telephone call with Dale Newell, June 21, 1991; deed description, Washington County Deed, vol. 395, p. 335; American Land Conservancy, "A Conversation with Alvin Hackathorn," *Newsletter* (Fall 1992): 5.

33. Harriet Burgess, letter to Alvin Hackathorn, July 3, 1991; Alvin Hackathorn, "Grandma's Story," as told to Harriet Burgess, July 3, 1991; handwritten recording of sale of property from John and Columbia McCollough to William Hackathorn, June 27, 1987.

34. U.S. Forest Service, "Wayne National Forest, History & Culture," www.fs.usda.gov/wps/portal, April 20, 2011; James M. Dyer, "Using Witness Trees to Assess Forest Change in Southeastern Ohio," *Canadian Journal of Forest Research* 31 (2001): 1708–18; U.S. Forest Service, "Celebrating—Ohio's Forests," www.fs.usda.gov/Internet/FSE_DOCUMENTS/fsm9_005960.pdf, April 20, 2011.

35. American Land Conservancy, "A Conversation . . ."; grant deed, 1971.

36. Title policy for Hackathorn property, Schedule A, July 1, 1987.

37. Dale Newell, appraisal report for USDA-Forest Service, Wayne National Forest, Alvin O. Hackathorn, et ux, Washington County, Ohio, April 21, 1988.

38. David Hanson, letter to Alvin Hackathorn, January 9, 1991; Nancy Shanahan, handwritten notes of telephone conversation with David Hanson, June 5, 1991.

39. Nancy Shanahan, handwritten note to Harriet Burgess, undated.

40. Hackathorn, "Grandma's Story."

41. Cowan, interview, November 17, 2008.

42. Dale Newell, photos of visit to Hackathorn property, July 9, 1991.

43. Harriet Burgess, letter to Alvin Hackathorn, July 19, 1991; photos of Harriet's visit to the cabin, July 9, 1991.

44. Handwritten notes, Harriet Burgess and possibly Nancy Shanahan, regarding the memorial, September 5, 1991, and undated; Harriet Burgess, letter to Dave Hanson and Dale Newell, September 6, 1991; Leslie King to Harriet Burgess, memorandum, September 12, 1991; Harriet Burgess, handwritten notes of telephone call with Emily Wallace, and Alvin Hackathorn, September 24, 1991; Leslie King to Harriet Burgess, memorandum, October 18, 1991; warranty deed granting the Hackathorn property to the United States, October 21, 1991; Harriet Burgess, handwritten notes of telephone calls with Dale Newell, November 18 and 25, 1991; American Land Conservancy, Hackathorn project summary, November 1991.

45. Emily Wallace and Alvin Hackathorn, letter to Harriet Burgess, December 8, 1991.

46. Ross de Lipkau, interview by the author, December 5, 2016; Harriet Burgess, letter to Ellen Tauscher, congresswoman from California's 10th district, July 24, 1997.

47. ALC purchased the gravesite January 6, 1995, for $191,041.93, which included $11,046.00 in interest from April 1, 1994, to January 6, 1995, and a $4.06 deduction for prorated county taxes. ALC, John Muir Gravesite audit summary, May 19, 1997; ALC, "John Muir Gravesite," n.d.; Harriet Burgess, letter to Barbara Salzman, Marin Audubon Society, February 19, 1997. Sondra Humphries told ALC's Bill Livermore that funding for the gravesite was dropped from the final 1997 federal budget review, but she had put it back in for 1998 as "just a must." Bill Livermore to Harriet/Nancy, memorandum, July 29, 1996.

48. Lauren Ward, fax to Harriet Burgess, Ted Reid, and Nancy Stryble, August 23, 1995; Bill Livermore, letter to Jim Caroompas, assistant city manager, Martinez, October 2, 1995; Harriet Burgess, letter to Ronald E. Peterson, assistant city manager, Martinez, March 5, 1996; C. K. Maclay, "Muir's Grave Site Finds No Takers in Martinez or D.C.," *Contra Costa Times*, April 1, 1996; Bill Livermore to Harriet Burgess, memorandum, October 3, 1996; Bill Livermore to Harriet Burgess, memorandum, January 2, 1997.

49. Margaret Wimmer donated the fence design in October 1995. Margaret Wimmer, letter to Bill Livermore, October 10, 1995; Harriet Burgess, letter to Margaret Wimmer, October 10, 1995. Carlos Campos of Artists Workshop donated the fence material valued at $6,564.80. ALC paid the $4,000 balance due for the construction of the fence. Carlos Campos, letters to ALC, November 6 and 9, 1995; Bill Livermore to Harriet Burgess, memorandum, November 14, 1995; Harriet Burgess, letter to Carlos Campos, January 18, 1996; Bill Livermore, letter to Carlos Campos, February 24, 1997. Campos was unable to install all of the post caps and spears on the gravesite fence. ALC contracted with Morgan Fence & Awning Company to complete the project at a cost of $477. Invoice from Morgan Aluminum Products, March 3, 1997. The John Muir 4-H Club of Martinez, led by Judy Pereira, contacted ALC and offered to adopt the gravesite as a community service project. Harriet Burgess, handwritten notes of telephone call with Judy Pereira, January 10,

1997; Judy Pereira, letter to Bill Livermore, February 4, 1997; Nancy Stryble, letter to Judy Pereira, April 8, 1998. Harriet Burgess, letter to Ross de Lipkau, February 13, 1996.

50. American Land Conservancy, newsletter (Winter 1994): 1.

51. National Association of Women Business Owners, "Harriet Burgess, Woman Entrepreneur of the Year, 1999," video available January 10, 2017, at https://www.youtube.com/watch?v=4n6w9KMc43g; Peter Sinton, "3 Women Who Dared—Keys to Success—Perseverance, Setting Goals, Flexibility," *San Francisco Chronicle*, April 21, 1999.

52. More detailed information about the LWCF may be found on the National Park Service website (www.nps.gov) and the LWCF Coalition website (www.lwcfcoalition.org). Congress often has used funds intended for LWCF projects for unrelated purposes. Political maneuvering threatened the availability of funds for the gravesite purchase when two subcommittee chairmen (Senator Slade Gorton, R-Washington, and Representative Ralph Regula, R-Ohio) refused for a time to release land acquisition money approved by Congress. The April 1999 appraisal of the gravesite property conducted by an NPS staff appraiser and approved by NPS valued the parcel at $210,000. ALC agreed to donate the difference of $10,000 that the 1999 appraisal exceeded the 1992 appraisal. After deducting settlement charges and taxes, ALC received a check from the NPS for $199,734.88. Mike McQueen and Edward McMahon, *Land Conservation Financing* (Washington: Island Press, 2003), 2–8; "Environmental Stalling in Congress," *New York Times*, April 24, 1998, http://www.nytimes.com/1998/04/24/opinion/environmental-stalling-in-congress.html, December 8, 2016; Robert C. Cirese, *Appraisal Report Tract 01-108, John Muir Grave Site Parcel, John Muir National Historic Site, Contra Costa County, Martinez, California* (San Francisco: NPS, 1999); Sondra S. Humphries, chief, Pacific land resources program center, NPS, letter to Harriet Burgess, June 18, 1999; ALC, grant deed to NPS, August 9, 1999; NPS, certificate of acceptance, August 13, 1999.

53. ALC, income statement: John Muir, 1/1/93-4/22/97; NAWBO, "Harriet Burgess."

54. Linnie Marsh Wolfe, *Son of the Wilderness: The Life of John Muir* (Madison: University of Wisconsin Press, 1945); Donald Worster, *A Passion for Nature: The Life of John Muir* (New York: Oxford University Press, 2008); information about Clair Vaughn McNeel provided by the Presbyterian Historical Society, Philadelphia, PA; Hunt, telephone interview, April 28, 2010.

55. Wolfe, *Son of the Wilderness*; Worster, *A Passion for Nature*; Hunt, telephone interview, April 28, 2010.

56. John Muir, letter to Jeanne Carr, December 6, 1869; John Muir, letter to David Muir, March 20, 1870.

57. Hunt, telephone interview, April 28, 2010; Hellman, interviews, June 30 and July 1, 2010; Kara Woodruff, telephone interview by the author, May 30, 2017; Worster, *A Passion for Nature*, 165 and 208.

58. Other Presbyterian conservationists include Theodore Roosevelt, Harold Ickes, and Wallace Stegner. Mark Stoll, *Inherit the Holy Mountain: Religion and the Rise of American Environmentalism* (New York: Oxford University Press, 2015), 2, 4, and 5. I am indebted to Stoll for substantiating my conclusion that Harriet's conservation work was grounded in her Presbyterian roots.

59. Tim Richardson, interview by the author, June 29, 2010.

60. Muir, *A Thousand-Mile Walk to the Gulf* (ebook 2013; William Frederic Badé, ed., Boston: Houghton Mifflin, 1916), 82; John Muir, *The Yosemite* (New York: Century, 1912), 1.

61. Bear Valley lies near the intersection of Highways 16 and 20 in Colusa County, California. Among the many varieties of wildflowers in the valley are the rare Adobe lily along with the more common yellow tidytips, orange California poppies, purple Ithuriel's spear, and blue lupine. ALC published a guide to the Bear Valley wildflowers that describes fifty of the most interesting or commonly seen flowers. A map with a suggested route for touring the valley was available on the Colusa County Resource Conservation District website, www.colusarcd.org/nodes/projects/documents/bearvalleywallkerridgelooop.pdf as of January 14, 2017. The land in the valley is privately owned, and the continued presence of wildflowers is guaranteed by conservation easements established by ALC and held by the California Rangeland Trust. The wildflowers may be viewed from the mostly dirt and gravel road that passes through the valley. Rancher Jim Keegan also has installed a spring-loaded gate on his Bear Valley property, what he calls a wildflower access gate, to permit public access to the fields without allowing the cattle to escape.

I had the pleasure of joining Keegan and a group of folks long associated with ALC—Russell Austin, Leslie and Darrel Cowan, Lauren Ward and his daughter, Bob Stephens and his wife, Al Jahns and his wife—on a misty day in April 2016 to tour the fields of wildflowers seated atop bales of hay in a truck-drawn trailer and have visited on several other occasions. Depending on the weather—the amount of rainfall and valley temperatures dramatically affect the wildflower bloom—the best times to view wildflowers in Bear Valley range from early March to late April. The display varies as the season progresses. American Land Conservancy, program briefing, Bear Valley, 1996; Monica Vaughan, "Wildflower Road Show Is Due to Bloom in Colusa," *Sacramento Bee*, April 4, 2013; Jeff Phillips, "The Wildflowers of Mr. Muir," *Sunset* (March 1998), 82; American Land Conservancy, Bear Valley Ranch, circa 1998; John Game and Richards Lyon, *Fifty Wildflowers, Bear Valley, Colusa County* (San Francisco: American Land Conservancy, 1996); John Muir, *Muir Among the Animals: The Wildlife Writings of John Muir*, edited by Lisa Mighetto (San Francisco: Sierra Club, 1986), 122.

62. Martin Litton, interview no. 53.32A.

63. Ibid.

64. Carlene Anderson, remarks at the celebration of Harriet's life, May 8, 2010.

65. Anderson, *Living at the Edge*, 94–95.

66. William C. Suran, *With the Wings of an Angel; A Biography of Ellsworth and Emery Kolb, Photographers of Grand Canyon* (1991), kaibab.org/kaiba.org/kolb/index.html, August 18, 2016.

67. Ibid.

68. Ibid. The quote from Leigh Lint's journal is included in chapter 8. The journal itself is available in the Leigh Lint Collection at Northern Arizona University, NAU.MS.388, 1920-1924, Box 1.4. Leigh Lint celebrated his twenty-first birthday during the expedition.

Chapter 6: Magnificent Obsession: Thunderbird Lodge

1. Henry David Thoreau, *Walden* (Boston: Ticknor and Fields, 1854; Minneapolis, MN: Lerner, 2014), 177; Mark Twain, *Roughing It* (Hartford, CT: American Publishing, 1872), 169, published as part of The Oxford Mark Twain (New York: Oxford University, 1996); John Muir, letter to Dr. and Mrs. Carr, Tahoe City, November 3, 1873, in Bonnie Johanna Gisel, ed., *Kindred and Related Spirits: The Letters of John Muir and Jeanne C. Carr* (Salt Lake City: University of Utah Press, 2001), 228–29.

2. Brendan Riley, "Tahoe Estate May Be a Park; Whittell Mansion on Federal Bloc," *Tahoe Daily Tribune*, February 5, 1996; John Trent, "Conservancy Working on Land Exchange," *Reno Gazette-Journal*, March 31, 1996.

3. www.keeptahoeblue.org (website of the League to Save Lake Tahoe) March 21, 2017; www.trpa.org (website of the Tahoe Regional Planning Agency) March 21, 2017. For more on Lake Tahoe's history and ecology, see Douglas H. Strong, *Tahoe, An Environmental History* (Lincoln: University of Nebraska, 1984); Lyndall Baker Landauer, *The Mountain Sea, a History of Lake Tahoe* (Honolulu: Flying Cloud, 1996); and David Beesley, *Crow's Range, an Environmental History of the Sierra Nevada* (Reno: University of Nevada, 2004).

4. Jack Dreyfus sold 10 percent of his interest in his Lake Tahoe properties to William P. Rogers, former secretary of State, June 12, 1974, for $330,000. He granted a third of his remaining 90 percent interest in the Tahoe properties to the Dreyfus Charitable Foundation September 22, 1993. Dreyfus had visited Thunderbird Lodge only once since 1984. John Trent, "For the People," *Reno Gazette-Journal*, March 31, 1996.

5. William K. Woodburn, letter to James J. Halley, November 16, 1970; Ronald M. and Susan A. James, *Castle in the Sky: George Whittell Jr. and the Thunderbird Lodge*, 2d. ed. (Lake Tahoe, NV: Thunderbird Lodge Press, 2005), 27–29.

6. James and James, *Castle in the Sky*, 30–42.

7. Whittell sold the nine thousand acres that he had acquired from the estate of Walter Hobart in the 1930s to the Nevada Lake Tahoe Investment Company for $5 million in 1959. One year later, the Crystal Bay Development Company purchased the land for $25 million and developed the new town of Incline Village in the 1960s. A jury verdict in November 1967 supported the condemnation action, and the state of Nevada purchased fifty-three hundred acres from Whittell for about $3 million. The U.S. Forest Service purchased 4,732 acres in 1970 for $1.5 million with money from the Land and Water Conservation Fund. The Forest Service purchased an additional ten thousand acres in 1972 for $10,685,000 after threatening condemnation. Dreyfus finally agreed to convey the land to the government because he wanted to "do what the government asked." Memorandum re Whittell Estate, October 22, 1970; Strong, *Tahoe*, 54–55, 83, and 93–94; warranty deed, January 6, 1972; Frankie Sue Del Papa, letter to Robert Armstrong, June 30, 1995.

8. Peter Laxalt, letter [draft] to unspecified members of the Nevada congressional delegation, June 19, 1995; Peter Laxalt, letter to The Honorable Harry Reid, December 3, 1996; Peter Dominique Laxalt, Obituary, *Reno Gazette-Journal*, March 23, 2010; Paul Laxalt, *Nevada's Paul Laxalt, a Memoir* (Reno: Jack Bacon, 2000), 74–78 and 151.

9. Peter Laxalt, letter [draft] to unspecified members of the Nevada congressional delegation, June 19, 1995; Liz Laxalt, letter to [Nevada] Governor Robert Miller, June 19, 1995; Ame Hellman to Harriet Burgess, memorandum, December 30, 1996.

10. Peter Laxalt, letter to The Honorable Harry Reid, December 3, 1996; Harriet Burgess, letter to Russell Austin, Julie Turrini, and Al Jahns, January 8, 1998; Harriet Burgess, letter to Robert Armstrong, August 7, 1995.

11. Addendum to buyer's broker employment agreement, February 15, 1995; Liz Laxalt, telephone call message for Harriet Burgess, February 28, 1995; Harriet Burgess, letter to Jack Dreyfus, February 28, 1995; Ame Hellman, interview by the author, June 30, 2010.

12. ALC staff, note to Harriet Burgess, March 9, 1995; Leslie King Cowan, e-mail to author, February 25, 2017.

13. Harriet Burgess, letter to Jack Dreyfus, April 28, 1995; Jack Dreyfus, letter to Harriet Burgess, May 1, 1995.

14. ALC, "The Anatomy of a Land Exchange," undated; Harriet's New York meetings with Dreyfus were noted on Ame Hellman's "Dreyfus Chronology" as occurring in August 1995.

15. Russell Austin, oral history interview.

16. Russell Austin, letter to William Rogers, October 10, 1995.

17. Harriet Burgess, letter to Michael Dwyer, district manager, Las Vegas District Office, BLM, June 27, 1995.

18. Summary of Nevada acquisition priorities, Lake Tahoe Basin Management Unit, February 1996.

19. Although Harriet first intended to acquire both Thunderbird Lodge and the Dreyfus property at Zephyr Cove, she focused her energies on Thunderbird lodge after Zephyr Cove went under contract to the Olympic Group, a private real estate firm, in December 1995. Shari Chase, letter to Liz Laxalt, December 5, 1995.

20. Harriet Burgess, handwritten notes of telephone calls on May 2, 1995, June 14, 26, 28, and 29, 1995; Harriet Burgess to "All Interested Parties," memorandum, July 7, 1995; Harriet Burgess to Mary Connolly, memorandum, October 13, 1995.

21. Frankie Sue Del Papa, letter to Robert Armstrong, June 30, 1995; Harriet Burgess, letter to Robert Armstrong, August 7, 1995.

22. Robert Harris, letter to Jack Dreyfus, September 11, 1995.

23. Peter Laxalt, letter to Barbara Vucanovich, Harry Reid, Richard Bryan, and John Ensign, June 29, 1995.

24. Russell Austin, letter to William Rogers, November 30, 1995.

25. Harriet Burgess, letter to Jack Dreyfus and William Rogers, January 3, 1996.

26. Harriet Burgess, letter to Martin Litton, January 4, 1996; Hunt, interview, April 28, 2010.

27. The first written offer for the Thunderbird Lodge is dated September 18, 1995; the second is dated December 22, 1995. Harriet Burgess, letter to Jack Dreyfus and William Rogers, January 4, 1996.

28. Harriet Burgess, letter to Martin Litton, January 4, 1996; agreement of sale, 29 January 1996.

29. National Association of Women Business Owners, "Harriet Burgess, Woman Entrepreneur of the Year, 1999," video available January 10, 2017, at https://www.youtube.com/watch?v=4n6w9KMc43g.

30. Harriet Burgess, letter to Jack Dreyfus and William Rogers, March 29, 1996; David Marlow, USFS, Lake Tahoe Basin Management Unit, lands officer, letter to Ted Reid, ALC, March 22, 1996; Ted Reid to Harriet Burgess, memorandum, March 28, 1996; Ted Reid, letter to Dave Marlow, April 15, 1996; Robison Engineering Company, Phase I environmental site assessment, Thunderbird Lodge Property, Washoe County, Nevada, March 8, 1996; Ronald B. Cecchi, USFS, Pacific Southwest Region, regional appraiser, letter to Harriet Burgess, March 22, 1996; G. Lynn Sprague, regional forester, Pacific Southwest Region, letter to Harriet Burgess, January 9, 1996; Harrison Appraisal Inc., appraisal of "Thunderbird Lodge," 5000 Highway 28, Washoe County, Nevada, date of value, February 26, 1996, prepared for American Land Conservancy, March 5, 1996; Harriet Burgess, letter to Jack Dreyfus and William Rogers, May 2, 1996.

31. Harriet Burgess, letter to Jack Dreyfus and William Rogers, March 29, 1996; Ronald B. Cecchi, USFS, Pacific Southwest Region, regional appraiser, letter to Harriet Burgess, March 22, 1996; G. Lynn Sprague, regional forester, Pacific Southwest Region, letter to Harriet Burgess, January 9, 1996.

32. Harriet Burgess, letter to Jack Dreyfus and William Rogers, March 29, 1996; Harriet Burgess, time sheet, 3/96 for March 7 and 8, 1996; Hellman, interviews, June 30 and July 1, 2010.

33. Harriet Burgess, fax sending the proposed BLM exchange for the Thunderbird Lodge and other properties around Las Vegas and elsewhere in Nevada to Lauren Ward; Mike Dwyer, BLM Las Vegas district manager; Ed Hastey, BLM California state director; Dave McIlnay, BLM; Jack Peterson for Matt Millenbach, BLM deputy director; Ann Morgan, BLM Nevada state director; Saundra Allen, BLM Nevada deputy state director; Jim Lawrence, USFS Pacific Southwest Region, deputy regional forester; G. Lynn Sprague, USFS Pacific Southwest Region, regional forester; Ron Cecchi, USFS Pacific Southwest Region, regional appraiser; Phil Bayles, USFS Pacific Southwest Region lands section; Bob Harris, USFS Lake Tahoe Basin Management Unit (LTBMU), forest supervisor; Dave Marlow, USFS LTMBU, lands officer, February 5, 1996; Harriet Burgess, letter to Mike Dwyer, BLM Las Vegas, March 1, 1996; ALC Nevada Land Exchange II, organizational meeting, agenda, February 7, 1996; Harriet Burgess tour with Jack Peterson, February 13, 1996; Jan Bernard, fax to Harriet Burgess, list of Las Vegas properties for exchange by appraisal number, February 7, 1996.

34. Harriet Burgess, letter to Margaret Owings, March 12, 1996 [the same letter was sent to all of the members of the Board of Councillors]; Martin Litton, fax to Harriet Burgess, March 13, 1996; Harriet Burgess, letter to Robert Stephens, March 14, 1996 [the same letter was sent to all of the members of the Board of Councillors].

35. Martin Litton, letter to Bruce Babbitt, March 13, 1996.

36. Galen Rowell, letter to Bruce Babbitt, March 26, 1996.

37. Bill Garrett, letter to Bruce Babbitt, March 22, 1996.

38. A. Brian Wallace, tribal chairman, Washoe Tribe of Nevada and California, letter to Bruce Babbitt, March 11, 1996; Rochelle Nason, executive director, League to Save Lake Tahoe, letter to Bruce Babbitt, March 14, 1996; Bob Miller, governor of Nevada, letter to Bruce Babbitt, March 28, 1996.

39. The bill introduced on March 19, 1996, by Senators Bryan and Reid (S. 1626) did not pass before the end of the legislative session. A similar bill was introduced by Senator Bryan (S. 94) on January 21, 1997, and by Nevada Congressman Ensign (H.R. 449) on January 20, 1997. See page 232 and footnote 85 (this chapter) for further discussion of these bills. "Sale May Pay for Lake Land; Proceeds from Las Vegas Land Could Buy Tahoe Property," *Nevada Appeal*, March 20, 1996; Keith White, "Public Land Sales Targeted at Environment," *Reno Gazette-Journal*, March 20, 1996; Harriet Burgess, notes of telephone call with Bruce Babbitt, March 28, 1996.

40. "Make Every Effort to Acquire Dreyfus Land, Lake Tahoe: The Transfer Could Be Difficult, But This Would Be a Marvelous Addition for the Public," *Reno Gazette-Journal* editorial, February 26, 1996; Ann Morgan, letter to Harriet Burgess, March 19, 1996.

41. John Trent, "Conservancy Working on Land Exchange," *Reno Gazette-Journal*, March 31, 1996.

42. Harriet Burgess, notes of telephone call with Mike Freed, September 18, 1995.

43. Resort Design Group to Harriet Burgess, memorandum, November 14, 1995; Loring Sagan, letter to Harriet Burgess, December 5, 1995.

44. Loring Sagan to Harriet [Burgess], Mike [Freed], Herb [McLaughlin], Nancy [Stryble], Leslie [Rosselli?], memorandum, January 9, 1996, that refers to a meeting January 5, 1996; Harriet Burgess, notes of telephone call with Loring Sagan, January 11, 1996; Gary Furumoto to Loring Sagan, memorandum, January 15, 1996; Loring Sagan to Harriet [Burgess], Mike [Freed], Herb [McLaughlin], Nancy [Stryble], Leslie [Rosselli?], memorandum, January 17, 1996.

45. Resort Design Group, Thunderbird Lodge proposal, County of Washoe, Nevada, prepared for the U.S. Forest Service, n.d. but probably April 1996; Harriet Burgess, letter to Robert Harris, supervisor, Lake Tahoe Basin Management Unit, May 2, 1996.

46. Harriet Burgess, letter to Jack Dreyfus and William Rogers, May 2, 1996.

47. Tom Walker, acting assistant director, Resource Assessment and Planning, BLM, letter to Joseph Fink, June 28, 1996.

48. Joseph Fink, comments at the celebration of Harriet's life, May 8, 2010.

49. Tim Willis, "Thunderbird Lodge Deal Complex," *Bonanza*, June 28, 1996.

50. Harriet Burgess, letter to Robert Campbell, May 15, 1996.

51. Ronald M. James administered the Nevada State Historic Preservation Office from 1983 until his retirement in 2013. Nancy Stryble, fax to Liz Laxalt, July 10, 1996; Harriet Burgess time sheet, July 15, 1996; Ron James, fax to Harriet Burgess, July 25, 1996; [Nevada Department of Museums, Library and Arts], prospectus; Lake Tahoe's Thunderbird Lodge: maintenance and development as a state-run facility, August 1, 1996; James and James, *Castle in the Sky*; Harriet Burgess, letter to Patricia A. Romeiro, July 22, 1996; Phil Caterino, interview by the author, March 4, 2017.

52. Friends of Hope Valley incorporated August 18, 1986, according to the registration on file with the California secretary of state. Phil Caterino, interview, March 4, 2017; Harriet Burgess, letter to Tom Knudson, August 10, 1998; Harriet Burgess, letter to Peter Stein, May 18, 1993.

53. Phil Caterino, interview, March 4, 2017; Annalise Kjolhede, "Diving Through Time," *Wink, the Collaborative Journal* (Winter 2013).

54. Willis, "Thunderbird Lodge Deal Complex."

55. Gordon Baxter, "Neptunus Rex and His Big Old Cessna," *Flying Magazine* (December 1984), 104; Lauren Ward, interview by the author, January 4, 2010; Joe Burgess, interview by the author, March 7, 2017.

56. Sinbad's Pier 2 Restaurant at 141 The Embarcadero in San Francisco served its last meal on November 23, 2015, ending a forty-year run after being evicted by its landlord, the Port of San Francisco. Leslie King Cowan, conversation with the author, December 2, 2009.

57. Harriet Burgess, letter to Jack Dreyfus and William Rogers, July 29, 1996; amendment to agreement of sale dated July 29, 1996.

58. Russell Austin, interview by the author, January 3, 2010.

59. John Trent, "Time Limited on Mansion Deal; Whittell Estate Land Swap; Waiting for BLM Policy Slows Process," *Reno Gazette-Journal*, September 27, 1996; Brendan Riley, "Land Swap for Tahoe Estate Called Still Alive," *Las Vegas Review-Journal*, September 27, 1996.

60. League to Save Lake Tahoe, invitation to the annual benefit luncheon, August 3, 1996; Pat Steger, "Summer Shades at Lake Tahoe," *San Francisco Chronicle*, August 7, 1996; Harriet Burgess, letter to Liz and Mick Laxalt, August 8, 1996.

61. Ame Hellman, interview by the author, June 30, 2010; Harriet Burgess, letter [draft] to Shari Chase, October 2, 1996.

62. Barry Smith, "Public Acquisition of Thunderbird Lodge in Question," *Nevada Appeal*, September 27, 1996.

63. Trent, "Time Limited on Mansion Deal"; "Cool: Making Whittell Estate Public," *Reno Gazette-Journal*, December 1, 1996.

64. Harriet Burgess, notes of a telephone call to Liz Laxalt, August 8, 1996; Nancy Stryble to Harriet Burgess, memorandum, August 8, 1996; Nancy Stryble, fax to Tom Martens, September 5, 1996; Ame Hellman, fax to Harriet Burgess, Nancy Stryble, October 2, 1996; Harriet Burgess, letter to Shari Chase, October 8, 1996; Nancy Stryble, fax to Ame Hellman, October 18, 1996; Harriet Burgess, letter to George Holman, October 25, 1996; Harriet Burgess, notes of a telephone call to Al Levy, October 28, 1996; Harriet Burgess, time sheets, 1996; Nancy Stryble, letter to Bob Braddock, November 5, 1996; Ame Hellman, notes of telephone call to Frankie Sue Del Papa, November 11, 1996; Harriet Burgess, notes of telephone call to Brent H[eberlee], November 21, 1996; Michael Dwyer, letter to Harriet Burgess, November 29, 1996; Peter Laxalt, letter to Senator Reid, December 3, 1996.

65. Harriet Burgess, notes of telephone call to Fritzi Huntington, November 8, 1996; Harriet Burgess, notes of telephone call with Dr. Charles Goldman, November 12, 1996; Harriet Burgess, letter to Fritzi Huntington, January 8, 1998.

66. Peter "Micky" Laxalt, letter to Senator Harry Reid, December 3, 1996.

67. Dennis Murphy, letter to Bruce Babbitt, December 19, 1996.

68. Joseph Crowley, letter to Bruce Babbitt, December 19, 1996.

69. Harriet Burgess, time sheets, 1996; Harriet Burgess, letter to Jack Dreyfus and William Rogers, December 24, 1996; Ame Hellman to Greg Ferraro, memorandum, December 30, 1996.

70. Russell Austin, letter to Jeffrey Weitzman, December 31, 1996; secured promissory installment note with interest added, December 31, 1996; Harriet Burgess, notes of telephone call with Put Livermore, December 30, 1996; Harriet Burgess, letter to Dolores Monroe, Western Title, December 31, 1996. ALC borrowed $180,000 from Putnam Livermore, $20,000 from Ken Hunter, and $10,000 from Glenn Miller. Thanking Harriet for the prompt repayment of the loan in early February 1997, Put Livermore wrote, "Those of us who were involved in the year-end loan were glad we could help you. . . . Meanwhile please call me any time for additional help . . . as an old friend who shares with many others a hope you succeed in this important project." Putnam Livermore, letter to Harriet Burgess, February 4, 1997.

71. Brendan Riley, "Buyout Plan for Lake Tahoe's Whittell Mansion Hits New Snag," *Nevada Appeal*, January 11, 1997.

72. The bird featured in the cartoon has also been identified as a crane and as a heron in other portrayals. Harriet Burgess, time sheets, 1997; Phil Caterino, interview by the author, March 4, 2017; Phil Caterino, fax to Harriet Burgess, December 28, 1997.

73. Russell Austin, letters to Jeffrey Weitzman, January 29 and 31, 1997; second amendment to agreement of sale, January 31, 1997; Harriet Burgess, letter to Ian Cumming,

February 14, 1997; Harriet Burgess, letter to Jack Dreyfus and William Rogers, February 18, 1997.

74. Jack Dreyfus, letter to American Land Conservancy, Attention: Harriet Burgess/Lesley Roselli, February 20, 1997.

75. Harriet Burgess, letter to Jack Dreyfus and William Rogers, February 27, 1997; Mick Laxalt, letter to Jack Dreyfus, February 26, 1997.

76. Ame Hellman, notes of telephone call to Joe Crowley, March 5, 1997; Patrick Mc-Cartney, "State and School Want Whittell Site But Option's Expired," *Tribune*, March 12, 1997; "Lawmakers Back Deal for Historic Tahoe Estate," *Reno Gazette-Journal*, March 16, 1997; Phil Caterino, interview by the author, March 4, 2017.

77. Mick Laxalt to Liz, Harriet, memorandum, March 13, 1997; John Trent, "Land Bill Boosts Whittell Deal Prospects," *Reno Gazette-Journal*, April 25, 1997; letter from Peter Laxalt to Harry Reid, April 2, 1997; Tony Batt, "Lawmakers Eye Lake Tahoe Property," *Las Vegas Review-Journal*, June 16, 1997.

78. Reinstatement of and third amendment to agreement of sale, April 15, 1997.

79. Chris Bowman, "Clinton Will Convene Tahoe Environmental Summit," *Sacramento Bee*, February 20, 1997; Bill O'Driscoll, "Clinton to Attend Summit at Tahoe," *Reno Gazette-Journal*, February 20, 1997; U.S. Department of Agriculture press release, June 8, 1997.

80. The UC Davis Tahoe Environmental Research Center and TRPA reported the average annual clarity level for 2016 at 69.2 feet, a 3.9-foot decrease from 2015. The average annual clarity level of 64.1 feet in 1997 was the lowest ever recorded until 2017 when the clarity level dropped to 59.7 feet. By mid-2018, the clarity level had improved to 65 feet. Irwin M. Goldberg, "President Clinton is Coming to Tahoe," *North Lake Tahoe Bonanza*, February 21, 1997; Batt, "Lawmakers Eye Lake Tahoe Property"; Tom Stienstra, "Summit at the Summit," *San Francisco Chronicle*, July 20, 1997; "Lake Tahoe Facts and Figures," July 26, 1997, terc.ucdavis.edu/research/lake-tahoe/water-clarity.html on September 3, 2017; Molly Sullivan, "Water Clarity in Lake Tahoe Sinks to All-Time Low, Report Finds," *Sacramento Bee*, June 13, 2018.

81. The Lake Tahoe Summit celebrated its twentieth anniversary in 2016 and continues to convene annually. Jeff DeLong, "Tahoe Summit Set for July 26–27," *Reno Gazette-Journal*, April 3, 1997; Tom Tuchmann, Western director and special assistant to the Secretary, USDA Office of the Secretary, and G. Lynn Sprague, regional forester, Pacific Southwest Region, letter to Harriet Burgess, May 16, 1997; U.S. Department of Agriculture press release, June 4, 1997.

82. Executive Order 13057, "Federal Actions in the Lake Tahoe Region," July 26, 1997.

83. "President Clinton and Vice President Gore: Actions to Protect Lake Tahoe," July 26, 1997.

84. ALC guest list, July 25, 1997; bills from valet and caterer, July 1997.

85. The bill (H.R. 449) passed by the House of Representatives eventually passed the Senate without amendment on October 2, 1998, and became law on 19 October 1998 as the Southern Nevada Public Land Management Act (P.L. 105-263), far too late to fund the Thunderbird Lodge acquisition. It allowed the BLM to sell public land within a specific boundary around Las Vegas. Revenue from the sale of these surplus BLM lands was split between the State of Nevada General Education Fund (5 percent) and the Southern Nevada Water Authority (10 percent), with the remaining 85 percent available

to the secretary of the Interior for expenditure on the acquisition and maintenance of environmentally sensitive lands (www.blm.gov/nv/st/en/snplma.html, March 7, 2017). Trent, "Land Bill Boosts Whittell Deal Prospects"; Patrick McCartney, "House Approves Nevada Land Swap, Whittell Estate Closer to Acquisition," *Nevada Appeal*, May 1, 1997; Fredreka Schouten, "House Okays Nevada Federal Land Sale; 20,000 Acres Near Vegas: Proceeds Will Be Used to Buy Other Land in Silver State—Including Lake Tahoe's Whittell Estate," *Reno Gazette-Journal*, April 24, 1997; Irwin M. Goldberg, "Whittell Estate Purchase Deadline Extended," *North Lake Tahoe Bonanza*, May 2, 1997; Senator Richard Bryan, press release, May 28, 1997; Senate Report 105-291 to accompany H.R. 449, July 31, 1998.

86. Harriet Burgess, time sheets, July through December 1997.

87. Russell Austin, letter to Harriet Burgess, February 26, 1997; Ann Morgan, letter to Harriet Burgess, October 5, 1997.

88. Phil Caterino, interview by the author, March 4, 2017; Phil Caterino, e-mail to the author, March 18, 2017.

89. Phyllis Martin, economic development administrator, city of North Las Vegas to Harriet Burgess, memorandum, June 24, 1997; Harriet Burgess to Mike Dwyer and Jim Abbot, memorandum, June 25, 1997; Harriet Burgess, letter to Mike Dwyer, June 25, 1997.

90. The budget included $700 million for the LWCF. John Ensign and Jim Gibbons, letter to Ralph Regula, July 10, 1997; Batt, "Lawmakers Eye Lake Tahoe Property."

91. JT, handwritten note, "Don't tell Harriet," on fax from Mary Alexander to Russell Austin, sending her final comments on memorandum of understanding between ALC and Del Webb, September 30, 1997; handwritten note on memo from Russell Austin to Mary Alexander, cc: Harriet Burgess, October 25, 1997; Julie Turrini, handwritten notes, undated but probably October 1997.

92. Russell Austin, letter to Jeffery Weitzman, November 11, 1997; memorandum of understanding, dated November 14, 1997, by and between ALC and Del Webb.

93. Phil Caterino, interview by the author, March 4, 2017; Phil Caterino, e-mail to the author, March 18, 2017; Russell Austin, letter to Jeffery Weitzman, December 15, 1997.

94. Chris Jehle, interview by the author, April 28, 2011.

95. Harriet Burgess, letter to Martin Litton, December 19, 1997; action of the executive committee of the board of directors of American Land Conservancy adopted by written consent, December 26, 1997.

96. Escrow would have closed on December 31, 1997, but Jack Dreyfus inadvertently failed to sign several of the closing documents delivered to him. His lawyer, Thomas J. Hall, had to travel to Miami to obtain the required signatures. Russell Austin to Thomas J. Hall, memorandum, January 3, 1998; agreement of purchase and sale, dated December 31, 1997 . . . by and between American Land Conservancy . . . and Del Webb Conservation Holding Corp.; Gerry Ring Waltz, First American Title/Scottsdale Centre Branch, letter to Mary Alexander, Diane Haller, Harriet Burgess, Julia Turrini/Russell Austin, Susan Lundquist, Dolores Monroe, and Jeffrey Weitzman, January 5, 1998

97. American Land Conservancy, press release, January 2, 1998.

98. Jim Sanders, "Record Price for Thunderbird Estate," *Sacramento Bee*, January 6, 1998; Bob Harris, letter to Harriet Burgess, January 13, 1998; Jack Dreyfus, letter to Harriet Burgess, January 13, 1998.

99. Sanders, "Record Price for Thunderbird Estate"; Harriet Burgess, letters to Harry Reid, Frankie Sue Del Papa, Myron Harrison, et al., January 8, 1998; Harriet Burgess, letter to Annaliese and Kirk Odencrantz, January 14, 1998.

100. Harriet Burgess, letter to Martin Litton, January 9, 1998.

101. Mike Henderson, "UNR Weighs Whittell Purchase," *Reno Gazette-Journal*, February 15, 1998; Thomas Ray, UNR counsel, letter to Diane Haller, Del Webb attorney, February 17, 1998; Harriet Burgess, letter to Mary Alexander, April 28, 1999; MOU [draft] between UNR and Del Webb, April 27, 1999; Phil Caterino, fax to Harriet Burgess, May 13, 1999; amended and restated sale agreement between Del Webb Conservation Holding Corporation, the UNR Board of Regents, and Thunderbird Lodge Preservation Society, July 15, 1999; Brendan Riley, "UNR, Nonprofit May Make Deal on Whittell Estate," *Reno Gazette-Journal*, July 28, 1999; Harriet Burgess, letter to Joseph Crowley, July 28, 1999; Jeff DeLong, "Round Hill Could Be Site of Tahoe Research Center," *Reno Gazette-Journal*, August 11, 1999; John Kerns to ALC Del Webb file, memorandum, March 13, 2000, revised April 3, 2000; Solem & Associates, fax to Russell Austin, Harriet Burgess, April 27, 2000.

102. thunderbirdtahoe.org/preservation-society March 21, 2017; James and James, *Castle in the Sky*, 70–76.

103. John Walker, chief state appraiser, to district manager, Las Vegas, memorandum, March 10, 1998; Irwin M. Goldberg, "Whittell Estate Closer to Public Domain," *Nevada Appeal*, April 1, 1998; Jeff DeLong, "Proposal Doesn't Present Threat to Whittell Deal, Senators Say," *Reno Gazette-Journal*, April 7, 1998; U.S. Department of Agriculture, Office of Inspector General, audit, Report No. 08801-5-SF, April 1999; BLM, amended notice of exchange proposal, December 23, 1998; assistant director, Minerals, Lands and Resource Protection, BLM, letter to state director, Nevada, December 23, 1998; Brendan Riley, "Tahoe's Thunderbird Lodge Deal Is Completed," *Auburn Journal*, October 17, 1999; John Kerns, memorandum to ALC Del Webb file, March 13, 2000, revised April 3, 2000; Phil Caterino, e-mail to author, March 14, 2017.

104. John Wesley Powell quoted in Buzz Belknap and Loie Belknap Evans, *Grand Canyon River Guide* (Evergreen, CO, 2010), 53.

105. Roderick Frazier Nash, *The Big Drops; Ten Legendary Rapids of the American West*, rev. ed. (Boulder: Johnson Books, 1989), 173–200; Belknap and Evans, *Grand Canyon River Guide*, 6–7 and 52–53; Arizona State University and Grand Canyon Association, "Nature, Culture and History at the Grand Canyon: Lava Falls," grandcanyonhistory.clas.asu.edu/sites_coloradorivercorridor_lavafalls.html, August 22, 2016.

106. Martin Litton, interview by Lewis Steiger, Flagstaff, Arizona, October 10, 1992.

107. Robert Hunt and Julie Walsh, interview by the author, June 29, 2010; Robert Hunt, telephone interview by the author, April 28, 2010.

Chapter 7: Crown Jewel of the Coast: Hearst Ranch

1. William Randolph Hearst, letter to Phoebe Apperson Hearst, circa September 1917, quoted in Victoria Kastner, *Hearst Ranch: Family, Land, and Legacy* (New York: Abrams, 2013), 72–73.

2. Martin Litton, conversation with author et al., at Sinbad's, San Francisco, November 17, 2008.

3. Sacramento is one hundred square miles or approximately sixty-four thousand acres. With the acquisition of some inholdings, the Hearst Ranch grew to eighty-three thousand acres

by 2019. Hearst Ranch and ALC, *Conservation Framework*, 2003; Kastner, *Hearst Ranch: Family, Land, and Legacy*, 10, 89, 145, and 163. Illustrated with many photographs, Kastner's *Hearst Ranch* is an excellent source for more information about the history of the ranch.

4. Russell Austin, conversation with author, April 5, 2017; Harriet Burgess, oral history interview; Shawn Connolly, telephone interview by the author, April 26, 2017; Stephen Hearst, telephone interview by the author, June 6, 2017; exclusive negotiating agreement (for Hearst Ranch conservation agreement) by and among the Hearst Corporation and the American Land Conservancy, November 27, 2002; Bill Hunter, e-mail to Cindy Starrett, Martin Cepkauskas, Stephen Hearst, cc: Henry Little, Thomas Macy, November 27, 2002, 12:27 p.m.

5. Kastner, *Hearst Ranch*, 191.

6. Kastner, *Hearst Ranch*, 125, 191; Coleen Bondy, "San Simeon Point: Natural Paradise or the Next Pebble Beach?" *San Luis Obispo County Telegram-Tribune*, July 22, 1996; Frank Clifford, "Hearst Corp. Plans Spark Coastal Fight," *Los Angeles Times*, June 30, 1996.

7. For additional information on the California Coastal Commission, see the commission's website, www.coastal.ca.gov; Kastner, *Hearst Ranch*, 191; David W. Myers, "Near San Simeon: Hearst Hotel Plan Stirs Controversy," *Los Angeles Times*, September 6, 1987.

8. According to Mark Massara, coastal director for the Sierra Club, "This area [the central coast where the Hearst Ranch is located] is the Yosemite of the California coast. It's [the battle over its development] shaping up as the coastal fight of the decade." Glen Martin, "'Coastal Fight of the Decade' Under Way in San Simeon," *San Francisco Chronicle*, May 26, 1997; Timm Herdt, "Pristine Point of Contention," *Ventura County Sunday Star*, December 14, 1997; William Claiborne, "Complex May Unleash Coastal Development," *Washington Post*, June 29, 1997; Todd S. Purdum, "Environmentalists and Hearst Heirs Locked in Battle at San Simeon," *New York Times*, January 14, 1998; Jane Kay, "Political Tides Collide on the Coast," *San Francisco Examiner*, January 11, 1998; Frank Clifford, "Will San Simeon Coast Become a Playground?" *Los Angeles Times*, January 11, 1998.

9. Glen Martin, "Coastal Commission Kills San Simeon Resort Plan," *San Francisco Chronicle*, January 16, 1998; John Hofschroer, senior planner, North Coast update to members of the San Luis Obispo County Board of Supervisors, memorandum, March 24, 1998.

10. Coastal Commission staff recommended a project with 375 instead of 650 rooms on one hundred acres around Old San Simeon and no golf course. Frank Clifford, "Coast Panel Rejects San Simeon Resort Plan," *Los Angeles Times*, January 16, 1998; Nathan Welton, "Competing Visions Undermine Unity of County Environmental Leaders," *The Tribune*, July 18, 2004; Tami Grove, Central Coast deputy director, California Coastal Commission, to commissioners, memorandum, May 20, 1998; Tami Grove to commissioners, staff recommendation on proposed San Luis Obispo County Local Coastal Program (LCP) major amendment No. 1-97 North Coast Area plan comprehensive update, memorandum, December 1997.

11. Kathe Tanner, "Keeper of the Kingdom," *The Tribune*, July 8, 2001; Stephen Hearst, interview by Rob Stewart, *Rob on the Road*, KVIE Public Television, 2014.

12. Kastner, *Hearst Ranch*, 202; Katharine A. Seelye, "Hearst Ranch Seeks Public-Private Balance," *New York Times*, July 3, 2003.

13. Marty Cepkauskas worked with Steve Hearst when they were both at the Hearst Corporation's San Francisco newspaper agency and moved with him to the division of Western Properties in January 1999. As of 2019, he is the senior director of real estate, Western

Properties. Seelye, ibid.; Jane Wells, "Hearst Castle Stayed Alone Thanks to a Huge Land Deal," CNBC, April 2, 2015, www.cnbc.com/2015/04/02/hearst-castle-stayed-alone-thanks-to-a-huge-land-deal.html, April 14, 2017.

14. Seelye, ibid.; Wells, ibid.

15. Glen Martin, "Hearst Renews Bid for Resort at San Simeon," *San Francisco Chronicle*, February 8, 2001; Kathe Tanner, "Conservation Easement for Hearst?" *The Cambrian*, February 8, 2001; Tanner, "Keeper of the Kingdom."

16. "Hearst Offers Conservation Bid in Development Discussions," (Monterey County) *The Herald*, February 9, 2001; David Sneed, "New Face of Hearst Draws Skepticism," *The Tribune*, February 10, 2001; Steve Hearst, letter to Sara Wan, chair, and commissioners, Coastal Commission, February 14, 2001.

17. Harriet Burgess and Daniel Macon, letter to Stephen Hearst re: Hearst Ranch: request for proposals for conservation easement, February 27, 2001.

18. Steve Hearst, letter to Harriet Burgess and Daniel Macon, March 22, 2001; Harriet Burgess, letter to Steve Hearst, April 9, 2001.

19. TNC and TCF announced their exclusive negotiating agreement with Hearst August 7, 2001. The last extension of that agreement expired September 30, 2002, but negotiations between TNC and Hearst continued through most of November. TNC and Hearst agreed to keep the reasons for the failure of their negotiations confidential, but a TNC spokeswoman said Hearst called off the talks. Some speculated that TNC's emphasis on science was a stumbling block, but the explanation here was confirmed by my sources who were present September 18, 2002, and at subsequent meetings. The original negotiating agreement between ALC and Hearst expired December 31, 2002. The expiration date later was extended to January 31, 2003, and then to February 28, 2003. ALC had a staff of fourteen while TNC's staff numbered a little under three thousand. "California Conserves 82,000 Acres: The Hearst Ranch as a Working Landscape," *American Landscapes: The Newsletter of the American Land Conservancy* (Winter 2006): 6; Kathe Tanner and David Sneed, "Hearst Drops Resort Plan; Smaller Hotel at Old San Simeon Village Possible in Deal," *The Tribune*, December 3, 2002; John Johnson, "Lengthy Talks to Preserve Hearst Ranch Collapse," *Los Angeles Times*, December 3, 2002; Kara [Blakeslee] Woodruff, telephone interview by the author, May 30, 2017; Stephen Hearst, telephone interview by the author, June 6, 2017; David Sneed, "A Small Group with a Big Plan, Conservancy Has Its Sights on Hearst Ranch," *The Tribune*, December 8, 2002.

20. ALC was also in the last stages of a five-year project concluded in 2003 to protect the 748 acres of Sea West Ranch with its three miles of coastline. Seven miles south of Cambria, Sea West Ranch is now Harmony Headlands State Park. Another significant ALC project in the area was the purchase of 175-acre Molinari Ranch between the southern boundary of Hearst Ranch and the northern boundary of San Simeon State Park in 2003 and its transfer to the state in 2005. Beth Van Valkenburgh, "East-West Ranch," *American Land Conservancy* [newsletter] (Winter 2000): 1 and 4.

21. Doug Buckmaster, letter to the Internal Revenue Service, February 20, 1996; Glen Williams, memorandum to Harriet Burgess, May 15, 1998.

22. Glen Williams, memorandum to Harriet Burgess, May 27, 1998; Glen Williams, letter to Doug Buckmaster [draft], May 26, 1998; Harriet Burgess, letter to Caroline Lee To, May 26, 1998; Glen Williams, fax to Harriet Burgess, July 22, 1998; Glen Williams, letter to Doug Buckmaster, July 22, 1998; Glen Williams, letter to Gavin Liau, July 30, 1998;

Glen Williams, letter to Ame Hellman, August 14, 1998; Ame Hellman, memorandum to Russell Austin, August 28, 1998.

23. Glen Williams, memorandum to Harriet Burgess, May 28, 1999; Harriet Burgess, letter to Bill Ahern, California State Coastal Conservancy, May 19, 1999; minutes of the Cambria Community Services District [CCSD], special meeting, August 11, 1999; Ken Topping, memorandum to CCSD board of directors, November 15, 1999; Glen Williams, memorandum to ALC executive committee, September 3, 1999; Ken Topping, letter to Glen Williams, October 14, 1999; Kathryn Hope McCrary, summary report for the community meeting on November 15, 1999, regarding community outlay of funds for purchase of the East West Ranch, November 15, 1999; Anne Russell, letter to Russell Austin, November 24, 1999; Abel Maldonado, letter to Glen Williams, February 22, 2000; Glen Williams, letters to Abel Maldonado and Jack O'Connell, February 3, 2000.

24. Esther and Martin Litton, conversation with author, September 20, 2008; Al Jahns, conversation with author, January 16, 2016.

25. Kathe Tanner, "'You Did It'; East West Ranch Deed Is Done," *The Cambrian*, November 23, 2000; Jo Ellen Butler, "10 Years After: 'Hi' Time to Celebrate Saving 'The Ranch,'" *The Cambrian*, November 3, 2010.

26. Kara Woodruff [formerly Blakeslee], telephone interview by the author, May 30, 2017; Kathe Tanner and David Sneed, "Hearst Drops Resort Plan," *SLO County Tribune*, December 3, 2002.

27. Tanner and Sneed, "Hearst Drops Resort Plan"; Hearst Corporation and American Land Conservancy, Hearst Ranch conservation framework, December 2002.

28. Hearst and ALC, ibid.

29. Among those in attendance at the February 2, 2001, meeting at Bianchi's house were Cambria Schools Superintendent Pam Martens, County Planning Commission Chairwoman Doreen Blanck, environmental activist Ken Butterfield, North Coast Alliance Chair Bill Allen, rancher Betty Fiscalini, and Cambria Community Services District General Manager Ken Topping. Kathe Tanner, "Conservation Easement for Hearst?" *The Cambrian*, February 8, 2001; Kathe Tanner, "Hearst Corp. Working with Locals," *The Tribune*, February 13, 2001; John Johnson and Kenneth Weiss, "Hearst Plan Is Latest Twist in a Long Saga," *Los Angeles Times*, December 8, 2002; Kathe Tanner, "Hearst Ranch Conservation Project Marks 10-Year Anniversary," *The Cambrian*, February 18, 2015.

30. Tanner, "Hearst Ranch Conservation Project Marks 10-Year Anniversary."

31. Proposition 50, the Water Quality, Supply and Safe Drinking Water Projects Act, was approved by the voters of California November 11, 2002. Coastal protection was among the programs designated for funding by the $3.4 billion bond measure. In addition to Proposition 50, funding from Proposition 40 approved March 5, 2002, was a strong possibility for the Hearst Ranch transaction. Known as the California Clean Water, Clean Air, Safe Neighborhood Parks, and Coastal Protection Act, most of the monies provided by the $2.6 billion bond measure had been appropriated by the end of 2002, including $300 million to the Wildlife Conservation Board and $200 million to the Coastal Conservancy. These two agencies ultimately would provide much of the funding for Hearst Ranch ($57 million), with all of the monies coming from Proposition 50 funds. Kara Blakeslee, e-mail to Russell Austin, Glen Williams, Harriet Burgess, Al Jahns, Beth van Valkenburg, Jeff Stump, and Shawn Connolly, December 9, 2002; Cambria Land Conservancy, letter to Roger Lyon, December 14, 2002; Kathe Tanner, "Hearst Ranch Conservation Wins

Support," *The Tribune*, December 24, 2002; William Johnson, Friends of the Elephant Seal, letter to Kara Blakeslee, n.d.; David Sneed, "Supervisors Support Hearst Plan," *The Tribune*, January 8, 2003; John Johnson, "Supervisors Endorse Hearst Ranch Deal," *Los Angeles Times*, January 8, 2003; Grant Deed, WCB to ALC, February 15, 2005.

32. Roger Lyon, letter to Jeff Stump enclosing twenty-four letters of support, April 30, 2003.

33. Johnson and Weiss, "Hearst Plan Is Latest Twist in a Long Saga"; Johnson, "Supervisors Endorse Hearst Ranch Deal"; Kathe Tanner, "Old Hearst Plans Could Affect New Ones," *The Cambrian*, December 5, 2002.

34. According to ALC's press release, "The option authorizes ALC to implement the Conservation Framework announced in December 2002 that would permanently restrict new commercial and residential development on the 128 square-mile ranch, protect resources, and increase public access to 18 miles of pristine California coastline." American Land Conservancy, announcement of conservation option agreement, February 19, 2003; Barbara Whitaker, "Conservancy Reaches Deal to Preserve Hearst Land," *New York Times*, February 20, 2003; Steve Hearst, "Clarifying the Conservation Agreement," *The Tribune*, July 10, 2003.

35. Russell Austin, conversations with author, January 13, 2010, April 5 and May 14, 2017; Sam Schuchat and Carol Arnold, memorandum to David Hayes, Cindy Starrett, Mary Nichols, Bob Hight, Al Wright, and Ruth Coleman, March 14, 2003; Russell Austin, e-mail to Al Jahns, Kara Blakeslee, and Jeff Stump, March 18, 2003.

36. Stephen Hearst, quoted in Kastner, *Hearst Ranch*, 206.

37. Russell Austin, conversations with the author, April 5 and May 5, 2017; Susan Lyon, Roger "Chopper" Lyon land conservation legacy tour, May 6, 2017; Greg Bettencourt, conversation with the author, during the Roger "Chopper" Lyon land conservation legacy tour, May 6, 2017; Steve Hearst, e-mail to author, June 8, 2017.

38. Seelye, "Hearst Ranch Seeks Public-Private Balance," July 3, 2003.

39. The letter, although attributed to Harriet, was written primarily by Kara Blakeslee and approved by Hearst before submission to the newspaper. Harriet Burgess, "Accord is 'one of the most significant deals in history,'" *The Tribune*, February 3, 2004.

40. Laura Mecoy, "Hearst Ranch Plan Twists in the Wind," *Bee Los Angeles Bureau*, May 25, 2004; Steve Hearst, letter to Secretary Chrisman, May 24, 2004; Kenneth R. Weiss, "Hearst, State Tentatively Agree to Coastal Land Preservation," *Los Angeles Times*, June 5, 2004.

41. John Johnson, "Hearst Land Plan Gains Support," *Los Angeles Times*, July 16, 2004; Kara Blakeslee, e-mail to Jeff Stump, Chris Jehle, Harriet Burgess, Shawn Connolly, Kerry O'Toole, Cynthia Berg, and Daniel Waggoner, June 22, 2004.

42. Johnson, "Hearst Land Plan Gains Support"; Laura Mecoy, "Restriction of Coastal Access Assailed in Hearst Land Deal," *Los Angeles Times*, July 13, 2004; Bruce Gibson, letter to Sam Schuchat, July 19, 2004; Hearst conservation transaction, answers to questions received July 15, 2004, Cayucos Veteran's Hall, n.d.

43. Minutes [draft] of the San Luis Obispo Council of Governments, May 5, 2004; Kathe Tanner, "State Transportation Panel OKs Caltrans' Plan for Hearst Coastline," *The Tribune*, May 13, 2004; www.hearstranchconservation/org/history.html#escrow, August 23, 2010. The California Transportation Commission voted unanimously to approve the $23 million grant.

44. Minutes of the Wildlife Conservation Board, August 12, 2004; Jeff Stump, conversation with author, May 12, 2017; Tim Reiterman, "Wildlife Board OKs Hearst Deal," *Los Angeles Times*, August 13, 2004; Stephen Hearst, telephone interview by the author, June 6, 2017.

45. Minutes of the Wildlife Conservation Board, August 12, 2004.

46. "The perfect is the enemy of the good" is an old saying popularized by Voltaire. Minutes of the Wildlife Conservation Board, August 12, 2004; Lauren Ward, conversation with author, May 12, 2017; Jeff Stump, conversation with author, May 12, 2017; Harriet Burgess, calendar 2004; Stephen Hearst, telephone interview by the author, June 6, 2017.

47. Liz Scott-Graham and Bruce Gibson along with Gary Felsman cochaired Hearst Ranch Conservation NOW (HRCN). Greg Bettencourt and Susan Mullen also were involved very actively in HRCN. HRCN placed a full-page ad in *The Tribune* July 14, 2004, encouraging supporters to attend the July 15 public meeting the state of California hosted in Cayucos. The ad proclaimed, "John Muir and Teddy Roosevelt's vision preserved the Yosemite Valley. We have just as great an opportunity right here, right now" and listed the community leaders who supported the conservation of Hearst Ranch. HRCN also played an important role in securing a key editorial in the *Los Angeles Times*, "The Hearst Deal Works," published August 12, 2004, the day of the WCB meeting. Minutes of the Wildlife Conservation Board, August 12, 2004; HRCN website, www .hearstranchconservation.org, February 1, 2010; Kara [Blakeslee] Woodruff, e-mail to author, December 13, 2017; Greg Bettencourt, conversation with author, May 7, 2017; *The Tribune*, July 14, 2004; HRCN, "Hearst Ranch Conservation Project Viewpoint and Response to Comments," August 2, 2004.

48. The three conditions were: (1) that the State Coastal Conservancy and the Public Works Board each consider the conservation transaction, and approve and authorize funding for the transaction as applicable; (2) that prior to funding the Board's portion of the Grant amount, staff and the Department of Fish and Game review and approve a baseline conditions report and monitoring protocol; and (3) that the following areas of concern be resolved to the satisfaction of staff: (a) application of viewshed protection standards for structures (i.e., buildings of sufficient size) that could impair the viewshed as seen from Highway One or Hearst-San Simeon State Historical Monument (Hearst Castle); (b) clarification that Highway One viewshed protection standards apply to the alignment of Highway One as it exists at the time of establishing each owner homesite parcel; (c) provision in the East Side Conservation Easement that the management plan shall prescribe actions consistent with sustaining a combination of agriculture operations, natural resources and habitats with the portions of the Easement Area used for range, cropland or other agriculture operations; and (d) incorporation of standards within the monitoring protocol to guide the California Rangeland Trust's determination regarding when there has been "impairment" of conservation values as defined in the East Side Conservation Easement. Minutes of the Wildlife Conservation Board, August 12, 2004.

49. Reiterman, "Wildlife Board OKs Hearst Deal."

50. The Coastal Conservancy hearing took place September 15, 2004. Sam Schuchat and Carol Arnold to David Hayes, Cindy Starrett, Mary Nichols, Bob Hight, Al Wright, and Ruth Coleman, memorandum, March 14, 2003; Kathe Tanner, "State Joins Hearst Ranch Negotiation," *The Tribune*, June 6, 2003.

51. Bob Balgenorth, chair, California Transportation Commission, letter to Paul Morabito, chair, California Coastal Conservancy, September 14, 2004; Mike Pool, California state director, BLM, letter to Sam Schuchat, SCC, September 8, 2004; Bill Garrett, letter to Sam Schuchat, SCC, September 9, 2004; Harriet Burgess and Nita Vail, letter to Chair Morabito and Board members, SCC, September 14, 2004; Coastal Conservancy, Hearst

Ranch Acquisition Staff Recommendation, File No. 04-048, Project Manager: Janel Diehl, September 15, 2004.

52. Jeff Stump, conversation with author, May 12, 2017; Marty Cepkauskas, e-mail to Jeff Stump, Al Jahns, Russell Austin, and Kara Blakeslee, September 14, 2004; Jeff Stump, oral history interview by Carol McLaughlin, April 25, 2006; Kathe Tanner, "Hearst Deal Clears Final High Hurdle," *The Cambrian*, September 23, 2004.

53. Kara [Blakeslee] Woodruff, telephone interview by the author, May 30, 2017.

54. Tanner, "Hearst Deal Clears Final High Hurdle."

55. The Public Works Board voted its approval November 10, 2004. The Natural Heritage Preservation (NHP) Tax Credit Program originally was authorized in 2000 but had been suspended in 2002 because of state budget shortfalls. Legislation passed by the Senate and Assembly in August 2004 and approved by the governor in September allowed the state to reinstate the tax credit by using Proposition 40 and Proposition 50 bond funds to reimburse the general fund for tax credits issued under the NHP act. The WCB, the agency that administers the tax credit program, the SCC, and the Department of Parks and Recreation signed the Hearst Ranch tax credit reimbursement agreement February 15, 2005, approving the Hearst donation of land for inclusion in the Natural Heritage Tax Credit Program, www.hearstranchconservation/org/history.html#escrow, August 23, 2010; WCB, letter to Jeff Stump, February 15, 2005; David Sneed, "Next Stop for Hearst Deal," *The Tribune*, November 11, 2004; notice of unrecorded tax-credit agreement (Junge Ranch portion of the Hearst Ranch, San Luis Obispo County, California), February 18, 2005, resources.ca.gov/hearst_ranch.html, May 15, 2017.

56. E-mail from Roger Lyon to Al Jahns, Russell Austin, and Kathy Hustrei; various e-mails among the lawyers in January and February 2005.

57. Russell Austin, e-mail to Jeff Stump, February 9, 2005; Russell Austin, e-mail to Kerry O'Toole, Al Jahns, and Kathy Hustrei, February 9, 2005.

58. Kathe Tanner, "Hearst Deal Is out of Escrow and Into History," *The Tribune*, February 19, 2005; Kara [Blakeslee] Woodruff, telephone interview by author, May 30, 2017.

59. The details of the conservation easement are specified in the 217-page deed of conservation easement and agreement concerning easement rights posted on the Resources Agency website, resources.ca.gov/hearst/2-18-05_pdfs/1687885_Doc_2005013388.pdf.

Epilogue: Grand Canyon Reprise

1. George Bernard Shaw, *Man and Superman; A Comedy and a Philosophy / Epistle Dedicatory* (New York: Penguin, 2004; New York: Brentano's, 1903), 32.

2. Harriet Burgess, "Woman Entrepreneur of the Year: Community Advocate, 1999," [video] NAWBO, 1999, https://www.youtube.com/watch?v=4n6w9KMc43g, uploaded April 22, 2010.

3. The Water Quality, Supply, and Infrastructure Improvement Act of 2014 (Proposition 1) authorized $7.545 billion in general obligation bonds to fund ecosystems and watershed protection and restoration, water supply infrastructure projects, including surface and groundwater storage, and drinking water protection (bondaccountability.resources .ca.gov/p1.aspx, on August 29, 2018). Proposition 1 was approved by 67.13 percent of voters November 4, 2014, https://ballotpedia.org/California_Proposition_1,_Water_Bond_(2014), August 29, 2018. California Proposition 68, the California Drought, Water,

Parks, Climate, Coastal Protection and Outdoor Access for All Act of 2018, was approved by 57.59 percent of the voters June 5, 2018 (https://ballotpedia.org/California_Proposi-tion_68,_Parks,_Environment,_and_Water_Bond_(June_2018), August 29, 2018).
4. "Everyone Deserves a Park," *Land + People* 29, no. 2 (Fall/Winter 2017): 31–39. Dis-advantaged communities (DACs) are areas throughout California that most suffer from a combination of economic, health, and environmental burdens including poverty, high unem-ployment, health conditions such as asthma and heart disease, air and water pollution, and hazardous wastes. California Senate Bill 535 passed in 2012 directed that a quarter of the proceeds for the Greenhouse Gas Reduction Fund go to projects that benefit DACs.

Selected Bibliography

The sources listed here include many of the books, articles, and oral histories that I consulted during the research for this book. Newspapers consulted are listed separately but not specific newspaper articles. Specific newspaper articles are fully cited in the notes. Letters, memoranda, emails, notes, and other unpublished materials from the American Land Conservancy files are cited in the notes but are not listed here. Government reports are not listed here but are fully cited in the notes. All the individuals that I interviewed are listed.

Books, Articles, and Oral Histories

Abbey, Edward. *Beyond the Wall*. New York: Holt, Rinehart and Winston, 1984.

——. *Desert Solitaire: A Season in the Wilderness*. New York: Simon & Schuster, 1968.

Abbott, Carl, Sy Adler and Margery Post Abbott. *Planning a New West: The Columbia River Gorge National Scenic Area*. Corvallis: Oregon University Press, 1997.

American Land Conservancy. "*[Newsletter]*." 1990–2009.

Anderson, Michael F. *Living at the Edge: Explorers, Exploiters and Settlers of the Grand Canyon Region*. Grand Canyon, AZ: Grand Canyon Association, 1998.

Anella, Anthony and John B. Wright. Photographs by Edward Ranney. *Saving the Ranch: Conservation Easement Design in the American West*. Washington, DC Island Press, 2004.

Ascher, Carol, Louise DeSalvo, and Sara Ruddick. *Between Women: Biographers, Novelists, Critics, Teachers and Artists Write About Their Work on Women*. Boston: Beacon Press, 1984; New York: Routledge, 1993 with new introduction.

Austin, Russell. Oral History Interview by Carol McLaughlin, Sacramento, California, 31 August 2006.

Babbitt, Bruce. *Cities in the Wilderness: a New Vision of Land Use in America*. Washington, DC: Island Press, 2005.

——, comp. *Grand Canyon: An Anthology*. Flagstaff, AZ: Northland Press, 1978.

Banerjee, Subhankar. *Arctic National Wildlife Refuge: Seasons of Life and Land*. Seattle: Mountaineers Books, 2003.

Banham, Russ. *The Fight for Fairfax: A Struggle for a Great American County*. Fairfax, VA: GMU Press, 2009.

Beesley, David. *Crow's Range: an Environmental History of the Sierra Nevada*. Reno: University of Nevada Press, 2004.

Belknap, Buzz and Loie Belknap Evans. *Grand Canyon River Guide*. Evergreen, CO: Westwater, 2007.

Beus, Stanley S. and Michael Morales. *Grand Canyon Geology*. 2d ed. New York: Oxford University Press, 2003.

Birchard, Bill. *Nature's Keepers: The Remarkable Story of How the Nature Conservancy Became the Largest Environmental Group in the World*. New York: Jossey-Bass, 2005.

Black, Brian and Donna L. Lybecker. *Great Debates in American Environmental History*. 2 v. Westport, Connecticut: Greenwood, 2008.

Blair, Bowen, Jr. "The Columbia River Gorge National Scenic Area, Its Genesis and Legislative History." *Environmental Law* 17 (1986–1987): 863–969.

Blaustein, John. *The Hidden Canyon: A River Journey*. San Francisco: Chronicle, 1999. First published in 1977.

Braun, Ernest. *Grand Canyon of the Living Colorado: Photographs and a Journal*. Edited by Roderick Nash with contributions by Colin Fletcher, Allen J. Malmquist, Roderick Nash, and Stewart L. Udall. Foreword by David Brower. New York: Ballantine, 1970.

Brewer, Richard. *Conservancy: the Land Trust Movement in America*. Lebanon, New Hampshire: University Press of New England, 2003.

Brinkley, Douglas. *The Wilderness Warrior: Theodore Roosevelt and the Crusade for America*. New York: HarperCollins, 2009.

Brower, David. *For Earth's Sake: the Life and Times of David Brower*. Salt Lake City: Gibbs-Smith, 1990.

———. *Let the Mountains Talk, Let the Rivers Run: A Call to Those Who Would Save the Earth*. New York: HarperCollins, 1995.

———, ed. *Wilderness: America's Living Heritage*. San Francisco: Sierra Club, 1961.

Brower, Kenneth. *One Earth; Photographed by More than 80 of the World's Leading Photojournalists*. Intro. by Michael Tobias. San Francisco: Collins, 1990.

———. *The Wildness Within: Remembering David Brower*. Berkeley: Heydey, 2012.

Burgess, Harriet. Oral History Interview by Carol McLaughlin, San Francisco, California, 12 January 2016 and Inverness, California, 17 January 2006.

Carson, Rachel. Photographs by Nick Kelsh. *The Sense of Wonder*. New York: Harper & Row, 1965; New York: HarperCollins, 1998.

Clark, Story. *A Field Guide to Conservation Finance*. Washington, DC, Covelo, London: Island Press, 2007.

Cohen, Michael P. *The History of the Sierra Club, 1892–1970*. San Francisco: Sierra Club Books, 1988.

Committee on Scientific and Technical Criteria for Federal Acquisition of Lands for Conservation. *Setting Priorities for Land Conservation*. Washington, DC: National Academy Press, 1993.

Cook, Janet. Photographs by Peter Marbach. *Columbia River Gorge National Scenic Area*. Woodburn, OR: Beautiful America Publishing, 2008.

Coontz, Stephanie. *A Strange Stirring: The Feminine Mystique and American Women at the Dawn of the 1960s*. New York: Basic Books, 2011.

Dagit, Rosi. "Topanga Creek Restoration: Rodeo Berm Removal." *Urban Coast* (November 2009): 37–41.

Dale, Regan. Interview by Lew Steiger, Flagstaff, Arizona, 6 November 1998. Grand Canyon River Guides Oral History Collection, interview no. 53.15, Northern Arizona University, Cline Library.

Davis, Wade. *River Notes: A Natural and Human History of the Colorado.* Washington: Island Press, 2013.

Dimock, Brad. "Articulate Outrage, Righteous Wrath—Martin Litton." *Boatman's Quarterly Review: Journal of the Grand Canyon River Guides* (Winter 2014/2015): 26–46.

———. *The Very Hard Way: Bert Loper and the Colorado River.* Flagstaff, AZ: Fretwater Press, 2007.

Dowie, Mark. *Losing Ground: American Environmentalism at the Close of the Twentieth Century.* Cambridge: MIT Press, 1996.

Dunlap, Thomas R. *Faith in Nature: Environmentalism as Religious Quest.* With a foreword by William Cronon. Seattle: University of Washington Press, 2004.

Durbin, Kathie. *Bridging a Great Divide: The Battle for the Columbia River Gorge.* Corvallis: Oregon State University Press, 2013.

Endicott, Eve, ed. *Land Conservation Through Public/Private Partnerships.* Washington, DC: Island Press, 1993.

Egan, Michael and Jeff Crane, eds. *Natural Protest: Essays on the History of American Environmentalism.* New York: Routledge, 2009.

Evans, Brock. *Environmental Campaigner: From the Northwest Forests to the Halls of Congress.* An oral history interview conducted in 1982 by Ann Lage, in *Building the Sierra Club's National Lobbying Program, 1967–1981,* Regional Oral History Office, The Bancroft Library, University of California, Berkeley, 1985.

Fairfax, Sally K., et. al. *Buying Nature: The Limits of Land Acquisition as a Conservation Strategy, 1780–2004.* Cambridge: MIT Press, 2005.

Fedarko, Kevin. "Ain't It Just Grand." *Outside Magazine* (June 2005). www.outsideonline.com/1927766/aint-it-just-grand.

———. *The Emerald Mile: The Epic Story of the Fastest Ride in History Through the Heart of the Grand Canyon.* New York: Scribner, 2013.

———. "They Call Me Groover Boy." *Outside* (7 July 2008). www.outsideonline.com/1892656/they-call-me-groover-boy.

Forbes, Peter, Ann Armbrecht Forbes, and Helen Whybrow, eds. *Our Land, Ourselves: Readings on People and Place.* 2d ed. San Francisco: Trust for Public Land, 1999.

Fradkin, Philip L. *Wallace Stegner and the American West.* New York: Knopf, 2008.

———. *A River No More: The Colorado River and the West.* New York: Knopf, 1981; Berkeley: University of California Press, 1996.

Friedan, Betty. *The Feminine Mystique.* New York: Norton, 2013; New York: Norton, 1963.

Game, John and Richards Lyon. *Fifty Wildflowers, Bear Valley, Colusa County.* San Francisco: American Land Conservancy, 1996.

Gessner, David. *All the Wild That Remains: Edward Abbey, Wallace Stegner, and the American West.* New York: W. W. Norton, 2015.

Ghiglieri, Michael P., and Thomas M. Myers. *Over the Edge: Death in the Grand Canyon.* 2d ed., expanded and rev. Flagstaff, AZ: Puma, 2012.

Ginn, William J. *Investing in Nature: Case Studies of Land Conservation in Collaboration with Business.* Washington, Covelo, London: Island Press, 2005.

Gisel, Bonnie Johanna, ed. *Kindred and Related Spirits: The Letters of John Muir and Jeanne C. Carr.* Salt Lake City: University of Utah Press, 2001.

Glidewell, Donna J. *It Endures Like the Wasatch Mountains: the History of Wasatch Academy.* N.p.: 1st Books, 2003.

Grua, Kenton. Interview by Lew Steiger, Flagstaff, Arizona, 30 December 1997. Grand Canyon River Guides Oral History Collection, interview no. 53.23C, Northern Arizona University, Cline Library.

Gustanski, Julie Ann and Roderick H. Squires, eds. *Protecting the Land: Conservation Easements Past, Present, and Future.* Washington, DC: Island Press, 2000.

Halberstam, David. *The Fifties.* New York: Villard, 1993.

Harvey, Brett. *The Fifties: A Women's Oral History.* New York: HarperCollins, 1993.

Heilbrun, Carolyn G. *Writing a Woman's Life.* New York: Ballantine, 1988.

Hilbruner, Roberta. *Columbia River Gorge: The Story Behind the Scenery.* Las Vegas, NV: KC Publications, 1995.

Holmes, Madelyn. *American Women Conservationists: Twelve Profiles.* Jefferson, NC: McFarland, 2004.

Hopkins, Alix W. *Groundswell: Stories of Saving Places, Finding Community.* San Francisco: Trust for Public Land, 2005.

Ingram, Jeff. *Hijacking a River: A Political History of the Colorado River in the Grand Canyon.* Flagstaff, AZ: Vishnu Temple Press, 2003.

James, Ronald M. and Susan M. *Castle in the Sky: George Whittell Jr. and the Thunderbird Lodge.* 2d ed. Lake Tahoe, NV: Thunderbird Lodge Press, 2005.

Johnson, Michele, ed. *The Topanga Story.* Expanded ed. Topanga, CA: Topanga Historical Society, 2012.

Kaledin, Eugenia. *Daily Life in the United States, 1940–1959, Shifting Worlds.* Westport, CT: Greenwood Press, 2000.

———. *Mothers and More: American Women in the 1950s.* Boston: Twayne, 1984.

Kastner, Victoria. *Hearst Ranch: Family, Land, and Legacy.* New York: Abrams, 2013.

Keller, Robert H. and Michael F. Turek. *American Indians & National Parks.* Tucson: University of Arizona Press, 1998.

Killion, Jeffrey and Mark Davison. *Cultural Landscape Report for the John Muir National Historic Site.* Vol. 1. Boston: National Park Service, 2005.

Kline, Benjamin. *First Along the River: A Brief History of the U.S. Environmental Movement.* 3rd ed. Lanham, MD: Rowman & Littlefield, 2007.

Labastille, Anne. *Women and Wilderness.* San Francisco: Sierra Club Books, 1980.

Landauer, Lyndall Baker. *The Mountain Sea: A History of Lake Tahoe.* Honolulu: Flying Cloud, 1996.

Lankford, Scott. *Tahoe Beneath the Surface: The Hidden Stories of America's Largest Mountain Lake.* Berkeley: Heyday; Rocklin, CA: Sierra College Press, 2010.

Laxalt, Paul. *Nevada's Paul Laxalt, a Memoir.* Reno: Jack Bacon, 2000.

Lear, Linda. *Rachel Carson: Witness for Nature.* Boston: Houghton Mifflin Harcourt, 1997.

Leopold, Aldo. *A Sand County Almanac.* New York and Oxford: Oxford University Press, 1949.

Levitt, James N., ed. *From Walden to Wall Street: Frontiers of Conservation Finance.* Washington, DC: Island Press, 2005.

Leydet, François. Edited by David Brower. *Time and the River Flowing: Grand Canyon.* With a foreword by David Brower. Abridged. San Francisco: Sierra Club and New York: Ballantine, 1968.

Litton, Martin. Interview by Lew Steiger, Flagstaff, Arizona, 10 October 1992. Grand Canyon River Guides Oral History Collection, interview no. 53.32A, Northern Arizona University, Cline Library.

———. Interview by Lew Steiger, Mile 196 camp in the Grand Canyon, 18 September 1994. Tape number: 1994.100.37, Northern Arizona University, Cline Library.

———. *Sierra Club Director and Uncompromising Preservationist, 1950s–1970s.* An oral history interview conducted in 1980–1981 by Ann Lage, Regional Oral History Office, The Bancroft Library, University of California, Berkeley, 1982.

Louv, Richard. *The Nature Principle: Reconnecting with Life in a Virtual Age.* Chapel Hill, NC: Algonquin Books, 2012.

McCairen, Patricia C. *Canyon Solitude: A Woman's Solo River Journey Through Grand Canyon.* Seattle: Seal Press, 1998.

McCloskey, J. Michael. *In the Thick of It: My Life in the Sierra Club.* Washington: Island Press, 2005.

McKibben, Bill, ed. *American Earth: Environmental Writing Since Thoreau.* Foreword by Al Gore. New York: Literary Classics of America, 2008.

McPhee, John. *Encounters with the Archdruid.* New York: Farrar, Straus and Giroux, 1971.

McQueen, Mike and Edward McMahon. *Land Conservation Financing.* Washington, DC: Island Press, 2003.

Merchant, Carolyn. *The Death of Nature: Women, Ecology and the Scientific Revolution.* San Francisco: Harper, 1980.

———. *Earthcare: Women and the Environment.* New York: Routledge, 1995.

Meyerowitz, Joanne, ed. *Not June Cleaver: Women and Gender in Postwar America, 1945–1960.* Philadelphia: Temple University Press, 1994.

Mighetto, Lisa, ed. *Muir Among the Animals: The Wildlife Writings of John Muir.* San Francisco: Sierra Club, 1986.

Mills, Stephanie. *In the Service of the Wild: Restoring and Reinhabiting Damaged Land.* Boston: Beacon, 1995.

Moore, Leonard J. *Citizen Klansman: The Ku Klux Klan in Indiana, 1921–1928.* Chapel Hill: University of North Carolina Press, 1991.

Muir, John. *John Muir: the Eight Wilderness Discovery Books.* Seattle: The Mountaineers, 1992.

———. *A Thousand-Mile Walk to the Gulf.* Boston: Houghton Mifflin, 1916; San Francisco: Sierra Club Books, 1991.

Nabhan, Gary Paul and Stephen Trimble. *The Geography of Childhood: Why Children Need Wild Places.* Boston: Beacon, 1994.

Nash, Roderick Frazier. Rev. ed. *The Big Drops: Ten Legendary Rapids of the American West.* Boulder, CO: Johnson, 1989.

———. *Wilderness and the American Mind.* 4th ed. New Haven: Yale University Press, 2001.

Newman, Lance, ed. *The Grand Canyon Reader.* Berkeley: University of California Press, 2011.

Papke, Keith G. and David A. Davis. *Mining Claim Procedures for Nevada Prospectors and Miners.* 5th ed. Nevada Bureau of Mines and Geology Special Publication 6. Reno: Nevada Bureau of Mines & Geology, 2002. A sixth edition was published in 2019.

http://minerals.nv.gov/uploadedFiles/mineralsnvgov/content/Programs/Mining/ MiningClaimProceduresSP6.pdf.

Patterson, James T. *The Dread Disease: Cancer and Modern American Culture*. Cambridge: Harvard University Press, 1987.

Pincetl, Stephanie S. *Transforming California: A Political History of Land Use and Development*. Baltimore: Johns Hopkins University Press, 1999.

President's Commission on Americans Outdoors. *Americans Outdoors: The Legacy, the Challenge, With Case Studies*. Washington, DC: Island Press, 1987.

Press, Daniel. *Saving Open Space: the Politics of Local Preservation in California*. Berkeley: University of California Press, 2002.

Porter, Eliot. Edited by David Brower. *The Place No One Knew: Glen Canyon on the Colorado*. With a foreword by David Brower. Abridged. San Francisco: Sierra Club and New York: Ballantine, 1968.

Reisner, Marc. *Cadillac Desert: The American West and Its Disappearing Water*. Rev. and updated. New York: Penguin, 1993.

Riley, Glenda. *Women and Nature: Saving the "Wild" West*. Lincoln: University of Nebraska Press, 1999.

Rosen, Martin J. *Trust for Public Land Founding Member and President, 1972–1997: The Ethics and Practice of Land Conservation*. An oral history interview conducted in 1998 and 1999 by Carl Wilmsen, Regional Oral History Office, The Bancroft Library, University of California, Berkeley, 2000.

Rowell, Galen. *Bay Area Wild; A Celebration of the Natural Heritage of the San Francisco Bay Area*. Photographs by Galen Rowell and Michael Sewell. Foreword by David R. Brower. San Francisco: Sierra Club, 1997.

Ryan, Kathleen, comp. and photographer. *Writing Down the River: Into the Heart of the Grand Canyon*. Flagstaff, AZ: Northland, 1998.

Sadler, Christa, ed. *There's This River... Grand Canyon Boatman Stories*. 2d ed. Flagstaff, AZ: This Earth Press, 2006.

Sandberg, Sheryl. *Lean In: Women, Work, and the Will to Lead*. New York: Alfred A. Knopf, 2013.

Scharff, Virginia J., ed. *Seeing Nature Through Gender*. Lawrence, KS: University Press of Kansas, 2003.

Schumacher, Geoff. *Sun, Sin & Suburbia: The History of Modern Las Vegas*. Rev. and expanded ed. Reno and Las Vegas: University of Nevada Press, 2012.

Shabecoff, Philip. *A Fierce Green Fire: the American Environmental Movement*. Rev. ed. Washington, Covelo, London: Island Press, 2003.

Simpson, John Warfield. *Yearning for the Land: A Search for the Importance of Place*. New York: Pantheon, 2002.

Stegner, Wallace. *Beyond the Hundredth Meridian: John Wesley Powell and the Second Opening of the West*. Boston: Houghton Mifflin, 1954; New York: Penguin, 1992.

Steiger, Lew. "My God, It's Waltenberg!" *The News (Grand Canyon River Guides)* 6, no. 1 (Winter 1992/1993). www.gcrg.org/bqr/6-1/waltenberg.htm.

Stoll, Mark R. *Inherit the Holy Mountain: Religion and the Rise of American Environmentalism*. New York: Oxford University Press, 2015.

Strong, Douglas. *Dreamers & Defenders: American Conservationists.* Lincoln: University of Nebraska, 1988.

———. *Tahoe: An Environmental History.* Lincoln: University of Nebraska Press, 1984.

Stump, Jeff. Oral History Interview by Carol McLaughlin, San Francisco, California, April 25, 2006.

Suran, William C. *The Kolb Brothers of Grand Canyon.* Grand Canyon, AZ: Grand Canyon Natural History Association, 1991.

Sutton, Ann and Myron. Photographs by Philip Hyde. *The Wilderness World of the Grand Canyon.* Philadelphia: J. B. Lippincott, 1971.

Teal, Louise. *Breaking into the Current: Boatwomen of the Grand Canyon.* Tucson: University of Arizona Press, 1994.

Trimble, Stephen. *Bargaining for Eden: The Fight for the Last Open Spaces in America.* Berkeley: University of California Press, 2008.

The Trust for Public Land. *Doing Deals: A Guide to Buying Land for Conservation.* Washington, DC: Land Trust Alliance; San Francisco: The Trust for Public Land, 1995.

Turner, Tom. *David Brower: The Making of the Environmental Movement.* Berkeley: University of California Press, 2015.

Udall, Stewart L. *The Quiet Crisis.* New York: Holt, Rinehart and Winston, 1963.

Unger, Nancy C. *Beyond Nature's Housekeepers: American Women in Environmental History.* New York: Oxford University Press, 2012.

Ward, Brian, ed. *The 1960s: A Documentary Reader.* Hoboken, NJ: Wiley-Blackwell, 2010.

Ward, Lauren. Oral History Interview by Carol McLaughlin, San Francisco, California, June 28, 2006.

Waterman, Jonathan. *Running Dry: A Journey From Source to Sea Down the Colorado River.* Washington, DC: National Geographic, 2010.

Wellock, Thomas R. *Preserving the Nation: The Conservation and Environmental Movements, 1870–2000.* Wheeling, IL: Harland Davidson, 2007.

Whitney, Stephen R. *A Field Guide to the Grand Canyon.* 2d. ed. Seattle: The Mountaineers Books, 1996.

Williams, Ted. "Fallen Forester: Did Whistleblowers Destroy a Fine Public Servant?" *High Country News.* (21 December 1998): 4–.

Williams, Terry Tempest. *The Hour of Land: A Personal Topography of America's National Parks.* New York: Sarah Crichton Books, Farrar, Straus and Giroux, 2016.

———. *Refuge: An Unnatural History of Family and Place.* New York: Vintage Books, 1992.

Wolfe, Linnie Marsh. *Son of the Wilderness: The Life of John Muir.* Madison: University of Wisconsin Press, 1945.

Worster, Donald, ed. *The Ends of the Earth: Perspectives on Modern Environmental History.* Cambridge: Cambridge University Press, 1988.

———. *A Passion for Nature: The Life of John Muir.* New York: Oxford University Press, 2008.

Young, Betty Lou. *Our First Century: The Los Angeles Athletic Club, 1880–1980.* Los Angeles: LAAC Press, 1979.

Zwinger, Susan and Ann Zwinger, eds. *Women in Wilderness: Writings and Photographs.* San Diego: Harcourt Brace, 1995.

Interviewees

Russell Austin
Bruce Babbitt
Ralph Benson
Senator Richard Bryan
Joseph Burgess
Phil Caterino
Shawn Connolly
Steve Costa
Leslie King Cowan
Rosi Dagit
Brock Evans
Jennie Gerard
Stephen T. Hearst
Ame Hellman
John Hunt
Robert G. Hunt
Al Jahns
Chris Jehle
Ruth Kilday
Ross de Lipkau
Esther Litton
Martin Litton
Kerry O'Toole
Lew Reid
Tim Richardson
Jeff Stump
Reynold Thomas
Julie [Hunt] Walsh
Lauren Ward
Kara Woodruff

Newspapers

Alexandria Gazette
Bonanza Times
The Cambrian
The Columbian
Contra Costa Times
Country & Canyon Times
Daily News of Los Angeles
The Huntsville Times
Las Vegas Review-Journal
Las Vegas Sun
Los Angeles Times
The Malibu Times
Monterey County The Herals
Nevada Appeal
New York Times
Orange County Register
The Phoenix Gazette
Reno Gazette-Journal
Sacramento Bee
San Francisco Chronicle
San Francisco Examiner
San Luis Obispo County Telegram-Tribune
Santa Monica Mirror
Seattle Times
Tahoe Daily Tribune
Topanga Messenger
The Tribune
Ventura County Sunday Star
Washington Post

Index

About the Author

Elizabeth Austin is a historian and former librarian with master's degrees in both fields. She knew Harriet Burgess and knew or was able to meet Harriet's family and many of her friends and business associates. She also had unrestricted access to the files of Harriet's organization, the American Land Conservancy. Elizabeth and her husband, Russell, live in Sacramento, California. This is her second book.